Land,

Livelihood,

and Civility

in Southern

Mexico

# Land, Livelihood, and Civility in Southern Mexico

*Oaxaca Valley Communities in History*

**Scott Cook**

UNIVERSITY OF TEXAS PRESS, AUSTIN

First edition, 2014

Requests for permission to reproduce material
from this work should be sent to:
Permissions
University of Texas Press
P.O. Box 7819
Austin, TX 78713-7819
http://utpress.utexas.edu/index.php/rp-form

♾ The paper used in this book meets the minimum
requirements of ANSI/NISO Z39.48-1992 (R1997)
(Permanence of Paper).

Library of Congress Cataloging-in-Publication Data
Cook, Scott, 1937–
Land, livelihood, and civility in southern Mexico :
Oaxaca valley communities in history / by Scott Cook.
    pages cm
Includes bibliographical references and index.
ISBN 978-0-292-75476-8 (cloth : alk. paper)
1. Zapotec Indians—Industries—Mexico—Oaxaca Valley.
2. Zapotec Indians—Land tenure—Mexico—Oaxaca Valley.
3. Zapotec Indians—Mexico—Oaxaca Valley—Social conditions.
4. Haciendas—Mexico—Oaxaca Valley—History. 5. Metate
industry—Mexico—Oaxaca Valley—History. 6. Brickmaking—
Mexico—Oaxaca Valley—History. 7. Oaxaca Valley (Mexico)—
Race relations. 8. Oaxaca Valley (Mexico)—Economic conditions.
9. Oaxaca Valley (Mexico)—Social conditions. I. Title.
F1221.Z3C57 2014
305.800972'74—dc23        2013023358
ISBN 978-0-292-77252-6
doi:10.7560/754768

*In memory of an unforgettable friend and colleague,*

## Cecil R. Welte,

*for his wise and informed counsel over the years; for his generosity in*

*providing space in his Oficina de Estudios de Humanidad del Valle de*

*Oaxaca during 1966–1968; for his lasting contribution to the people*

*of San Sebastián Teitipac by surveying and mapping their village lands*

*and their disputed boundaries with ten contiguous settlements in a*

*grueling week-long trek in hostile terrain; and for his contribution to*

*the historical, demographic, cartographic, and anthropological under-*

*standing of Oaxaca*

# CONTENTS

MAPS

TABLES

This book was written to document and explain how nine communities in the Oaxaca Valley of Mexico have endeavored over centuries to secure land, livelihood, and civility.[1] There is nothing remarkable about this theme for anyone familiar with rural life in the central valleys and mountains of Oaxaca. Three facets of this region's social life have been interconnected and interactive from colonial times to the present: community land as a space to live and work; a civil-religious system of community service requiring expenditures of labor-time and money to meet obligations of citizenship, office, and festive sponsorships by means of reciprocity and market activity; and occupation. Without land for agriculture and resource extraction, occupational options were restricted, livelihood was precarious and contingent, and civility was jeopardized. In short, land, household maintenance through occupational practice, and community reproduction through civility were intimately bound together in a historical embrace.[2]

In the grips of this embrace, agricultural and nonagricultural occupational cultures have been passed down from generation to generation in local communities with shared historical identities. Intergenerational continuity of craft cultures is the rule, as implied in popular expressions by peasant-artisans throughout the Oaxaca Valley emphasizing that "our craft comes from our ancestors" (nuestro oficio viene de los antepasados). Nevertheless, occupational cultures are not immutable, as will be shown by case studies in subsequent chapters.

In the Zapotec and mestizo communities of central Oaxaca in the second half of the twentieth century, there were relatively few indigenous-language monolinguals; most Zapotec-speaking villagers also spoke Spanish. Zapotec was spoken in many households, but few households lacked Spanish speakers.

Most rural communities in the Oaxaca Valley have economies with a mix of agriculture, animal husbandry, and other forms of livelihood or employment, including crafts and other nonagricultural occupations. Differences between them relate to such variables as size, location, topography, role in the regional division of labor and specialization, degree of adherence to "traditional" cultural practices (usos y costumbres), and receptivity to outsiders and outside influences. A major difference in the twentieth century was between communities in which Zapotec was still widely spoken and those that were exclusively Spanish speaking. In the district of Tlacolula, this indígena-mestizo divide was illustrated by several communities historically related to Hacienda Xaagá, like San Lorenzo Albarradas, Maguey Largo, and the congregation of Xaagá, that were identified collectively as "castellano" and were surrounded on all sides by Zapotec-speaking communities. These castellano/mestizo communities did not have civil–religious hierarchies, a cycle of mayordomía (saints' cult) celebrations, or institutionalized reciprocity (guelaguetza), all of which characterized Zapotec communities.

The passage of time complicates generalizing about fieldwork experiences in an "ethnographic present" (the time when fieldwork was conducted). Changes inevitably occurred between the 1960s, when I first began fieldwork in the region, and 1990, when my last fieldwork was conducted. Rural electrification, the introduction of potable water, school construction, and road improvements, to cite a few major events, were symptomatic of changes in demographics, culture, and material well-being over the decades.[3]

Migration has been both a cause and a consequence of change in rural Oaxaca, even to the point of leading to the formation of communities of expatriates throughout the United States. Migration has given rise to a wide gamut of transactions and processes that have transformed communities on both sides of the border—demographically, economically, and culturally. Arguably, such transformations in Oaxaca Valley communities had already assumed measurable proportions in the 1940s and 1950s as a consequence of significant participation by male villagers in the Bracero Program. Still, evidence from communities like San Sebastián Teitipac and Xaagá showed that migratory labor did not lead to the abandonment of craft occupations such as metate making and weaving by return migrants. Indeed, in Xaagá's case, remittances and saved earnings fueled the expansion of family weaving enterprises.[4]

The most serious risk for fieldworkers in Oaxaca Valley communities, aside from roaming dogs, derived from the consumption of mezcal by villagers in local stores/cantinas and in connection with fiesta-cycle celebrations (birthdays, weddings, and saints' days). Most of my bad experiences during fieldwork were due to random encounters with drunks, who could be cantankerous, disruptive, and violence-prone. Accordingly, I developed a strategy to assure undistracted fieldwork by avoiding places or events where heavy drinking was occurring. When I saw a drunk staggering down the street, I went in the opposite direction or got off the street (cf. Dennis 1987, 11–12).

Avoidance is not necessarily helpful in establishing rapport, and sometimes risk taking in fieldwork had positive outcomes. A case in point involved male banter in the quarries where metateros (people who make or sell metates) worked in cooperative groups or companies (compañías) to blast and extract stone. Some metateros were particularly adept at playing a game of aggressive verbal communication that could potentially escalate if participants failed to maintain their composure.

I experienced wordplay (relajo) in Puerto Rico before coming to Oaxaca and also had some knowledge of the Texas-Mexico border word game known as "toss flies" (echar mosca). So I knew that verbal exchanges had to walk a fine line between joking and annoyance without escalation into open hostility. One day, in a San Sebastián Teitipac quarry, a metatero at work whose nickname was Macario exclaimed for all to hear: "Hey, gringo, I bet your sister would be a good lay." I quickly retorted: "Not nearly as good as your sister would be, Macario." This produced more raucous laughter from several of his coworkers than Macario's initial comment. Macario mumbled something like "Pinche, desgraciado gringo," and the exchange ended. From that point on, he was friendly and cooperative, if occasionally pugnacious, in his interactions with me. Context set the rules of male banter, which could escalate dangerously in situations involving alcohol consumption (Lauria 1964a, 1964b; Cook 1965; Spielberg 1974; Limón 1994, Ch. 6).

Fieldwork in Oaxaca was especially challenging in the middle and late 1960s, when Mexico's political culture was infused with anti-Americanism growing out of opposition to the Vietnam War and to CIA operations in Central America and Cuba and, to make matters worse, lingering official outrage over Oscar Lewis's study *The Children of Sanchez*. Lewis's study, published in English in 1960, was banned in Mexico, and Lewis himself was declared persona non grata, all because his Mexican informants made direct criticisms of the ruling party, the Partido Revolucionario Institucional (PRI), and controversial comments about intimate social relations. On more than one occasion, rumors circulated in at least one village where I was working that I was, in fact, an undercover CIA agent. When confronted with these accusations, I attempted to deflect them, first by straightforward denial and then by expressing my own critique of the Vietnam War and of the CIA fiascos in Central America and Cuba. This way of handling these rumors seemed to reduce their impact on fieldwork.

On my first official visit to San Juan Teitipac, which had a long-running land feud with its neighbor San Sebastián Teitipac, where I was staying, I remember being escorted into the municipal building (ayuntamiento). The councilmen (regidores) were seated along the wall, and the presiding official (presidente municipal) was seated behind an imposing, modern metal office desk. After I explained my project, the official looked at me with a serious expression on his face and, to my amazement, exclaimed, "I hope that you are not an Oscar Lewis kind of anthropologist." He then proceeded to give me the ruling party's line about how Lewis had defamed the Mexican nation by portraying its citizens as poverty-stricken, whoring haters of central government. I recovered my composure and explained, as best I could, that all anthropologists were not like Oscar Lewis, and that I would never willfully engage in any behavior that would earn me persona non grata status in Mexico. I never mentioned that I knew and respected Oscar Lewis, and had briefly worked for him in Puerto Rico during the preparatory phase of his "La Vida" project.

Upon my arrival that day at the government office in San Juan Teitipac, I supplied the secretary with my credentials, which included letters of introduction from both the national and regional offices of the Instituto Nacional de Antropología e Historia (INAH); from the state governor; and from the state representative (diputado federal) for that region of Oaxaca in Mexico City, who was from a prominent Oaxaca City family. Thankfully, these credentials, together with an explanation of my project, served to obtain approval to conduct fieldwork in their community.

My research excursions in Oaxaca overlapped at different times with those of two historians, Bill Taylor and Brian Hamnett. We shared information and impressions, but one memory stands out for me in each case. Taylor was frustrated with having to dig and compile systematic information out of documents rather than being able to do so from behaving human subjects; but, more to the point, he was discouraged about prospects for accomplishing a detailed study of particular branches of activity in the Oaxaca Valley's colonial economy. He wrote (1971, 1): "In principle, the time dimension could shed light on any facet of the market economy of Oaxaca; but in fact, the kinds of questions and hypotheses which an historian can pose and hope to answer hinge directly on the nature of the historical records at his disposal. The documentation for colonial Oaxaca would not permit the duplication of Scott Cook's work for metateros." Be that as it may, Taylor's pioneering study *Landlord and Peasant in Colonial Oaxaca* (1972) was an indispensable guide in writing this book and set a very high standard for insightful interpretation of historical records.

One evening in Oaxaca City's Posada San Pablo, where we both happened to be staying in separate quarters during overlapping research stints, I shared with Brian Hamnett the gist of my late-afternoon discussions about Oaxaca politics with acquaintances in a neighborhood bar frequented by an assortment of prominent local citizens. He listened intently and then expressed his frustration at not being able to do the same in a similar establishment in previous centuries rather than having to find his information exclusively from dusty, musty archives, and on that basis infer the content of phantom conversations. Ironically, his pioneering study *Politics and Trade in Southern Mexico, 1750–1821* (1971) shed light on that topic as if Hamnett had been a virtual witness to phantom conversations in eighteenth-century Oaxaca.

In short, the pioneering work of historians like Taylor and Hamnett provides a comprehensive basis for interpreting ethnographic data from several Oaxaca Valley communities in a deeper time frame.

Since the 1960s and 1970s, public access to archival materials related to the conduct of official business by communities throughout the state has been transformed. The tons and miles of documents bundled and stored haphazardly in depositories of the state government, mostly in the southern patio of the ex-convent Los Siete Príncipes, were essentially inaccessible until the 1980s as described by Anselmo Arellanes Meixueiro (2002, ix–x). The main state archive (AGEO, Archivo General del Estado de Oaxaca, or, in its longer official name, AGEPEO, Archivo General del Poder Ejecutivo de Oaxaca) was considered a zona de castigo (punishment zone) for public employees sent there "to swallow dust" (a tragar polvo; ibid., ixn4).

Through the scholarly efforts of dedicated public servants like Manuel Esparza, these materials were processed and organized to the extent that they are now accessible through detailed guides (Arellanes Meixueiro 2002; Esparza 1991a and 1991b). I personally examined only a few documents in this archive but have consulted several sources that have done so systematically and exhaustively (Arellanes Meixueiro 1988, 1999; Esparza 1988; Ruiz Cervantes 1988; Chassen-López 2004; Smith 2009).[5]

Many of the archival materials used in the course of writing this book were found in Oaxaca's Archivo de la Secretaría de la Reforma Agraria (ASRA). ASRA had sets of publicly accessible files (expedientes) organized by locality that contained copies of documents sent to offices of the state government or the federal government in Mexico City. A few key documents were found in public and private archives in Oaxaca, including the Archivo Municipal de San Sebastián Teitipac, the Archivo de la Agencia Municipal de Santa Cecilia Jalieza, and the Fundación Bustamante (Sala Oaxaca), and in Mexico City, such as the Tierras section of the Archivo General de la Nación (AGNT) and the Archivo del Departamento de Asuntos Agrarios y Colonización (ADAAC).

Finally, many of the publications listed in the bibliography were consulted at the following libraries: Biblioteca del Estado de Oaxaca (BEO); Biblioteca del Instituto de Investigaciones Sociológicas-Universidad Autónoma Benito Juárez de Oaxaca (BIIS-UABJO); Benson Latin American Collection, University of Texas; Collection of Cecil R. Welte (CCRW); Hemeroteca Nacional-Universidad Nacional Autónoma de México; and the Hemeroteca Pública de Oaxaca.[6]

## ACKNOWLEDGMENTS

I gratefully re-acknowledge the cooperation, hospitality, and assistance of all those communities, persons, agencies, offices, and organizations in the United States, Mexico, and Oaxaca too numerous to relist here but acknowledged in my previous research publications. To the authorities and people of San Lorenzo Albarradas, Xaagá, San Juan Teitipac, San Sebastián Teitipac, and San Antonio Buenavista, in the district of Tlacolula; and of Santa Cecilia Jalieza, Santo Domingo Jalieza, Santo Tomás Jalieza, and Magdalena, in the district of Ocotlán, I express my deepest appreciation for their cooperation and tolerance, and hope that my work will prove helpful to their future generations in understanding the lives and struggles of their forerunners.

All of my postdoctoral fieldwork prior to 1990 was made possible mostly through grants from the National Science Foundation, the Social Science Research Council, the Fulbright Academic Specialist Program in Mexico, and the University of Connecticut Research Foundation. The expert and courteous staff of the Benson Latin American Collection at the Long Institute of Latin American Studies at the University of Texas at Austin were a crucial resource in locating published materials unavailable to me from other sources. Also, I express my appreciation to the reference librarians at the Alkek Library of Texas State University in San Marcos for allowing me to access periodicals through JSTOR; and to Adam Mathews, skilled cartographer of the Department of Geography at that same university, for his work in redoing and improving the maps included in this book.

Arturo Solís V. provided friendship and camaraderie during several decades of my work in Oaxaca; his lubrication service kept my vehicle in top condition during long stays, and during shorter stays he generously provided me with lodging and transportation. Thanks to his unique social network and deep appreciation of Oaxacan and Mexican life, I met people and visited places that I would not have without his good offices and hospitality.

Special mention for their indispensable assistance during the writing of this book must be made of Manuel Esparza of INAH-Oaxaca and Jorge Hernández-Díaz of IIS-UABJO. Also, John Chance, Colin Clarke, and Brian Hamnett demonstrated unusual patience and attention as discerning readers of earlier versions of the manuscript. Mike Chibnik and Joe Whitecotton provided helpful commentaries as readers for the University of Texas Press.

I am enormously grateful for the advice and input of all of the above readers, and I hope the final version is not displeasing to any of them and meets their own high standards of scholarship. Also, I want to express my appreciation to Theresa May, Editor-in-Chief of the University of Texas Press, for her interest in this project, and to her and her editorial staff for getting the book to press.

Finally, my wife Hilda and the rest of my family have provided love, support, and understanding during the trials and tribulations of this project and all the others that preceded it, for which I am truly grateful.

Land,

Livelihood,

and Civility

in Southern

Mexico

# Introduction

The modern nation-state of Mexico geographically encompasses roughly three-quarters of the territory of the ancient New World civilization of Mesoamerica. Together with Mesopotamia, Egypt, India, China, and Peru, Mesoamerica was one of the independent centers of civilizational development in world history, and it was the homeland of two great pre-Hispanic empires, the Maya and the Tenochca (Aztec or Mexica), which were still in existence at the time of the Spanish Conquest (Kirchhoff 1968; Sanders and Price 1968, 6–7; Ribeiro 1968, 55).[1]

Within Mesoamerica, the Valley of Oaxaca was a "key area" in the Southern Highland region (between the Sierra Madre de Oaxaca and the Sierra Madre del Sur) that in each period of history exhibited "the highest degree of urban development, together with the largest and densest population" (Palerm and Wolf 1957, 29). It was precisely here that the "Zapotecs achieved their highest level of cultural development" thanks to its 700 square kilometers of flat land and high level of agricultural potential and productivity (Whitecotton 1977, 18). Many archaeologists, sociocultural anthropologists, and ethnohistorians have specialized in studying Zapotec civilization, as well as the Tenochca and Mixtec intrusions into the Oaxaca Valley.

Archaeologists have collected abundant data from multiple sites that lend themselves to evolutionary interpretation as a sequence of transformations in Oaxaca Valley life dating from the Late Ice Age to the Spanish Conquest (Marcus and Flannery 1996, 25). This process was characterized by uneven spatial development and shifting centers and peripheries.

The central Oaxaca landscape, shaped by a mountain chain known as the Mesa del Sur, is dominated by a large system of contiguous valleys or basins, drained by the Río Atoyac and its tributaries, like the Río Salado, which is located roughly 5,000 feet above sea level. Given the region's arid environment, moderated by seasonal rainfall and a temperate climate, the river and its tributaries typically have significant flows of water only during the rainy season. This has been sufficient to foster human settlement and the practice of agriculture in the region for thousands of years. Agriculture has provided, even to this day, a basis for the region's status of having some of the most densely settled rural areas of Mexico.

The Central Valleys region is the most extensive valley area in the entire state of Oaxaca (Map 1). The Valley of Oaxaca is the largest of these valleys and is the most densely populated of the contiguous basins composing the central Oaxaca system. It encompasses some 3,600 square kilometers and includes four branches: Tlacolula-Mitla to the east, Etla to the north, Ocotlán-Ejutla-Miahuatlán to the south, and Zaachila-Zimatlán-Ayoquesco to the southwest. The southern branch of the valley, its largest, is known as Valle Grande, which, due to its relatively high rainfall, also has an extensive zone of very productive irrigable land (Blanton et al. 1999, 34).

The Oaxaca Valley is interconnected with a series of smaller basins like those of Río Mijangos–Totolapan to the southeast, of Ejutla-Miahuatlán (Río Miahuatlán) to the south, and of Sola de Vega to the southwest. The entire landscape of interconnected valleys and basins is enclosed by ranges of the Sierra Madre whose highest peaks rise to altitudes of 7,000 to 13,000 feet (West 1964, 63; Welte 1976, 283–284; Whitecotton 1977, 18).

## Contours of the Pre-Hispanic and Colonial Social Formations

The Spaniards first settled at a central place where three arms of the Oaxaca Valley converged. This place, named Huaxyacac by the Tenochca, was fortified and had a garrison of over one hundred troops in 1521. By 1526, the settlement had grown to fifty Spanish families and was named the Villa de Antequera. By the end of 1529, Antequera came to look very much like other Spanish towns founded in the densely inhabited Mexican highlands: a small core of Spaniards occupying a carefully planned grid of streets surrounded by a number of Indian settlements (Chance 1978, 36).

In the arms of the valley to the west, east, and south of Antequera, Spaniards encountered a population of at least 160,000 people (Marcus and Flannery 1996, 13) composed ethnically of a Zapotec majority and a minority of Nahuatl and Mixtec speakers. The region was divided socially into hierarchical divisions or groupings based on status, descent, and differential access to economic resources best understood as estates rather than classes. There were three primary estates: the nobility, the commoners, and the priests. The nobility was divided into higher (caciques) and lower (princi-

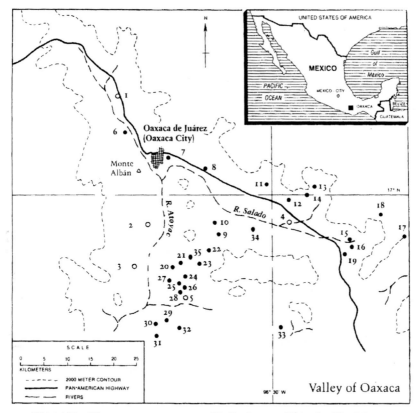

**District Head Towns**

1. San Pedro y San Pablo Etla
2. Zaachila
3. Zimatlán de Alvarez
4. Tlacolula de Matamoros
5. Ocotlán de Morelos

**Villages by District**

6. Santa María Atzompa, Centro
7. Santa Lucía del Camino, Centro
8. Santa María del Tule, Centro
9. San Juan Teitipac, Tlacolula
10. San Sebastián Teitipac, Tlacolula
11. Teotitlán del Valle, Tlacolula
12. Santa Ana del Valle, Tlacolula
13. San Miguel del Valle, Tlacolula
14. Díaz Ordaz, Tlacolula
15. San Pablo Villa de Mitla, Tlacolula
16. Xaagá, Tlacolula

17. San Lorenzo Albarradas, Tlacolula
18. Santo Domingo Albarradas, Tlacolula.
19. Santiago Matatlán, Tlacolula
20. San Martín Tilcajete, Ocotlán
21. San Pedro Guegorexe, Ocotlán
22. Santa Cecilia Jalieza, Ocotlán
23. Santo Domingo Jalieza, Ocotlán
24. Santo Tomás Jalieza, Ocotlán
25. San Jacinto Chilateca, Ocotlán
26. San Juan Chilateca, Ocotlán
27. San Isidro Zegache, Ocotlán
28. San Antonio Castillo Velasco, Ocotlán
29. San Pedro Mártir, Ocotlán
30. San Pedro Apóstol, Ocotlán
31. Magdalena Ocotlán, Ocotlán
32. Santa Lucía Ocotlán, Ocotlán
33. San Baltazar Chichicapan, Ocotlán
34. San Juan Guelavía, Tlacolula
35. Rancho Guelaviate, Tlacolula

MAP 1. **Valley of Oaxaca Showing Five District Head Towns and Thirty Selected Communities**

pales) ranks. Each estate had land, and commoners cultivated their own land as well as land belonging to the nobility and the priests (Whitecotton 1977, 142). All of these social groupings had separate names in Zapotec (Whitecotton 1977, 142–143; Marcus and Flannery 1996, 13–14).[2]

Caciques and principales were entitled to exact tribute, in kind and in labor, from their subject populations. Many caciques also held land grants that were worked by tenant farmers (Whitecotton 1977, 186). Nobles and priests lived in sumptuous masonry palaces, and commoners lived in wattle-and-daub or adobe houses with thatched roofs. Most caciques resided within the local community, in which case cacicazgo lands and the community were an integral unit. Others resided on cacicazgo lands outside the bounds of their tributary communities. Family-owned plots of commoners were dispersed around the settlement but not far from lands of the nobility (Taylor 1972, 40–41; Whitecotton 1977, 149). Spatial separation of commoners, living in dispersed hamlets, was compatible with membership in the same larger social unit. Indigenous settlements were less nucleated and more dispersed than they would become under Spanish control; they often were hamlets in or near the fields. In the Teitipac and Jalieza areas, hilltop settlements were predominant (Taylor 1972, 76; Gerhard 1993, 26, 191).

Commoners working for caciques, principales, or priests were not share-croppers or renters like most of the serfs (terrazgueros) on colonial haciendas would be. They were obliged to cultivate plots of land for their superiors and perform additional services (Taylor 1972, 41). No clear social distinction between serf and commoner was present in Zapotec culture. Traders, artisans, and other occupational specialists were essentially commoners. There is little evidence to suggest upward mobility for them, as was possible among the Tenochca (Katz 1958, 22–23; Whitecotton 1977, 149–151; Berdan 2005, 51–52, 69–72).

Archaeological research in central Oaxaca in recent decades has produced impressive new findings on craft production and exchange, especially about how these articulated with social and political organization, as well as with different consumption destinations (e.g., commoner vs. elite, utilitarian vs. luxury). The vast majority of these studies has ignored the commodity status of pre-Hispanic artifacts. This is strange, considering that Mesoamerica, including Oaxaca, was one of the independent centers of commodity cultural development in the world civilizational process. Developments like specialized markets or markets subdivided according to specialties, merchants who were also spies, and the *tianguis* (local markets) were elements of a commodity economy. Typical Mesoamerican products like maguey paper, the metate and mano, pyrite mirrors, mantas (cotton cloth) and other woven goods, cut and polished obsidian, and pottery, all made for use and exchange, represented commodity cultures well established in Mexico long before the arrival of the Spaniards (Kirchhoff 1968, 24–25; Cook 2004, especially 165–174; Cook 2006, 184–185, 188–190). Very special commodities—mantas (*quachtli* in Nahuatl), woven lengths of white cotton cloth suitable for cloaks and other garments—served as money or "generalized means of payment" in the Tenochca economy (Berdan 1989, 91; 2000, 192; Warman 2003, 197–198; Cook 2006, 195).[3]

Perhaps the most successful effort to synthesize scholarship about the Mesoamerican way of life, in its pre-Hispanic prime, is Frances F. Berdan's (2005) work on the Aztec (Tenochca). In addition to providing an updated compilation and interpretation of scholarly knowledge about Tenochca economy, society, and culture, Berdan explains in a perceptive and balanced way three complementary methods available to anthropologists to undertake such a reconstruction: archaeology, ethnohistory, and ethnographic analogy (2005, 15–19). In traditional anthropological parlance, the term "ethnographic present" referred to a sort of timeless, essentialist past understood as the pre-European contact period of any non-European culture (Hannerz 1992, 228; cf. Rosaldo 1993, 42). In this sense, Berdan succeeded in synthesizing knowledge about the "Aztec" segment of the Mesoamerican ethnographic present.

Joseph Whitecotton (1977) also employed these complementary methods in his comprehensive interpretation of pre-Hispanic Zapotec society and culture, drawing heavily on archaeology and ethnohistory. He broadened the scope of his study to cover postconquest Zapotec history from colonial times into the twentieth century, employing conventional historical and ethnographic methods. Since its publication, Whitecotton's book *The Zapotecs* has been an indispensable resource by combining historical and ethnographic approaches to expand and deepen our understanding of the struggle for land, subsistence, and civility in Oaxaca Valley communities. I consulted Whitecotton's work as a guide, a source of understanding, and an interpretative springboard to clarify and strengthen my own arguments.

In the sixteenth century, the indigenous Mesoamerican social formation was invaded, penetrated, and transformed by Spaniards bent on pursuing their separate, but intertwined and sometimes conflicting, interests. Confronted with varying degrees of native resistance, the Spaniards succeeded in eliminating indigenous military, political, and religious organization. Indigenous nobility were co-opted and slowly reenculturated. Spaniards did what they could to appropriate and develop land not directly controlled by established indigenous communities or cacicazgos.

Ancient pre-Hispanic organization was replaced by a new system through which the inclusion and dependency of the indigenous population on the

Spanish regime was guaranteed. This system was controlled from Europe for the benefit of the new ruling class. Indigenous political structures were reduced to the level of small communities. Local governments remained in the hands of caciques in many cases. In other cases, they were controlled by new indigenous authorities who were stripped of authority outside of their small localities and had very limited power within them. They essentially functioned as instruments of Spanish power for the exploitation of the rest of the indigenous population. Supported by a policy of nurturing community life, this system of dominance fragmented indigenous society and isolated its settlements (Olivera and Romero 1973, 279).

Given the need of Spanish colonizers for indigenous labor, initially for construction and subsequently for agricultural and mining enterprises, the Zapotec nobility (caciques and principales) were forced to compete. In most areas of the valley, they lost economic power, social status, and political clout after 1650 (Whitecotton 1977, 186–187). Rapid population decline in the second half of the sixteenth century exacerbated the competitive scramble for indigenous labor in the Oaxaca Valley. Combined with the Spanish policy of congregating dispersed indigenous populations, this resulted in settlement reconfiguration in which some settlements disappeared and new ones emerged (Taylor 1972, 26–27; Gerhard 1993, 27).

By the early 1600s, the Oaxaca Valley population bottomed out and began a slow process of recovery. Every undertaking in the colonial economy from that point on was negatively impacted by huge attrition in the ranks of tribute payers (Taylor 1972, 29–34; cf. Gerhard 1993, 24–26). Zapotec-speaking communities in the Oaxaca Valley during the colonial period lost considerable population, but most of them lost very little land (Taylor 1972, 77). They were by then communities of peasant-artisans with language being the most distinctively Zapotec element remaining of their culture and society (Whitecotton 1977, 219).

The development of civil-religious organization during the colonial period in the Oaxaca Valley is not well documented. It most likely occurred through the intertwining of local government (cabildo) and religious brotherhoods (cofradías) introduced by the Spaniards. Service in civil posts typically followed menial assignments for the church or the cult of a particular saint, and then alternated with increasingly prestigious cofradía service. Less plausible is the view that this evolving civil-religious system functioned to level out wealth differences to the point of destratifying peasant Indian communities (Whitecotton 1977, 217–218). Dating at least from the eighteenth century, empirical evidence exists to support the supposition of class differentiation in local Oaxaca Valley populations, especially with specific regard to access to land and agricultural means of production (i.e., ox teams, plows, carts). The historical struggle for land, subsistence, and civility in the Oaxaca Valley took place within socially differentiated communities with hierarchical civil-religious systems, in which household economic fortunes fluctuated without changing an underlying structure of inequality.

Communities and households were not alone as organizational actors in the development of the Oaxaca Valley economy. From the seventeenth century into the early twentieth century in several areas of the valley and its mountain hinterland, haciendas (and mines) operated as enterprises occupying land and labor to produce wealth for the benefit of the elites that owned, rented, and managed them. This was uniformly to the detriment of workers and their communities, as illustrated by the cases of Xaagá, San Antonio Buenavista, and San José la Garzona.

Oaxaca Valley haciendas were as much about social status and lifestyle as they were about significant capital accumulation. Being an hacendado meant possessing a title of high social position, belonging to an elite intimately linked to power, and having membership in a privileged class approximating a criollo aristocracy (aristocracia criolla). The political and economic presence of hacendados reflected the extent and number of landed properties under their ownership and these properties' market potentials. Hacendados lived according to their pretensions and relationships, which encouraged luxury consumption and the use of large retinues of personal servants. Excess constituted a way of life that could not be paid for with the income derived from the hacienda and its workers, especially in periods of agricultural crisis. Hacendados' deficits were covered by mortgaging their properties with the clergy, their principal source of financial aid (refaccionador de dinero; Arellanes Meixueiro 1999, 29; Taylor 1972, 141–142, 154–158).

The haciendas of Xaagá, San Antonio Buenavista, and San José were among the Oaxaca Valley's largest and were dominant players in the histories of communities examined in this book. The fact that three communities—San Lorenzo Albarradas, Xaagá, and Magdalena Ocotlán—benefited from substantial ejido grants in the 1920s and 1930s demonstrated how persistent struggle against despoliation by haciendas resulted in the recovery (reivindicación) of ancestral lands to reinvigorate community life in the region.

## Time Perspective and Understanding Change

Mexican history can be viewed as a series of transformations from the sixteenth century to the present conceived as phases in the uneven development of capitalism (Semo 1973; Cook and Diskin 1976a, 266–275; Cook and

Binford 1990, 35–39). These can be sequentially periodized in conventional terms as colonial, independence, revolution, and postrevolution. The latest period encompasses processes like continentalization (the emergence of NAFTAmerica) and globalization (Cook 2004, Ch. 10), which were well under way in the 1990s. Each of these periods and their transformations enveloped processes and relations that have differentially influenced daily life in local communities in ways selectively explained in a wide range of studies.

Fundamental discontinuity occurred between 1500 and, say, 1600 in the transformative change of constitutive institutional elements of Oaxaca Valley civilization. The existential transformations wrought by the Spanish Conquest and colonization upon the inhabitants of the Oaxaca Valley were at least as significant as sedentarization, the rise of agriculture, and state formation in the preconquest period. Sociocultural carryovers from the preconquest period appeared in the civilizational repertory forged during the colonial period. Nevertheless, a new sociocultural order was created by a decimated indigenous population and Spanish/criollo elements after 1700.

Transformative change accelerated through the nineteenth-century independence movement, the Juárez reforms, and the early twentieth-century agrarian revolution. At the end of this series of existential transformations, the "Indian peasant" as a social category of commoners in the Oaxaca Valley was replaced by a class of relatively acculturated campesinos whose status as national citizens was played out by and large in their communities of residence and, to a lesser extent, regionally (cf. Whitecotton 1977, 272–273).

From the perspective of the ethnographic phase of my research from 1965 to 1990, a temporal baseline was delimited by the oral record of testimonial accounts, supplemented by direct examination of archival documents. This baseline did not extend much beyond the last quarter of the nineteenth century; its extension necessarily entailed full reliance on knowledge of the past as reconstructed by archaeologists, historians, and chroniclers and from supplementary documents. In this process, historical material provided background, context, and meaning to ethnographic data. It also exposed important threads of continuity or discontinuity between past and present and, in some cases, yielded insights about patterns and processes not discernible from ethnographic data alone. An obvious example is provided by haciendas examined in this book: inoperative ruins that could be brought to life only through oral history and consultation of primary and secondary documentary sources.

Existential circumstances of Oaxaca Valley communities have been progressively more entangled in world history since the sixteenth century. Their lives increasingly became part of a "Global Ecumene" (Hannerz 1992) that immerses the study of culture in the study of history. Nevertheless, this book rests upon the thesis that "in the peripheries of the world system, the present, the real present, has its own characteristics" (Hannerz 1992, 228). This approach implies an appreciation of idiosyncratic or particular cultural forms without losing sight of universal processes in world history.

Ethnographic research in the Oaxaca Valley yielded enough evidence of change in the struggle for land, subsistence, and civility to evoke an expectation of finding similar evidence in the historical record, and to posit change in that struggle as a constant. Change is not uniform and does not occur at the same pace in different time periods, institutions, or cultural dimensions. On a decade-by-decade basis, demographic profiles of communities, reflecting the natural life cycle, always changed. Variables like languages spoken, agricultural technology, and social and political organization were less susceptible to change. They did so gradually or, more unpredictably, as a consequence of social upheaval, as occurred in the early decades of the nineteenth century in the struggle for Mexican independence from Spain, and in the Mexican Revolution during the early decades of the twentieth century.[4]

In some general sense, the nine communities examined in this book have collectively experienced unilineal change roughly measured in terms of polarized continua like folk-to-urban or closed-to-open. Nevertheless, deviations, detours, or regressions from idealized linear trajectories were common. Shifts in relationships between center and periphery in Oaxaca Valley history were less common; most communities examined in this study remained (and remain) peripheral subjects over the centuries. The exceptions were San Juan Teitipac, which enjoyed high regional politico-religious status during the preconquest and early colonial periods but lost it during the postcolonial period, and Santo Tomás Jalieza, which in the late preconquest/early colonial period as Mecatepeque had a greater sphere of political influence than it did in the twentieth century as a municipality with only two dependent agencies, Santa Cecilia and Santo Domingo.

## Oaxaca Valley Communities in the Twentieth Century

The twenty-first-century urban viewer of twentieth-century photos from rural Oaxaca will find the people, objects, and activities represented to be quaint and rustic. One of the features that originally attracted me to rural life in Oaxaca in the second half of the twentieth century was its low-tech lifestyle in which manual labor exerted at the household level, accompanied by animal power (and mostly without the aid of machines), was the main source of productive energy and livelihood. In the process of making and earning a living, rural Oaxacans participated in regional marketplaces to exchange the products of their household labor for goods and services produced or offered by other households and enterprises in the wider economy. In many ways, this appeared to resemble a world that had long been lost in mid-twentieth-century United States (and Europe) and, consequently, exemplified economic otherness south of the border. Upon closer scrutiny, this characterization's accuracy diminished somewhat in the face of an ancient, pervasive, and persisting commodity cultural disposition (Cook 2004).

By the end of the colonial period, Oaxaca Valley settlements conformed to a grid pattern combining streets and residential blocks organized symmetrically around a central plaza where a church and government buildings (including schools) were situated. Each block contained several residence lots (solares) of varying sizes with houses and outbuildings constructed of adobe, thatch, brick, tile, or some combination of these materials. Most public events took place in the area of the central plaza; residence lots were usually fenced and were open to nonfamily members by permission only. This pattern for the most part persisted into the twenty-first century.

With the exception of small herb gardens in residence lots, the typical mid- to late twentieth-century Oaxaca Valley rural settlement was surrounded on all sides by agricultural fields, as well as by other land unsuited to agriculture because of hostile topography or poor soil quality but used to hunt and gather, graze animals, cut wood, or to exploit other resources like stone. The settlement area (pueblo) was divided into named neighborhoods or barrios. The campo, land surrounding the pueblo, was also separated into named localities known as parajes.

The topography of the Oaxaca Valley landscape is striking and unique in its balanced mix of mountains, hills, and flat lands. The most distinctive features of the built environment in the twentieth century derived from the imaginative use of locally available materials. Three basic building types prevailed: the casa de adobe (adobe house); the tejabana (house with low-pitched tile roof laid over a tied-reed platform and adobe, reed, or wattle-and-daub walls and open front); and the jacal (wooden frame, high and steep roof, covered with thatched cornstalks, palm fronds, and reeds). In communities that had resident specialists who made and fired clay tiles and brick, some residences were made of these materials, which, in the later decades of the twentieth century, were also available for purchase through the regional market system. The typical residence lot had more than one type of building: adobe buildings (either single- or multiroomed) were primary residences, with adjacent or attached tejabanas used as secondary residences or kitchens.

Public activities usually occurred in conjunction with the annual ceremonial/festive cycle but also on weekends or secular holidays. Many communities had basketball courts, usually in the area of the village plaza, where men and boys played regularly, usually in the late afternoons. Games of chance involving dice or cards were also played by men on street corners or in public spaces. San Sebastián Teitipac in the 1960s and 1970s was one of a handful of villages in the Oaxaca Valley where a traditional ball game known as pelota mixteca was played in a special area resembling a soccer field on the periphery of the village.

The annual life cycle for most twentieth-century Oaxaca Valley communities was driven by the festive calendar and, particularly, by saints' days and the Day of the Dead (Todos Santos/Día de los Muertos). Like secular holidays, these occurred on the same dates year after year and were markers around which households and communities planned and organized expenditures of time, money, and energy. In addition, there were weddings (bodas or fandangos), baptisms (bautizos), and other events that occurred regularly, if on different dates, that rounded out the annual festive calendar. The manner in which these festive occasions were celebrated and the scale of the celebrations varied from community to community, even with regard to the traditionally important saints' celebrations (mayordomías) that potentially involved sizable expenditures.

In twentieth-century Zapotec-speaking communities, the most important and prestigious mayordomía sponsorships involved a year-long series of expenditures culminating in the week of the actual saint's day. These typically entailed several thousand pesos in sponsorship expenditures in addition to a substantial time commitment for preparations. The reciprocity (guelaguetza) system was pressed to its limits to help provision the festive needs of the sponsoring household. In San Sebastián Teitipac in the 1960s, there were specialized occupations (oficios), like candle maker (velero) and fireworks maker (cohetero), geared to supplying the ceremonial-festive cycle when large numbers of fireworks and wax candles were used.

Mestizo communities like Xaagá, San Lorenzo Albarradas, and Santa Lucía del Camino traditionally had much-reduced and more secularized festive calendars than Zapotec communities. By 1980, conspicuous consumption of saints' cult sponsorship was mostly absent, but there were still cases of individual voluntary or official celebrations of the patron saint or other religious or secular dates.

In most Zapotec-speaking communities, the long-term trend by the 1980s was toward weakening the civil-religious ladder or cargo system of festive sponsorships that had been practiced for nearly two hundred years. According to this system, individual households were assigned sponsorship by village authorities, or sponsorship was tied to a particular elective or appointed office. By the 1980s, voluntary (by individual households) and official (paid by community tax assessments) forms of sponsorship were becoming the rule (Chance and Taylor 1985; Chance 1990; Stephen 1991, Ch. 7).

Important political-administrative issues were discussed in open gatherings (juntas) of male heads of household (ciudadanos) held in front of the main community political office, the presidencia municipal (also municipio or ayuntamiento) or agencia. I witnessed many of these gatherings in the 1960s and 1970s, and though generally quite orderly, when controversial issues were being discussed, they could become raucous. When voting was involved, such assemblies had specific, definitive outcomes; decisions on many important matters were also made by elected officials behind closed doors.

To obtain a systematic, empirically grounded overview of community life, basic demographic, social, and economic data were collected through a survey of twenty Oaxaca Valley communities in the period from 1978 to 1980 (twelve in the Ocotlán district, seven in the Tlacolula district, and one in the Centro district). A random sample of households found that two-thirds were nuclear in organization (Hu + Wi with or without offspring) with exclusive occupancy of the residence lot; 10 percent of these were either childless or one-parent units. Fifteen percent of the sample households were virilocal-extended in organization; 11 percent had a compound form of organization, typically joining a nuclear household with some sort of appended member or unit. Both types shared a common residence lot, often with multiple residences. Approximately 10 percent of these households were female headed, mostly by widows. The average age of household heads was 50.5 years (only .5 percent were under the age of 20, and 15 percent were in the 20–30-year age range). Of the households surveyed, 35 percent had 7 or more members (mean of 5.3 members for 951 households sampled).[5]

The dynamics and realities of domestic organization were not always evident from statistical analysis of survey data. In 1965–1966 in San Sebastián Teitipac, there was a high incidence of residence lots with multiple dwelling units whose residents, considered collectively, formed extended-family households. Closer scrutiny of the situation showed that residents in separate dwelling units on the same lot did not necessarily sleep in the same quarters, prepare food and eat together, store their fodder and crop harvest together, or operate from a common budget.

In San Sebastián, there was also a tendency for household heads in contiguous residence lots to be related consanguineously. The usual pattern was for a father and one of his sons to reside together with their respective families on one lot, with a second son (or other paternal relative) residing with his family on a contiguous lot (Cook 1969, 152–155).

In our 1978–1980 survey, the most important variables for understanding Oaxaca Valley rural households as economic enterprises were size, composition (which determines consumer/worker ratios), and stage in the developmental cycle. The relationships between these variables were rigorously examined as the basis for discerning patterns and trends in social organization (Cook 1984b, 21–22; Cook and Binford 1990, 47–56).[6]

It is difficult to make region-wide generalizations about population pressure on carrying capacity due to intervening variables like land distribution, quality, access, use, tenure, and so on. Poverty in land and agricultural means of production led, by 1900 if not earlier, to seasonal migration and permanent emigration from regional communities. Recent studies point to an intensification of migration owing to shifts in national and global political economy starting in the 1990s (Cohen 2004, 148–149).

The social reproduction of many rural communities in the Oaxaca Valley was far from self-sufficient for centuries and was dependent on interaction in a regional intercommunity division of labor and specialization (Cook and Diskin 1976a, 255–266). The diversity and fragmentation of the regional population complicates generalizing about how the institutional structure and process of social life related to the lived experiences of villagers. There was always a time lag for state- or national-level policies, programs, or events to trickle down to the local level. Sometimes these had no measurable effect, or only a minimal effect, on the daily routines of making and earning a living and other dimensions of community life. The nature and extent of nation-to-state-to-locality articulation was strictly a matter for empirical determination.

During my fieldwork periods, state and federal government policy and programmatic initiatives were viewed by villagers skeptically or cynically, if with seeming obeisance and gratitude. When taxation or police/military intervention was involved, attitudes changed to outright hostility, contempt, and dissemblance, if not organized resistance. Local officials of Teotitlán del Valle, for example, regularly dissembled in their communications with state or federal agencies regarding the nature and extent of weaving production to avoid bureaucratic entanglements (Stephen 1991, 100).

After 1924, when the Oaxaca state government was readmitted into the federal system following a period of secession in 1915 during the revolution, many rural Oaxacans began to benefit from central government actions, especially regarding land reform, education, and infrastructure. After 1940, each successive sexennial regime contributed incrementally to positive change in these three key areas. This was true despite the fact that until the 1970s, "Oaxaca failed to excite the concern of the centralizing federal authorities" (Clarke 2000, 31). In short, communities like San Sebastián Teitipac or Santa Cecilia Jalieza, which had ongoing conflicts over land, "never imagined resistance as entirely at variance with voting for the PRI candidate, marching in a mass meeting, or signing on to the local party organization," since these activities "were perceived as being conterminous with the individual's ultimate goal, whether it was individual survival, economic betterment, or community autonomy" (Smith 2009, 413).

## Change in Occupational Cultures, Crafts, and the Plaza-Mercado System

All of the craft occupations examined in this book, even those involving full-time artisans, were practiced in communities where agriculture was the predominant economic activity of a majority of households. Most artisans worked at their crafts on a part-time basis, often in those times of the year when the work demands of seasonal or rainfall-dependent agriculture were at a minimum. Peasant-artisan households shared a relative lack of access to land and basic agricultural means of production, and an annual deficit in staple foods like corn and beans from own-household output. This translated into a need for earning income to buy staples and other necessities in order to subsist (Cook and Binford 1990, Ch. 2).

In the 1960s and 1970s, oxen pulling locally made plows or carts were still more widely used than tractors, and communal tenure and labor existed in many communities on designated parcels of arable land, but private tenure predominated, except in ejido communities like San Lorenzo Albarradas, Xaagá, San Antonio Buenavista, and Magdalena Ocotlán. Agriculture was mostly rainfall-dependent, although there was some irrigation, which permitted more than one annual planting of corn, beans, and squash or other crops like chickpeas or alfalfa. Some villages with well irrigation specialized in intensive year-round production of flowers or vegetables, whereas mountain villages like San Lorenzo and Santo Domingo Albarradas grew drought-resistant crops like maguey that did not require irrigation.

A whole realm of work in Oaxaca Valley rural life occurred outside the structure of the intercommunity division of labor and specialization, and strictly within the community and household division of labor. Work was allocated primarily according to gender and age and was performed either daily, like most household chores, or seasonally, usually in the dry season (temporada seca) when agricultural work is at its low ebb for the year. During the rainy season (temporada de agua or de lluvia), work activity took a decided shift toward agriculture, which typically lasted through the main harvest.

Women worked at household chores like food preparation, washing clothes, tending gardens and small animals (e.g., chickens, pigs), and gathering firewood, whereas men did heavier household work like home construction and repair, or raising/tending large animals (e.g., oxen, horses, mules, burros). Young girls helped their mothers; young boys often tended grazing animals, especially goats, or helped their fathers. In the interhousehold division of labor, some men were butchers, bakers, barbers, large animal raisers and caretakers, and adobe makers, whereas some women were seamstresses, tortilla makers, and petty traders.

Gender crossover rarely happened in these divisions of labor, except with regard to agriculture, where both men and women planted. Men, however, managed the ox teams during plowing and hauling and did most of the field maintenance and crop harvesting, whereas women prepared food and beverages that they brought to men in the fields. In these divisions of labor, older people simply did less of what their younger gender counterparts did. Agroindustries like mezcal distilling and sugarcane processing, and the agricultural activities involved with them—planting, harvesting, and hauling maguey, in the first instance, and planting, harvesting, and hauling sugarcane, in the second—tended to be, without exception, male activities.

Less universal than agriculture, but also an indispensable source of livelihood in many Oaxaca Valley households and villages of the region in the twentieth century, was craft commodity production. The most important industrial branches of craft commodity production developed historically as integral parts of an intercommunity division of labor and specialization linked to the periodic marketplace system. Examples were weaving, sewing and shawl knotting, wood carving (utensils, plows, ox yokes), pottery making, metate making, palm plaiting (mats, baskets, fans, brooms), and hard fiber work (rope from *ixtle*, baskets from bamboo-like reed known as carrizo).

These industries produced utilitarian commodities that through design and usage could be infused with particular cultural or symbolic significance, as was the case for metates and wedding chests (baúles) among others. Through the combined impact of ethnography, a gamut of public and private promotional activities, and tourism beginning in the early decades of the twentieth century, artisanal occupations in the Oaxaca Valley came to uniquely identify communities, significantly boost incomes, and stimulate local and regional economic development.

Many Oaxaca Valley craft villages in the 1970s and 1980s had artisans practicing ancestral crafts with roots in the pre-Hispanic regional division of labor and specialization. This included metateros of the Teitipac villages and Magdalena Ocotlán; wood-carvers of Santa Cecilia Jalieza who carved spoons (cucharas), beverage stirrers (acahuetes or agitadores), and beaters (molinillos); and several pottery-making communities, including Atzompa and San Marcos Tlapazola.

A host of other villages had traditions of intergenerational practice of particular indigenous crafts where ethnohistorical and oral traditions were ambiguous or silent, and where the organic ties between past and present had been disrupted, broken, or reinvented. The cases of weaving in Teotitlán del Valle, Mitla, and Santo Tomás Jalieza come to mind in this regard.

Mitla, where weaving was the dominant craft industry in the late decades of the twentieth century, had only a handful of female backstrap loom weavers in the 1930s producing woolen cloth for locally worn wraparound skirts, as their ancestors had done, and one treadle loom introduced from Teotitlán del Valle. In the 1950s, treadle looms built in Oaxaca City were introduced in Mitla to weave shawls and tablecloths (Beals 1975, 257–258).

Santo Tomás Jalieza, the Oaxaca Valley's best-known and most prolific community of backstrap-loom weavers in the late twentieth century, had only a few such weavers at the beginning of the century. Evidence points, however, to an unbroken tradition in that activity dating from the colonial period and involving a trade in wraparound sashes with the Sierra de Villa Alta (Clements 1980; Aranda Bezaury 1989, 63–65).

Teotitlán del Valle, by contrast, was associated exclusively with treadle-loom weaving as a male occupation following its introduction by Spaniards during the colonial period (Stephen 1991, 20). At that time, Teotitlán was already practicing backstrap-loom weaving of cloth for own use (e.g., wraparound skirts and sashes) and for tribute, so there would have been an impact on the gender division of labor (with women becoming less involved in backstrap-loom weaving and more involved in tasks related to the new treadle-loom technology; Hernández-Díaz and Zafra 2005).

Several twentieth-century Oaxaca Valley craft commodity cultures had relatively short histories, spanning no more than two or three generations. This is the case of needlework in communities like San Antonino and San Isidro Zegache, wood carving in communities like San Martín Tilcajete and Arrazola (Chibnik 2003; Hernández-Díaz and Zafra 2005), and basketry in San Juan Guelavía that was introduced after World War II by a group of promoters who successfully established an export industry for the U.S. market there—even though the main raw material, carrizo, had to be purchased in neighboring communities (Martínez Ríos and Luna Méndez 1960, 280–285).[7]

A short craft tradition had no necessary implications for the legitimacy, quality, or integrity of artisanal practice in specific communities. It simply underscored the adaptive and innovative nature of commodity cultures in an area of long settlement, like the Oaxaca Valley, with often conflictive or opportunistic relations and behaviors within and between communities and regions. Local and regional craft traditions were not immutable, uncontested, or immune to innovation, invention, or opportunism. Given the conflictive and sometimes tumultuous periods in the histories of communities in which their very existence has been threatened, it is amazing that so many of them survived over the centuries with their particular craft traditions intact, as in the case of Santa Cecilia Jalieza and its wood-carving tradition.

Observable differences could be discerned in the quality of products manufactured by different artisans in particular village industries, as well as between different village industries in the same branch. These differences were not necessarily apparent to the untrained eye but became more apparent through side-by-side comparisons.

In those branches of craft production where multiple communities participated in the manufacture of more or less the same product lines, comparative product evaluations invariably favored villages that had the longest history of participation in the craft, as was the case with Teotitlán del Valle in the woolen products branch of treadle-loom weaving, Santo Tomás Jalieza in backstrap-loom weaving, and San Antonino in embroidery. Exceptions could be found to this general rule, but it generally held.

Some product categories lent themselves more readily to differential quality evaluations or measures of artistry than others. Both backstrap- and treadle-loom weavings, for instance, could be readily judged according to a continuum of tightness and design complexity of the weave—looser and less complex design requiring less skill than tighter and more intricate design. The same could be said of embroidery. However, such evaluations became more challenging within similar groupings of woven products (e.g., tightly woven + complex design). Here, expertise was required, and the outsider often had to follow the artistry rankings obtained from the artisans themselves by inquiring who were the masters (maestros) of their craft and why.

The best representatives of a craft by local consensus were usually those artisans who had been practicing it the longest. This tended to be the case in occupations like backstrap-loom weaving and wood carving but less so in metate making. In the latter occupation, strength, eye-hand coordination, and dexterity were all required to exceed average levels of output with above-average product quality. It was in the realm of perceived differences in quality that craft production got personal and differences in skill and experience were on display.

Oaxaca Valley artisans of the second half of the twentieth century viewed their crafts in pragmatic market terms and proudly acknowledged that their trade or occupation (oficio) was ancestral. They recognized their role as stewards of ancestral traditions and, accordingly, took precautions to protect certain secrets of this heritage from being shared with others who might be or become competitors, thus, preserving natural monopolies.

A pragmatic market orientation did not imply a lack of appreciation of skilled traditions of work, or of artistry, but a desire and need to obtain proper compensation for these. If they were unable to sell a time-consuming, especially artistic version of a product for a fair price (e.g., a more tightly woven garment or finer, more elaborate needlework), they would cease to make it, or make less time-consuming or less costly (in terms of raw materials) versions. They also withdrew from the craft temporarily, either to work longer in agriculture or to seek wage labor. The commodity status of crafts and the businesslike attitudes of craftspeople were compatible with intergenerational transmission of craft traditions or the continuous practice of craft traditions by many artisans in defiance of market fluctuations and changes in consumer demand.

The rhythm and vibrancy of making and earning a living in the Oaxaca Valley at the end of the twentieth century continued to be attuned to the workings of a complex marketing organization with deep historical and cultural roots, linking village, town, and city. The entire gamut of agricultural and artisanal commodities destined for local and regional consumption and produced through the local and regional division of labor still found its way to consumers mainly through the periodic sectional marketplace or plaza-mercado system. Labeling this system "traditional" masks uncertainty regarding its origins and historical development. It had uncertain antecedents and assumed a form during the colonial period that has persisted into the twenty-first century (cf. Beals 1975, 38–39; Cook and Diskin 1976c, 11).

The system operated seven days each week, with market activities shifting location from Sunday in Tlacolula, to Monday in Miahuatlán, to Tuesday in Ayoquesco, to Wednesday in Etla and Zimatlán, to Thursday in Ejutla and Zaachila, to Friday in Ocotlán, and culminating in the large Saturday market in Oaxaca City. In this way, the entire regional village population was able to adapt trading activities to a schedule involving a major subregional town or the region's largest city.

Every market was organized sectionally by commodity category, the section location remaining the same from week to week, and sellers paid a fee to occupy a particular space within each section. There were also permanent stalls, usually occupied by intermediaries, and permanent stores within the precinct of the market. This sectional organization facilitated buying and selling among villagers, between villagers and intermediaries/storekeepers, as well as between villagers and nonvillagers, including urbanites and tourists. Prices were determined through haggling between buyers and sellers of locally produced commodities but were fixed in permanent businesses that carried inventories of nonlocal commodities. Most transactions were on a cash basis, although permanent businesses did sell on credit or accept local commodities (such as corn or eggs) in cash-mediated barter for nonlocal commodities (e.g., canned goods, cooking oil, bottled beverages).[8]

Daily, weekly, or periodically in conjunction with the festive cycle, seasonal crops and certain utilitarian craft commodities like clay pots (ollas) and griddles (comales) were bought, sold, or bartered in officially designated local marketplaces. Patron saints' festivals and the Virgin of Juquila mayordomía in the Oaxaca Valley were typically occasions for special market days in villages, as were the days preceding the Day of the Dead (Día de los Muertos) celebration in the regional head town (cabecera) and the Oaxaca City marketplaces attended by village-based buyers and sellers.

The complex division of labor and specialization of the Oaxaca Valley and its surrounding mountain hinterlands evolved over centuries under a variety of ecological, demographic, social, and economic conditions. Its constituent households and communities had sufficient space to adapt or change without damaging the surrounding integrative structure. Over the centuries, some specific content of that integrative structure changed, but even as it has been integrated into farther-reaching structures of national, continental, and international scope, the plaza-mercado system continues to play a role in the twenty-first-century regional economy.

## The Case-Study Communities: Rationale for Selection and Order of Presentation

Table I.1 lists and compares the communities selected for case study according to criteria that influenced their selection and their order of presentation in the book. Two of these criteria are closely related and were instrumental in community selection: (1) inclusion in the OVSIP household survey listed in column 4, and (2) fieldwork intensity estimated in column 11. Together with the criterion presented in column 10, which estimates the amount and quality of accessible archival and other historical source materials, these criteria are accurate indicators of the quantity and quality of the data corpus by community. According to these criteria, San Sebastián Teitipac and Magdalena Ocotlán ranked high. I spent more research time in these two communities and, consequently, had more information about them than I did about others. Nevertheless, in only two of the nine selected communities, San

Juan Teitipac and Santo Domingo Jalieza, was my experience limited to one research period; in all of the other communities, I had two or more separate research stints either in the same decade or spread over several decades.

Absent from the communities selected for case study is Santa Lucía del Camino, located in the Centro district, which was included in the OVSIP survey in 1980 and was the focus of additional fieldwork that year and in 1985 (Cook 1984a; 1985, 70–71). Given Santa Lucía's periurban setting, its large and heterogeneous population, and the specialized focus of my research there on the handmade-brick industry, I decided not to include it in this book.

Despite the many ways in which rural communities in a region like the Oaxaca Valley can be classified, a strong case can be made for emphasizing prevailing conditions of local citizenship, forged during the colonial period from either precolonial or colonial origins, rather than ethnicity, as the primary marker of fundamental division (Robichaux 2005; 2009, 24). Whether or not communities were settlements founded in pre-Hispanic or early postconquest times, they have been engaged for centuries in defending their settlement and communal land from outsiders through specific forms of governance based on exchange and obligatory community assessment (Robichaux 2009, 27). Consequently, such communities merit distinctive categorization and recognition that crosscuts identifiers like indigenous, mestizo, and transitional (Cook and Joo 1995, 40–41). From this perspective, the most critical division in Oaxaca Valley life is between city and countryside and their respective communities' contrasting systems of civility (Cook 1993, 316–323). It is not being Zapotec or mestizo that matters so much as being a citizen/taxpayer (ciudadano/contribuyente) of community X, Y, or Z.[9]

Table I.1 shows variation among the nine communities regarding indigenous versus mestizo identity markers like language and preconquest origin. One notable correspondence, though limited to San Antonio Buenavista and Xaagá, is between land tenure and hacienda influence, which indicates their common background as totally encapsulated, subaltern hacienda communities. Historically, neither community had access to nonhacienda land; they were always renters or sharecroppers without access to communal land and without private landholdings. As will be shown below, landlessness had serious consequences for their struggle for livelihood and civility, and superseded any concern with their status as indígena or mestizo.

Chapters 1, 3, and 4 explore the depths of the livelihood/civility struggle in two ancient communities, San Juan Teitipac and San Sebastián Teitipac, with mixed communal and private tenure regimes and a neighboring adjunct hacienda community, San Antonio Buenavista, examined in Chap-

TABLE 1.1. Nine Case-Study Communities Compared

| Community Name | District | District Population 1960/1970 | OVSIP Survey | Languages | Preconquest Origin | Land Tenure | Craft Industry | Hacienda Influence | Historical Record | Fieldwork Dates/ Intensity |
|---|---|---|---|---|---|---|---|---|---|---|
| 1. San Juan Teitipac | Tlacolula | 2,701/3,180 | No | Z, S | Yes | C, PP | metates | peripheral | CE, MG | 1966–1967 (5) |
| 2. San Sebastián Teitipac | Tlacolula | 1,257/1,677 | No | Z, S | Yes | C, PP | metates | peripheral | CG, MG | 1965, 1966–1967, 1985, 1990 (10) |
| 3. San Antonio Buenavista | Tlacolula | 106/— | No | Z, S | No | E | none | dominant | CL, ML | 1966–1967, 1985 (3) |
| 4. Santo Tomás Jalieza | Ocotlán | 424/537 | 11–12/78 | Z, S | Yes | C, PP | weaving | minimal | CE, ML | 1978, 1985 (6) |
| 5. Santo Domingo Jalieza | Ocotlán | 644/613 | 11–12/78 | Z, S | Yes | C, PP, E | weaving | minimal | CL, ML | 1978 (2) |
| 6. Santa Cecilia Jalieza | Ocotlán | 220/308 | 10–11/78 | Z, S | Yes | C, PP, E | wood carving, embroidery | minimal | CE, ME | 1979–1980, 1985 (7) |
| 7. San Lorenzo Albarradas | Tlacolula | —/2,057 | 1–3/80 | S | ? | C, PP, E | palm work | dominant | CL, ME | 1980, 1985 (7) |
| 8. Xaagá | Tlacolula | 468/— | 10–11/79 | S | No | E | weaving | dominant | CL, MG | 1979–1980, 1985 (8) |
| 9. Magdalena Ocotlán | Ocotlán | 583/703 | 2–3/79 | Z, S | Probable | C, PP, E | metates | dominant | CL, ME | 1967–1968, 1985 (10) |

NOTE: In column 3, 1960 population figures are from Welte 1966 and 1970 figures are from Cook 1978; in column 5, Z = Zapotec, S = Spanish; in column 7, C = communal, PP = private property, E = ejido; in column 10 (estimating the accessible historical record), C = colonial, M = modern, E = excellent, G = good, L = limited; in last column, intensity of fieldwork is estimated on a scale from 1 to 10, with 10 being most intense.

ter 2, which twentieth-century agrarian reform transformed into an ejido. These three communities, especially the Teitipacs, had variants of the traditional civil-religious hierarchy and fiesta system, institutionalized reciprocity, and other institutions regulating the terms of local citizenship.

Chapters 5 and 6 return to the exploration of life in communities dominated by haciendas launched in Chapter 1 through case studies of San Lorenzo Albarradas and Xaagá. In contrast to the Teitipac communities and San Antonio Buenavista, which were of Zapotec identity, the castellano identity of San Lorenzo and Xaagá sets them apart and poses challenging historical questions.

Chapters 7 and 8 compare three mixed-craft communities in the Jalieza cluster and focus especially on the weaving community of Santo Tomás and the woodworking and embroidery community of Santa Cecilia. The case study of Santa Cecilia in Chapter 8 explores the vicissitudes of the struggle of a small settlement for survival in a hostile neighborhood.

Finally, Chapters 9 and 10 deal with the community of Magdalena Ocotlán, which, like San Lorenzo Albarradas, was submitted historically to despoliation by adjacent haciendas. Here the theme is once again how changes in land tenure had repercussions in Magdalenans' struggle for livelihood and civility, with a particular focus on metateros as members of a cofradía dedicated to Nuestro Señor de las Peñas and as market-oriented producers.

There is always some sense in which events or processes observed in one community in Oaxaca are unique, but the degree to which this is true can only be ascertained through comparative analysis with several other communities. Claims to single-community uniqueness usually have to be modified and relativized, if not abandoned altogether, the wider the net of comparative analysis is cast. Still, most anthropologists who have worked in several Oaxaca Valley communities would probably agree that even though there may be nothing new under the Oaxacan sun, there is always a particular local nuance that adds to understanding more general phenomena.

## CHAPTER 1

# The Teitipac Communities:

## Peasant-Artisans on the

## Hacienda's Periphery

The Teitipac cluster of three communities (San Juan, San Sebastián, and Magdalena) provides a good point of departure for a historical inquiry into the struggle for land, livelihood, and civility in the Oaxaca Valley. The community known as Zeetoba/Quehuiquijezaa in Zapotec and as Teitipac in Nahuatl, and renamed San Juan Bautista in the sixteenth century by the Spaniards, was a major religious-ceremonial center in pre-Hispanic regional civilization. Moreover, owing to the Teitipac area's early colonial involvement in mining, especially near Magdalena, this cluster is well represented in the colonial archival record and in key historical sources like Burgoa (1934). Spanish colonizers purchased cacicazgo lands in the Teitipac area and combined them with royal land grants (mercedes) in the eighteenth century to form a full-fledged hacienda known as San Antonio Buenavista, which would necessarily affect the economies of its neighboring communities.[1]

San Juan's prominence as a Zapotec religious center carried over into the colonial period as it became the site of a church-monastery complex for the Dominican order's spiritual conquest of the region. San Juan became the focus of a special campaign by the Spanish clergy to extirpate pagan religion.

San Sebastián and Magdalena were satellite communities of the San Juan parish; as such, both communities had churches but no resident priests. San Sebastián and San Juan, being less than 2 kilometers apart and separated by a hilly area, were more directly engaged with each other, often in conflict over land boundaries or grazing and watering rights; Magdalena was some 6 kilometers southeast of San Juan at the edge of a high range of mountains.

During the second half of the nineteenth century, San Sebastián was the center of operation of Matías Marcial, who became the dominant landowner and merchant in the Teitipac subregion of the Tlacolula arm of the valley, exercising political and economic influence over villagers in competition with the hacendado in San Antonio Buenavista. The Mexican Revolution reduced the influence of Marcial and his heirs but did not result in the redistribution of their landholdings. It did effectively end the hacienda by redistributing most of its land to terrazgueros and establishing an ejido. The demise of the hacienda, combined with the dismantling of the Porfirian "jefe político" system, created a vacuum filled in the late 1920s and early 1930s by local militias under the command of ex-revolutionary general Juan Brito. These developments affected all of the Teitipac communities and the ex-terrazgueros of the hacienda; most of the latter resided in the Buenavista congregation (which would become an ejido), but some permanently relocated to San Juan and San Sebastián.

The entry of these communities into the period of modernization, launched by the 1940 opening of the Pan-American Highway 10 kilometers or so to the north but accessible by unpaved roads, was encumbered by a history of oppression and exploitation as well as a system of civil-religious obligations that complicated household economics. The latter topic will be developed more fully in Chapter 2, whereas the present chapter will examine the themes outlined above by historical period.

### The Pre-Hispanic Period

Since San Juan Teitipac was one of the major pre-Hispanic Zapotec settlements in the Oaxaca Valley, its early colonial history overshadows that of its smaller neighbor, San Sebastián. In Zapotec, according to Francisco de Burgoa (1934, 2:70), San Juan was best known as "Quehuiquijezaa, which means palace of stone, of teaching, and doctrine, because it was built over a very large rock, and the kings of Teozapotlán [renamed Zaachila] placed caciques here of great capacity, and intelligence in their rites, and the worship of their gods, for their veneration of them." Burgoa (1934, 2:95) also noted that Quehuiquijezaa "in pre-Christian times was very celebrated, with a large population and a multitude of people, who lived together for a distance of one league, and in their characters and figures, refer to the fact that their principal founders were two valiant captains, who came out of the pueblo of Macuilsuchil." These two captains, Baaloo and Baalachi, conquered the Teitipac area for the Zapotec; the identity of their opponents is uncertain, though it has been speculated that they were Mixe (Carriedo 1949, 1:108) or Chatino (Gay 1950, 1(1):233). The Codex Mendocino, using the Nahuatl name Teitipac, referred to Quehuiquijezaa as one of the eleven principal indigenous towns in the province of Coyolapan (now the state of Oaxaca), which was incorporated into the tribute system of the Culhua Mexica (Tenochca) Empire (Barlow 1949, 118; Carrasco 1999, 304–305). The 1580 *Relación geográfica* for Teitipac asserted that it "always has been known as a principal settlement of large population" (Del Paso y Troncoso 1905, 109) but gave slight importance to its subjection to the Tenochca Empire (Carrasco 1999, 308).

San Sebastián, in Zapotec, was called Quiaguia, meaning "above the stone." It is listed as the first of eleven Zapotec-speaking sujetos of Teticpac in the first list of corregidores in the mid-sixteenth century (Olivera and Romero 1973, 259). In the early colonial literature, the Nahuatl word "Teiticpac," which had been given to Quehuiquijezaa by the Tenochca invaders, was used originally by the chroniclers to refer only to San Juan Bautista, but eventually the surname was also used with reference to San Sebastián (Quiaguia) and to Magdalena (Taba).

In 1559, the cacique of San Sebastián Teitipac sold a portion of his hacienda, which belonged to his cacicazgo, on the condition that it could not be subsequently sold; it would be reintegrated into the cacicazgo if the buyers or their descendants lacked heirs. This exemplified how various legal tactics were employed in the sixteenth century by Indian caciques to circumvent the Spanish colonial law against alienation through sale of estate land following the precedent in Spain vis-à-vis mayorazgos (Taylor 1986, 162–163).

San Juan and San Sebastián were cacicazgos under the political control of Teotzapotlán prior to their incorporation into the Tenochca tribute system in the fifteenth century (Del Paso y Troncoso 1905, 111; Spores 1965, 966). The tribute paid by Teitipac populations to their Zapotec and Tenochca rulers consisted of identical products: hens, hares, rabbits, deer, and honey (Carrasco 1999, 308). It is possible that under the Tenochca, tribute also included woven blankets, gold disks, cochineal, and various seeds. The precise nature of the relationship between tributaries like the Teitipac pueblos and the Zapotec lords at Teotzapotlán is unknown, but it did require tributaries to wage war against "mountain peoples" like the Mixe and to provide dogs, children, and Indian slaves for sacrifice (Del Paso y Troncoso 1905, 112). Teitipac (Quehuiquijezaa) was one of five Zapotec towns reported in the *Relaciones* to have taken slaves in war for purposes of ceremonial human sacrifice (Whitecotton 1977, 151).

Chroniclers associated Teitipac with a division between the nobility (caciques) and commoners (macehuales), which translated into differential consumption patterns (Del Paso y Troncoso 1905, 112). Agriculture, both rainfall-dependent and irrigation- or high-water-table-dependent, was the backbone of the local economy. Principal cultigens were maize, beans, squash, certain grasses and seeds (e.g., quelites and pepitas), and various types of fruits and vegetables. Maguey was extensively cultivated on hilly or rainfall-dependent land, especially for the *ixtle* fiber obtained from mashing its leaves and for the aguamiel, obtained from the center of the plant, which was fermented to make pulque. Nopal (agave) cactus was grown as a source of food (tender leaves cooked and eaten), and its fruit known as tuna was also harvested and eaten. The nopal was also a habitat for a small bright-red insect (*Dactylopius coccus*) used to produce a highly coveted dyestuff known as cochineal (cochinilla).

Hunting and gathering were significant subsidiary economic activities. Rabbits, hares, deer, and other varieties of small game animals and birds were hunted, and a wide variety of wild herbs, roots, and fruits were collected for food and medicinal purposes. Only four animals were under domestication in the Oaxaca Valley at the time of the Spanish Conquest: the dog, the turkey, the honeybee, and the cochineal insect (Spores 1965, 967).

Salt was extracted from local deposits and was traded with other communities, and cotton was purchased by Teitipac traders in Tehuantepec (Paso y Troncoso 1905, 113). Although not specifically with reference to Teitipac, the seventeenth-century Spanish chronicler Fray Francisco de Burgoa (1934, 1:416), referring to the Oaxaca Valley Zapotec peoples, characterized them as "very officious and solicitous regarding commodities" and as having "stone quarries from which they make metates or ordinary grinding stones for corn." To my knowledge, this is the only such reference in colonial chronicles dealing with the Oaxaca Valley. Burgoa did not specify Teitipac as a site of such activity.[2]

The early historical record is revealing about the role of Teitipac as an important pre-Hispanic Zapotec religious center known in Zapotec as Zeetoba, or the "other sepulchre" (to distinguish it from Mitla, the burial place of kings). It was the principal burial place of the Zapotec nobility, as well as a major residence and teaching center of priests (Gay 1950, 1(1):207–208). The 1580 *Relación* (Del Paso y Troncoso 1905, 111) contains a brief, dramatic, and judgmental description of devil-worshiping rituals involving dog and human sacrifice, and consumption of hallucinogenic mushrooms, presided over by Zapotec priests.

## The Colonial Period

The Spanish conquest of Teitipac was apparently a bloodless affair, as it was throughout Zapotec territory (Mendieta y Núñez 1949, 109–110; Gay 1950, 1(2):97; Iturribarría 1955, 53). Soon after Hernán Cortés returned to

Mexico from Spain in 1529 with his royal designation as Marqués del Valle, Teitipac was awarded in encomienda (or señorío) to a Spaniard known only as Colmenero (Del Paso y Troncoso 1905, 110; Iturribarría 1955, 61). Prior to that, Teitipac was one of several towns assigned to Cortés for tribute collection; tribute was paid in gold, corn, beans, chiles, turkeys, clothing, and slaves (Chance 1978, 38). In 1560, a royal decree referring to Teitipac and twenty-four other Zapotec towns stated that they should be considered as "head towns of your Majesty in New Spain that cannot be separated from the Crown nor granted to any person" (Iturribarría 1955, 98). Teitipac was selected in 1536 as a corregimiento to serve as a jurisdictional center of royal authority in matters relating to colonization and administration (Mendieta y Núñez 1949, 144–145). Its encomienda status was still in effect in 1579, at which time five of the original ten encomiendas had been reclaimed by the king, but was rescinded before 1600 (Taylor 1972, 36–37).[3]

A folktale or "foundation story" (Dennis 1987, 51–56) for the Teitipac area related to me in 1966 by Pablo Rojas, municipal president of San Sebastián, described the influence that Spanish colonization had on the area. According to the tale, after the arrival of the Spaniards in Mexico, the Indians suffered. They were treated like beasts of burden; their sandals were torn to pieces; they were badly fed; their clothing was ragged. The Spaniards tried to eliminate the indigenous races.

When the Spaniards came to Teitipac, the tale continued, the Indians did not understand the Spanish language, and the Spaniards did not understand the Indian languages. To solve this lack of understanding, those illustrious men who brought the Castilian language captured an Indian and forced him to learn Spanish. After he learned some Spanish, the Spaniards sent him out to bring more of his companions. The Indian went off into the hills (los montes), where his companions were hiding. He returned and told the Spaniards that his people were afraid to accompany him. The Spaniards took out their drums and began to play them as a sign for the Indians to come down and assemble. The Indian was sent back into the hills and, this time, returned with four other Indians, who were afraid, as were all of them. The Spaniards told them not to be afraid, that they all would be well treated. The Spaniards finally succeeded in gathering the Indians together to instruct them.

Once those Indians learned a little Spanish, they were sent back out to the hills to convince more of their companions to come down. Five Indians went out and brought back fifteen others. Then those twenty Indians were sent out to bring others, until the Spaniards were able to gather together a larger group to instruct them and to attract others. In that way the Spaniards were successful in bringing the Indians together. They made them congregate and establish settlements (poblados). And to this day those pueblos exist.

According to the tale, at the time of the Spanish Conquest, Indians lived in distant ranchos in the mountains, and others lived and buried their dead near the twentieth-century village plaza as indicated by visible pre-Hispanic mounds and ruins. Afterward, the tale continued, the Spaniards began to build; they built the steeples of the church first, causing much suffering to the Indians. They were badly fed and treated like beasts of burden, and many perished. Their huaraches were worn out, and their clothing was torn and ragged. The situation remained that way until the time when a man referred to as the "priest of the devil" (el cura del diablo) came and organized an uprising; an army was formed, war spread, and people were killed.

This folk history can be summarized as follows: At the time the Spaniards invaded Teitipac, the indigenous population was dispersed in smaller hamlets, barrios, or estancias around the periphery of a ceremonial-administrative center that was chosen as a town site by the Spaniards. When the Spaniards arrived, many indígenas fled into the surrounding mountains. The Spaniards, to initiate their colonization plans, had to find the means to congregate the dispersed indigenous population in a central place. They built a church near the indigenous town center, identified by the ruins mentioned in the account that were adjacent to the present-day municipio on the east side. The last lines of the story referred to the sixteenth-century religious clash instigated by a campaign of the Dominican missionaries to erase indigenous beliefs and rites and forcibly Christianize them.[4]

In 1547, the Teitipac population resisted Spanish rule, initiating a period of rebellion and religious revitalization among the Zapotec and convincing the Dominicans of the necessity of accelerating evangelization in the area (Jiménez Moreno 1942, 14, 18). The Dominicans launched a program to terrorize Indians through the visitation of the Holy Inquisition in 1560 and, in so doing, wrote one of the blackest pages in the early colonial history of the Oaxaca Valley and Mexico. The priestly instrument of this inquisitorial visitation was Fray Domingo de Grijelmo, a student of the Zapotec language and a fervent proselytizer who, his chief apologist, Burgoa, alleged, "preached to them with great understanding of their language and customs" (1934, 2:85–86).

Given his fanatical dedication to the missionary cause, Grijelmo confirmed shocking rumors that secret pagan ceremonies were regularly celebrated not only in San Juan but elsewhere in the region (Burgoa 1934, 2:87). Under the authority of Bishop Bernardo de Albuquerque, the leader of the nine-member cult was apprehended, jailed, and sentenced to a public punishment by burning at the stake for maximum effect in terrorizing the population. The affair was attended by the bishop himself, by a representative of the alcalde mayor, and by a crowd of onlookers. As it turned out, only the cult leader was incinerated; his followers apparently were spared (Burgoa 1934, 2:88–90).

In the aftermath of the event, on a platform not far from the pyre, the terrified survivors recounted to the judge that the deceased cult leader "had an altar in his house with idols." The judge went to the house of the cult leader, found a space between two walls lined with various jade figurines and other ritual paraphernalia, including obsidian razors for bloodletting and incense burners, under the care of an elderly "sacristan of the idols." All of this paraphernalia was brought back to the platform in the theatrical setting and ritually purged of evil spirits by Grijelmo. The eight "repentant and crying" survivors were jailed, and the elderly pagan attendant disappeared (Burgoa 1934, 2:91).

All of the accounts of this Teitipac incident were written by clerics who were biased and defensive in their evaluations of Grijelmo and the church's role in the affair (Gay 1881, 1:441–444; Arroyo 1961, 104–112; cf. Martínez Gracida 1883). There was widespread negative reaction throughout New Spain to the trial and execution, including hearings to investigate them in the University of Mexico (Burgoa 1934, 92). Juan Carriedo (1949, 1:70) assigned the role of martyr in this distasteful episode to the unfortunate pagan cult leader of Teitipac, who was burned alive by the Holy Inquisitional torch, and not to the troubled priest Grijelmo, who, according to Burgoa (1934, 2:91), "requested a leave from saying mass, so as to avoid the scandal of the impassioned."[5]

The Dominicans were resolute in carrying out their evangelical program; in 1580, four priests were residing in San Juan as the center of a jurisdiction that included Tlacolula, Macuilxochitl, Teotitlán del Valle, and nine smaller settlements (Paso y Troncoso 1905, 110–111, 145; Arroyo 1961, 216). Also, by 1580, a large church and monastery were nearing completion in San Juan (Del Paso y Troncoso 1905, 109; Burgoa 1934, 95). According to Burgoa (1934, 64, 76–77), by the late sixteenth century, the Dominican establishment there "was the best of this Nation . . . among the largest of the Zapotec area, of a very active and abundant population."

The Teitipac incident occurred under conditions of stress and crisis in the region's economy and demography. Economic stress was the inevitable outcome of the twin oppressive colonial institutions of encomienda and repartimiento, and it can be measured through the abusive operation of these institutions in construction and mining activities that, together with epidemic disease, caused a marked decline in the Indian population. Around 1550, in an attempt to reign in clerical abuses of Indian tributaries,

Viceroy Antonio de Mendoza ordered that Teitipac's tribute to the Dominicans be reduced to three hundred pesos annually (Gay 1881, 1:380). Around this time, the citizenry of Teitipac was providing free labor to the Dominicans for the construction of the church and monastery located there.

The exploitation of indigenous communities intensified in 1561 when Teitipac, along with nine other communities, was ordered by the viceroy, through the corregidor of Antequera, to send laborers to work on construction projects in the city (Gay 1950, 2(1):548). Teitipac was surely among the indigenous communities required to contribute a fixed number of workers (apparently either male or female) to constitute the repartimiento of Antequera, a labor force at the command of city authorities and residents for the performance of various menial and other labor services (Gay 1950, 2(1):549).[6]

By 1580, the Spaniards had established silver mines and sugar haciendas, complete with slaves, in Magdalena Teitipac (Del Paso y Troncoso 1905, 113), and in 1590, the hacienda of Los Negritos (later Santa Rosa Buenavista) was founded on lands bordering San Sebastián Teitipac to the north. Teitipac labor (both San Juan and San Sebastián) was negatively affected by these developments.

The opening of mining activities in Santa Catarina Minas around 1580 had dire consequences for nearby pueblos. Burgoa (1934, 2:42–44, 96; cf. Gay 1950, 1(2):101–103) provided especially vivid descriptions of the abuses suffered by Teitipac workers in the Santa Catarina mines who were recruited by repartimiento and were apparently the principal labor supply for the mine operators. The labor drain was so great that construction work on the Dominican church and monastery in Teitipac was suspended for a time (Burgoa 1934, 2:96; cf. Gay 1950, 1(2):101–103 and 1881, 2:76). It can be assumed that these conditions diminished Teitipac's tribute role and also the wealth, power, and status of its cacique by the end of the sixteenth century; this was the trend in most parts of the Oaxaca Valley at the time (Olivera and Romero 1973, 276–277).

Between 1580 and 1787, San Sebastián was within the political jurisdiction of Santa Catarina Minas, where the alcalde mayor resided. The combined consequences of Spanish exploitation and epidemic disease were devastating to the Teitipac population. Of 4,000 married males residing there prior to the opening of the Santa Catarina mines, only 40 remained when these operations were terminated in the seventeenth century (Burgoa 1934, 2:96; cf. Gay 1950, 1(2):104). The 1580 Relación (Del Paso y Troncoso 1905, 110) indicated that at the time of Spanish contact Teitipac had a population of 2,000 adult males ("indios") but by 1580 had only 1,000; the decline was attributed to illnesses and epidemics.[7]

During the seventeenth and eighteenth centuries, available data for Teitipac were sufficient to support the positing of four trends. First, there was
a slow but steady regrouping and increase of the population, as occurred
throughout the central region of New Spain that included the Obispado de
Antequera, after it bottomed out in the middle of the seventeenth century
(Romero Frizzi 1988, 147). Second, there was an escalation in disputes with
neighboring communities linked with efforts to legitimize communal land
titles. Third, the cacicazgo was still partially intact through inheritance, as illustrated by Beatriz de Montemayor, who, at the end of the seventeenth century, inherited a cacicazgo in San Sebastián, apparently following matrilin-
eal succession dating from the previous century (Taylor 1986, 164). Finally,
there was substantial landownership outside the control of the cacicazgo,
sale of cacicazgo land itself, and evidence of the fractionalization of parcels
through inheritance. Factionalism in these pueblos is also indicated by the
fact that following a disputed election in 1701, the barrio of Loyuse in San
Juan was vacated (Taylor 1972, 28). Land controlled by lesser Indian nobility
was subject to partition through inheritance.

Taylor (1972, 72) found that in 1624, a native nobleman, Juan López,
bequeathed 15 medidas (about 7 acres) with the stipulation that the land
become the property of the community for the use of citizens who had no
land of their own. Landless Indians might enter into terrazguero relationships with the community, obligating them to perform services in exchange
for the use of land. Citing records of purchases of eleven cattle ranches and
one mill by Indian communities, including San Sebastián, Taylor (1972, 79)
concluded that it exemplified how "purchases and bequests from caciques
and non-Indians constituted another source of Indian lands in the colonial
period."

Documents from later in the seventeenth century, referring to the same
individual, Juanito López, as a principal, showed that his will involved the
fractionalization of eleven land parcels through a modified rule of primo-
geniture to four sons and a grandson as follows: his eldest son received
two complete parcels and a share of two others, his second son obtained
a complete parcel and shares of three others, the third son received half
shares of four parcels, the fourth received the other half, and his grandson
received one intact parcel and a share of another. The eleventh and last parcel was donated to the local parish (Taylor 1986, 164–165). This pattern of
fractionalization of land parcels among heirs, at the discretion of the owner,
was typical among subsequent generations of San Sebastianos (Cook 1969,
88–96).[8]

Documents from the San Sebastián archive dated 1691 pertaining to local inheritance exposed considerable inequality in landownership: seven in-

dividuals owned more than 550 medidas of arable fields (at least 322 acres); many tracts were classified as highly fertile moist bottomlands (de humedad) (Taylor 1972, 105, 247n164). There is evidence that landowners during this period were pressed to recruit agricultural laborers. An indigenous principal in San Sebastián in 1716 advanced the sum of 339 pesos to five men in the community on the assumption that the debts would be repaid through work in the fields; he would later complain that the men in question "refused to work" (Taylor 1986, 162).

In 1748, San Juan was reported to have 872 Indian families (which indicated recovery from its seventeenth-century low point), and it was administered by a Dominican priest of the town parish, which included other "barrios" (Villaseñor y Sánchez [1748] 1952, 124). By that date, mining activity had been supplanted by the cultivation of cochineal and certain grains as the principal economic activity (ibid., 123). San Juan was one of three communities in the Oaxaca Valley during the colonial period that had a sector of irrigated fields. It had fewer offices in its cabildo slate than smaller communities like Macuilxochitl: one tequitlato, four topiles, one juez de sementeras, one alguacil de doctrina, one escribano, and two topiles de iglesia (Taylor 1972, 11, 50–51n).

San Juan's population had decreased by the year 1777, when Fray Agustín de Aguilar estimated that it had 400 "indios" (adult male household heads; Esparza 1994, 309). Most of the nearby mines, like Santa Catarina, had shut down by that time, but, reportedly, "Some Spaniards still claimed to operate mines and secured repartimientos that they then used for agricultural work or rented out to hacendados" (Taylor 1972, 144–145). The situation in 1777 in Magdalena de Minas (Teitipac) was bleak compared to previous times when it had twenty-five gold, silver, and copper mines: "Having had men of great wealth, today one sees said mines in such ruin that the poor watchmen guard only waste (los pobrecitos velavistas de desechos) and content themselves with discovering one or another trial pit where hardly a lode can be found" (Fray Agustín de Aguilar in Esparza 1994, 310).

An anecdote surviving from the second half of the eighteenth century shows that Sanjuaneros themselves continued to engage in mining activity, albeit on a small scale (Portillo 1910, 195). The village council expressed to the parish priest that they were ashamed that their church had less fancy adornments than those of neighboring communities. The priest asked them to bring him all the precious metal they could find to make candlesticks, lamps, crosses, and images. A few weeks later, the astonished priest was visited by a group of the faithful loaded down with numerous bundles of small rods and bars of sparkling silver with no explanation of source. He learned afterward that the villagers had clandestine placers of gold and silver; he also found on an arid slope a provisional ore-smelting oven made from stones and sand. This anecdote left open the question as to the proportion of Spanish versus preconquest elements in Teitipac's mining and smelting culture.

In 1777, Fray de Aguilar (Esparza 1994, 309) implied that San Juan had an agricultural basis for expanding its population from four hundred households: "For greater increase in its population, there was a plantation of fruit trees from the door of the convent all the way to Santa Cecilia, a distance of one league (2.6 miles)." He also described the northern and eastern surroundings and neighbors of San Juan: San Sebastián was "about the distance of a slingshot" to the northeast, and Santa Cruz Papalutla was about a half league's distance (Esparza 1994, 312).

Between 1691 and 1701, San Sebastián initiated efforts to define its territorial boundaries and legitimize titles to its communal lands. All but the southern boundaries of the pueblo were disputed during this period with Santa Cruz Papalutla, Santa María Guelacé, and San Bartolo Coyotepec and with private landholders, including the estancia of Los Negritos (Santa Rosa Buenavista), the cacicazgo of Lucas de Grijalva, the cacicazgo of Domingo de Montemayor, and the hacienda of Mateo Salazar. The dispute with Santa Cruz Papalutla lasted from 1691 until 1720 (Taylor 1972, 209).

The dispute between San Sebastián and Coyotepec over rights to exploit forest products in the mountains lying between them (to the west of San Sebastián) was serious enough to be ruled upon by the Royal Audiencia in Mexico City on March 29, 1697. The official directly involved in settling the dispute was the alcalde mayor residing in Santa Catarina Minas. The disputed lands were inspected by a surveying party headed by the alcalde mayor and including several officials from the disputing communities (e.g., alcalde, regidores, alguaciles mayores), a scribe (escribano), and an interpreter. Prominent in these disputes was Lucas de Grijalva, cacique of San Juan and owner of a sitio de ganado mayor contiguous with San Sebastián. The surveying party found several boundary markers already in place, which community informants assured them had been there for as long as anyone could remember; other markers were placed by the party. This record of Teitipac land conflicts supports Joseph Whitecotton's generalization that "violence, strong community xenophobia, and constant litigation between pueblos" was characteristic of the Tlacolula wing of the Oaxaca Valley during the colonial period (1977, 199).

Between 1751 and 1765, San Sebastián rented portions of the Bethlemite hospital estate, then known as Hacienda Santo Domingo Buenavista but later renamed as Santa Rosa Buenavista. It was primarily a cattle estate but had some arable land suited only for corn cultivation (Taylor 1972, 184–185). In 1769, San Sebastián purchased title to the sitio de ganado mayor, which had been in the hands of the heirs of Lucas de Grijalva, for 1,100 reales. In 1807, the great-grandson of Lucas initiated a lawsuit against San Sebastián for the purpose of repossessing his great-grandfather's lands, claiming that they had not been sold outright but only mortgaged. The court in Zimatlán rejected his claim and upheld the validity of the 1769 transaction. The territorial jurisdiction of San Sebastián remained intact after the acquisition of Grijalva's land, although exact boundaries were the subject of many subsequent disputes with neighboring villages. Documents dated 1781 disclosed that San Sebastián's lands included a sheep ranch that had also been purchased.

### The Nineteenth Century: Peripheral Haciendas and a Local Cacique

Life in San Sebastián and its immediate environs during the nineteenth century revolved around two contiguous haciendas, San Antonio Buenavista and Santa Rosa Buenavista, and a self-made cacique, Matías Marcial. The haciendas were operated along the lines of the feudal-like latifundio system described for other areas of Mexico in which the hacendado was the patrón or amo and his workers were terrazgueros or share-cropping serfs (medieros) and peons. Both haciendas had permanent settlements of workers outside their walls, but some residents in neighboring villages like San Sebastián also worked the hacienda's land as day laborers (jornaleros). Both haciendas had extensive irrigation systems; San Antonio Buenavista cultivated sugar cane and had a trapiche. Overall, corn and livestock production were the basis of the hacienda economy. Maguey was also widely grown in the Tlacolula arm of the valley. Statistics from the first decade of the nineteenth century list San Sebastián as having 4,000 maguey plants, more than San Juan, which had 3,100. The leaders in maguey cultivation were Tlalixtac with 8,000 and Matatlán, a commercial mezcal-producing community, with 6,000.[9]

In 1826, San Sebastián had a population of 729 distributed among 153 households consisting of a conjugal pair with (116) or without (37) children, and either married (casado) (68) or not (85); there were also 77 single-headed households consisting of widows, widowers, divorced or single persons with or without live-in relatives. Presumably, "married" in this census meant couples united in Catholic weddings. Over half of the conjugal pairs in the 1826 census were living in consensual union. This reflected the lack of a resident priest in San Sebastián throughout its history; a few Masses were held annually by a parish priest from San Juan. Only prosperous families could afford the luxury of a church-sanctioned wedding and accompanying celebration (fandango), a condition that still prevailed in the 1960s and 1970s. The presence and influence of Dominican priests substantially declined in Oaxaca after independence, and by 1850, in monasteries and parishes like those in San Juan Teitipac, their numbers were minimal (Berry 1981, 23).

The 1826 San Sebastián census also included the livestock population: there were 192 oxen, 35 cows selected for reproduction (vacas de vientre), 2 horses, 130 male sheep (carneros), 2,108 female sheep (ovejas), 12 male goats (chivos), 83 female goats (cabras), 11 male donkeys (burros), 12 female donkeys (burras), 84 male hogs (marranos), 53 female hogs (marranas), 2 female mules (mulas), and 5 male mules (mulos). These data indicated a significant specialization in sheep raising at the time, undoubtedly for wool production. Even more significant was the fact that there were only 96 ox-team owners (yunteros). This indicated that around 40 percent of the households had to cultivate their arable land with borrowed or rented oxen. Somewhat surprising was the relatively small number of pack animals or beasts of burden, burros and mules, since these were indispensable for hauling products from the campo to the pueblo and for long-distance transport.

Matías Marcial and his wife, Casimira Larita, began their careers in relative poverty around the middle of the nineteenth century, earning their livelihood by making weekly trips to Oaxaca to sell tortillas and other village products and from Matías's earnings as an agricultural wage laborer. It was Casimira's inheritance of lands upon the death of her father that provided a boost in their rise to wealth and power in the community. Their grandson, Guadalupe, served as municipal president in 1943–1944 and was eighty-five years old when I interviewed him in 1967. With reference to his grandparents, he remembered: "Their wealth grew and grew. Before you knew it, they had mozos, and were buying and renting land. Then they were selling shelled corn and hogs they had fattened. Then they kept on buying more and more land parcels. That is how their wealth grew." The Marcial surname appears only once on the 1826 census, for forty-year-old Apolinar, married to Nicolasa, with three children: nineteen-year-old Isidro, fourteen-year-old Francisca, and seven-year-old Davida. Matías was the son of Isidro.

As the Marcial couple's landholdings and wealth increased, they opened a general merchandise store, operated by Casimira, in which everything from pulque, tepache, and mezcal to machetes, baskets, and cloth was sold on a cash, barter, or credit basis. Their practice of extending credit inevitably led to a form of debt peonage according to which the debtor could work off his debt or, alternatively, could satisfy his debt by signing over his land titles to them. Several informants told me that their fathers and grandfathers signed over land titles to Matías during and after drinking and gambling bouts in the store.

According to Pedro Valeriano, who grew up in the Marcial household as a mozo tending cows for 2 pesos a month (plus food and lodging), "Men went to Matías's store and bar to drink away their land (iban a tomar allí sobre la tierra). That was how Matías accumulated so much land. They drank mezcal, and the tab kept growing day by day. The mezcal drinkers got into debt for their land (se endrogaban de la tierra). When the time came to pay the tab, their land was already sold." Chico Larita, now deceased, was identified by Pedro as someone who lost his land that way.

Pedro Valeriano's mother was abandoned by her husband and left with five children to raise. She arranged for Pedro to move to the Marcial household to earn his keep. "He gave me corn, beans, and money," said Pedro with reference to Matías Marcial, "and I had to pay him with my work." Pedro grew tired of tending cattle and asked Matías to allow him to learn to plow fields with a yunta, or "surquear" (i.e., surcar, or "plow furrows"). Matías agreed, and Pedro was rewarded with a salary increase to 3 pesos monthly, although his payment was always in kind through store credit for his mother. All Pedro remembered his work yielding was "pure debt, pure debt. I never earned anything in cash."

Pedro also remembered working a corn-shelling machine (desgranadora) for Marcial. "We began to shell corn by machine. Only two of us, and we worked hard, very hard. One of us cranked the handle, and the other tossed ears of corn into the machine. The rest of the mozos were cleaning up the mess, hard work, very hard work." Every afternoon, the Marcial store filled up with clients from the neighboring villages of Santa Cruz Papalutla and San Juan Teitipac in addition to those from San Sebastián—all of whom were there to buy shelled corn. According to Pedro: "During the time of the hunger of the government (Cuando estuvo el hambre del gobierno), Matías planted more land and was able to maintain people."

The economic dominance of the Marcials and a few other relatively prosperous families who were categorized as "ricos" was reinforced by a culture of "respect" and "discipline" in class relations. Pedro remembered that there was discipline in those days. When the presidente municipal walked along the street at some distance, or when he passed by in the street in front of one's residence lot, men had to remove their hats and say "Good morning" or "Good afternoon, sir." If they did not do this, along came the police (topil) to haul them off to jail. In those days, everybody had respect for the rich. (Entonces hubo respeto. Todas las gentes tenían respeto a los ricos.)

The Marcials' fortune rose as they accumulated more and more property in land and animals, whereas many other households in the community became impoverished. Between 1880 and 1915, Matías Marcial controlled local government. He was the principal link between San Sebastián and the district jefe político in Tlacolula, and he became a well-known figure regionally. During this period, Marcial not only acquired control of a large proportion of San Sebastián's first-class lands but also acquired significant holdings within the jurisdictions of several neighboring villages, like Abasolo, Tlacochahuaya, and Santa Cruz Papalutla. He was municipal president for five separate terms, with his sons serving for several others, and his dominant role as employer, provisioner, and creditor on a regional basis was still a topic of lively discussion in San Sebastián in the 1960s.

In 1912, Matías Marcial purchased the extensive Meixueiro holdings in the neighboring village of Santa Cruz Papalutla, one year after he managed to take control of San Sebastián's communal terrenos del santo, located in a paraje called El Pirú, for the sum of 789 pesos. In 1915, when Pedro Valeriano was about fifteen years old, Matías and Casimira both died of "enfermedad" (probably typhoid). Maximiano Hernández, an ex–municipal president (1953–1954), a political opponent of the Marcials, and head of one of the two wealthiest households in San Sebastián in the 1960s, explained that prior to Marcial's acquisition of the terrenos del santo, it was customary for the mayordomo (sponsor) of the patron saint's festival to be allowed to cultivate and harvest one-half of this land to help meet the expenses of the sponsorship. That practice ended in 1910 when Marcial acquired the parcel. It remained in his family's possession until 1942, when, according to Maximiano, "We took that land out of pawn," and its communal and religious status was reinstated.[10]

Matías Marcial had always claimed that he bought the land outright from the local government when it was in need of money to build the ayuntamiento, or town hall, and his heirs insisted that they had a title to prove this. Upon further investigation during Maximiano's administration, it was learned that the land had been pawned rather than sold. (Cuando nosotros gestionamos ese terreno con el gobierno, vimos que son empeñados, no más, y por eso pudimos hacer la devolución.) Maximiano said that they were told by state government officials, "You people do not understand the need that they had when they pawned that land." A town meeting (junta) was held, and it was decided to levy a 2-peso surtax on each household to buy out the lease. This meant that income from the sale of the harvest went into the treasury of the local government rather than into the pockets of the Marcial family, which had profited considerably over the thirty-one years since Matías's original 789-peso investment.[11]

The prerevolutionary career of Matías Marcial in San Sebastián was similar to that of Marcial López in San Juan Guelavía with regard to the ways in which land was accumulated, relationships to workers were organized, and local political power was exercised (Martínez Ríos and Luna Méndez 1960, 216–221). Nevertheless, Marcial's land interests, unlike López's, remained essentially unaffected by agrarian reform. Marcial's heirs did have to relinquish titles to certain tracts of land that had been leased from the village during a period when its treasury was depleted; they maintained possession of all the land that had been acquired outright (except for those properties outside the jurisdiction of San Sebastián). Some of the Marcials' direct descendants in the 1960s were still among San Sebastián's wealthiest households on the basis of land inherited from Matías and his wife, Casimira Larita.[12]

## The Modern Period

In a general economic developmental sense, the logical starting point for the modern period is the opening of the Pan-American Highway in the early 1940s and the introduction of regular bus service to the village of San Sebastián from Oaxaca City and Tlacolula by 1942. It was around this time that the first San Sebastianos left the village to work as braceros in the United States, a program that at the time of its cessation in 1965 had involved nearly one hundred village men in at least one trip to the United States. Permanent emigration began on a large scale in 1950, so that by 1966 some sixty San Sebastianos had established permanent residence outside the village, most of them in Mexico City.[13]

An expanded and improved school program, together with the introduction of bus service, also boosted modernization. Beginning in 1965, new modular buildings were constructed to house the school, new equipment was provided, and additional teachers were employed to provide instruction through the sixth-grade level. Evening classes in reading and writing were offered to illiterate adults. Finally, a project for the introduction of potable water was approved by San Sebastianos in 1966, and construction of the system was initiated in 1967.

Some people consistently opposed these changes, and many more were hard-pressed to pay the assessments required to finance them. Nevertheless, the momentum for change appeared to be irreversible. In the early 1970s, San Sebastián was integrated into the rural electrification program. This meant that nighttime meetings of men on certain street corners that proved to be an important source of rapport and information for me in the

1960s would henceforth be conducted under a streetlight instead of by moonlight, flashlights, or candles.

John Krejci (1976), who conducted three months of fieldwork in San Sebastián in the early 1970s, described the role of the head teacher as a change agent in the community who promoted the school construction project, as well as the potable water and electrification projects. Unfortunately, the teacher also became embroiled in problems related to land rental and was expelled from the community. This led to temporary setbacks for supporters of change in the community, most of whom lived in the more affluent first section; the setbacks included a reduction in school attendance, interruption of the potable water system for residents' refusal to pay a 1-peso-per-month fee for the purchase of diesel fuel to pump water to the reservoir, and shutoff of electrical service for the second section because of their widespread refusal to pay (Krejci 1976, 193). These setbacks were later remedied by a new set of local officials.

A crucial juncture in relations between San Sebastián and the state government came in 1954 when a large contingent of heavily armed police was sent into the village to quell an outbreak of violence over land boundaries with Santa Cruz Papalutla. At least ten San Sebastianos were killed in a gun battle with the police, and a police detachment remained stationed there for several months afterward. This episode ended organized hostility between San Sebastián and outsiders, although isolated incidents continued to occur, either related to the ex-hacienda of San Antonio Buenavista or to competition between private groups for control of bus routes to the Teitipac villages from Oaxaca City. In 1967, a fare collector (cobrador) on one of these buses was shot and killed by unknown assailants hiding in dense thickets of brush along the road between San Sebastián and San Juan Teitipac.

Modernization inevitably brought Protestantism to San Sebastián and its message of prosperity through frugality, clean living (i.e., no alcohol consumption or gambling), hard work, and Bible study. One young villager, Raúl Martínez, who had periodically entered the migratory stream during the late 1950s and early 1960s, became an evangélico and decided to enter the ministry. With missionary training under his belt and a wife also dedicated to the cause, he returned to San Sebastián in 1966, opened up a place of worship adjoining his residence—where he also opened a small store—and began to preach the Gospel. His activities caused bitterness among some members of his own family and other villagers, all of whom were Catholics, but he did find support among some ex-braceros and tolerance from others.

Since San Sebastián never had a resident priest, given the village's subordinate position in the San Juan–based parish, their Catholicism was very much in the hands of the local traditional hierarchical organization of the village faithful and the cult of the saints, or mayordomía, celebrations. The resident priest in San Juan included San Sebastián on his circuit, but Masses were held only on special occasions. Although the cult of the saints in San Sebastián no longer involved obligatory sponsorship of the patron saint's or other saint's day festivals, it was very much alive and flourishing in the 1960s and 1970s through a system of voluntary, promesa-driven sponsorship and expenditure. The entire fiesta cycle, including the celebration of weddings, birthdays, and confirmations, was always accompanied by the consumption of food and alcohol, especially mezcal, and showed no signs of waning during those years, much to the chagrin of the evangelicals who definitely had their work cut out for them to change the ways of the majority of their co-villagers.

## CHAPTER 2

# Hacienda San Antonio Buenavista

# from Two Perspectives:

## Hacendado and Terrazguero

As oppressive as life was for San Sebastianos under the Marcial cacicazgo, it was even more oppressive under the hacienda regime experienced by the terrazgueros of Hacienda San Antonio Buenavista (see Map 2, center bottom, for location vis-à-vis San Sebastián). One afternoon in 1966, in the shadows of the ruins of the hacienda, I interviewed eighty-eight-year-old Eduardo Mendoza (b. 1878), whose testimony provided a compelling depiction of exploitation, oppression, and violence that he, as the oldest founding ejidatario and ciudadano, and other Buenavistans experienced during their lifetimes. Although exact dates were absent in Eduardo's account, and chronology was somewhat disordered, his memory regarding events, activities, people, and relationships was vivid. Don Eduardo's demeanor throughout the two-hour tape-recorded interview was dignified and dispassionate, even when the subject matter involved abuse, violence, and death. Sometimes his narrative was laced with humor and sarcasm but never with anger regarding the unequal nature of the amo (master)-terrazguero (serf) relationship. His social consciousness was matched by his pragmatism; he came across more as a community leader than as a rebel.

To counterbalance and complement Eduardo Mendoza's account, I was able to acquire a copy of a document written by the hacendado, Lic. Carlos Castro Castillo, that is best described as a memoir focused on two subjects, himself and Hacienda San Antonio Buenavista. He was born in 1853 as the son of Don José María Castro and Señora Luz Castillo de Castro. His father was a prominent member of the Oaxaca Valley elite (Vallistocracia) who served as state governor on two separate occasions, once during the republican government between 1867 and 1876 and, again, at the beginning of the Porfiriato (1877–1910; Rojas González 1949, 172).[1]

Owing to his father's acquisition of the Hacienda San Antonio Buenavista in 1879, especially for the purpose of providing him with a job closer to the city of Oaxaca (Castro Castillo n.d., 5), Castro was involved in its operation into the 1920s. Given Castro's training as a lawyer, his prominent role in the state judicial system and business sector (especially mining), and his historical bent, his account of the hacienda's formation, development, and ownership is probably as accurate and complete as we are going to get in view of the apparent disappearance of many records as a consequence of legal and business maneuverings in the aftermath of the 1850s disentailment and nationalization laws.

## Origin and Development of the Hacienda: The Hacendado's View

The hacienda originated in a 1620 land grant to Don José María Vásquez, captain in the royal army, of "five caballerías of mountainous land for cattle raising" (cría de ganado mayor). The grant was described as "a hollow of vacant land (hueco de terreno baldío) located between the pueblos of San Juan Teitipac, Santo Domingo Jalieza, San Pedro Guegorexe and the hacienda de Reyes that is today Mantecón" (Castro Castillo n.d., 11). As an estancia de ganado mayor, the property was known as San José Guelaviate, and Vásquez "built a house with a chapel, corrals and housing, introduced cattle, and opened up land to cultivation. He built a system of tubing all the way to the house and made the farm productive" (Castro Castillo n.d., 11–12).

Without citing specific supporting documentation, Castro estimated that by the end of the seventeenth century, another owner of the estancia acquired additional land from the last cacica of Teitipac "to complete the whole that today forms the perfect property of Hacienda San Antonio." He confessed that he had been unable to find documents that definitively dated that transaction but reiterated: "One clearly understands that when the Hacienda San Antonio formed part of the Mayorazgo Magro, the two estates of San José Guelaviate and the cacicazgo were already united" (Castro Castillo n.d., 14).

Castro's late seventeenth-century dating of the Magro purchase of Hacienda San Antonio was about a century premature, since none other than José Mariano Magro was a prominent member of the official retinue (comitiva) involved in the 1820 hearings and survey of Santa Cecilia Jalieza's boundaries. It is documented that José Antonio de Larrainzán, corregidor of Antequera, owned the hacienda in the 1770s (Taylor 1972, 159). The Magros may well have acquired the hacienda from de Larrainzán during the peak years of the cochineal trade.[2]

Castro attributed to the Magros the construction of the first water reservoir (toma de agua), as well as the construction of the hacienda house, which together must have cost several thousand pesos. The Magros also had a brass chapel bell cast, which in the late nineteenth century was still in use to call the workers and could be heard clearly in the neighboring communities of San Sebastián and San Juan. Castro was also impressed by the Magros' construction of a pond (estanque) constructed about 20 meters outside the caserío (house and outbuildings) proper that was designed to capture water left over from serving the needs of the interior of the house that came from the cisterns on top of the house, and that also served to irrigate some of the lands below.

The Magros acquired the hacienda near the end of the eighteenth century. Castro was unable to pinpoint the exact date when the hacienda was sold to Don Agustín Mantecón, but the sale was after 1820. His 1837 dating of Mantecón's exchange (permuta) of the hacienda with the Catarina nuns or "Dominican Sisters" (Berry 1981, 173) in Oaxaca City for ownership of some molinos de harina (flour mills) is accurate (Castro Castillo n.d., 15).

The nuns' properties, such as Hacienda San Antonio, were managed, presumably on site and in Oaxaca City, by priests. In 1860, the hacienda was sold to Sr. Manuel José Toro by D. Nicolás Vasconcelos, canon and administrator of the properties of the Catarina nuns in accord with the laws of reform, disentailment, and nationalization of property of deceased owners, convents, communities, and all civil and religious foundations (Castro Castillo n.d., 15–16). The official valuation of the hacienda was 15,806 pesos; it was sold to Toro for 10,000 pesos (Berry 1981, 173).

This complicated process involved liquidation, sequestering, and hiding of assets of the hacienda at the direction of Canon Vasconcelos but carried out by Don Juan María Acevedo, the man in charge of San Antonio at that time, who witnessed the extraction and distribution of livestock, grains, and other assets (llenos) of the farm (Castro Castillo n.d., 15–16). According to Charles Berry (1981, 171): "Toro, who purchased San Antonio Hacienda in Tlacolula District, found after the sale that his hacienda had been stripped and he threatened to reduce his payments by the value of the cattle that had been carried off." He added that Toro was "a bureaucrat, a local official of the Ministry of the Treasury, and a supporter of the Liberal Party" (ibid., 172).

The hacienda foreman, Juan María Acevedo, was a native of San Sebastián Teitipac, and presided over a change in the boundaries of Hacienda San Antonio involving 2 kilometers from northeast to southwest through an agreement with his community that clearly favored the latter. This transaction involved substantial windfall profits for the new hacienda owner, Manuel Toro, resulting from manipulation of land values and financial arrangements (Castro Castillo n.d., 16–17). In this process, land titles pertaining to the consolidation of the hacienda by the Magro brothers, and to subsequent transactions up to and including those involving the Catarina nuns, were permanently lost or misplaced (ocultación o extravío de los títulos). Inconsistencies in Castro's chronology of transactions for the hacienda prior to its purchase by Toro in 1860 can be attributed to this disappearance of pertinent records.[3]

By 1862, the process of liquidation of the Catarina nuns' properties had transferred possession of the somewhat reduced hacienda from Toro to Don Ygnacio Atustaín and Don Luis Medrano in 1863. They, in turn, quickly sold it to Don Carlos Esperón, who moved there with his family with the intention of bringing the hacienda back to life as a viable enterprise. Esperón dealt with the consequences of the War of the French Intervention, and due to "scarcity of resources" and "lack of communication with the nearby populations," found himself having to provide lighting for his house by using candle wax from the chapel (tuvo la necesidad de alumbrarse con la cera de la Capilla). In 1867, Esperón, whose relative José served as governor around that time (Rojas González 1949, 172), sold out to Don Luis Moya, a grocery merchant from Oaxaca City (Castro Castillo n.d., 18).

Moya was too busy to attend to the hacienda and reportedly also had bad experiences involving threats from locals (Castro n.d., 7). Even when he was showing the property a few years later to José María Castro, who had an interest in buying it, he showed only the fields bordering San Juan Teitipac then quickly headed directly to the monastery in San Juan to seek lodging and food (posada) from the resident priests. Moya's only benefit from ownership of the hacienda was a weekly shipment of a barrel of mezcal from foreman Acevedo. In 1877, he rented the hacienda to Don Apolinar Rojas, head ranchero of the nearby dairying community of Rojas de Cuauhtémoc, for a two-year term, and then sold it to José María Castro in July 1879, "the farm reduced to a complete skeleton" (Castro Castillo n.d., 7).

Given Castro's lack of early documentary sources, one can cautiously accept his contention that the hacienda originated in a 1620 grant of "cinco caballerías" to Captain Don José María Vásquez, who proceeded to build an estate known as San José Guelaviate, "half of which was sold by the last cacica to the owner of San José Guelaviate in order to complete the property of the Hacienda San Antonio" (Castro Castillo n.d., 13–14). The location of this site was a few kilometers south of the site that would become Hacienda San Antonio Buenavista. The person involved in that sale may well have been Beatriz de Montemayor, who, as a direct descendant of the first cacica of San Sebastián Teitipac, was considered to be the last cacica there as of the end of the seventeenth century.[4]

Carlos Castro, José María's son, after finishing his law degree in Mexico City in 1875, went to work in the gold, silver, and lead mining business in Villa Alta, where his family already had properties and investments. His stay in Villa Alta included a stint in the Casa de Moneda as an assayer. He contracted malaria in 1879, so he and his family moved back to Oaxaca City for a change in climate to promote his recuperation and, also, for him to run the Hacienda San Antonio that his father had bought for that purpose. They arrived in Oaxaca City in late October, and Carlos went to the hacienda for the first time "for the purpose of visiting its fields, housing, and inhabitants" on November 6, 1879, and a few days later settled in to repair the buildings and review the planted fields and livestock that constituted the farm's total assets (revisar las sembradas y los ganados que eran los llenos que constituían el haber de la finca; Castro Castillo n.d., 6).

Carlos was less than enthusiastic about the conditions of the estate but managed to inject a bit of sardonic humor into his appraisal (Castro Castillo n.d., 7): "I took my family there on the ninth of December after having cleaned rooms, fixed the plumbing, the fountain, and the patios. To give some idea of the lamentable condition that I found everything to be in, the living room, and the rooms adjacent to it, had served as a stable for the milk goats (las cabras de ordeñar), the chapel for the suckling kids (los cabritos mamones), and the fountain to deposit the manure from those animals. This is what happens to rented farms!"

He was more positive regarding the condition of the fields and farm equipment. The corn harvest was in maturity and not bad. He decided that the harvest of fodder (la pastura de zacate) should proceed and be stored in the granary (gavillero), in perfect condition and located about 150 meters or so below the house; it had good doors with lock and key. The granary, which measured 10 meters in length by 11 in width and 12 in height, was filled halfway with fodder (zacate). He prepared carts, nets for hauling (barcinas), yokes, ox teams, and everything else required to proceed with the corn harvest.

During this period of orientation, repair, and preparation for harvest, Castro frankly admitted that he was "alone and at the mercy of the mayordomo, Don Juan María Acevedo, and his wife, who helped for several weeks" (Castro Castillo n.d., 6). Somewhat surprisingly, he made no reference to his terrazgueros, who obviously did most of the work. It was almost as if everything was being done by himself and his mayordomo, as if there were no workers, much less an entire community of them, at his doorstep. In Castro's entire manuscript, the word "terrazguero" is mentioned only once: in the context of his survey of the hacienda's animal population, where he observed that in 1880 he bought twenty head of cattle, two ox teams, and six mares in Tlacolula and, in addition, "the shares of newborn goats and sheep that had been in different flocks raised by the terrazgueros, augmented those born belonging to the hacienda and estate" (Castro Castillo n.d., 8).

When describing the forged brass bell installed by the Magro brothers, Castro mentioned that it was used "to call the workers," and when describing relations between the hacienda and its neighboring communities of San Juan and Santa Cecilia, he noted that "not one nor the other of those two pueblos has even imagined that ranch hands (los rancheros de la hacienda) have once done them harm, since they are all good friends and some are even bound together by kinship ties" (Castro Castillo n.d., 13, 14).

In sum, Castro made only three references to his workers—once as terrazgueros, once as trabajadores, and once as rancheros—in the entire document. The social distance between hacendado and worker was formidable.

Castro had a keen interest in the hacienda's boundaries and relations with neighboring communities. After Don Juan María Acevedo, mayordomo of the hacienda, died of pneumonia in his native village of San Sebastián Teitipac in November 1880 at the age of eighty-four, Castro immediately undertook a detailed survey of the boundaries (linderos) of the hacienda with his new mayordomo, his primo hermano (cousin) Ramón Castillo. During a period of several days, equipped as if on safari, they inspected every boundary marker (mojonera) and also hunted game animals such as deer, javelinas, jackrabbits, and cottontails (Castro Castillo n.d., 8–9). Castro emphasized that "all these boundaries and their straight lines and distances from one to the other, whatever their direction, are and have been from remote times recognized and well respected by all contiguous neighbors (colindantes), whether they be pueblos or haciendas." He also observed that a unique feature of the hacienda's footprint was that its borders were contiguous with three separate political districts of the Oaxaca Valley: Centro, Ocotlán, and Tlacolula (Castro Castillo n.d., 10).

Castro was well versed on the historical enmity between San Juan Teitipac and Santa Cecilia Jalieza. He seemed inclined to view Santa Cecilia as a sort of rogue community while also acknowledging San Juan's imperfect behavior vis-à-vis its smaller neighbor. He observed that "Santa Cecilia has belonged sometimes to the jurisdiction of Ocotlán and other times to that of Tlacolula because that pueblo, although small with respect to its rival, has contested, both judicially and extrajudicially, in ways that have brought disastrous results for the lives and property of both communities" (Castro Castillo n.d., 10). This was simply because San Juan Teitipac, its adversary, denied Santa Cecilia the right to make good use of a part of its mountainous land that was once assigned to it as an ejido. Authorities in Tlacolula believed that removing Santa Cecilia from their jurisdiction would make it easier for the corresponding parties to moderate their hostile relations. To the contrary, the jefes políticos of Ocotlán were bothered by the frequent complaints of Santa Cecilia against the pueblo of San Juan associated with juridical proceedings to retrieve bodies of unburied victims of unknown assassins without being able to prove their pueblo of origin (Castro Castillo n.d., 10–11).

Castro's concerns regarding Santa Cecilia and San Juan Teitipac were mostly legal or jurisdictional in nature, with a tinge of humanism. They also reflected his effort to understand why the combination of market forces and government adjudication had failed to eliminate violent struggles over land in his neighborhood. He was justifiably concerned that the violent relations between two neighbors might spread to his hacienda.

By 1883, the hacienda had 110 head of cattle, 35 mares and foals, 700 goats, 22 ox teams, 4 horses, and 2 burros (Castro Castillo n.d., 8); starting in 1880, Castro and his father were dedicated to restoring and improving its physical plant and lands to achieve better security and productivity. They plowed and planted three hundred furrows of sugarcane on a parcel irrigated from a reservoir built by the Magros, remodeled a gallery to install a mobile trapiche (trapiche movible), and constructed a new reservoir with tubing. The following year, a new planting of sugarcane was completed with seed cane (camotes) taken from the first planting. The harvest from the second planting was sufficient to produce six hundred cakes of panela under the direction of a specialist hired to run the trapiche who oversaw the installation of new boilers, vats, benches, and other equipment. In short, the hacienda's venture into sugarcane planting and panela production in the early 1880s was successful enough to merit expansion (Castro Castillo n.d., 18–19).

Castro accepted a civil judgeship in Oaxaca City in 1883, and for the next ten years, until his father's death in Mexico City in 1893, the hacienda was run by his cousin Don Félix Salazar, who lacked enthusiasm for sugarcane cultivation and processing. Castro blamed Salazar for allowing the cane fields to go to ruin and for squandering the investment that had been made in sugarcane production (dejó que las cañas se arruinaran, perdiéndose con ese abandono un capital en construcciones, siembras y maquinaria; Castro Castillo n.d., 19).

After Carlos's father's death, ownership of the hacienda passed to his father's widow (who was not Carlos's mother), Doña Guadalupe Gómez, who promptly rented it to Doña Josefa Mimiaga until 1898, when the lease expired. The widow Gómez, who lived in Mexico City, ran the hacienda through a mayordomo under the supervision of Carlos's fourteen-year-old brother, Manuel. Finally, in 1901, by which time the hacienda had a 6,000-peso lien owed to Archbishop Eulogio Guillow, the family sold the hacienda to Carlos. He was able to buy it with funds raised from the sale of Hacienda Santa Rosa (which he had purchased for 40,000 pesos on credit provided by the Banco Oriental) for 60,000 pesos, and did so "for the love of family lineage that links me to it" (por el cariño de abolengo que me liga a ella; Castro Castillo n.d., 20).

Castro's manuscript provided no substantive information regarding the hacienda's operation under his ownership after 1901. That gap will be filled by the account of Eduardo Mendoza. It can be inferred from Castro's references to Santa Cecilia Jalieza cited earlier and, in the same context, to their 1917 petition for an expansion of its ejido at the expense of San Juan Teitipac, that he was experiencing some anxiety regarding the future of his hacienda (Castro Castillo n.d., 11), noting that "their petition did not contain anything new with respect to the farm." The specter of agrarian reform and its potential negative effect on his hacienda was clearly on Castro's mind as he wrote these words. He must have been pained by the realization that historical events beyond his control would prevent him from continuing to "exploit to good advantage" (explotar con provecho) the hacienda that he and his father had restored to relative prosperity in the early 1880s.

## Eduardo Mendoza: The Terrazguero's Perspective on Hacienda Life

Eduardo Mendoza's belief was that Hacienda San Antonio had been founded by friars (frailes) as part of an estate that also included a rancho known as Guelaviate. This was in accordance with oral tradition in Congregación San Antonio, and was supported by a legend that one of the friars who died there came down the steps every night directly to the chapel from the rectory. These ghostly visions were reportedly witnessed by servants living within the hacienda compound. This folkloric rendering of the hacienda's history probably referred to the period of time during the nineteenth century when it was in the hands of Catarina nuns. It could also derive from the earlier presence of Dominican priests who, already ensconced in their parish headquarters in nearby San Juan Teitipac, consecrated the chapel after it was built, presided over Masses, and were at the beck and call of the hacendado who periodically stayed at the hacienda.

Local oral tradition, as related by Eduardo, was not far off the track in believing that the friars sold the hacienda at some point in the second half of the nineteenth century. He did not remember the exact date when the hacienda lands were expropriated and the ejido established, but thought that it occurred after ownership had passed from the Castro family to Taurino Barriga of Rojas (who may have leased it from Enrique Luis Audiffred Bustamante, who owned the estate after Carlos Castro).

Eduardo referred to himself and other hacienda workers interchangeably by the terms "campesino," "terrazguero," or "mediero," and to the owners by the terms "hacendado" or "amo." The hacienda administrator who assigned work and kept accounts was referred to as the "mandador" (foreman). Those who worked directly for the hacendado were referred to as "mozos de pie" or "criados."

Eduardo's narrative was framed in a straightforward style with an emphasis on the unequal economic relationship between amo (master) and terrazguero (tenant), as evidenced by his opening statement: "We have always been peasants (campesinos). That has been our work from the time we were growing up. That is our life, suffering." (Esa es la vida de nosotros, sufriendo.) He further explained that they worked all day long for 25 centavos. The hacendado obligated them to do household chores (y nos obligaba hacer faena) such as sweep the patio of the hacienda. If the worker did not do it, the hacendado charged him 6 centavos a week and stopped assigning chores like sweeping. He told them that due to their disobedience, they would be forbidden to come near the big house. At the end of the year, he charged workers a cumulative fee of 6 centavos weekly as punishment.

Workers lived in close proximity to the hacienda on residence lots (solares) owned by the hacendado but selected by the workers with the approval of the mandador (foreman). The settlement pattern of the workers' community of fifty households was dispersed; it had a total population in 1900 of 247 (Arellanes Meixueiro 1999, 39). The casas de adobe, jacales, and tejabanas were built by the workers and recognized as belonging to them. The residence lot and house could be passed on to a son upon the death of the household head but would revert back to the hacendado in those cases where the deceased worker left no male heir.

Eduardo characterized the nature of the amo-terrazguero relationship as sharecropping and specified that the hacendado did not provide seed for planting. Workers saved seeds used to plant beans, corn, or whatever crop the hacendado instructed them to plant. The hacendado charged rent for land cultivated: 10 centavos per almud for corn planted but also in kind. Workers were charged two hens (gallinas) for every fanega (24 almudes) of corn planted and one hen for a half fanega of corn (12 almudes) planted. Each hen was worth 15 pesos. This enabled the hacendado to accumulate wealth in the form of poultry. "Just for planting one fanega of corn," lamented Eduardo, "a poor campesino came up embracing his two hens and had to give them to the master." Eduardo saw an entire room in the hacienda filled with hens.

These were unusual variations on the theme of the mediero-hacendado relationship previously reported for the Oaxaca Valley. The surcharge levied on medieros, in addition to the obligatory payment of a share of the crop harvested, was especially onerous.

The assignment of plots to be planted, and of the tasks to be performed during the agricultural cycle, occurred through a permission system strictly controlled by the mandador. The hacendado lived most of the time in Oaxaca City, and the hacienda was run by a resident mandador who assigned and supervised the workforce. The mandador kept weekly accounts of work performed by mozos; the hacendado came on Saturdays to pay his workers (a rayar).

At harvesttime, the mandador assigned mozos de pie to pick the hacendado's share. (Él metía mozos a sacar la media.) Three or so mozos de pie worked for the hacendado year-round, although not on a permanent basis, since they were regularly rotated. At harvesttime, thirty to thirty-five mozos picked and processed the harvest (piscar, deshojar, desgranar). After the hacendado's share was processed, medieros were permitted to pick their shares. (Después iba uno a pizcar lo de uno.)

The hacendado had several foremen for different sections of the estate that included Rancho Guelaviate. There was constant turnover in staff. If one foreman did not work out, then another replaced him. A foreman rarely lasted beyond a year or two. When tasks needed to be done, the foreman simply instructed the community leader to "Call Fulano [So-and-So] to come to work for me." Individual work assignments lasted from two or three days to an entire week.

During harvest, the foreman walked parcel by parcel, inspecting to make sure that not one ear of corn was missing, and to make certain they had been harvested or plowed. To go to the fields and bring back a basket of corn, the mediero had to ask permission from the mandador. Those were the "things that one had to put up with" (así eran las trabas de la gamarra), complained Eduardo. "Any little thing you wanted to do, you had to get permission from the foreman. You needed his permission to go and pick a few green beans (ejotes) or squash. You needed permission for everything. You could not just go to the fields and pick what you wanted like we do now."

The share and surcharge system, enforced by the foreman, operated with regard to crops as well as animals. If a mediero raised goats, he did this on a share basis (al partido). The same arrangement applied to cows. In the month of October, goats that were to be left in a mediero's care were branded, and if one of them died or disappeared, the mediero had to pay the hacendado. In January, all of the goats given out on a share basis were herded into a corral and counted. If one had died or had been eaten by a coyote, the mediero had to pay the hacendado. "You had to pay," said Eduardo, "in goats." The goats were kept on a share basis because they grazed and ate grass on the hacendado's land (campean en el cerro, comen de la pastura del hacendado).

This strict regime of control was described in Eduardo's discussion of what he termed the frightening year of hunger (el año de hambre) in 1915 (Ruiz Cervantes 1988, 380). The hacendado hid corn from government officials requesting feed for cavalry horses (la caballada) and never complied with their requests. There was grudging compliance with requests for fodder (zacate). Eduardo remembered that workers hauled bundles of zacate for cavalry horses to a place near the chapel, where they were loaded onto a government truck.

During the 1915 crisis, the hacendado doled out corn rations at night to needy tenants. Eduardo remembered that "around 10 o'clock at night, we went to get corn, according to the work we had done." The mandador kept the accounts. He would record the exact amount of corn given for household consumption, typically about 1 almud per day. "Every night it was like that," declared Eduardo, "and when the accounts were added up, you had to pay for the corn you got with days of work. We worked a week to pay for the corn we consumed. Clothing? We had only mended clothes during the famine. It was ugly. That was the way it was."

The practice of "pedir maíz" (to request corn) was the only form of credit relationship between hacendado and mediero. Medieros were accustomed to asking the hacendado for a fanega of corn to supplement their share when the harvest was poor; the corn they got was repaid through other assigned work. There was no tienda de raya or hacienda store, and no cash loans or advances at Hacienda San Antonio.

Violations of the mandador system were punished by reducing the amount of land the offending mediero could cultivate. Land cultivated by the offender was reassigned by the foreman to another mediero. Eduardo insisted that they had no other choice but to adapt to this controlling regimen: "To do something, you had to ask the foreman," he explained. "'Patrón, I want you to give me permission to parar surcos (plow after harvest) on my plot,' and he would respond, 'Go and do it.' If you didn't ask permission, the foreman would ask you, 'Why did you go there to such and such a paraje? Why did you go to plow furrows? Why didn't you get permission from me first?'" Thus there was a strong incentive for the mediero to follow the rules requiring sanction by the mandador for any activity undertaken on hacienda land: land assigned to violators would be reassigned.[5]

The Castros were not only conservative in their administration of the hacienda but intransigent regarding changes in the payment and surcharge system. When Eduardo served as community president, he received an official correspondence from the state government, through the municipal president in San Sebastián, ordering the hacendado to grant a 5-centavo pay raise from 25 to 30 centavos for a day's work. The raise was grudgingly granted but was accompanied by a new compensatory surcharge of 25 centavos levied per bundle of firewood cut on hacienda land.

The hacienda regime in San Antonio operated for decades with a resident mandador and an absentee hacendado. The Castros, who lived in Oaxaca City, typically came to their hacienda only on weekends in a wooden coach driven by a coachman (cochero) and pulled by four or five mules kept at the hacienda for that purpose.

Social interaction between the hacendado and the terrazguero community was limited. His only participation in community life was during the patron saint's mayordomía when he attended festivities and ate. The fiesta's sponsoring mayordomo relied on the *guelaguetza* system to assemble the requisite ceremonial consumables: mezcal, cigarettes, tortillas, cacao, turkeys, and so on. "We didn't ask for anything on a *guelaguetza* basis from the hacendado," Eduardo emphasized, "we celebrated the fiesta by using reciprocity (*guelaguetza*) only among ourselves." One evening was designated for *guelaguetza* collections of a kilo of chocolate, a package of cigarettes, a gallon of mezcal, or 5 almudes of tortillas. Donations were written down. Every household in the community participated. "Once we understood what was required for the person who was mayordomo," said Eduardo, "we gave *guelaguetzas*, since we knew we would be paid back what was given."

Eduardo did not remember exactly when the ownership of the hacienda passed from José María Castro's widow to his son Carlos, only that it occurred prior to the incursion led by General Juan Brito, commander of a brigade in the Ejército Soberanista de Oaxaca, around 1915.[6]

Rancho Guelaviate, also known as Hacienda San José Guelaviate, was the original part of Hacienda San Antonio Buenavista. The Castros had two foremen: one at the hacienda proper and another at Rancho Guelaviate. The residents of Guelaviate originated there but belonged to the hacienda. The ranch served to guard the mountainous lands of the hacienda that bordered Santa Cecilia Jalieza, Santo Domingo Jalieza, and San Pedro Guegorexe. There were forty or so contribuyentes in Guelaviate, and fifty or so in the hacienda. The ranch also had cultivable land. Among the victims of the 1908 typhoid epidemic in Guelaviate were the parents of the Sumano brothers: Juan, Antonio, and Marcelo. Many people in Rancho Guelaviate died of typhoid (tifo). People were afraid to attend wakes for the victims for fear of contagion.

Eduardo personally knew all of the inhabitants of Guelaviate and recalled the names of several heads of household and "terrazgueros del amo" who lived there when he was a young man: Antonio Martínez, Pedro González, Donaciano Hernández, Teodardo Hernández, Trinidad Mendoza, Porfirio Mendoza, Cornelio Sumano, Eugenio Platas, Francisco López, Nacho López, Alfonso Gabriel, and Antonio Gabriel. He remembered that Eugenio Platas "was a warden (guardamonte) for the master his entire life" and looked after the brushland and mountains to prevent poachers from cutting firewood.

Things went from bad to worse in Guelaviate in the aftermath of the epidemic, apparently due to a combination of family feuds, intercommunity land feuds, and factionalism. According to Eduardo, "They shot Trinidad Mendoza (unrelated to him), and the ranch began to disintegrate (así fue que se descompuso el rancho). They had their clashes," said Eduardo, "who knows with whom? (¿quién sabe con quién?) Nobody knew the people who invaded there." The end result was that Rancho Guelaviate was sacked and the Sumano brothers, including Juan (whom Eduardo described as a "muchachón"), left for San Juan, while others left for Santa Cecilia and San Pedro. Eduardo admitted that the Sumano brothers "were known as tough guys (valientes) in Rancho Guelaviate," and that they upheld their reputation after moving to San Juan, where they became embroiled in political violence and gangsterism before, during, and after the reign of ex-General Juan Brito and his defensas sociales.

### The Revolution in San Sebastián and Buenavista

San Sebastianos who personally experienced the 1910s and 1920s remembered those years as marked by hunger, poverty, and suffering. For them, those decades did not represent the end of one political epoch and the beginning of another but rather a tumultuous and unsettled time. Armed encampments of soldiers requisitioned scarce provisions, mounted intruders stole animals, and wealthy families like the Marcials were temporarily forced to abandon their homes and lands in the village and go into temporary exile in Oaxaca City. It was a period of political turmoil involving "Serranos" (members of the highlander anti-Carranza movement) against "Carrancistas" (followers of Venustiano Carranza) and a scattering of other "-ista"-suffixed movements whose causes of the moment were vague and had little local meaning to most San Sebastianos. Maguey was cooked and

eaten as a sole means of sustenance. In short, the revolution for San Sebastianos was a time of instability, hunger, and deprivation that resulted
in meaningful agrarian reform only for a relatively small group of households who had been terrazgueros on the adjoining Hacienda San Antonio
Buenavista.

The first incident that San Sebastianos recalled as being associated with
the revolution occurred on May 28, 1912. To my knowledge, this is the only
incident from that period involving Teitipac residents that found its way into
published history. The account, written by Cayetano Esteva (1913, 388–389),
a Oaxaca historian unsympathetic to the revolutionary cause, reported that
on May 28, 1912, seventy revolutionaries from Valle Grande penetrated the
Hacienda of Santa Rosa Los Negritos and, after consummating their "con-
temptible deeds," moved toward San Sebastián Teitipac for the purpose of
"inciting its peaceful and industrious inhabitants." When the municipal
president was informed of this situation, he went out to greet the "outlaws"
and took them to the village. They never had an inkling of the ambush that
was being prepared for them. When the leader of the group spoke to the San
Sebastianos of socialism and invited them to expropriate hacienda lands
for redistribution to sharecroppers, the San Sebastianos demanded that his
words be written up and signed in a municipal act. Just when the revolutionaries thought they had persuaded the San Sebastianos to initiate a general
uprising, one infuriated individual rebuked the words of the revolutionary
leader, fired a shot into the air, and gave a call to arms. The crowd disarmed
the revolutionaries, and with their own weapons killed sixteen of them in
the village and wounded several others, five of whom later died in Papalutla
while others died on the road. Animals that had been robbed from the Los
Negritos Hacienda were recuperated.

Pedro Valeriano, who was a teenager at the time, recalled that "they ad-
vised us that the thieves (ladrones) who robbed Hacienda Santa Rosa were
coming toward our community by ringing the church bells so that people
would assemble." The "infuriated individual" mentioned in the above account was identified by Valeriano as none other than Matías Marcial himself: "When the people gathered, the thieves turned around and attacked.
The now-deceased (difunto) Matías led the chase on horseback, shooting
his rifle into the air. They captured the thieves over there by the river, near
where the guava trees (palos de guayaba) are. All of the thieves were shot
(fusilados)."

This was the first of several incidents in San Sebastián set in motion by
the revolution. Oral tradition in the community did not view these incidents
in ideological or political terms but rather as acts of undesirable intruders
identified as ladrones or bandidos (thieves or bandits). The only real monu-

ment to the revolution in San Sebastián was not a statue of a revolutionary hero but rather a large mound covered with a dense thicket of thorn bushes at a paraje near the habitation area known as El Espinal de los Ladrones (The Thieves' Briar Patch). There, the bodily remains of many of those 1912 revolutionaries from Valle Grande were buried in a common grave by the San Sebastianos who killed them.

Land-poor San Sebastianos sympathized with the revolutionary program of agrarian reform. The more affluent minority, especially the Marcials and other village leaders, supported the counterrevolutionary Serranos, one of whose leading generals, Licenciado Guillermo Meixueiro, was a close relative of the largest landowner in the adjacent community of Santa Cruz Papalutla (Ruiz Cervantes 1988, 366–380; Bailón Corres 1999, 170–177;).

When the Carranza forces arrived in San Sebastián in 1916, counterrevolutionary supporters, including the brothers and sons of Matías Marcial (who died in 1915), had their homes sacked and most of their movable property destroyed or stolen. The Marcial family and their supporters fled the village. Afterward, when the revolutionary fervor died down, they all returned to the village, reoccupied their houses, and took up where they left off, with one significant difference: village politics was characterized by shorter periods of control by one faction after the revolution. Between 1940 and 1990, only four municipal presidents were direct descendants of Matías Marcial.[7]

The first event in San Antonio Buenavista during the years of the Mexican Revolution remembered by Eduardo Mendoza was a 1914 incursion by forces led by General Juan Brito, who represented Meixueiro's Ejército Soberanista de Oaxaca. This was part of the Serrano campaign to topple the "liberal" governorship of Miguel Bolaños Cacho and install a regional government resistant to the Federalist/Constitutionalist forces loyal to Carranza (Bailón Corres 1999, 170–171; cf. Ruiz Cervantes 1988, 384–388; Arellanes Meixueiro et al. 2000, 45). Brito's troops were encamped in the vicinity of San Juan Guelavía and issued requisitions to nearby settlements for provisions: "Brito and his forces asked for everything: onions, garlic, beans, salt, tortillas," according to Eduardo. Brito was among those who requested "corn for the cavalry horses" (maíz para la caballada) from the hacendado, and like the rest, was refused. In Brito's case, the refusal had repercussions: a nighttime raid of the hacienda by Brito's militia during which the granary was emptied of corn and all of the horses, mules, and cows in the corral were taken.

Eduardo recalled that during the raid, nineteen workers, including him, were locked up in a room of the hacienda, while the hacendado, who happened to be at the hacienda at the time, hid in another room. After the raiders left, according to Eduardo, all of the calves were braying; and the hacendado, in fear of his life, left for Oaxaca. Castro was arrested and jailed for a time in Oaxaca by political opponents. Upon his release, a new foreman was sent to manage the hacienda. During this period of political unrest, the foreman "went to Oaxaca to bring money for the payroll because the hacendado, the poor man, was afraid to come himself."

Not long afterward, the hacienda was raided by a group of Carrancistas. "I was working as a mozo de pie in the hacienda with a cart (carreta)," explained Eduardo, and "I was seated on a pile of rope (montón de reatas) used for making three or four trips daily to haul firewood, good-sized logs (puros trozos), to San Sebastián Tutla. We heard shouts of 'People are coming!' (allí viene la gente). They came mounted on horseback in a big hurry with rifles in their hands (vinieron a caballo a toda prisa, traían armas en la mano). They stole horses from the master."

The military phase of the revolution, and the concomitant breakdown of the Porfirian system of regional governance, created conditions for the emergence of new forms of local and regional caciquism and political gangsterism. Ancestral enmities between pueblos regarding territorial and communal land boundaries and land-use patterns were exacerbated. In the case of San Antonio Buenavista, these ancestral enmities involved their larger, aggressive neighbor, San Juan Teitipac.

Ironically, the 1920s agrarian reform process caused an escalation in local violence. "Congregación Buenavista," observed one scholar, "complained that they had not been able to use the land conceded to them in the definitive dotación [land endowment by expropriation], because San Juan did not allow them to do so—they were attacked by armed men causing a number of dead and wounded; the remainder of the population had to take refuge in a nearby pueblo" (Arellanes Meixueiro 1988, 54).

The "nearby pueblo" was San Sebastián Teitipac; Eduardo Mendoza remembered the names of several victims of that attack by San Juan. "The question of violence began," he recounted, "when those from San Juan came (cuando entraron los de San Juan), when they killed Genaro Alvarado and Joaquín Alvarado and also killed Pioquinto Hernández and Pancho. They killed five, all from the hacienda. San Juan has never allowed us to live our lives. (Los sanjuaneros nunca nos han dejado vida.) They invaded our community because they knew that there were only a few of us." All of these killings occurred near the boundary with San Juan after the ejido had been established. Eduardo believed that this provided a motive for the attacks; San Juan had failed to petition for an ejido because they were not considered terrazgueros.

Eduardo also remembered an earlier murder of residents of Congregación San Antonio by unidentified Sanjuaneros: "The night when Ubenses, nicknamed 'Barquillero,' was baptized, Sanjuaneros invaded, killing his mother, father, and brother. Three, a woman and two men, died on that occasion. It was me who took the baby 'Barquillero,' who was breast-feeding, from his dead mother's arms. I carried him to my aunt's house. That was the first invasion by San Juan, when they killed the parents of that child. They declared war on us because there were only a few of us." (Ellos han hecho una guerra con nosotros, como somos pocos.)

Eduardo did not remember the exact year when the ejido was officially established in San Antonio but estimated that it had occurred by the early 1930s. Eduardo's view was that those who wanted land only had to petition the government for it. (Nos fuimos al gobierno para que el gobierno nos diera esa repartición.) He remembered that Lic. Carlos Castro was still alive when hacienda land was expropriated by government order. (Era orden que el gobierno daba. Le quitamos su terreno.) By the time the dotación became definitive, Castro's widow was owner of the casco and the remaining lands of the hacienda.[8]

Castro's widow leased or sold her interest in what remained of the hacienda to an individual from Rojas named Taurino Barriga. Barriga, whose surname when not capitalized means "stomach," was derided by the ejidatarios because he had a potbelly (era panzonsote). He got the last laugh, however, by forcing the ejidatarios to remove their residences from hacienda property following the repartition.

Eduardo did not disclose, perhaps for lack of knowledge, that Don Taurino Barriga was a "cattle magnate" whose herd was stolen (in the late 1930s incident described by Malinowski and De la Fuente near the Cerro de Mantecón) as the cattle were being driven by herders from Ocotlán to Oaxaca (Drucker-Brown 1982, 94). Ironically, the linkage between this incident and Barriga's involvement with Hacienda San Antonio and San Juan Teitipac in the 1930s was probably not coincidental. Circumstantial evidence gives reason to speculate that the robbery may have been an inside job perpetrated by Barriga's own hired thugs or persons affiliated with them.

Eduardo explained that it was none other than the Sumanos, refugees from Rancho Guelaviate then living in San Juan, and other Sanjuaneros who served as the ex-hacienda's enforcers and caretakers of its remaining land and cattle. When their ejido was granted, Buenavistans were still living on hacienda land. Taurino's people came to remove them by force with Chico Sumano, Taurino's mandador and Juan Sumano's uncle, heading the removal party. The ejidatarios were told that since they now had an ejido, they could not live on hacienda land. They complied and made provisional housing by tying together strips of thatch (zacate) on poles.

Barriga had either leased or bought the ex-hacienda. All of the Sumanos were his followers (allegados); they worked his land and always carried weapons. (Todos ellos andaban armados, todos. No les faltaba su arma.) "He couldn't stand the sight of us," Eduardo stressed regarding Barriga, "because we got the ejido. He had become owner of the hacienda. He told us to 'go and raise vultures so they will pick out your eyes' (críen zopilotes para que les sacan los ojos)."


## Memories of Juan Brito, the Sumanos, and the Defensas Sociales

The Mexican Revolution had both positive and negative legacies for the peasant population of Hacienda San Antonio Buenavista. Buenavistans during the Porfiriato had an identity as Congregación Buenavista and were an "agencia," or administrative dependency, of the municipality of San Sebastián Teitipac. By 1930 or so, they were granted an ejido from the lands of the hacienda. For the first time in their lives, Buenavistans were able to make and earn their livelihoods free of the onerous mandador system of the hacienda regime.

Following the decommissioning of his troops in 1920 (Martínez 1985, 318; Bailón Corres 1999, 175–176), Juan Brito spent time in prison (Santiago Tlatelolco jail in the D.F.) as punishment for his service in the Ejército Soberanista. After his release, he returned to Oaxaca and settled in San Juan Guelavía, his wife's hometown, where they owned and operated a store. His military career with the Soberanistas in the Tlacolula arm of the Oaxaca Valley (which included a battle with Carrancista forces near Santa Ana del Valle; Cohen 1999, 29–31) gave Brito a great deal of local knowledge, as well as a local and regional political base. It was not surprising that he was resurrected as a leader of the defensas sociales in 1928, and that for a few years prior to his assassination in his store in San Juan Guelavía on March 27, 1936, he was the de facto jefe político in the Tlacolula arm of the Oaxaca Valley.

In the early 1930s, Eduardo Mendoza, as president of the ejido and congregación of Buenavista, went on official business to San Juan Guelavía to inform Brito (fuimos a darle parte a Brito) of the murder of Luis Gabriel that occurred in Rancho Guelaviate. Gabriel was working in his cornfield (milpa) when he was ambushed and left to die. Eduardo told Brito that he had an official report for him. Brito asked, "About what?" And Eduardo read the report alleging that Marcelo Sumano, who was on Brito's payroll, shot and killed a man from the hacienda. Brito asked: "How did that happen? Was there a fight between them?" Eduardo responded in the negative and reported that Gabriel was just working on his plot of land, weeding, when Marcelo came down from the mountain where he had been cutting firewood and ambushed him. Brito listened and replied: "Tomorrow we will go to investigate the matter." An abbreviated investigation took place, Marcelo denied the accusation, and the investigators concluded their proceedings with a culpatory interrogative directed to the Buenavistans: "The entire affair was just among you, perhaps?" (¿Entre Uds. mismos, tal vez?) End of story.

The connection between Brito and the Sumano family was that he came to San Juan Teitipac from his base in Guelavía to recruit militia members (a conquistar gente). Juan Sumano became the head of Juan Brito's group in San Juan Teitipac. Rancho San Antonio, Eduardo insisted, had no factional leaders (no había gente de nadie). Buenavistans did not want to get mixed up with Brito because of his reputation for committing robberies. (No quisieron meterse con Brito porque Brito andaba no más robando, vaya.) Brito had gangs (palomillas) in San Juan Teitipac and in Guelavía guarding his house and store, where Eduardo went regularly to report on conditions in Buenavista. He described Brito as the strongman in that area of the valley (era el poderoso de todos esos pueblos por allí—Eduardo made a sweeping gesture of his hand toward the east and southeast of Buenavista; see Map 2).

Eduardo's wife was a cousin of the Sumano brothers. She no longer considered them to be part of the Guelaviate/San Antonio community, since they had moved to San Juan in the second decade of the twentieth century: "We no longer respected them as our people. (Ya no los respetábamos como gente de nosotros.) They were considered as belonging to San Juan. They got themselves involved with evil. They became bad guys. (Se metieron a la maldad. Se metieron a valientes.)" Eduardo made clear that he knew all of the Sumanos because they were his wife's relatives.

Some Sumanos had separate trajectories from those who moved to San Juan. Felipe Sumano moved from Hacienda San Antonio to live in Rojas because the hacendado demanded that he tend his herd of goats on a share basis. Since Felipe had a lot of goats, such an arrangement did not appeal to him. He told the hacendado, "You can have your hacienda without me," and he left. (Lo exigía con el partido de sus chivos y, como tenía hartos chivos, eso no le convino. Dijo Felipe: "Que se queda el amo con su hacienda, yo me largo.") Felipe, a first cousin of Juan and son of Teófilo Sumano, bought land and a house in Rojas and took his animals there. Teófilo was Juan Sumano's uncle and Eduardo's father-in-law, and lived in the Congregación Buenavista. According to Eduardo, Felipe was never involved with the activities of the San Juan branch of his family.

Pedro Valeriano, a native of San Sebastián Teitipac, served in Juan Brito's militia for about three years, starting in the late 1920s. He remembered that Brito brought people together to be soldiers (juntaba gente para soldado) in what was known as the defensa. In San Juan Teitipac, Juan Sumano was in charge; in San Sebastián, Fidel Martínez was in charge. The defensa was about land. That is why Pedro and others got involved, to get land near the hacienda. The government gave them land and money to buy ox teams. (Fué cosa de tierra, dice Brito. Por eso nos metimos, para conseguir tierra al lado de la hacienda. Dió el gobierno tierra y dinero para comprar yuntas.)

Pedro said that he moved to San Antonio, built a jacal there, bought an ox team, and lived there for one year as a member of Brito's militia. In disagreement with Eduardo Mendoza's account, Pedro remembered that there were five militia members in the Congregación Buenavista (ex-terrazgueros de la hacienda), including Eduardo Mendoza's own son, Gustavo, and "el difunto Efrén."

Pedro recalled that on one occasion, General Brito, always on horseback and in uniform, came to Congregación Buenavista to meet with assembled militia members who then went to San Juan Teitipac to meet up with more militia members; then the assembled militia went to Magdalena Teitipac to pick up a prisoner who was in jail there. According to Pedro, "We arrived at the jail, and since General Brito had the key, he opened it up and took out the prisoner." As the militia was leaving town, Magdalenans opened fire: "Gunshots (balazos), many, many gunshots were fired at us." Brito commanded the militia to walk in single files along each side of the road, and to avoid the middle of the road, but did not permit them to return fire. Several militia members criticized the order, complaining that they were carrying rifles not sticks and should be allowed to use them to defend themselves.

Pedro did not remember how many times he responded to Brito's call to arms in the three-year period he served, but he emphasized that "those of us from San Sebastián and San Juan Teitipac went to San Juan Guelavía whenever he wanted. When he sent for us, we went there." Pedro did not admit to having committed acts of robbery or murder in Brito's service. He was clear, however, in describing Brito's role as sort of a regional Oaxacan equivalent to West Texas's Judge Roy Bean. Whenever there was a dispute (pleito) or a fight (pelea) in San Sebastián over land, animals, or something else, the matter was settled in San Juan Guelavía with Juan Brito. The armed militia in San Sebastián escorted plaintiffs directly to San Juan Guelavía, not to Tlacolula. The municipal president in San Sebastián took the position that serious matters had to be resolved by Brito in Guelavía. (El presidente aquí no hizo nada. Dijo, "Mejor se resuelva con Juan Brito; él nos va a arreglar el asunto.")

Pedro remembered the day when San Sebastián militia members were called to a meeting with Brito in Santa Cruz Papalutla. When they had assembled in front of the municipio, Brito told them that an order had been received from Oaxaca City requiring them to disarm: "Now, boys (mucha-chos), the time has come. I am sorry to tell you, but an order has come down from Oaxaca that everyone is to be disarmed." This news was not well received, and the San Sebastián contingent withdrew to deliberate their re-sponse. Their main concern was that the order was unjust; they had paid for their rifles and considered them to be private property. Nevertheless, after a heated discussion, the San Sebastianos decided to comply and turned in their rifles. On that day, with that act, San Sebastián's official participation in Brito's militia ended. Their period of service lasted about three years, from the late 1920s to the early 1930s.[9]

## The 1966 Petition to Expand the Ejido[10]

Even though most of the Hacienda Buenavista's land had been redistributed to the ejido community made up of ex-terrazgueros living in Congregación San Antonio decades earlier, in 1966 there was a new petition for ampli-ación of the ejido pending with agrarian officials; it was filed on behalf of twenty-eight landless contribuyentes/ciudadanos of San Sebastián. The land in the ex-hacienda was under the control of a new absentee owner; it had been cultivated for a time by hired hands and sharecroppers but was finally allowed to go fallow by 1960. The majority of petitioners were land-less metateros, but the petition originated in collaboration with Buenavistan ejidatarios. It was considered by all concerned as a way to minimize future conflict with San Juan Teitipac, especially over grazing rights. There were troubling signs in 1966 that further conflict might not be avoided before an official decision was made on ejido expansion.

According to Ismael Bautista, one of the signers of the petition, the own-er of the land in question was Enrique Luis Audiffred Bustamante or simply Don Luis: "Earlier there was a boss at the ranch, and his mozos worked those lands. He didn't intend to sell them. Now that the owner has died, his widow and son-in-law remained owners but left the land uncultivated."[11]

Maximiano Hernández and his wife, Artemia Díaz, of San Sebastián had some sort of connection to these remnant hacienda lands and their absentee owners. Ismael mentioned that "Doña Artemia got mad and told us that we were bandits and intended to steal land from the hacienda." She lodged a formal complaint with the Ministerio Público in Tlacolula against the five leaders of the San Sebastián petitioners, who were subpoenaed to attend a hearing.

Ismael, in describing the visit to the Ministerio Público, noted that the agent in charge there said nothing to them. The lawyer representing the owners of the hacienda, in a veiled threat, told them not to get involved in the matter because it was not in their interest to do so. They were told not to continue with the petition because they were going to end up badly. (Nos dijo que no nos metiéramos en ese asunto porque no conviene. Dijo que no está bien que ustedes siguen haciendo la lucha esa; van a salir mal.) Ismael and the others told the lawyer that it was up to the government to resolve the case. If the government decided not to give them the land, then the matter would end there.

Not long after the hearing, a pistolero entered the residence lot of the group's leader, Manuel Hernández, and attempted to murder him. The attempt failed when the pistol jammed. Ismael, Manuel's first cousin, and the others were convinced that the murder attempt had been arranged by Maximiano and Doña Artemia, who had some involvement with the ex-hacienda landowners.


## Conclusion

The most notable sources of continuity from the colonial period to the 1960s in the history of the Teitipac communities and San Antonio Buenavista, aside from the Zapotec language, were several cultural practices regarding economic matters and elements of social organization. The division of labor and specialization with respect to gender, age, and occupations was replete with examples of such continuity, as were kinship, residence, and inheritance. There was evidence of continuity in land tenure, regarding the division between communal and private domains, and in the lingering institution of cacicazgo.

The territorial boundaries of San Sebastián Teitipac were essentially set in the eighteenth century with the community's purchase of a tract of land from the heirs of Lucas de Grijalva, cacique of San Juan, and the Hacienda San Antonio Buenavista also seems to have completed its expansion during the same century by acquiring land from a person described by Carlos Castro as the last cacica of Teitipac. It is tempting to view the emergence of the cacicazgo of Matías Marcial in San Sebastián during the second half of the nineteenth century as foreshadowed by a pre-Hispanic institution reinforced by the early colonial encomendero system.

Overall, given the combined effects of epidemic disease and exploitation through the institution of repartimiento, especially in mining, and the near-genocidal decline in population by the late sixteenth century, the economic record of the seventeenth and eighteenth centuries represented a decisive break with the pre-Hispanic period. Even pre-Hispanic cultigens like corn and nopal were cultivated differently, and in the case of nopal, cultivated on an expanded commercial basis due to its hosting of the cochineal insect. Many new crops and herd animals introduced by the Spaniards transformed local land use and the agrarian economy. This set in motion a process of discontinuity and change, upsetting one of continuity, persistency, and gradual transition.

In the postcolonial period, a complex relationship existed between the two Teitipac communities, San Sebastián and San Juan, and Hacienda San Antonio Buenavista. San Sebastián was more closely related to the hacienda in terms of land boundaries, labor relations, and kinship. The fact that the long-serving foreman of the hacienda, Juan María Acevedo, was a native of San Sebastián cemented this relationship during the second half of the nineteenth century. All of this exacerbated relations between San Sebastián and its larger and relatively land-poor neighbor, San Juan.

The bifurcated organization of the hacienda between the community of San Antonio and the outlying Rancho Guelaviate, which bordered San Juan and Santa Cecilia Jalieza, led to a schism in the hacienda population in the early twentieth century; the Guelaviate community was more closely related socially to San Juan, and the San Antonio community was more closely tied to San Sebastián. During the postrevolutionary period of local militias and banditry, these divisions culminated in considerable internecine violence involving San Sebastianos, Sanjuaneros, Santa Cecilians, and Buenavistans.

## CHAPTER 3

# San Juan Teitipac:

# Metateros Here and There

We do not know for certain if metate production originated in San Juan or San Sebastián, or exactly when metate production originated as an industry in the Oaxaca Valley. Popular archaeological evidence supports the thesis that metates were being made in Teitipac when the Spaniards arrived. In the early 1960s, Rosendo Carranza, a metatero from San Juan Teitipac, uncovered ancient remains in his quarry. I visited and photographed the site and the artifacts recovered by Carranza, but these were not examined by professional archaeologists.

Uncorroborated testimonial evidence from San Sebastián suggests that the quarry in question may, in fact, have originally belonged to San Sebastián and not to San Juan. Be that as it may, it is likely that the ancient stone tools found by Carranza were partially replaced by Spanish steel tools (barretas and cuñas) in the late sixteenth century when stone was quarried to build the large Dominican church and monastery in San Juan. Oral testimony also indicated that some steel tools like sledgehammers were by no means uniformly adopted by metateros in San Sebastián and San Juan during the colonial period, and were not adopted in many cases until the early twentieth century when sledgehammers replaced heavy wooden mallets.

A main theme in this chapter is instability in San Juan's metate industry owing to factionalism. This led to emigration and circulatory migration to the district cabecera, Tlacolula. An alternative to emigration for some Sanjuaneros was to become aggressive buyers-up of metates and manos from the neighboring community of San Sebastián, which had a larger, more stable and diverse supply of stone. The entrepreneurial bent among San Juan's metateros is illustrated by the cases of Efrén Carranza, a pioneer trader, and Inocencio Morales, who, over a period of several decades of permanent residence in Tlacolula, established a unique and thriving metate workshop with in-house employees and outworkers.

Another notable aspect of San Juan expatriates' struggle for livelihood and civility was the tendency for them to remain involved in reciprocity and other elements of the usos y costumbres system of their natal community. Some recent evidence suggests that this tendency may have weakened over the decades (Gabbarot and Clarke 2010, 199).

### The Origins of the Metate Industry and Rosendo Carranza's Discovery

To my knowledge, the earliest reference to metates in the historical litera-ture dealing with Oaxaca Valley Zapotec communities was by Fray Fran-cisco de Burgoa, a native Oaxacan born in 1600 who entered the Dominican order in 1629 and in 1674 published his *Geográfica descripción*. He cred-ited the Oaxaca Valley Zapotec for making and transporting commodities, specifying that they had "quarries for stone, from which they make metates, or ordinary corn grindstones" (Burgoa 1934, 1:416). It is not inconceivable that Burgoa, as a high-ranking member of the Dominican order, visited San Juan Teitipac during the years that the church and monastery were under construction there; if he did, he probably visited the nearby quarries where stone was being extracted. It is likely that among the quarry workers were metateros who had knowledge of quarrying and stonecutting. One can only speculate that Burgoa became aware of that connection, since he failed to explicitly express it in his discussion of Teitipac.

Metates are referenced three times in Malinowski and De la Fuente's (1957) classic study of the Oaxaca market system. In the same paragraph where they described marketplaces as "an ephemeral, dramatic museum of the day" (1957, 19), they noted that ancient customs and traditional ways are revealed in certain pre-Hispanic articles like the metate (ibid., 19–20). In another passage (ibid., 91), they noted that molinos de *nixtamal* competed against the pre-Hispanic metate, which had still not been displaced. Finally, in four paragraphs they explained the utilitarian and cultural importance of the metate (ibid., 154–155; cf. Drucker-Brown 1982, 169–170 and photo 27), including its specific role in gender relations and marriage ceremonies as witnessed by Malinowski himself.[1]

Malinowski and De la Fuente's reference to the metate as a pre-Hispanic artifact was based on the cumulative knowledge of Mesoamerican archae-ology rather than their own field research. Long before their study was written, archaeologists had excavated and classified the remains of many metates and manos from a variety of Mesoamerican sites, hence establishing these artifacts' antiquity beyond a doubt. Metates were of great interest to archaeologists mainly as indicators of maize cultivation and processing but also as indicators of other cultigens like cacao, spices, and even pigments (Searcy 2011, 76). Archaeologists have systematically inferred from metates what they could about consumption and use, and then put them in storage. This record improved somewhat as a result of archaeological research dating from the 1970s in the Oaxaca Valley that documented metate and mano production by an estimated 52–104 individuals at Monte Albán at around AD 500, presumably for use by the resident population that may have been as large as thirty thousand (Blanton 1978, 58).[2]

In 1966, Rosendo Carranza took me to the quarry where four years earlier he had serendipitously uncovered remains of an entire family together with various stone tools positioned around them in circular fashion (Cook 1973; 1982, 181–184). He left the human remains in situ, kept the artifacts he found, and, out of respect for the original burial site, suspended further quarrying activity there.

The discovery of ancient stone tools, together with evidence of metate manufacture, reinforced Rosendo's identity as a metatero and pride in his craft. When people asked him why he continued to work in an occupation that involved so many hard blows with heavy tools, his answer was that he was destined to be a metatero because his ancient progenitors were. Rosendo learned about his craft's antiquity from oral history, but logic told him that the stone tools he found in the quarry were used "before the conquest when the white race (raza blanca) came."

Rosendo explained that he came to the quarry with his son to start clearing away waste stone in order to begin excavating to find bedrock and a vein of stone for making metates. After three weeks of listening to his son complain about the hard work, one day they uncovered a slab of stone measuring about 6 feet long and a few feet wide. The slablike rock had a thin top about 3 inches thick. It was like a wooden plank, like a door (como una tabla, un pedazo de madera, como una puerta), which they inferred to be the surface of a vein of bedrock (ya nos ayudó la suerte; ya nos tocó la de bueno).

In anticipation of blasting sufficient stone for dozens of metates, Rosendo and his son began to clear away all the dirt covering the slab. Using his sledgehammer to sound out the slab of stone to find out if it was embedded or simply lying on top of smaller pieces of stone, Rosendo determined that it was lying on top. When he tapped it, it sounded hollow (oí que sonaba coco). He inferred from this that the slab was provisional, not native or solid bedrock, so they proceeded to clear away more dirt to completely uncover the slab. Rosendo inserted the point of his barreta under the slab for leverage to try to pry it loose. Suddenly, the slab loosened and started to slide off, and Rosendo's son had to jump out of the way to avoid being crushed.

Rosendo explained: "The slab completely rolled over, and if my poor son had not jumped out of the way, he would have been crushed. The slab fell away and there before us was a chamber (vamos viendo un subterráneo allí). A stench was let off (cuando se soltó el olor), it smelled so bad you could not stand it, like the stench of chiles that burn while being roasted for mole; it burned your nostrils. After the stench died down, little by little I approached the chamber to see what might be down there. My son warned me: 'Don't go near it, there might be something down there, there might be a devil down there' (puede haber una cosa adentro, puede haber un diablo allí). By then it was 6:30 or 7:00 p.m. and it was getting dark, so I said to my son that we'd better go home and come back tomorrow morning."

They returned to the quarry the next morning around 10:00 a.m., and what they found shocked them: human remains. Rosendo made the following interpretation of what they saw: "Those poor people, the condition they must have been in back then! Out of fear of the white man (la raza blanca), as history tells us, well those people were so fearful and surprised to hear that their country had been invaded by another race. Those people hid in a hole, grabbed that large slab of stone to use as a cover, and enclosed themselves down there. They starved themselves to death, those ingrates (estos ingratos). That's why I found an entire family buried down there. The two oldest ones were in the center, and the rest of the family was spread out around them. Their remains were here, there, and over there [motioning in circular fashion]. That's why it smelled so bad. The poor innocents were down there, hiding in fear, and decided to bury themselves down in that chamber. That was the condition of those people when the Spaniards arrived in Mexico. When they realized they were incompetent to defend themselves, they hid away in those caves, in underground chambers, so they would not witness what was happening. The entire family died of starvation and thirst down there."

Rosendo provided more details regarding the discovery. When the chamber was uncovered, the hammerstones were inside. The layer of material on top of the covering slab consisted of flakes/pieces of waste stone from making metates (de pura laja de metate); underneath was a layer of pulverized earth, then another layer of flaked stone, and finally big slabs on top of black earth, just like the foundation of a house. (La segunda capa lo mismo, tenía laja. Y de allí una tierra negra y sobrepuestos las piedras enteramente como un cimiento de casa.)

Rosendo speculated about the identity of the people whose remains he had discovered in the midst of stone tools. The layers of stone flakes on top of the burial chamber, he reasoned, were from metates that people were making and finishing (labrando) back then. He also found used metates and manos. All of the above led him to conclude that "those people we un-covered were metateros before the Spanish Conquest," and he added: "This craft has been here for a long time, they had it in ancient times. That is why we think the craft was born here."

We need not agree with Rosendo's speculation about the circumstances that led to the burial to appreciate the significance of his discovery, which was supported by artifactual evidence that I photographed (see photo essay), as well as by the detailed description he provided. When I asked Rosendo what additional evidence he had—apart from his discovery of the burial in the quarry area—to support the pre-Hispanic origins of his craft, he simply cited oral tradition familiar to all of his fellow metateros. His serendipitous ethnoarchaeological project was remarkable, even without the intervention of archaeologists, which would have secured the site a place in the official record.[3]

## Metatero Lives and Business

The Carranzas were one of San Juan's major metatero lineages, including Rosendo's father, Marcelino, who was seventy-five and living in the extend-ed household with Rosendo in 1966; his son Isaías; his brother Eliseo; his uncle Efrén, seventy-two; and three cousins, Otón, Armando, and Bulmaro. Armando had permanently relocated to Tlacolula, where he pursued his oficio full-time. Armando's first cousin (FaSisSo, or father's sister's son) Emilio Alvarado, like Armando, also permanently relocated to Tlacolula "to get away from disputes (pleitos) and to avoid difficulties."

Armando explained more fully why he had relocated to Tlacolula: "I left due to the troubles (los líos) from bad elements (por malos elementos) there." He said that on any given day he would hardly start work before an incident occurred involving "bad things some people do, they abuse you (atropellan a uno)." Someone from another section of town would come to talk to him, and immediately neighbors or others began to raise questions or gossip. You could not be seen talking to anyone, he reiterated, because there were serious conflicts between different sections of town, especially the second against the third. During the twelve years that he served on the municipal police force in San Juan, every year involved interventions due to shoot-outs between the sections.

"If you walked from one section of the town to another," explained Armando, "immediately you were asked, 'Where do you think you are going?' or 'What are you doing here?' People complained about you (reclaman a uno) even when you simply went to visit family. Immediately they asked you: 'What is it you are bringing here from over there?' or 'What is your business here? Are you coming to judge us?'" (Luego dicen, '¿Algo llevarás de acá para allá?' Y ya los otros dicen, 'Tú, ¿a que vienes? ¿No más vienes a juzgar aquí?') One was not free simply to walk around the streets of San Juan. The people in charge of each section were sometimes betrayed by their own constituents. He cited the case of a man named Lorenzo who was assaulted by a bad element of his own faction. Armando, in short, viewed Tlacolula as a safer and more neighborly town than his native San Juan.

A further illustration of internal factionalism and conflict in San Juan was provided in an October 1967 article in an Oaxaca City newspaper entitled "Cacique of San Juan Teitipac Wounded, Now Protected by the Authorities" (*Carteles del Sur*, October 17, 1 and 4). The article, based on information from several Sanjuaneros who came to the newspaper office, reported the "grave wounding" of a San Juan gang leader (capitán de gavilla) who was responsible for rapes, robberies, murders, and shoot-outs (zafarranchos).

The first San Juan metatero to relocate to Tlacolula was Porfirio Mateo Cruz, who was forty-eight years old in 1966. His reasons for relocating were similar to those expressed by Armando: "Because of the troubles there, I told myself I was tired of fighting, and it was better for me to get away and come to Tlacolula." He did so in 1947. Porfirio began to learn metate making at the age of twelve; at the time, he was living with his uncle, Vicente Martínez, who taught him by example.

After living and working in Tlacolula for eighteen years, Porfirio returned to San Juan in reaction to an ownership dispute in the Tlacolula quarry between comuneros and a private property owner. He had been buying his supply of stone from Tlacolula quarrymen and working on it at home. The dispute temporarily disrupted this arrangement, so he worked out a share arrangement back in San Juan in a quarry owned by his uncle, Ángel Martínez. Their arrangement was to split quarried stone equally between them, and then each, in turn, split his share with coworkers. If enough stone for twelve metates was quarried, Ángel got six and Porfirio six. Porfirio, who had two workers, kept two stones for his own use and gave two stones to each worker. He lived with his wife and a nine-year-old daughter and had no agricultural land to cultivate because his one small parcel was being cultivated by his recently married son. In Porfirio's words: "I don't have anything, only my craft. Every day I get up, drink my coffee, and go to work in the quarry."

## The Extraordinary Career of Inocencio Morales

Porfirio Mateo was the first San Juan metatero to move to Tlacolula in 1947, but Inocencio Morales arrived in 1950 and had a greater influence on the industry there. Born in the first decade of the twentieth century in San Juan, Inocencio married in 1926, and he and his wife lived with his parents until 1933. His parents had land, and he worked only as a campesino. He explained: "I was a peasant from the beginning. Corn, black beans, broad beans (habas), chickpeas, all of that we cultivated to eat, but I didn't have money to spend." He was ashamed to seek work as a jornalero to earn money ("A mí me daba vergüenza ir a trabajar como jornalero"), so he asked his compadre, Efrén Carranza, to teach him the craft of stoneworking. Efrén asked for a peso to buy a hand pick for him but instead brought him a used hammer that Inocencio took to a local blacksmith, who made two hand picks from it. On that same day, Inocencio finished his first mano from several unfinished ones he bought from an old metatero for five cents each. He was apprehensive at the end of that day because a chip of stone had flown into his eye, but he persisted and finished all of the manos as fast as he could, sold them in the Oaxaca City market, and bought some sunglasses to protect his eyes—a practice that stayed with him over the years.

"Little by little I kept finishing manos until I could finish two or three in one day," explained Inocencio. "Two was enough," he said, "since in those days a day laborer earned 25 centavos for a day's work, from sunrise to sunset. I was able to cut alfalfa for my animals, and then finish two manos by six in the afternoon." He earned 50 centavos a day just by finishing manos. It was during this period that Inocencio described street-corner competition in San Juan between him and other stoneworkers to see who could make the best manos. (Nos reuníamos en la esquina en San Juan y nos poníamos en competencia a ver quién la sacaba mejor.) This competition improved his skill to the point that he took manos to the Oaxaca City market, where they sold quickly because they were so well made.

Once Inocencio started earning cash from finishing and selling manos, and then metates, he continued to cultivate his own fields, especially alfalfa used by his wife to fatten cattle. By 1936, Inocencio and his wife, who never had children, accumulated sufficient capital to open a small store in San Juan, tended by his wife. This gave him the opportunity to "earn a few cents more from stones" by exchanging cigarettes, matches, and other items for metates and manos and, subsequently, buying them for cash rather than by bartering. He was among the first Sanjuaneros to acquire metates and manos through indirect barter for store goods, and he stayed in the business as an intermediary until leaving San Juan in 1946.

Inocencio learned to play guitar and sing at home by the age of twelve, but neither his parents nor other relatives encouraged him to pursue that interest because it was associated in their eyes with drinking and debauchery. On the advice of an uncle, but without the knowledge of his parents, he began to study with the local priest to become a cantor. He had taken forty-one lessons when his parents heard that he was studying music. When he clarified to them that he was doing so to become a cantor, and not to be a member of the village band, they permitted him to practice at home.

In 1928, Inocencio studied in the choir room (cantoría) of the local church, and in 1930 he began to play for Masses in the San Juan church; he was still doing so in the Tlacolula church when I interviewed him in 1966. The instrument he mastered was the harmonium (armónico). It had a keyboard that produced tones by forcing air through metallic reeds by means of a bellows driven with leg power by pedals. In San Juan, Inocencio's only economic reward for this service was to be exempted from tequio work on communal land held in the name of the patron saint (los terrenos del santo).

Toward the end of 1946, he left San Juan for Nochistlán, where he was recruited by the church to become a cantor. He and his wife lived there until 1950. Through the good offices of a priest he met in Nochistlán, who was subsequently assigned to the church in Tlacolula, Inocencio was recruited to replace the retiring cantor there. Until that time, he had retained his house and property in San Juan. He sold it in 1950 to buy a house in Tlacolula, where, in addition to working for the church as cantor, he again took up metate making. In 1966, he was working at both jobs, and his wife operated a successful restaurant in the market.

Inocencio considered both of his occupations to be artistic. For him, metate making was an art because not everybody could do it (cualquiera no puede hacerlo), and because it took time to learn it (se dilata para poder hacer un metate regularcito), unlike the work of a campesino (cualquiera puede entrar en el campo y pronto aprende). He liked working as a metatero because it was monetarily rewarding (tengo la plena seguridad que tiene salida el trabajo) but admitted that it was heavy work, and he realized that when he grew old and weaker, he would stop doing it. Music was artistic in his view because "not everyone knows the notes," and it had the added advantage of involving lighter work (trabajo más liviano). Even though he was not paid for being a cantor in San Juan, he did earn a salary in Nochistlán and Tlacolula for that work.

Before leaving San Juan for Nochistlán, after mastering the technique of finishing manos, Inocencio taught himself how to finish metates. His ingenious procedure began with a used metate, taking its measurements and studying its form. Then he used a pencil and a carpenter's square to trace out patterns on trozos he bought in the quarries. He started to use a small chisel to smooth out rough surfaces and, by 1939, began to chisel designs on the sides and undersides of metates that gave them more value in the market. At that time, he did not have his own quarry in San Juan and did not have time to do quarry work, so he bought eight, ten, or twelve pieces of stone for metates in the quarries and hauled them home with a wagon. He did all of the cutting and finishing work on his residence lot, a pattern he would later continue in Tlacolula.

In 1944, two years before he accepted his appointment as cantor in Nochistlán, he paid 30 pesos for access to a section of a quarry whose owner considered it unpromising for finding suitable stone. Inocencio hired five mozos and began to excavate, and within half a day, encountered a treasure trove of fifteen or so buried trozos. The owner was chagrined by this discovery, so Inocencio gave him a trozo in consolation. The next day, he and his crew set a powder charge in the exposed bedrock, and the blast yielded several more trozos for metates and manos. Afterward, Inocencio began excavating a site on land owned by his father and succeeded in finding sufficient stone to produce manos. That was to be his last experience of actually working in a quarry.

Upon arriving in Tlacolula from Nochistlán, Inocencio and his wife lived in a room in the rectory (curato); he bought stone from local quarrymen and hauled it to the rectory to work on it. When the priest and sacristan saw several unfinished roughed-out metates (metates destroncados) beside the curato, they laughed and cast doubts on Inocencio's skill as a metatero. When the sacristan returned later and saw the finished metates, he was persuaded that the cantor was also skilled as a metatero. Later that year, Inocencio bought a house in Tlacolula, and with stone bought and trucked to his residence lot, he began to make metates for sale in the Sunday plaza. He also bought finished metates for resale from San Sebastián and San Juan sellers and resold them at a profit of 5 to 10 pesos per metate.

As his metate business prospered, Inocencio cultivated relationships with expatriate San Juan metateros like Porfirio Mateo and Emilio Alvarado. In the case of Emilio, Inocencio provided him with roughed-out metates to finish during his period of apprenticeship, but he bought finished metates from Porfirio on a regular basis. Once Emilio learned how to make metates, he left Inocencio's house, ended their relationship, and began to compete with Inocencio for stone in the Tlacolula quarries. To replace Emilio, Inocencio hired a live-in mozo from San Juan, Silverio Molina, who made metates and manos for him for about three years.

In the 1950s, Inocencio's nephew from San Juan, Luis Alvarado, came to reside in his house and became an apprentice in the metate business. He was followed, in 1962, by another nephew, Luis's brother Constantino, who did the same. Inocencio's metate workshop was thus born and consolidated. Under his direction, both Luis and Constantino became expert at making high-quality metates and manos. By 1965, they had developed a market identity for Tlacolula metates as the largest, best-crafted, most durable, and most expensive metates in the Oaxaca Valley.

Inocencio, pridefully, attributed the difference between their metates and those made in San Juan and San Sebastián to his use of the right tools, including carpenter's squares and measuring tapes, and patience to make sharper angles and straighter lines. In comparing his products with those made by Porfirio Mateo, whom he credited with being an excellent metatero, Inocencio considered his to be even better owing to an extensive inventory of tools and his own bellows to forge sharper points without depending on the local blacksmith. His attention to detail and desire to excel, exemplified in terms of both capital expenditure and entrepreneurial conduct, were the keys to Inocencio's unique status in the Oaxaca Valley metate industry.

As an outsider (afuerano/afuereño) in Tlacolula, Inocencio encountered obstacles both in the conduct of his metate business and in his position as cantor. Although a district head town and more urbanized than any other community in its district, Tlacolula in the mid-1960s still had some vil-lage-like characteristics regarding issues like envy (envidia), participation in the civil-religious hierarchy and reciprocity relations, boundaries between communal and private land, and notions of legitimate citizenship that em-phasized nativity and kinship. All of these factors, taken together, were the source of Inocencio's difficulties.

Inocencio's service as cantor in the local Catholic church was rewarded by an exemption from tequio work on communal agricultural land in San Juan but not from service in the civil-religious hierarchy. While living in San Juan, Inocencio served as a mayordomo twice, once in 1937 and again in 1945; this cost him a few thousand pesos the first time, and 5,000 or 6,000 for his second sponsorship.

In 1961 in Tlacolula, as Inocencio expressed it, "When they saw that I was making progress, they came to ask me to be mayordomo." He elabo-rated: "Since they knew I was from another community and saw me with a good job, they decided that I should be named mayordomo, but I refused to do it. I told them that I had gone through two expenditures as mayor-domo in my home community and I did not want to spend again here." The selection committee, made up of the incumbent and ex-mayordomos, complained to the priest and demanded that Inocencio be replaced as cantor for his refusal to accept mayordomía sponsorship. The priest rejected their request but visited Inocencio and convinced him to accept a compromise.

The priest told him to satisfy the selection committee by accepting their offer, pay for the Mass, and it would be over and done with. Inocencio followed the priest's advice and became mayordomo of the fiesta of San Juan Bautista. Much to his chagrin, the sponsorship cost him 3,000 pesos over a three-day period because his wife insisted on celebrating "more than just a Mass" as the priest had suggested.

The quarries in Tlacolula were located in an area of mixed or disputed tenure between communal and private property. Quarrying was done by comuneros in good standing (they had to be originarios and contribuyentes with all taxes paid in full) and privately. At first, Inocencio worked in a group headed by José, one of the comuneros; he, in fact, advanced money to José to hire workers. That arrangement ended when José changed to another quarry area. Inocencio was then obliged to make arrangements with another group of comuneros. This required permission from the síndico municipal and communal representative (representante de bienes comunales) that cost Inocencio several hundred pesos in bribes.

In the 1960s, difficulties developed between the canteros comuneros and a private landowner, Aureliano Sánchez, who claimed that the entire quarry area was his private property, since he had cleared the land on which the quarry was located in 1950. This dispute resulted in periodic suspensions of quarrying activities. Following an official determination that the quarries were in fact communal property, another problem arose: the government announced plans to build a public water tank just above the quarry and prohibited further blasting in the area.[4]

Inocencio's strategy for adapting to the uncertainties of stone supply was to buy and stockpile as much stone as possible. He had a storage area on his residence lot for that purpose. At one point, I counted more than one hundred metate trozos piled up there. He also hired trucks to haul back to Tlacolula stone he bought from quarries in San Sebastián Teitipac and Magdalena Ocotlán. He bought finished metates in the Tlacolula and Oaxaca City marketplaces at relatively low prices, refinished them according to his specifications, and resold them at a higher price.

Inocencio's business did not simply depend on sales in the marketplace. As his reputation grew and his business became established, he also had an increase in special-order (encargo) sales. During the period 1965–1968, metates made in his workshop, combined with those made by two other San Juan expatriates, Armando Carranza and Emilio Alvarado, accounted for 60 percent of metate sales in the Tlacolula plaza.[5]

Among the San Juan metateros influenced by Inocencio was Emilio Alvarado, who, like Luis and Constantino, was a nephew of Inocencio's wife. Emilio tried to make a go of it in San Juan, where he was a campesino and carbonero but had also started to work on manos with a cousin who was more experienced and gave him semifinished products to finish. He liked stoneworking, as opposed to charcoal making, because it required less time outside the village in the mountains. After learning to finish manos and metates in San Juan, he moved to Tlacolula in 1954, at the age of twenty-five, to become an apprentice to Inocencio.

Emilio's period of apprenticeship with Inocencio was not the first time in his life that he had left San Juan for Tlacolula. As a twelve-year-old, he ran away from home because his father mistreated him, and worked for three years tending animals (cuidando borregos, cuidando vacas) until his parents took him back to San Juan. He married there in 1945 and worked in agriculture and as a charcoal maker before returning to Tlacolula. He retained ownership of a house and three plots of land in San Juan, which were cultivated by his brothers on a share basis.

During nine months of apprenticeship with Inocencio, Emilio finished metates and manos in return for one unfinished metate weekly to finish for himself, but he also improved his finishing techniques. Once Emilio felt confident about the quality of his work, he moved into a rented room but still worked on a share basis for a time with Inocencio. He looked for an independent work alternative, which hinged upon finding a stone supply. Emilio and other expatriate metateros, like Armando Carranza and Porfirio Mateo, bucked heads with Inocencio precisely over that issue.

Inocencio's business plan involved using money and influence to control as much stone as possible produced by the Tlacolula canteros-comuneros through exclusive contractual arrangements. The only way Emilio and the other Sanjuaneros could compete with Inocencio's strategy was to offer to work in the quarries in exchange for stone.

From 1960 to 1966, Emilio emphasized that no metatero from San Juan could operate independently because Tlacolula quarries were communal and Sanjuaneros were excluded from being comuneros. At first, they bought stone weekly from the quarrymen. But Inocencio managed to corner all of the stone for himself through contracts with the quarrymen, in effect cutting off the supply to other metateros. This led to their falling out with Inocencio. Emilio and other San Juan metateros had no choice but to go to work for the comuneros in exchange for stone.

Not to be outmaneuvered, Inocencio made a deal with José, a comunero and cantero, to buy dynamite, fuses, and supplies for him in exchange for stone. He also hired workers for José so that he would not hire metateros through an in-kind arrangement. Other comuneros-canteros also made deals with Inocencio to do the same for them as he was doing for José. Inocencio ended up controlling output in the Tlacolula quarries, paying workers, buying stone for metates, and selling stone for construction. He accumulated an inventory of two to three hundred blocks of stone for metates on a lot next to his house.

In sum, Inocencio partnered with the quarry bosses through cash advances to meet payrolls and quarrying costs in exchange for a guaranteed share of quarry output, including construction stone. He cornered the Tlacolula stone market. Unfortunately for him, this strategy backfired in 1966 when he was denounced by one of his partners for selling construction stone at discounted prices that were prejudicial to the quarry business for all of the comuneros.

Emilio, by that time, earned income by combining quarry work with making metates. Despite Inocencio's arrangements, quarrymen allowed Emilio to work one or two days a week in exchange for a few pieces of stone for metates. In addition, he managed to buy enough stone on a cash basis for his two sons to help him finish metates. During the rainy season, when metate sales declined, Emilio tended to work more days per week as a hired hand (jornalero) in agriculture than he did working in the quarries or making metates.

### The Carranza Family in San Juan and Tlacolula

Armando Carranza, unlike Emilio Alvarado, learned metate making from his father, Efrén, in San Juan. He began at the age of twelve and within one and a half years had, more or less, completed his apprenticeship. His father traced out the pattern of a metate on the trozo and showed Armando how to cut it out. His customary way of working in San Juan, both in his father's quarry and later in his own, was to employ one or two helpers to quarry stone on a product share basis: one trozo to each mozo and the remainder for him, since he was the quarry owner; he provided the blasting powder, fuses, and all of the tools, and the mozos provided labor. Armando moved to Tlacolula in the early 1960s at the invitation of his wife's family, who were native Tlacolulans; bought trozos for metates from the communal quarrymen; hauled the trozos to his house; and made metates and manos there.

Like Emilio, Armando did not remain independent of Inocencio Morales, who lent him cash whenever he needed it, apparently with no strings attached. However, Inocencio tried to convince Armando to work in the quarry for trozos, and then sell semifinished metates (barreteados) to him for finishing. Armando declined this proposition because he had other tasks to do at home, like getting firewood (leña) and hauling water from a neighborhood well, so it was more convenient for him to work independently.

His wife also made tortillas for sale in Tlacolula, a business that she could not pursue in San Juan, since households there made their own tortillas. Armando found it more convenient and financially rewarding to transport his unsold finished metates to Oaxaca City, where there were several dealers. In San Juan, his only recourse had been to sell semifinished metates to intermediaries for a much smaller cash return than he received in Oaxaca City for metates finished at his adopted home in Tlacolula.

Aside from escaping from "bad elements" in San Juan by moving to Tlacolula, Armando also cited the freedom from tequio service and from punishing expenditures of obligatory mayordomía sponsorship in San Juan as advantages of living there. When he lived in San Juan, he was named to serve as mayordomo of San Francisco and spent 1,500 pesos. Even though he relied completely upon the *guelaguetza* system to defray this expense by calling in loans he had made to others, he still incurred new debts and new obligations for future repayment. Also, sponsorship of a relatively minor mayordomía like San Francisco did not free him from the possibility of being named in the future for a more costly sponsorship. Even though he was living in Tlacolula, he still had to meet *guelaguetza* obligations previously incurred in San Juan. He had made four repayments to Sanjuaneros since moving to Tlacolula; the last one involved a payment of 6 almudes of corn and 10 pesos in cash.[6]

Otón Carranza, who at thirty-nine in 1966 was a few years younger than his brother Armando, left San Juan as a teenager to work in Tlacolula as a house servant for a priest in exchange for room, board, and schooling. Prior to that, his father, Efrén, had taught him to make metates by drawing the outline of a metate on a trozo with a green leaf from a nearby bush, helping him to shape it with a hammer, and then showing him how to further reduce or cut it out with a barreta.

After his stint with the priest in Tlacolula, Otón worked in various wage-labor jobs (cleaning public baths, construction) either in Oaxaca City or in regional highway construction. He aspired to be a bus or truck driver but never had the opportunity to learn how to drive. He wanted to be something other than a campesino and metatero but lacked the money and resources to succeed. By 1950, he was back in San Juan working in his father's quarry with his father; two brothers, Armando and Bulmaro; and a cousin, Leopoldo Noriega. Within a year or so, his father gave him a promising section of the quarry to work on his own, and he began to work on a share basis with two mozos. By that time, he had married Guadalupe Cruz, set up an independent household on a lot loaned to him by a paternal uncle, and started a family.

Otón had two plots of privately owned land (a first-class plot inherited from his father and a third-class plot from his wife) and two plots cultivated on a share basis. As an ox-team owner, Otón managed to make and earn a living by dividing his time between subsistence agriculture and metate making. Metates supplied him with money for clothing, for a piece of meat, and for bread for his children, and agriculture supplied him with corn and beans. He could not sell corn and beans to raise cash because he needed them for his household's own consumption. When he had stone available to make metates or manos, and he had an urgent need for cash, he would simply go to an intermediary and ask for a loan in return for manos or metates.

As one of the most adept members of his craft, Otón was among the youngest of San Juan's master canteros and metateros. He was disappointed that metate work was not more remunerative and considered it to be hard, tiring, and damaging to his lungs.

With an annual estimated harvest of 9 fanegas of corn (900 kilograms), Otón was better off than nine of his colleagues I surveyed whose estimates ranged from a high of 8.5 fanegas (850 kilograms) to a low of .5 fanegas (50 kilograms), with the average being 5.4 fanegas, or 540 kilograms. All of these households also cultivated beans, squash, and other supplementary crops like chickpeas (garbanzos) and broad beans (habas) to contribute to their subsistence. Still, none of them produced enough corn to fully supply their annual household needs.

The corn harvest estimates of Otón Carranza, Rosendo Carranza, and Miguel Cruz, all of whom owned an ox team, had the same high degree of reliability but demonstrated the difficulty of establishing formulaic global standards for measuring agricultural output. The possible mixes of land types, extent of land cultivated, and differential crop yields complicated measurement. Otón had four plots of land, only one of which was first class, measuring a combined total of 1.42 hectares. This compared with Rosendo, who had seven plots, none of which was first class, measuring a combined total of 2.22 hectares; and with Miguel, who (together with his father, Pablo, with whom he resided) had thirteen plots, only one of which was first class, for a combined total of a meager .4 hectares. Otón did own an ox team, an advantage shared by only three of eleven Sanjuaneros in the sample.

Efrén Carranza was among the oldest living maestros in San Juan and was also a pioneer long-distance trader (regatón). He was born in 1894, and in 1966, at the age of seventy-two, had been in the craft for sixty years. He was still active, both as an intermediary and as a manufacturer of small sets of metates and manos that he sold to tourists or as toys in the Tlacolula market. At the age of seventy-two, Efrén was making the same products he had made as a twelve-year-old apprentice with a young metatero named

Francisco, who allowed him to come to his quarry, where he gave him tasks to do like making miniature metates and pestles.

Efrén's father owned a quarry but was a full-time peasant, not a metatero. After a year or so of working with Francisco and others, Efrén learned how to cut and finish small metates and manos, and one day his father suggested that he start working in the quarry. Efrén explained that he still did not know how to blast stone and had to work for other metateros to learn. He did so for about five years and then found a companion to work with him in his father's quarry.

By the age of seventeen, Efrén was performing all of the tasks of a master metatero in the quarry owned by his non-metatero father. From that point on, until he married and his sons were old enough to work, he worked with three or four hired hands (mozos) who helped haul debitage from the quarry in exchange for trozos to make metates. In those years, there was never a shortage of workers willing to learn the craft as apprentices. During the 1940s and 1950s, his quarry's peak years of production, Efrén supervised and worked with his three sons (Armando, Otón, and Bulmaro) and a nephew.

Efrén finally withdrew from quarrying around 1960, after which he acquired stone from his son Otón or from other metateros working in his quarry on a share basis. He realistically recognized that he was just another employer with share workers. "They get their share and I get mine," he said, and "there are other maestros now, my time has passed. I don't deceive myself." He also admitted that his vision was failing, which impaired precision cutting and finishing tasks required for making good-quality, full-size metates and manos. Basically, his main source of cash income from the craft was selling his share of trozos to other metateros.

Efrén's decades-long career in the metate industry was notable, not only for his role in production as a master of quarrying and stonecutting but also as an innovative trader. Over a period of four decades, he sold products from his own quarry but increasingly specialized in the sale of products he purchased for resale from other producers. In taking his own products to market in Tlacolula, Ocotlán, and Oaxaca City, Efrén learned that intermediaries profited from buying cheap and selling dear, and since there were no traders in the San Juan metate industry in the 1930s and 1940s, he decided to start buying up locally, paying cash advances of 2.50 pesos per metate for resale regionally and in the Isthmus of Tehuantepec for 4–6 pesos each, first traveling by burro and then by bus.

After the Oaxaca-to-Isthmus stretch of the Pan-American Highway was finished in 1940 and bus service became available, Efrén hauled as many as fifteen or twenty metates to Oaxaca City. He accumulated an inventory over a period of a week or two of ten to twenty metates and several dozen manos, and then plied the market circuit: Tlacolula on Sundays, Zaachila and Ocotlán on Thursdays and Fridays, Oaxaca City on Saturdays. When he had accumulated an especially large inventory of twenty-five or so metates and six dozen manos, he traveled to the Isthmus, where he could sell 30-peso metates for 60 or 70 pesos each.

Efrén calculated costs and earnings by a formula of "mitad y mitad," explaining that "the first part and the second is what you lost; the third part is what you earned." The "first part" consisted of transportation costs; the "second part" consisted of room, board, and other costs (e.g., market fee); and the "third part" was earnings to reinvest in new purchases. When he went on those trips, he also bought hats, huaraches, machetes, chicozapote (fruit), mangos, coconuts, and gourds (jícaras) to resell in San Juan. The earnings from this second business paid his transportation costs.

There was an ironic twist in Efrén's career as San Juan's sole metate intermediary, which happened during a womanizing stage in his life (cuando yo estaba en la época de aprovechar con las viejas). Efrén made an offer to teach Esperanza, an attractive widow, the metate trade to strengthen their relationship but came to regret his decision. In his words: "That was my mistake. I taught her and she learned the business so well that before long she was buying more metates than I was. Since she was a good-looking woman, when she came looking for metates, the metateros sold to her. So, now there were two regatones in San Juan."

With the Esperanza affair, which occurred in the mid-1940s, Efrén unintentionally set in motion a process of increased competition between San Juan buyers-up in the metate market, in which the "merry widows"—Esperanza, María, and Jacinta—cultivated a network of single or philandering married metateros by offering sexual favors in order to accumulate metate inventories.

Efrén explained that, following his precedent with Esperanza, these seductive regatonas took many metateros as "lovers" (queridos): "The metateros sell cheap to the female buyers-up because they also go to bed with them. Male intermediaries have less success in buying up metates because the metateros prefer to sell to the women." By the mid-1960s, the ranks of the "merry widows" were reduced by the murder of Esperanza. Competition among traders escalated to the point at which Jacinta (who was widowed in 1950 and started her metate business in 1951) complained (in a 1966 interview with me) that she had difficulty competing with two new, aggressive, and well-financed male intermediaries. They entered the trade by outbidding her with generous cash advances and higher prices in buying metates, and then lowered their profit margins when selling, depending on higher volume sales to offset lower sales prices. Under these conditions, Efrén was eliminated from the standard metate market altogether and had to survive purely from sales of his line of miniatures.

### San Juan Regatones and the San Sebastián Metate Trade: The Case of Ramón Ramírez

In 1966–1967, several traders were actively competing in the San Juan metate market to the extent that cash-hungry metateros found it more rewarding to sell to them rather than in the Tlacolula or Oaxaca City plazas. A few small-scale metate traders were operating in San Sebastián, but they were poorly capitalized and did not offer competitive prices. This restricted their business only to metateros in San Sebastián who were especially receptive of cash advances. Consequently, the more highly capitalized San Juan traders exploited this opening in the market and began to aggressively buy up metates and manos in San Sebastián.

Among the ranks of the San Juan traders was a relative newcomer to the business of buying for resale, Carlos Sánchez Martínez, fifty-one years old, who was taught to make metates in 1937 in a quarry belonging to his maternal uncle, Florentino. Carlos was among the most accomplished of San Juan's metateros, renowned for his expertly carved gift metates. His five sons, ranging in ages from fifteen to twenty-seven when I interviewed him in 1967, still lived in his household, and all of them worked in their father's oficio.

San Juan's quarries in the mid-1960s were quite deep and lacked drainage; consequently, they filled up with water during the spring-summer rainy season that was particularly active in 1966. This created a supply crisis in the San Juan metate business, as production in local quarries was suspended due to the water problem. Carlos decided to make it through this difficult period by buying up metates and manos in semifinished condition and, with the help of his sons, finishing them for resale. His twenty-year-old son, Tiburcio, nicknamed "Bucho," had a particular affinity for commerce and became his father's business agent. He bought unfinished metates in San Sebastián, painted decorations on them after they were finished by his other brothers and father back in San Juan, and then sold them in Oaxaca City's Saturday market.

During this period, Carlos's eldest son, Jaime, had experimented with working on a share basis in a San Juan quarry but decided that it was not rewarding. Carlos and his sons also tried to pump water out of their flooded quarry only to have it fill up again. Finally, it was decided that the water could be used for domestic purposes. In short, they decided that it was to their advantage to strengthen (amarrar) their business relationships in San Sebastián.

Even under normal conditions, stone for metates was more abundant in San Sebastián than in San Juan and was reputed to be easier to work. Therefore, San Juan buyers-up were particularly motivated to establish patron-client relationships with San Sebastián metateros. In November 1966, Carlos was in the process of assembling an inventory of small metates to take to Santa Catarina Juquila for the annual celebration of that town's patron saint's festival (la Virgen de Juquila), attended by pilgrims from many regions of Oaxaca, that included a large market. Given Juquila's location in coffee-growing country, there was a brisk demand for smaller metates that were suited to transport by burro or mule from the district cabecera back to isolated coffee-growing communities.

Carlos planned to take twelve metates to Juquila, and already had six on hand, recently purchased from Ramón Ramírez in San Sebastián. He said that he had purchased fifty metates barreteados from Ramón since early September. Carlos paid 25 pesos each for metates in this semifinished state. When finished by himself and his sons, the amount invested per metate rose to 40 pesos. To cover travel and hauling expenses by bus to Juquila, he intended to sell at prices averaging not less than 50 pesos per metate; his business plan was to earn between 10 and 20 pesos per metate.

In the 1960s, San Juan had slightly more total personnel in quarrying and metate making than San Sebastián (estimate of 100 vs. 75; see Cook 1969, 320). Historically, San Sebastián developed many quarries located in several different terrain sectors (see Map 2), in contrast to San Juan, where quarries were concentrated in only one sector. The larger number and wider dispersal of quarries in San Sebastián meant that they were less likely to suffer flooding from scattered showers during the rainy season than San Juan quarries. San Sebastián never had quarry production stoppages like those affecting the San Juan industry in 1966–1967. In short, San Sebastián had a larger, more diverse, and more reliable supply of stone for the metate industry than did San Juan.[7]

This is why Ramón Ramírez, the most productive of San Sebastián's full-time metateros, had done business with at least three San Juan regatones, including Carlos Sánchez, during the fall of 1966. At the time, he was thirty-two years old, married with one child, and landless. He started working as a metatero at the age of fourteen, learning from his older brother. Like many of his cohorts, Ramón participated in migratory agricultural labor, including four separate stints in Texas and California and one in the coffee harvest in

Pochutla; he also worked for one month in Oaxaca City on construction jobs and for six months in Mexico City as a painter's assistant. He worked several half days yearly in local agriculture on a sharecropping basis; he did so in 1965 for eight half days in return for a cartload of unhusked corn equivalent to 500 kilograms of shelled corn.

Most years, Ramón worked all day, every day as a metatero. As he put it: "I sustain myself from my oficio; it maintains me. From my earnings I buy corn and other food staples, and I also pay for curing illnesses and for clothing. From my craft, I earn enough money to support my household."

I observed Ramón at work in San Sebastián's Mesa Grande quarries on several occasions; he was a formidable worker in all phases of production but was outstanding in the "barretear" phase of cutting out a semifinished metate from a trozo, easily finishing two in one afternoon. This is why Carlos Sánchez's assertion in 1966 that "we have found that Ramón in a month supplies us with as many as six, eight, or even ten metates weekly" was perfectly credible. My data on average gross monthly returns for fifteen San Sebastián metate sellers over the period from September 1966 to July 1967 put Ramón in first place among the producer-sellers at 225 pesos (Cook 1982, 319). That amount was exceeded only by two regatonas: Crispina and María Luisa.

Ramón achieved high output and earnings largely by avoiding cooperative work arrangements; he preferred to work alone as much as possible, since he was faster, more efficient, more goal oriented, and harder working than most of his cohorts (Cook 1982, 216–218). When working on a cooperative basis, he arrived at work before his companions did and worked more skillfully but ended up earning the same as they did. This did not sit well with Ramón, so he decided to go independent.

Despite Ramón's success as an independent metatero, he rated agriculture as a better occupation. The only problem with agriculture, from his standpoint, was that an ox team was required to be able to plant and harvest enough crops for household needs. This was a viewpoint shared by most of his full-time metatero colleagues. Like Ramón, they remained "peasants without land and the means to work it" (Cook 1982, 129–139) and were metateros by default.

Ramón's participation in a rationalized form of production that permitted him to make only semifinished products for sale at fair prices to San Juan intermediaries was not destined to last. His arrangement caught my attention because during my fieldwork in San Sebastián during the summer of 1965, I interviewed Ramón, observed him at work in the quarry during the week, and kept track of his activities as a seller in the Oaxaca City market on Saturdays. When my fieldwork resumed in 1966, I was surprised by Ramon's absence from the metate sales area on Saturdays in Oaxaca City. This led me to examine his case more closely.

Pricing in the metate market was a complex process that generated many prices based on product differences (i.e., size, type of stone, stage or quality of workmanship, and finish), where they were produced, to whom and where they were sold, time of year when they were sold, and so on. Buyers-up who purchased regularly throughout the year in bulk quantities were able to negotiate lower prices from sellers than individual buyers for own use. The pricing agreement between Carlos Sánchez and Ramón Ramírez operating in the fall of 1966 for standard-sized semifinished metates at 25 pesos each was reflective of a temporary moment in an ongoing marketing process driven by a combination of structural, conjunctural, and situational factors.

Ramón, by virtue of the high quality and steady supply of his products, was identified by buyers-up locally and regionally as a preferred supplier. In 1966, Ramón decided to sell semifinished metates in San Sebastián to San Juan regatones for a blanket price of 25 pesos each. He explained this using the metaphor of "binding himself to his employers" (amarrarse con mis patrones) by mutual agreement to assure an acceptable price floor during low-market periods.[8]

This followed a precedent Ramón had set with a female trader (regatona) from Tehuantepec between 1953 and 1955 at a year-around blanket price of 35 pesos per finished metate. The regatona approached Ramón on the street in the Oaxaca market where the San Sebastianos sold metates and told him that she liked the look of his products. He was puzzled, since all of San Sebastian's products were made from the same stone in the same sizes. She explained that his were more finely worked and had a more luxurious appearance that the others. So, they made a deal: for two years, twice a month on Saturday, Ramón delivered his metates to the regatona's hotel near the market to receive payment at a blanket price of 35 pesos per finished metate.

In his words: "She brought me little gifts for Holy Week, she brought me dried fish, she was a real nice, good-looking brunette (morenita)." This statement prompted a follow-up question from me as to whether or not her gifts had included sexual favors, and he responded with a sort of qualified negative, implying that nothing had ever happened between them but that there was a certain chemistry and that he was not opposed to the idea (No. Nunca. Pero, ¿quién sabe, pues?—smiling). In any case, in 1955 the Tehuana inexplicably stopped coming to the Oaxaca plaza, and Ramón returned to his previous practice of lining up his products on a street together with other San Sebastián sellers on Saturday market days.

Starting around 1958, Miahuatlán-based Serafín, who was the most active of several wholesale interplaza intermediaries who bought metates regularly from San Juan and San Sebastián sellers, started buying metates from Ramón with a guarantee of 30 pesos per metate during low-market periods and a promise to increase this price as the market shifted upward. This was an offer that appealed to Ramón, even though Serafín's low-market price of 30 pesos was below the 35-peso blanket price paid by the Tejuana. Ramón's expectation was that Serafín "in good times will pay me 35, 40, 45, up to 50 pesos per metate. That's the guarantee he gave me. When the market price is 55 or 60 pesos, I sell to him for 45 or 50 pesos delivered to his hotel." Between 1962 and 1965, Ramón sold finished metates to Serafín according to a sliding price scale pegged to market fluctuations, but never below 30 pesos per metate.

The possibility of selling unfinished metates at a rewarding price in the village and bypassing the plaza began to emerge in 1965, thanks to the increased activity of intermediaries from San Juan in response to the scarcity of stone and metates in San Juan. According to Ramón, four San Juan regatones, operating separately, "walked from one house to another here in San Sebastián asking if they had metates for sale." Initially, they offered 18 to 20 pesos for semifinished metates. Ramón began to sell to them but became concerned regarding their increasing competitiveness. This became troubling to him when problems emerged between an uncle (Chico) and his nephew (Cornelio) who had been Chico's business apprentice. Ramón wanted to avoid becoming embroiled in San Juan family disputes, and one day stated his position, indicating his wariness, clearly to Cornelio: "The day that your uncle says something to you about our business, I will no longer sell to you or to anyone else from San Juan. I won't sell to any of you because I don't like that type of behavior. Later on something bad could happen and I would be blamed because I am selling to you and not to them." It was with this practical, cautious orientation that Ramón approached the escalating competition among the San Juan regatones for his and other San Sebastián products.

Ramón met yet another of the new San Juan regatones, Tiburcio (son of Carlos Sánchez), on June 8, 1966, at a special market held on the patron saint's day in San Pablo Huistepec, where metate sales had been brisk over the years. Ramón took five small finished metates and by noon had sold four of them for 50 pesos each. Tiburcio agreed to buy his remaining metate for 35 pesos, which enabled Ramón to "buy some fruit, the kinds that are grown around here," and return home. In early August, Tiburcio showed up at Ramón's residence lot in San Sebastián and bought two standard-size finished metates for 35 pesos each, the same price he had paid in San Pablo. He told Ramón that he was willing to buy his entire inventory of finished or unfinished metates, and Ramón agreed to sell him unfinished metates for 25 pesos each. Tiburcio offered to pay in advance for future purchases.

It was common knowledge among all participants that the Oaxaca Valley metate market was characterized by ups and downs that roughly overlapped the festive cycle and the agricultural cycle. The latter corresponded to the precipitation cycle: rainy season from April through September and dry season from October through February. Generally speaking, prices rose during the dry season and bottomed out during the rainy season (Cook 1982, Ch. 7 especially).

Since Ramón already had a satisfactory sliding price agreement for finished metates with Serafín in Oaxaca City, his decision making focused on the possibility of matching that arrangement with a San Juan regatón for the sale of unfinished metates in San Sebastián. He heard a rumor that trouble was brewing again between the San Juan regatones and that one of them, who was known to belong to a local gang, was plotting to assassinate Tiburcio on the road between San Juan and San Sebastián. This worried Ramón, not so much for Tiburcio but for himself as potentially being dragged into a San Juan feud, and made him rethink his situation. He told Tiburcio about the rumor and said: "Something bad can happen; they can beat you up and then come the results that could damage my reputation or put me in the position of being a rival to someone who might take revenge on me (que me quieren traer de rival, me revancha o una cosa así)." Then he reasserted his claim to business independence by telling Tiburcio, "I sell my own work, and I can sell it wherever and to whomever I want. I am free to sell however I want to. I sell what belongs to me, not what belongs to someone else (vendo lo que es mío, no vendo el ajeno). If I don't like the way we are doing business, then it's better for me not to do business with you."

Tiburcio assured Ramón that the rumors were just that, and that nothing would happen between him and other Sanjuaneros. He made Ramón an offer to establish a more permanent business relationship (vamos a hacernos marchantes) based on cash advances. Ramón accepted this offer and, in anticipation of the Día de los Muertos celebration in October, he sold Bucho five unfinished metates for 25 pesos each and received advance payment on another five. Bucho gave him 250 pesos, so Ramón still owed him five semifinished metates. Ramón admitted that the relation between them was purely monetary: "I have five metates here right now and I don't plan to take them to Oaxaca to sell, since Bucho is going to give me 125 pesos in advance for another five metates."

Looking down the road to the prospect of higher metate prices by December's fiesta of Juquila, Ramón insisted that he was going to tell Bucho that metates had doubled in price, implying that he could finish and sell them himself in the Oaxaca City market for 50 pesos each. After explaining that with an extra day's work he could transform a 25-peso semifinished metate (barreteado) into a 50-peso finished (labrado) metate, he intended to demand that Bucho pay 40 pesos each for unfinished metates. If that demand was rejected, as Ramón anticipated, then he would take twelve finished metates to Oaxaca and sell them to his patrón, Serafín, for more than 500 pesos.

This prospect definitely appealed to Ramón, yet at the end of his ruminations, he returned to the position that his best option would be to convince Bucho to pay 40 pesos each for metates barreteados. Given Ramón's weekly output capacity of five metates, he concluded that the return on his labor at that price would be 200 pesos weekly. Ramón noted that this was 50 pesos more than he could earn in Mexico City for working six days a week from 6:00 a.m. to 6:00 p.m. Moreover, working in San Sebastián as a metatero was preferable: "I get up at 8:00 in the morning and arrive in the quarry by 10:00, and I am back home by 6:00 p.m. and I am working as I like."

Clearly, Ramón's thinking and rethinking about the business of being a metatero was symptomatic of discontent. Underlying cost-accounting considerations and the possible implications of doing business with conflictive Sanjuaneros was his sense of loss of full market participation in commodity circuits as a producer-seller-consumer. Even though, in strict cost-accounting terms, Ramón could justify selling semifinished metates without going to the plaza, he was troubled by not selling finished metates there. "Right now," he explained, "I feel strange for not going to market in Oaxaca, not taking my metates there to sell. I was accustomed to doing that. Now when I go to Oaxaca only with money and no metates, I don't feel good about myself." He summed up his feeling of alienation from market participation by emphasizing that "it is a very strange feeling to go to the marketplace without anything to sell and to just walk around. One has to take something there to sell and then bring something back that was bought with one's earnings."

Ramón Ramírez was an exceptional metatero who was subjected to higher-than-average competitive pressure from intermediaries seeking to do business with him. His case highlights market conditions and factors, including the allure of the marketplace and personal relationships and concerns, that influenced decision making by all Teitipac metateros in the mid-1960s (cf. Cook 1976, 162–163; Cook 1982, 281–282).[9]

## CHAPTER 4

# San Sebastián Teitipac:

# Metateros and Civility

The most direct route to San Sebastián was by an unpaved road that departed from the Pan-American Highway at the 559-kilometer marker 3 kilometers east of Tule and wound its way through the pueblos of Güendulain, Rojas de Cuauhtémoc, and Santa Rosa Buenavista. After departing Rojas, located about 2.5 kilometers from the highway, the road gradually rose from the valley floor as it skirted the range of mountains to the west for the roughly 3 kilometers to Santa Rosa Buenavista. Before reaching Santa Rosa, high up on a mountain to the southwest a white area was visible on the green slopes. This was an extensive complex of quarries on the Mesa Grande (Map 2) that I would visit many times in the company of metateros. Just beyond Santa Rosa, as the road briefly turned eastward, the entire expanse of the Tlacolula arm of the Oaxaca Valley was on panoramic display. As the road curved southward, again hugging the slope of the nearby mountains, a formidable expanse of agricultural land was visible to the east along the Río Salado basin belonging to the pueblos of Guelacé, Abasolo, Tlacochahuaya, Lachígolo, Guelavía, Papalutla, and San Sebastián itself. Continuing in a southerly direction for a short distance, only several hundred yards from the road and midway up a hillside to the west, another quarry area came into view where men could be seen cutting stone in open patios. At that point in the trip the habitation area of San Sebastián became visible in the distance, some 9 kilometers or so off the Pan-American Highway.

After arriving in San Sebastián in early June 1965, I chatted with men sitting around the village plaza, one of whom, Luis Gutiérrez, happened to be a metatero who would later become my first field assistant. I learned from him that the quarry I had passed on the road, the Mesa Chiquita, belonged to San Sebastián, and that the men I had seen working there were metateros. I decided then and there that this would be an ideal community for a

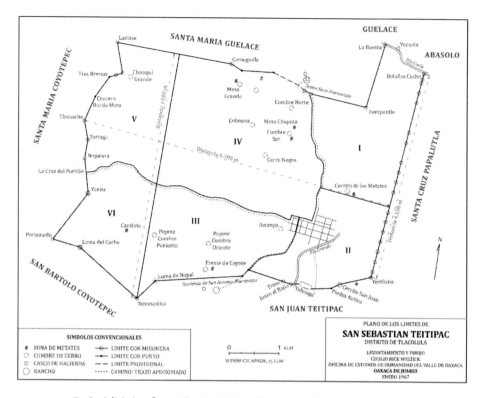

MAP 2. **Territorial Limits of San Sebastián Teitipac Showing Physiographic Sectors and Parajes**

summer fieldwork project, so I met with Presidente Municipal Wenceslao Gutiérrez Marcial, a serious, soft-spoken, intelligent, and friendly man, to see if the community would be receptive. He showed interest and promised to consult with his village council (regidores) regarding my request. To make a long story short, official permission was granted during a subsequent meeting with the ayuntamiento (village council), and I rented a spare room in the municipal president's casa de adobe, where I took up residence within a few days. I resided there during that summer and, also, for twelve months in 1966–1967 when Pablo Rojas was municipal president.

My research plans in San Sebastián in 1965 and 1966–1967 did not involve random sampling, but followed a method that relied heavily on the social networks of my field assistants: first, Luis Gutiérrez, and later, Filomeno Gabriel. Luis and Filomeno both shared similar backgrounds of extensive experience as braceros in U.S. agriculture, especially in California and Texas, and also work experience in Mexico City and Oaxaca City. Their life experiences bridged the traditional peasant-artisan culture of Oaxaca Valley Zapotec speakers and the wider urban-industrial cultures of Mexico and the United States. Owing to their personal experiences of adapting to unfamiliar cultural contexts in distant places, and to their relatively success-ful stints as migrant laborers, they were flexible, friendly, and quick to grasp my purpose in being in their community. They were amenable to cooperat-ing with my project as part-time field assistants and as key informants, espe-cially after I clarified that my policy would be to pay them for the time they spent doing so. Each of these men in his own way seemed to be genuinely interested in the history and culture of their community and craft, and in helping to communicate this to outsiders through my project.[1]

Luis, like his father, Gregorio, a maestro metatero and retired quarry boss, was especially important in introducing me to the culture of the hard-core, essentially full-time metateros. He was strongly positioned through kinship, marriage, and career to give me access to the traditions, daily lives, and work of his colleagues. By early 1967, I relied more on Filomeno, who as a peasant-artisan and a trader (regatón), and through social networks, was well connected with the wider community of peasant-artisans and traders, not only in San Sebastián but also in San Juan, San Antonio Buenavista, and Santa Cecilia Jalieza. My interactions with San Sebastianos in 1965 and 1966–1967 were filtered through my relationships with Luis and Filomeno, as was much of the cultural knowledge acquired from them as key infor-mants.

Given the exigencies of making and earning a living in the market econ-omy of the Oaxaca Valley, the most efficient, pragmatic, and culturally ap-propriate way for my project to proceed was to compensate informants for the time required to conduct a household census and follow-up interview. I paid a gratuity that exceeded the going day wage for casual labor. Informal data-gathering situations were not wage-mediated. These included casual conversations with individuals or in a group context and observations of work activities and of ceremonial, festive, or public events. When I began to commute weekly in my own vehicle every few days or daily to San Sebastián from Oaxaca City in 1967, I regularly gave free rides to San Sebastianos, and also did so in a few emergency situations. During typical photographic ses-sions, I used two cameras, one of which was a Polaroid; this enabled me to present instant snapshots to the family in exchange for taking a wider range of photos of their household setting and activities.

It was the presence of quarries and, especially, metate making that served to identify San Sebastián Teitipac as special in the panoply of Zapotec-speaking peasant-artisan communities in the Oaxaca Valley. In the mid-1960s, it was without electrification, potable water, water or sewer lines, indoor plumbing, paved roads, or other elements of modern public infrastructure. With the exception of the unpaved road to the Pan-American Highway, a school, a municipal government building, and a small rainfall-retention dam and channel irrigation system, there was no significant infrastructure that represented federal or state government participation.

The services of San Sebastián's church, housing, health care, recreation sector, and basic economy were provided mostly through a homegrown and home-staffed division of labor and specialization, necessarily supplemented by commodities and services imported from external markets. With just over three hundred households, it was not an autarky but had the capacity to provide a surprisingly wide array of necessary commodities and services required for subsistence and for achieving a regionally acceptable standard of living.

## The Lay of the Land and the Paraje System

One of the most impressive dimensions of daily life among San Sebastianos was their landscape culture. This shaped work scheduling and task and time allocation in the short and long term, kept them attuned to their collective past, and oriented them in the present. Their landscape culture was organized around and through an intermeshed series of taxonomies pertaining to all aspects of the physical habitat. It focused primarily on the area beyond the settlement proper, referred to as the campo, and involved everything from particular features in specific places to the conditions and uses of different categories of terrain. It provided San Sebastianos with a cognitive map of their habitat without the benefit of an actual map.[2]

At 1,680 meters above sea level, San Sebastián's habitation area was some 130 meters higher than the floor of the Oaxaca Valley. This altitude was just high enough to eliminate the disadvantages of the tropical climate proper to the geographical area, without giving to it the rigor that characterized the high mountains (Schmieder 1930, 1). The mean annual temperature was 20 degrees C (68 degrees F), and the mean annual rainfall was around 570 millimeters (23 inches). The basic contrast in this temperate climate was between a rainy season that typically began in April or May and lasted through September or October, and a dry season from November through March.

According to the 1960 Mexican Federal Census, there were 1,496 San Sebastianos (746 males and 750 females) dispersed among 313 households, of which 259 were male-headed and 54 were female-headed. The settlement had a gridlike layout with streets running north–south and east–west forming residential blocks around an off-centered plaza (there was no settlement in the northwest quadrant) where the church, municipal offices, and schools were located. The habitation area occupied about 1 square kilometer in the southeast corner of a 25-square-kilometer territorial jurisdiction (see Map 2). The 24 square kilometers beyond the habitation area composed the habitat from which San Sebastianos made and earned their livelihood—primarily through agriculture and animal husbandry but also from hunting and gathering (mostly the latter) and a variety of craft occupations, including, most prominently, stone quarrying, metate making, charcoal making, basketry, and broom making.

Most workdays would find some member of a San Sebastián household engaged in economic activity in the campo; even children regularly took goats and sheep to pasture and elderly women collected firewood. This was true during the wet season, when agricultural work peaked, and the dry season, when agricultural work ebbed but did not disappear. Alfalfa grown on irrigated land had to be regularly cut, bundled, and transported back to the village to feed draft animals or cows, and there were other irrigated crops that required tending during the dry season.

The San Sebastián landscape consisted of three zones: flat, mixed (hills and mountains), and mountainous. The flat zone comprised Sectors I and II; the mixed zone, Sectors III and IV; and the mountainous zone, Sectors V and VI (see Map 2). None of these zones has been free of the consequences of human activity. In 1966–1967, there were still some large trees, mostly coniferous, on the slopes near the ridge lines along the mountain summits, but there was also evidence of new growth and of deforestation. In Sector VI at Cacalote, there was a large quarry area where stone was extracted for making metates and manos. Sectors III and IV had some cultivated fields on rainfall-dependent land with slopes and rocky, low-quality soil. Sector IV had the largest and deepest quarries at Mesa Grande, which were visible high up on the side of the mountain on the drive from Santa Rosa, as well as two quarry areas closer to the road at Mesa Chiquita. Sector III had two less accessible but important quarry areas, Piedra de Sal (not shown on Map 2), with stone especially prized for its green color and durability, and Frente de Coyote.

The entire southern portion of Sector IV, which abutted the village in its southeast corner, was agricultural lands. Sectors I and II contained the village's most productive agricultural zone, capable of yielding two harvests annually, and nearly all of the irrigated and naturally moist lands (terreno de humedad). An important hilly quarry area, Cerrito de los Metates, was on the border between these sectors (see Map 2). The small dam and reservoir and the channel irrigation system originating there integrated these two sectors. On the banks of the Río Grande and the irrigation canals in

Sector II, stands of reeds (carrizo) used for baskets, roofing, and fencing flourished. With quarries also located there, Sectors I and II were the most heavily exploited areas in the San Sebastián landscape.

The landscape was subdivided into cultivated land (terrenos labrados, de labranza, or de labor); scrub/uncleared land or wasteland (monte, terreno en bruto, enmontado, or baldío); and cerro, or mountainous terrain. Although unsuited for agriculture, the cerro was put to economic use by cutting and gathering firewood (leña), otate (a bush used by the escoberos, or broom makers, for brooms), and several types of trees used mostly for construction purposes or charcoal making, and for harvesting fruits, nuts, or leaves from a variety of wild medicinal and food plants. The mountainous terrain had additional economic importance as a source of spring water, as pasturage for sheep and goats, as an area for hunting small game animals, and, as mentioned above, as a source of stone that was quarried for use in the metate industry and construction. Monte or terreno enmontado, when cleared of brush, thorn thickets (espinal), and stones, could be cultivated but was limited to beans and a low-yield variety of corn.

Arable lands (terrenos de labranza) were subcategorized into three categories: humedad propia (naturally moist due to a high water table), riego (irrigated), and temporal (literally "seasonal" but more accurately "rainfall-dependent"). These subcategories were further classified by San Sebastianos into four ranked classes. Land categorized as humedad propia or riego was ranked highest as first class (primera clase), and rainfall-dependent land (temporal) was ranked as second, third, or fourth class, respectively, according to its characteristics with regard to the following set of criteria: topography (from low and flat to high and steeply sloped), soil (moisture content and retention, depth of topsoil, rock or sand content, and color), annual crop yield, and use for which suited (type of crop that could be planted on it or suitability as pasturage).

First-class land was low and flat and could either be naturally moist due to a high water table (it is said to have "jugo propio") or have a high rate of retention from adjacent rainfall-fed water courses (river, stream, or arroyo) and was said to be "de humedad." Irrigated land also was classified as first class. This class of land had thick, fertile topsoil (often black in color and called "tierra negra") with no rocks; it had a high crop yield (especially of alfalfa, which, as a perennial, gave several cuttings per year), often yielding two crops a year of corn, broad beans, and chickpeas. Some pot irrigation (from wells) was practiced, but there was an extensive channel (zanja) irrigation system, starting at a small retention dam, using water captured late in the rainy season from the Río Salado, in Sector II in paraje 11 (Calicanto del Río Grande). The moist, nonirrigated type of first-class land was cultivated only by hoe (coa); ox-drawn plows are used in cultivating irrigated land. The quantity and quality of harvests on first-class land was also said to be influenced by precipitation patterns: too much rain might flood out a crop, and too little might diminish the yield.

By contrast, fourth-class land had extremely thin, rocky topsoil known variously as delgado, pedregoso, or pedregal but could also be clayish (arcilloso), sandy (arenoso), or have a high gravel content (cascajudo). In good rainfall years, it yielded a modest crop of corn or beans but, otherwise, served only as pasture for goats, sheep, and cattle. Second- and third-class lands were all rainfall-dependent and suited to planting a wider range of crops—such as castor beans (higuerilla), broad beans (habas), and squash (calabaza)—than fourth-class lands.

A fascinating domain of San Sebastiano landscape culture pertained to their village's toponymy or system of place-names. The Spanish term "paraje" was generally used for named places in the landscape. They recognized the individuality of every morphological feature—a slope, a gully, a dale, a little flat in the valley, and so on—by giving each a proper name (Schmieder 1930, 14–15). A paraje, according to one of my informants, was "a place that had a name." Another explained that they found their way around in the campo by means of different signs (señas) that existed in a place. The sign was a thing that was seen, a thing that was used to guide them to where they wanted to go.

Within parajes, locations were further pinpointed by environmental signs. The paraje named Detzdañi in Zapotec (detrás del cerrito, or "on the other side of the little mountain") had a more precise location, or a sub-paraje, known as El Huajal, because at that location there was a huajal tree. When referring to this precise location, a San Sebastiano would say in Zapotec, "yalaa niy zub detzdañi" (el huajal que está detrás del cerrito, or "the huajal that is behind the little mountain"). Another paraje known as Río Guela ("Ruw Gel" in Zapotec) had four sub-parajes: Nueve Surcos (Gazhurk Ruw Gel), or "Nine Furrows"; Esquina Río Guela (Skiyn Ruw Gel), or "Corner of the Río Guela"; Espinal Rio Guela (Guetch Ruw Gel), or "Thorn Thicket on the Río Guela"; and Máquina Río Guela, or "Machine on the Rio Guela." The latter was named for the remains of a stone pumping station built either by the nearby Hacienda Santa Rosa Buenavista or by a local cacique.

A cross-tabulation of the 144 parajes (Cook 1969, 83) by land type disclosed that 27 percent (39 of 144) did not have land suited to cultivation, and that of the parajes with arable land, only one-quarter of that land was first class. The most predominant land class in such parajes was third class (27 percent of the total). Twenty-eight percent of the 144 parajes contained more than one class of land, with the combination of cerro, monte, and fourth-class land being predominant. Although only a rough approximation, this exercise suggested that there would be little room in the future to expand the amount of arable land in San Sebastián. Future increases in agricultural output would have to be achieved through more efficient or intensive cultivation of existing arable land.

The most frequently occurring referents in San Sebastián's toponymy in descending order were: terrain, water courses, trees, human-made or -influenced elements in the environment, rocks or rock formations, local history, plants, animals, religious/magical association, water sources, rain, and communal land (Cook 1969, 331). Many place-names had oral histories associated with them or, at least, had historical implications. The paraje known as El Espinal de la Estancia referred to one of the landholdings associated historically with caciques in the early colonial period. The paraje called Río de la Matanza, known as the killing ground of the ill-fated revolutionaries from Valle Grande, was located in the same sector (IV) as El Espinal del Ladrón, known as their burial place.[3]

One of the most prominent and central topographic features in the San Sebastián landscape, Cerro Negro, is shown in Map 2 in Sector IV. A legend regarding this mountain was narrated by Maximiano Hernández, San Sebastián's largest landowner and a former presidente municipal, on November 1, 1966, in an evening bull session with various neighbors and me on the street corner near his residence. His story was that the Santo Patrón San Sebastián had some cows in a place that was known as Corral de Vaca. Nearby, on Cerro Negro, there was a very large black bull that began to attract the cows in the corral of the patrón. A nagual, or sorcerer, of unknown origin was believed to have brought the bull to Cerro Negro. When the bull left, the cows began to die until none remained. The bastard nagual (ese cabrón) brought a huge snake that coiled up around the mountain, which was then surrounded with sadness.

In this disjointed folk legend, the juxtaposition of the bull and the serpent can be interpreted symbolically to represent the Spaniards and the Indians. Also, the paraje "Corral de Vacas," or Cattle Corral, probably belonged to the Dominicans as part of their colonization enterprise in San Sebastián, or conceivably to a local cacique. Again, speculatively, the displacement of the serpent that wrapped itself around the mountain by the bull that attracted the cows may be a metaphor for the sixteenth-century Spanish Conquest and colonization and the subjugation of the Indians. The "sadness" referred to would be an indigenous response to their subjugation.

In casual discussions evoking tales of the community's founding or ancient identity, several San Sebastianos referred to the image of the mythical serpent that wrapped itself around Cerro Negro. They always emphasized that this cerro was said to be enchanted (de encanto). Cerro Negro was one of the favorite sites for San Sebastianos to trek to on New Year's Eve to exchange stories and gossip, stargaze, and receive the New Year with libations.

## Civility, Social Class, and Community Reproduction

Culturally, San Sebastián in the 1960s possessed most of the customs and institutions essential for reproducing community life for Oaxaca Valley Zapotec speakers: a civil-religious hierarchy and associated fiesta system; a system of land use and tenure only minimally influenced by the agrarian reform inscribed in the 1917 constitution (e.g., no ejido but mixed private and communal tenure); civic status of household heads validated by payments in cash, kind, or service to the community (e.g., tequio, impuestos, cuotas); reciprocity (*guelaguetza*) as a mutual assistance mechanism; and, most important, a household division of labor by gender and age that had some fifty agricultural and nonagricultural occupations (oficios) providing a diverse range of commodities and services.

There were various types of specialists in animal husbandry, including beekeeping, and specialists in cutting firewood, working stone, making adobe and tiles, making charcoal, baskets, and brooms, as well as at least one or more butchers, animal castrators, wool shearers, seamstresses and tailors, adobe house builders, bakers, blacksmiths, carpenters, harness makers, plow makers, wagon makers, millers, barbers, midwives, bonesetters, gravediggers, musicians, scribes, ceremonial flutists (chirimiteros) and drummers (tamborilleros), marriage brokers (huehuetes), healers (curanderos), candle makers (veleros), and fireworks makers (coheteros).

The interhousehold division of labor was complex enough to reduce dependency of the San Sebastián household on the intervillage system of rotating marketplaces, and to promote the reproduction of its economy and culture (see Cook 1969, 99–104). The relationship between community reproduction, production for own use, and production for exchange in local and regional markets was so tightly and finely calibrated that it defined the economic landscape without leaving much room for the entry of new economic elements (Diskin 1986, 262). The complex development of commodity value and culture in the Oaxaca Valley economy following Spanish conquest and colonization was not incompatible with local values of community service and reciprocity in work and festive life. These also had a basis in the commodity culture of pre-Hispanic Mesoamerica (Cook 2004 and 2006; cf. Diskin 1986, 260).

Migratory wage labor was an important external source of exchange value for the San Sebastián economy, even before the heyday of the Bracero Program in the 1940s and 1950s and before the intensification of undocumented migratory labor to the United States in subsequent decades. This factor alone contradicted a tendency in the 1970s to view San Sebastián as an example of a closed corporate peasant community in a tightly integrated regional system (Diskin 1986, 263–264).[4]

The identity of a community like San Sebastián and of its individual household heads rested upon a concept of shared citizenship (ciudadanía) that implied not only common nativity and residence but also an obligation of service—especially of payment of taxes and fees (cuotas) in cash, in kind, and in labor but also in civil, religious, and festive capacities. So long as a contribuyente (taxpayer and service provider) was in good standing, that obligation was understood to be reciprocated by important privileges: the use of communal land and resources, including the achievement of the status of quasi ownership (como dueño) through such use; and the capacity to acquire rights to noncommunal land by purchase, rent, pawning, or sharecropping. Noncitizens could not directly gain access to land in San Sebastián (Cook 1969, 85–86; Diskin 1986, 264).

Filomeno Gabriel explained the civic obligations of San Sebastián's household heads as "having to do with the law (ley) of our community" (Cook 1990, Tape 1560, 7–9). For example, when the authorities requested a fee for some public project to benefit the community, citizens were obligated to work without pay (tequio) and to pay a surcharge (cuota). When they were named to a post such as representative of a public works committee, they had to collect and pay money. Those who had children in school had to serve on the school committee and pay fees. Also, citizens who had money and wanted to build a better house could get wood, stone, sand, and gravel from communal land.

Filomeno also mentioned that mayordomías were voluntary; citizens were no longer obligated to sponsor them. The citizen who sponsored one did so "voluntarily" according to his own thinking and was exempted from serving in public office during the period of sponsorship. Only those who had served as mayordomos were eligible to serve on church committees (ibid.). His discussion suggested that, as of 1990, something remained of the civil-religious hierarchy and fiesta system from the 1960s (Cook 1969, 117–120, 161–172) observed in attenuated form by Diskin (1986) in the 1970s.

Diskin found the barest outlines of civil-religious hierarchy in San Sebastián in the mid-1970s. He emphasized the importance of marriage and mayordomía festive sponsorships in his analysis of ceremonial expenditures and the role of the *guelaguetza* system in managing them. There was no longer a religious hierarchy, but Diskin considered religious cargos (one of the fourteen annual mayordomías) equivalent to municipal cargos (1986, 284). Regarding the use of *guelaguetza* to mobilize ceremonial wealth to consume in fiestas, he found that households sought to balance debt liquidation with donations to position themselves for possible sponsorship of costly and prestigious ceremonial sponsorships.

By equating religious cargos with mayordomía sponsorships, Diskin implied a lack of non-mayordomía cargos entailing religious service. This did not accord with the results of my fieldwork in San Sebastián in 1965–1967 (Cook 1969, 161–177). If Diskin's position was correct, then major changes occurred in a very short period of time. Just on the basis of Filomeno Gabriel's 1990 statement quoted above, I doubt that such changes were progressing as rapidly in the 1970s as Diskin's interpretation implied.

According to my 1960s fieldwork, it was through their participation in civil-religious posts or cargos, in combination with mayordomía sponsorships, that San Sebastián's household heads were organized into a social system in which they were informally ranked in terms of prestige and graded on an age basis. Service in the hierarchy was obligatory for all adult male villagers eighteen years of age and older, and carried no monetary remuneration, since it was considered to be a social service. Recruitment into the posts was by public vote or appointment at set intervals of one or three years, although a few of the posts like sacristan (encargado de la iglesia) were filled only when the incumbent chose to resign or was dismissed. Recruitment was increasingly selective for the more important or prestigious cargos.

Lower-level cargos were filled by young unmarried males or by adult married males aged thirty years and younger. Younger males could enter service at ten to twelve years of age as an acólito (acolyte), or at thirteen to fifteen years of age as a topil de la iglesia (helper for church officials), or at the age of eighteen as a member of the policía. Mid-level cargos were occupied by mature adult male heads of household between the ages of thirty and forty-five. All cargos at this level had an incumbent turnover at regular intervals of one to three years, with each ex-incumbent being granted a one-year rest period from service.

The cargo careers of many, perhaps most, San Sebastianos in the 1960s did not progress beyond this level; many never attained the post of regidor (councilman). The highest tier of cargos had three-year terms and were occupied only by those San Sebastianos, typically forty-five years of age or older, who had served as regidores. Ex-incumbents were granted three-year periods of grace from service in the hierarchy. The cargo of municipal president was the most important and demanding of these executive posts, and the man occupying it was recognized as the political leader of the community and was its chief administrator. The post of fiscal was the most honorific and respectful in the hierarchy and was occupied by a village elder who typically had been municipal president and most certainly mayordomo of San Sebastián, the annual patron saint's festival.

Until around 1920, the civil-religious hierarchy in San Sebastián incorporated several religious cargos immediately below that of fiscal, which subsequently disappeared: alcalde nazareno, regidor del alcalde nazareno, and topil del alcalde nazareno. The incumbents in these cargos nominated candidates to succeed themselves; the nominations were made mandatory by the civil authority. These were purely ceremonial offices related to a prolonged Holy Week celebration known as the labranza de cera in which the mayordomo, who was called the alcalde nazareno, sponsored all attendant festivities at a cost of several thousand pesos.

The cargo career of the father of one of my informants, who died in 1938, illustrated how this series of offices on the religious side of the hierarchy combined with civil offices to form a ladder system. He entered service on the religious side as a topil del alcalde nazareno, then moved up to regidor del alcalde nazareno and, afterward, on the civil side, became topil del mayor. From that point on, the alternation continued to alcalde nazareno, regidor municipal, mayordomo de San Sebastián, alcalde municipal, and culminated in service as fiscal, the top religious cargo (Cook 1969, 176). Under this older system, an individual household head's service alternated between civil and religious cargos but began on the religious side. This contrasted with the system in place in the 1960s in which individual cargo careers could start on either side of the ladder.

In 1966, the ladder system incorporated two additional sets of cargos, one in the civil sector consisting of a series of committee and secretarial posts, and the other in the religious-ceremonial sector consisting of sponsorship of saint's day celebrations, or mayordomías. There were two major mayordomías (patron saint, San Sebastián, January 12–24, and the Virgen de Juquila, December 2–11) and six of lesser importance: San Juan (June 24), San Pedro (June 29), Virgen del Rosario (first Sunday of October), the Virgen de Guadalupe (December 12), the Virgen de Soledad (December 18), and Navidad (December 24–25; the Navidad mayordomo also sponsored fiestas on January 1 and February 2).

In addition to these major and minor mayordomías, celebrations occurred throughout Holy Week (Semana Santa) that, according to tradition, were sponsored by civil office holders. On Palm Sunday (Domingo de Ramos), the juez (judge) sponsored a celebration; on Ash Wednesday the tequitlatos (village criers) and the mayor de vara (jail keeper) were sponsors; on Holy Thursday (Jueves Santo) and on Easter Sunday (Domingo de Pascua), the regidores (community councilmen) sponsored celebrations. These obligatory ceremonial expenditures by civil cargo holders were referred to as gastos and would typically involve reliance on *guelaguetza* relations like the other array of festive commitments.[5]

Civil cargos were occupied through election or appointment and entailed only limited financial expenditures by the incumbent. Mayordomía sponsorships, by contrast, were essentially voluntary and entailed the expectation of heavy expenditures by the incumbent. Both sets of cargos placed demands on the incumbent's time, with the period of incumbency varying from one year in the case of the mayordomías, and from one to three years in the case of the others.

Committee and secretarial posts tended to be conferred on the most educated San Sebastianos or those judged to be most competent. Religious cargos, by contrast, were filled by those household heads who had the requisite assets and financial means and who made a vow (promesa) to a particular saint as a gesture of gratitude for some favor granted or anticipated. Occupancy of either of these two accessory sets of cargos in the civil-religious hierarchy had equivalent effects on incumbent careers: to qualify them for service in more prestigious cargos without necessitating service in less prestigious ones.

Obviously, there was idealization in how the system was understood and represented by San Sebastianos, and the only way to separate the ideal from the real was through the aggregate analysis of many representative individual cargo careers. In the absence of such aggregate data, case studies had to suffice.

More important than the organizational scheme of the civil-religious hierarchy was the institution that facilitated the economics of fiesta sponsorship: reciprocity (*guelaguetza*). The reciprocity system operated on the principle that the household receiving goods or services was obligated to reciprocate in kind, at some time in the future, at the request of the donor household. It typically involved households in a continuous process in which the donor-recipient relationship alternated through time, and it was employed to accumulate wealth in the form of cash or consumables for purposes of festive celebrations like mayordomías and fandangos. Households participating in major festive expenditures such as mayordomía sponsorships kept an account book (libreta de *guelaguetza*) with an itemized list of its assets (future payment claims for donations made) and liabilities (payment obligations for donations received) within its circle of reciprocity partners. These claims and obligations were respected intergenerationally and even in the case of relocation of the participant household to another community. In the words of one informant, "Guelaguetza never dies" (Cook 1969, 126; cf. Diskin 1986, 286–287).

The case of the household of Saúl Gutiérrez and his wife, Juana, regarding their sponsorship of the Virgen de Juquila mayordomía in 1966, is illustrative. Saúl was thirty years old and was serving as mayordomo of the Virgen de Juquila, San Sebastián's second-most-prestigious and -costly religious sponsorship. By volunteering for this sponsorship, Saúl applied a strategy to preempt service in the lower tiers of the ladder system and broke the mold in undertaking a major mayordomía sponsorship at such a young age. "By serving as mayordomo," he told me, "they are not going to occupy me as a policía or as a topil. The person who serves as sponsor of a large mayordomía will never be assigned to those cargos; instead they will give him cargos like suplente (substitute) or will appoint him to a committee like the School Committee (Comité Escolar). But," he hastened to add, "I did not sponsor the mayordomía for that reason." Still, his alternative explanation for volunteering was rather cryptic: "The promesa to be mayordomo of the Virgin is like a mandate, since the Virgin has miraculous powers." (La promesa de ser mayordomo de la Virgen es una manda porque la Virgen es milagrosa.)

Saúl was the son of a recently retired presidente municipal, Wenceslao Gutiérrez Marcial, who was a grandson of Matías Marcial, and may have been exercising an option available only to elite households. Diskin (1986, 288) correctly emphasized elite households as the main players in major mayordomía sponsorship and the ceremonial *guelaguetza* system. Saúl and Juana raised a total of 8,450 pesos ($676.00) in cash by selling an ox team for 5,600 pesos, a fattened steer for 1,900 pesos, and a cow for 950 pesos.[6]

Approximately six months prior to the December celebration, Juana began lining up donors among relatives, compadres, and friends to provide specific donations on preassigned days during the fiesta period. She succeeded in lining up ninety-three new donors in addition to the forty who owed them from previous donations and were asked to reciprocate. As these donations (new and reciprocated) flowed in during the fiesta period, separate entries were made in their household account book, with each entry specifying the nature and quantity of the donation. When totaled up, these donations included the following items: 351 pesos in cash, 85 1/2 dozen eggs, 17 turkeys, 66 1/2 almudes of tortillas, 150 pesos' worth of fireworks, seven almudes of beans, and lesser quantities of sugar, chocolate, candles, mezcal, and cigarettes.

Regarding the social relationships of the ninety-three new donors to Saúl and Juana, fifty-four were described simply as friends and ten others as compadres, underlining the extent of extrafamilial support. Of the remaining twenty-nine donors, eight were first- or second-degree consanguineal relatives of either Saúl or Juana, thirteen were more distant consanguineal relatives, and eight were affinal relatives (Cook 1982, 111–112).

Saúl and Juana anticipated that a substantial proportion of the ninety-three donations received would be repaid in full and, perhaps, with an increment during their lifetimes. Through a selective process, reciprocity relations would be continued with some of the new donors by reciprocating their initial donation with an increment. A donation of two dozen eggs would be repaid with an increment of an additional two dozen, and so on. This pattern of repayment with an increment depended on the cargo career plans or aspirations of specific households. In the case of Saúl and Juana, who had several young children, there was less likelihood of future mayordomía sponsorships other than expenditures for weddings and birthdays.

The first page of the libreta de *guelaguetza* for Luis Gutiérrez Antonio and his second wife, Irene Antonio Rojas, listed *guelaguetzas* owed by them as of May 1, 1966. Their largest previous expenditure had been a fandango, or boda (wedding), which occurred several years after they started living together in 1952, following a sort of elopement and a period of several years living in consensual union. "I had to ask for *guelaguetzas*," explained Luis, "because I don't have much money. I bought this notebook (libreta) to record the date, the item, and who gave it so that when they come in the future and ask me for a return, I can check and see if what they ask for, and what I owe, is correct."

Luis's libreta had only thirteen donor entries, more than half of them relatives. The sixth listing was for the incoming mayordomo of Juquila, who was owed 2 almudes of corn, 10 pesos, and three dozen eggs. Luis commented regarding this debt that he planned to pay all of it and, if possible, an increment ("I will give them more than they gave us"). Since that expenditure was scheduled for December, he had already been reminded to prepare for the payback by the wife of the incumbent mayordomo. He explained his payback plan: "That señor gave me 10 pesos, 2 almudes of corn, and three dozen eggs. I will give him three dozen eggs that I owe him, and an additional three dozen as a gift that will become a new debt he owes to me." Another household on the list to whom he owed a turkey of twenty-six pounds, and who had a fiesta sponsorship scheduled for February 1967, had also reminded Luis and Irene of the forthcoming obligation. According to Luis, the wife came and told them to get prepared to give a turkey in February and that she wanted them to help her out with an extra turkey or 20 pesos. Instead of helping out with another turkey, their preference was to help with money or with tortillas.

The general rule was for creditors to remind debtors of their obligation at least two months in advance. It was up to debtors to pay on time and to renew the relationship with another donation. Households that failed to comply with payment could be jailed if a formal complaint, backed up by libreta entries, was made to local authorities. The violators would also suffer the penalty of being stuck with the reputation of "tramposo" (untrustworthy) or "no legal" (unreliable) and be shunned as a future *guelaguetza* partner in the community (Cook 1969, 120–122).

The mayordomía of the Virgen de Juquila was complicated by the fact that it had two mayordomos, the first and the second, for each annual celebration. Each mayordomo had similar obligations but, for the most part, at different times during the calendar year. Agustín Martínez, who was a sponsor of this mayordomía in 1962, explained the process of changeover (entrega) of mayordomos as starting on the first Sunday of September; the incoming mayordomo received sponsorship, and the outgoing mayordomo had to foot the bill (gasto). They drank chocolate and had a lunch of turkey soup, and the incoming mayordomo gave a bottle of mezcal and cigarettes to the outgoing one. They drank the mezcal, smoked cigarettes, and then went to the church to weigh the candle wax.

The weighing of candle wax was recorded in a book kept in the church. Each piece of candle wax was laid out on a palm mat and then weighed, and the weight was recorded in the book. If it was determined that there had been a reduction in weights in the changeover, then the old mayordomo had to replace the amount of the difference before the new mayordomo could receive the candle wax. Once he received it, with everything weighed and counted, the municipal president came and a recount was conducted in his presence.

Then the outgoing mayordomo had to give equal portions of tejate with sugar to everyone there. An increase in candle wax made by the outgoing mayordomo was voluntary. Everything was recorded and the book returned to the archive. Then came the counting of money in the power of the old mayordomo, which was handed over to the new mayordomo. Once the old mayordomo handed over the money, the key to the storage chest was retained by the new first mayordomo. He received all the ornaments and paraphernalia that were recorded in the book, such as candleholders and flower vases.

The fact that portions of this ceremony had to be witnessed by the presidente municipal reinforced the civil-religious nature of major mayordomías. Also, the fireworks burned at particular points in the celebration were paid for by surcharges levied upon each household in the community by civil authorities on behalf of the two mayordomos.

The history of the Virgen de Juquila mayordomía in San Sebastián is intertwined with the reproduction of the community's identity and San Sebastián's conflictive relationship with the neighboring community of San Juan. According to Agustín Martínez's account, his great-great-grandfather (tatarabuelo) was grazing animals on the slopes of Cerrito San Juan (see Map 2, Sector II), not far from his homestead, when the Virgin appeared to him. (Le apareció la Virgen donde está la lomita allí, tendrá como dos o tres siglos yo creo.) Reportedly, there was a dispute (pleito) with San Juan when the news spread that the Virgin appeared in that place; combatants fought with stones, machetes, and lances. San Sebastián won the fight and, afterward, Agustín's ancestor invited people to come to his house with flowers, candles, and other offerings for the Virgin. People went there to leave their offerings (dar su limosna) on a regular basis. When Agustín's ancestor was very old, the image of the Virgin was moved to the church. After the Virgin went to the church, the mayordomía was established in her honor alongside a preexisting one for the patron saint. It was not clear from Agustín's account precisely how the vision of the Virgin on the hillside led to a physical image in the visionary's house or how it came to be identified as the Virgin of Juquila.[7]

His account did include details regarding financing of major mayordomía sponsorships. Communal land assigned to the patron saint, San Sebastián, earmarked pasturage for livestock, including oxen, that were made available to the mayordomos for cultivating sections of the communal land, with the harvest being used for the mayordomía ("from the animals that were tended in the name of the patron saint, from those animals the mayordomos would get ox teams, one for the first mayordomo and another for the second, and the lands of the patron saint were divided between the mayordomos to grow corn for use during the mayordomía").

When Agustín served as mayordomo of the patron saint's celebration in 1962, there was no access by the sponsor to revenues from communal harvests, a practice that probably ended in the aftermath of the 1857 disentailment laws (Whitecotton 1977, 222). According to his estimate, he spent around 5,000 pesos in cash, apart from what he collected through *guelaguetza*. The cash was spent on the band, the drummer (tamborillero) and flutist (chirimitero), the priest for the Mass, plus 500 pesos for bread and 500 pesos for chocolate, sugar, firewood, and four fattened hogs, "para que alcanza para toda la familia." He added: "Here we help each other out, the mayordomo is given *guelaguetzas* of corn, of turkeys, tortillas, eggs, and so on. A person helps me out and, later on when he sponsors a mayordomía, then I return what he helped me out with and I double that help (le doblo la ayuda)."

Agustín's reason for volunteering to serve as mayordomo was a promesa (vow) he made to the Virgin in a prayer if she would help him escape from two robbers during an incident in Chihuahua at a staging area where laborers were contracted for migratory labor in the United States. As he was being escorted across a river at gunpoint, one of the robbers crossed the river, and Agustín grabbed a stone and hit the second robber, who was walking behind him and carrying a pistol, and managed to escape. The robber apparently died from the blow, but Agustín attributed his escape to the Virgin's miraculous response to his prayer for help.

Diskin's detailed study of the consumption and nutritional dimension of the festive cycle in San Sebastián found that there was a definite redistributive process at work. He observed that "some (of the invited guests) live in the house (of the large fiesta sponsor) up to 15 days and are fed during that period" and that this was "the richest and most nutritious food that they consumed during the year." Ceremonial meals represented up to 25 percent of the total number of meals San Sebastianos ate during the year (Diskin 1986, 286).

Diskin also emphasized that land-and-equipment-poor household heads participated in the *guelaguetza* system, exchanging use of equipment for labor on an equivalency basis, but they were also agricultural wage laborers (jornaleros or peones) for the land-and-equipment-endowed households (1986, 278). Even as wage laborers, they expected and received food and drink from their employers as part and parcel of a culture that discouraged impersonal conduct and accentuated neighborliness, to the extent of employing kinship and fictive kinship terminology to redefine the employer-employee relationship (ibid., 278–279; cf. Martínez Ríos 1964, 103).

The above factors, Diskin argued, combined with the effects of differential household size, composition, and developmental cycle on San Sebastián's social relations of production, and a system of equivalences permitting means-deficient households to access land and means of production like ox teams and carts in exchange for labor (1986, 267), tended to promote long-term turnover and relative leveling of household statuses. A factor that Diskin did not mention in this regard but that had a similar effect was the inheritance system. Among other things, inheritance tended to keep land-ownership under the control of senior male household heads and also promoted the fractionalization of plots (Cook 1969, 88–94).

The end result was that turnover and leveling disrupted the "creation of a system of social stratification based on social classes, with capitalist relations," which, from Diskin's perspective, would be tantamount to rupturing the "tissue of community life" (1986, 283). Taking into account all of the above factors in the context of reciprocity relations and the fiesta system,

Diskin concluded that San Sebastián in the mid-1970s was being reproduced as a noncapitalist ethnic community (ibid., 289).[8]

All of the factors and conditions Diskin included in his analysis were
operative in San Sebastián in the 1960s and 1970s. There were others, however, that qualify the conclusions he reached: an enduring structure of inequality in ownership of land and agricultural means of production, and a
series of money-mediated social relations between debtor and creditor, as
well as employer and employee, on record at least from the second half of
the nineteenth century.

Diskin (1986, 267, 277) found that more than a third of households had
no oxen, three-fourths had no carts, and that land was unequally distributed, with a typical family having access to eight plots of land, amounting to
one-half hectare. I previously found that twenty metateros owned, rented,
or pawned an average of just over five plots, amounting to roughly .8 hectares; less than half of them owned ox teams, and most did not own carts.
Another survey I conducted of thirty-five households (of which only twelve
had metate making as a principal occupation of the head) showed them to
have an average of 2.1 plots of first-class land and 4.1 plots of lesser-quality
land, and just over one-third had ox teams and carts. Finally, fourteen of
these households reported being in debt to moneylenders at the time of the
survey (for an average of 477 pesos, or $38, per household).[9]

These data should be considered together with three additional factors:
every household surveyed in 1966 participated in wage labor as employer or
employee, or regularly sold agricultural or craft commodities they produced
for cash. All of the commodities and labor involved in household festive
and reciprocity-based transactions not only had monetary equivalents (Diskin 1986, 267) but also circulated in the market economy. These additional
factors were strong indicators that community reproduction in the Oaxaca
Valley in the decade from 1965 to 1975 was realized within a commodity
economy where capitalist relations of production were widespread.

This does not mean that community reproduction was capitalist, but it
does suggest that the commodity element of noncapitalist relations and culture was compatible with, rather than representing obstacles to, the "entry
of capitalism" (Diskin 1986, 292). Capitalism had a natural seedbed within
San Sebastián's petty commodity culture. Capitalist relations were not uniformly incompatible with noncapitalist relations but potentially supported
or nurtured them by adding additional circuits for the circulation and realization of commodity value between households, as well as between the
entire community and the wider world (Cook 2004, Ch. 8).

## Metateros and Their Industry

A postcard photograph taken in the early 1950s of the metate sales area at the Saturday market in Oaxaca City showed several San Sebastián metateros with their products (see the first photo in the photo essay). In the center of the photo is Gregorio Gutiérrez, flanked on his left by his son, Luis, and on the right by members of the Antonio lineage: Jorge, Gregorio, Bernabé, and Urbano. Gregorio's wife was also an Antonio, a family surname that, together with Cruz, was historically predominant in metate making in San Sebastián. The inventory shown in the photo, spread out on the ground against a backdrop of large baskets just outside the entrance to a main marketplace building, included at least eighteen metates with companion manos and several extra manos. The metateros were dressed in typical peasant garb of the day: white cotton calzones (pants), sombreros de dos dobleces (double-creased hats), and huaraches tapados (closed sandals). Only two of the metates, in the center of the array, were in the luxury or gift category, having been bordado (engraved) and pintado (painted) by Gregorio Gutiérrez, who was the master (maestro) metatero in the group. The rest of the inventory was composed of standard undecorated metates.[10]

The photo was taken around the time that Gregorio was serving as presidente municipal of San Sebastián (1951–1952), only one of two metateros to hold that office after 1940 (the other was Margarito Ruiz, 1945–1946). Gregorio held this office during a fifteen-year interim when local politics was not controlled by the Marcial family (Guadalupe Marcial had held the post in 1943–1944, followed by Mateo Marcial, 1960–1962; Wenceslao Gutiérrez Marcial, 1963–1965; and Jesús Gutiérrez Marcial, 1968–1971). This was undoubtedly a time of some political advantage and pride for the metatero population, who were a distinct minority in San Sebastián, where the better-off landed agriculturists, storeowners, and moneylenders were usually in control of local politics.

Gregorio, in his midsixties in 1966, lived on a large residence lot with three jacales. He occupied the largest jacal (hut with adobe walls and thatched roof) with his second wife, Silveria, and son Alejandrino; the other two (made of reed walls with thatched roofs) were occupied by his sons Aristeo and Bartolo and their families. The residence lot also had a separate kitchen and washing area, a well, and a small corral for animals.

Gregorio learned metate making from his father, Diego, who was a first-generation full-time metatero who had access to very little agricultural land. Nevertheless, Gregorio said that by the time he was in his early teens, he began to help his father in agriculture while he worked in the quarry. A few years later, he spent five months as a contract laborer on a sugarcane plantation in tierra caliente (hot country) in Chiapas for 1.25 pesos per day. This compared with an agricultural day wage of 25 centavos at the time in San Sebastián. That Chiapas experience in tierra caliente taught him to appreciate more the tierra templada (temperate country) in San Sebastián; he spent the next twenty-five years working full-time there as a metatero. Over the years, he managed to gain access to a few plots of land but always had to rent an ox team during the agricultural cycle.

In 1920, when Gregorio began to work daily as a metatero, he earned about 4 or 5 pesos weekly during the first year; afterward he earned an average of 8 to 10 pesos weekly. He was able to provide for his family on that salary, since corn sold for only 25 centavos per almud. In comparing the situation at the beginning of his career in the 1920s with the 1960s, he noted price changes but insisted the bottom-line cost of subsistence changed little: "In the old days, I sold a hen for 35 centavos, and paid 25 centavos for a half day of ox-team use, and I had 10 centavos left over. Today I sell a hen for 15 pesos, and pay 10 pesos for a half day of ox-team use, and 5 pesos are left over. It's the same; I compare the two situations as being equal."

Gregorio's career as a metatero was marked by major changes in technology, which, in his estimation, clearly improved productivity and work organization. Large, heavy wooden mallets were replaced by steel sledgehammers in his lifetime, but "we simply used brute force—blows with a 4- or 5-kilo bar (barreta) to split stone" and noted that subsequent generations adopted the use of steel wedges with hammers to make this process less punishing and quicker. Tool kits also were diversified to include different steel tools (barreno and pulseta) to facilitate perforation of bedrock for inserting blasting powder. Before wedges (cuñas) and sledgehammers (marros) were used to split stone, it was impossible for metateros to work alone; they had to cooperate in groups in order to blast and split large stones into metate-sized blocks (trozar). Large slabs of stone were blasted out of a quarry wall by perforating holes in the wall with a barreno (bar with a specially shaped, sharpened tip) in combination with a large wooden mallet that was eventually replaced by the steel sledgehammer. Then, after being equipped with steel wedges and sledgehammers, an individual metatero could split large stone blasted from a quarry wall unassisted, thus eliminating the imperative of cooperating with others to quarry and cut stone.[11]

When I first met Luis Gutiérrez in 1965, he was forty-two years old and lived in a residence lot adjacent to those of his father and two brothers. Later, after remarrying, he moved to another residence lot containing three separate households: his own, which included his wife, Irene Antonio Rojas, and two sons of his deceased wife (María Valencia Martínez), Onésimo, eleven, and Tomás, nine; another headed by his wife's mother, Micaela Rojas; and a third headed by his wife's uncle, Felipe Rojas.

Luis began making metates at the age of seventeen under the guidance of his father. By the time he was pictured together with his father, Gregorio, in the Oaxaca City metate sales area around 1950, Luis had long since moved through the ranks as aprendiz (apprentice), to mozo metatero (journeyman metatero), and was on his way to becoming a maestro, although still acquiring knowledge about the finer points of quarrying and cutting stone. His progress was interrupted by several experiences as a migratory agricultural worker, first as a bracero, mostly in California but also in Texas, for a cumulative total of 17.5 months, and then in a 6-month stint in a cookie factory (fábrica de galletas) in Mexico City. His saved earnings amounted to more than 21,000 pesos (1,680 dollars), which enabled him to acquire, mostly through pawn (empeño) arrangements, seven plots of arable land (three of which were irrigated)—though it was not enough to acquire an ox team.

By comparison, the average number of agricultural plots owned or leased by nineteen of Luis's colleagues in 1967–1968 was just under five, covering an area of .82 hectares, but less than half of them owned ox teams. Only one member of this group, Cresencio Cruz, who not only owned an ox team but also owned fifteen separate agricultural plots inherited from his father, typically harvested sufficient corn to meet his annual household needs. Luis and the rest of the metateros all had to either buy corn during several months of the year or work as sharecroppers to supplement the annual harvest from their own land.

It was Luis's contention that a maestro differed from ordinary metateros by his outstanding skill as a metate maker but mostly for his knowledge about quarrying, realized by a high output of suitable stone. He had to direct others how to study bedrock and prepare a blast properly to get stone, how to cut big blocks of stone the right way to reduce waste. A master metatero, aside from patience in cutting stone, also had to own a complete tool kit to cut and finish stone: barreta, marro, cuñas, barreno, cucharillas, and pulseta.

Luis emphasized that while he did not need advice from others regarding work, he did regularly require assistance with quarrying to clear debris, move large stones, and in the preparation of a blast that required tiring, repetitive blows with the heaviest tools (pulseta, barreno, and sledgehammer) to perforate bedrock. In contrast to Ramón Ramírez and a few other metateros like Salvador Martínez and Ignacio Juárez, who excelled as independent workers, Luis, like his father, Gregorio, mostly thrived in the context of work companies that included his brothers Aristeo and Bartolo and his nephew, Florencio Cruz.

Aristeo Gutiérrez, Luis's younger brother (thirty-five years old when first interviewed in 1965), learned quarrying and stoneworking initially from his father but also from other maestros he worked with, like his uncle Joaquín López. After his father gave him a barreta, he would go to the quarry accompanied by his younger brother Bartolo, who tended grazing cows and did not yet concentrate on stoneworking. His uncle, who worked in a nearby quarry, encouraged him to spend more time to learn stonecutting, but he was more inclined to become a charcoal maker (carbonero). His father finally convinced Aristeo that although metate making was hard work, it had the advantage of a flexible work schedule and enabled you to spend more time closer to home compared to charcoal making, which required longer hours away from the village in the mountains than did metate making. Aristeo resolved to work with his father and become a metatero.

In 1990, after a career of working in company with others in many different quarries, Aristeo was working essentially alone in a quarry in the Cerrito de los Metates sector (Map 2, Sector I) on a half-day (medio día) schedule. Since he was no longer a young man, he preferred to work alone, which allowed him to spend less time in the quarry and schedule metate work at his own pace. Given the Cerrito's status as communal property, Aristeo was recognized as a quasi owner (como dueño). As a citizen who paid taxes and provided tequio service, he had the right to work in a quarry on communal property like the Cerrito; by contrast, he had no right to look for stone "where the land belongs to people" (a dónde hay terrenos de la gente) or "where there are owners." "So," he concluded, "we look for stone in the mountains or lands that are communal" (Cook 1990, Tape 1554).

Considering that San Sebastián's quarries were all located in terrain sectors where access to land was regulated through a system of communal tenure, before a maestro/dirigente could direct quarry operations, he had to satisfy the rules in order to gain recognition as having exclusive usufruct rights "como dueño" (as a quasi owner). Gregorio Gutiérrez provided the most straightforward statement of the rules for establishing quasi ownership of a quarry: "You clear away a sort of semicircle, then, if good stone is found there, that spot is recognized as belonging to you 'as if' you were an owner (como si fuera dueño). You have to be respected as if you were owner because you cleared and worked there." He cautioned that such recognition does not automatically happen when the metatero first asks permission from village authorities to work in a particular quarry, but is a consequence of the continuous work he does there.

Recognition as a de facto or quasi owner of a quarry came with a civic obligation. When stone was required for a public project, recognized owners had to supply the required quantity of stone with stipulated specifications; by so doing, they officially legitimized and reproduced their quasi-ownership statuses. Gregorio reiterated the conditional rather than absolute nature of this status: "Being recognized 'as if' you were owner, AS IF (emphatic raising of voice: COMO dueño) you were owner, not owner. Nobody else can work in that part of a quarry without your permission, and you are considered by other metateros as owner of the quarry."

On some occasions, quasi-ownership status was contested. Likewise, the apportioning of shares of stone by a quarry boss (encabezado) to members of work companies was problematic and also led to disputes. These two issues were joined in the case of Cresencio Cruz, who explained a situation that occurred in 1960 in the Mesa Chiquita quarry area (Map 2, Sector IV) and involved his first cousin (primo hermano) Odilón and two companions. In this case, Cresencio had decided to look for stone in a quarry where his patrilineal relatives had worked for generations, and where he had learned the craft from his father, Florentino, as his cousins Odilón and José Ricardo had from their respective fathers, Tereso and Apolonio. Since Cresencio had not worked there for quite a while, his right to do so was contested by his patrilineal relatives on a day when Cresencio arrived early to successfully prepare a blast and semifinish a metate from one of several trozos he had blasted loose. According to him, "envy" (envidia) was the cause of tension with his cousin, who expected Cresencio to ask permission from him before returning to work there. Such disagreements tended to occur where quarrying activity was discontinuous and on-again, off-again, even when dealing with a quarry where a particular metatero had a history of working with patrilineal relatives.

Cresencio's experience was not unique and exposed an important factor explaining turnover in the composition of quarry work groups. Even the best quarry bosses experienced turnover in work companies and adopted a "share and share alike" attitude regarding the stone distribution process. Individual metateros accepted the basic principle that stone shares earned in the quarrying process were to be apportioned equitably and roughly in accordance with labor-time expended, with the only exceptions favoring the boss/quasi owner. The critical consideration for each metatero was to keep labor-time per trozo as low as possible. The most difficult and time-consuming task was removing debris and waste stone by filling and dumping baskets (wheelbarrows or carts were not used). Several days were often spent at this task without exposing a promising vein of underlying bedrock. This process, along with deciding where and how deep to blast, was precisely where the knowledge and skill of the quarry boss and the patience and loyalty of workers were most sorely tested.[12]

During 1965 and 1966–1967, the largest work company I observed was headed by Aurelio Martínez in his quarry in the Mesa Grande area. He was thirty-five years old and had begun working in the metate industry at the age of fifteen. At first he made manos, and then, when he helped clear debris and so on in the quarries, he was compensated with trozos to make metates. Over time, he learned to do so by watching others and getting tips from them. Aurelio also was the principal blacksmith for all of San Sebastián's metateros, a trade he learned as an apprentice to a blacksmith in the neighboring community of San Juan Teitipac. He could usually be found at his bellows (ventilador) early in the morning, tempering tools before departing to the quarry. In 1966, he had no agricultural plots of his own but cultivated three that he had leased (por empeño) for 700 pesos. Moreover, since he had managed to acquire an ox team, he was able to access land on a cash-plus-sharecrop basis with landowners (10 pesos each half day plus 2 fanegas of corn at harvesttime).

Aurelio achieved recognition as quasi owner of the quarry by stages. First, he began clearing and sorting stone in an area that had not previously been quarried, discarding stone that was not useful for making manos or metates and setting aside useful stone. This process exposed underlying bedrock (paderones grandes de piedra) that he began to extract through blasting. Five workers volunteered to assist Aurelio as mozos, clearing and sorting stone under his direction in exchange for a share of stone suitable for manos and metates. He strictly applied his prerogatives as quarry boss; work was suspended in his absence and was conducted only according to his plan and under his supervision.

Aurelio's formula for sharing was ad hoc. When pieces of rock were blown loose by a blast, he told mozos where to make cuts. He measured large blocks of rock to estimate how many trozos could be cut and where to make the cuts. After the trozos were cut, he distributed them equitably among his mozos. His company of eight workers—which included one of his brothers, Felipe, and one of his cousins, Lauro López—performed tasks under Aurelio's direction in pairs (trabajan dos con dos); each worker, including Aurelio, partnered with another. Two worked together to blast, another two cleared away waste stone and dirt, two more cut up slabs into trozos, and so on. Stone for metates and manos was informally distributed in Aurelio's presence, with each worker taking his share, knowing that Aurelio would say something if the share was perceived as being too generous or otherwise inequitable.

Share arrangements and ownership claims in the San Sebastián metate industry were conditional and brittle. Aurelio, it turned out, had worked for many years with his maternal uncle Juan López in the Mesa Grande quarry (where Juan had worked since 1930). Following his uncle's death around

1960, and according to inheritance tradition pertaining to previously un-used communal agricultural land that had been cleared and cultivated, the ownership of the quarry was contested by Juan's widow, Herlinda. Her ac-tion was based on the agricultural tradition that the citizen who prepared and used a parcel of land established quasi-ownership rights over it by vir-tue of that activity. Unlike agriculture, however, quarrying involved a con-tinuous cycle of activity to obtain useful stone, and each new blast may or may not expose such stone, thus causing suspension of quarrying activity in one particular area and exploration of a more promising area. This led to a hit-or-miss pattern of quarrying and a cycle of starting, abandoning, and restarting activity in the same quarries (Cook 1969, 220–225).

Inevitably, quarrying promoted competitive jockeying for quasi-owner-ship rights to particular quarries among metateros who also needed to work cooperatively. The bottom line was that the cards were stacked against a widow such as Herlinda, a non-metatero, to retain quasi ownership of a quarry worked by metateros on a share basis. Metateros shared product ac-cording to the principle "to each according to his work," and without a male metatero proxy, Herlinda could not be a player. When no usable stone was extracted over time in a quarry, work in that particular place would be sus-pended but could be resumed later. Consequently, quarrying cycles were typically short and discontinuous.

The case of Aurelio and Herlinda became the focus of a great deal of at-tention in 1967, resulting in two contentious public hearings that involved various members of local government, including the presidente municipal, the síndico, and the representante de bienes comunales, as well as sever-al metateros. The hearings themselves were triggered by a series of com-plaints lodged with the síndico by affected parties, starting with a complaint by Herlinda against Aurelio and, subsequently, by different metateros with conflicting claims to ownership rights in the same quarry. The process al-lowed various government officeholders to exercise their limited author-ity and enabled the metateros to defuse or reduce tension in their ranks through the intervention of local authorities.

Herlinda first attempted to work out matters with Aurelio directly through an informal verbal agreement that, essentially, placed him in the position of having to recognize her ownership rights and provide compen-sation in kind for his continued use of the quarry. During this initial stage, Aurelio foolishly agreed to pay Herlinda four metates monthly but did not follow through on the agreement, since, after further consideration, he real-ized it was untenable. This led Herlinda to file a complaint with the síndico, who proceeded to draft an official agreement obligating Aurelio to provide Herlinda with two metates every fifteen days. This document, referred to as an Acta de Conformidad, was signed by the contending parties and by the síndico. Aurelio had to sign for fear of having his quarrying rights suspended. Afterward, Aurelio spoke with the members of his quarry team and supposedly extracted a verbal agreement from them to contribute one metate each per month to satisfy the ruling. Aurelio managed to give Herlinda four metates over the period of one month but did not comply further, having decided that it was in his best interest to move on to another quarry where he would not be bound by the ruling. This move would safeguard his long-term rights to communal quarry access.

The start of the new calendar year coincided with a change in municipal officeholders, including the síndico. With a new síndico in place, Aurelio and his brother Felipe decided to test the waters by returning to his old quarry and picking up activity where they had left off. This prompted Herlinda to file another complaint with the new síndico, supported by the old Acta de Conformidad. In addition, new claims to ownership of the quarry were lodged with the síndico by other metateros, some of whom had worked previously with Aurelio or with his deceased uncle Juan. This flurry of complaints, claims, and counterclaims compelled the síndico and the representante de bienes comunales to organize a site visit to the disputed Mesa Grande quarry. The end result of their inquiry was that they issued an official rejection of the previous síndico's ruling that had recognized Herlinda's ownership claim, and they suspended all activity in the contested quarry. In short, all of the plaintiffs lost, and local officials asserted their authority to resolve disputes regarding communal land. Such a suspension rarely outlasted the incumbency of the issuing officials.

I attended and tape-recorded the two public hearings triggered by the Aurelio-Herlinda case and, with Luis Gutiérrez as a Spanish-to-Zapotec translator, interviewed Herlinda López. I had already interviewed Aurelio and spent considerable time observing activity in his Mesa Grande quarry, and I had also interviewed Filomeno Gabriel regarding his knowledge of the case. My review of this material for this book reminded me that aside from the conflict-resolution role of the process, the proceedings provided a forum for discussion of the rights and duties of ciudadanos vis-à-vis the use of communal land, as well as for conveying information to the public about a particular occupational subculture many of them were less familiar with than agriculture, the community's most widely practiced and understood occupation.

From the perspective of metateros, the original ruling in favor of Herlinda violated the unwritten rules of their occupational culture, which assigned quarry ownership on the basis of continuous activity by the originator of a given quarrying cycle, that is, from clearing a path to exposed bedrock; to blasting, sorting, and finding usable stone; to cutting and shaping the usable stone into vendible products; and then reinitiating the sequence until the supply of usable stone was exhausted. Once a particular quasi owner broke the cycle and withdrew from a particular quarry, metatero culture viewed ownership rights to have ended, with the implication that any other metatero subsequently had the right to establish a new claim by starting a new quarrying cycle in that spot. This unwritten rule was contested and, sometimes, overcome by sheer bravado or intimidation by individual metateros; the metateros doing this were said to insert themselves by the weight of their testicles (se metió por sus güevos). I never heard of the violation of this rule resulting in physical violence, but it definitely led to threats and hostile relations.

Aurelio admitted that his uncle began working in the Mesa Grande area years before he did but claimed that his uncle had moved on to quarry in another spot and that he, together with his brother Felipe, started working another area in his uncle's old quarry. When he realized that stone in the new area was suited to metate manufacture, he invited his uncle back to work with them. They had a successful run of luck, so much so that Aurelio within a few months was able to save enough money from metate sales to buy an ox team. He then told his uncle to take charge of the quarry again because he was going to work full-time cultivating his land (ya me voy a cultivar mis mergitas).

Aurelio did not return to the quarry until after his uncle passed away and he resumed his duties as boss of a company that included his brother Felipe. Even though he had taken a leave of absence from the quarry, Aurelio was clearly caught in a dilemma by his aunt Herlinda's claim to a share of the quarry's output. Luis Gutiérrez, after hearing the story told by Herlinda, culminating with her success in convincing the síndico to draft an Acta de Conformidad in support of her claim against Aurelio, commented: "Frankly, the síndico was not familiar with the work we do and made a poor decision."

As if to confirm Luis's thesis of official misunderstanding, during the hearings, various members of the municipal authority took every opportunity to make disparaging characterizations of metatero behavior. Pablo Rojas, municipal president at the time, who as a young man in need of quick cash had attached himself as an apprentice in a quarry to learn how to make metates but ended up losing time and money instead, declared (still bearing a grudge from his early fleeting experience in metate making) that metateros capriciously did whatever they wanted in violation of local law. They sold land without official permission, despite their obligation to first get such permission, since quarries were on communal property.

Rojas explained that when ciudadanos needed a plot of agricultural land, they were welcome to clear, plow, and plant on communal lands, so long as they did so with the permission of the representante de bienes comunales and the presidente municipal and with a receipt for a required fee. Luis Gutiérrez, in a rebuttal to Rojas's statement, insisted that comparing agricultural land and stone quarries was like comparing apples and oranges, and emphasized that a great deal of work and expense was incurred by metateros to get usable stone—many times without success. There was no recourse or possibility of recovering their investment, unlike peasant cultivators who could always recoup their investments through a better harvest next year from communal land they had cleared without having to clear the land again. Even when there was some success in extracting usable stone and making a few metates and manos, Luis explained, there was no guarantee that those products would sell at prices that prevented a metatero from incurring debt just to feed his family.

Another officeholder, the suplente del síndico, weighed into the discussion at this point, arguing that the reason for pleitos among metateros was their tendency to aggressively assert ownership rights by declaring "I am owner" and that, in reality, none of them had receipts (comprobantes) from local authorities to back up their claims. According to the Mexican constitution, he insisted, no local officeholder—not the alcalde, or the presidente municipal, or the síndico—was empowered to sell communal land that was federal patrimony. Metateros engaged in a series of "free-for-alls" (luchas libres), and not one of them could claim that he was legally an owner. All that really happens, according to the suplente, was that "some metateros die and others are born, none is owner and stone lasts for years and years" to create problems for village officials.

Another official chimed in with a threat regarding the possible loss of use rights. He opined that the metateros were stupid because they would not work together peacefully, and warned that if they failed to shape up, they should be collectively banned from quarrying on communal land.[13]

Near the end of this hearing, Luis Gutiérrez, the most persistent and avid defender of the metateros, summed up the matter of quarry ownership in one sentence, clearly rejecting the precedent set in the Aurelio-Herlinda case with an Acta de Conformidad and an official receipt of payment (comprobante): "The matter of ownership of quarries is really something that is determined among the metateros themselves, not by local authorities citing codes of law."

The San Sebastián landscape included several hilly and mountainous sectors that had proven over the generations to be suited to quarrying for purposes of making metates, manos, grinding stones for corn mills, mortars and pestles, and pilas (troughs) to hold water for animals, as well as for construction. Each sector's quarries were associated with particular classes or types of stone, graded by color, workability, and vendibility. Also, accessibility of the sector and its quarries is an important consideration—especially for construction stone that is transported by truck. Metateros preferred to work in quarries that were either located relatively near the village or to agricultural fields or pastures, which made it easier for them to plan daily allocations of labor-time, as, for example, cutting alfalfa on the way to or from the quarry or grazing animals while cutting stone. Between 1965 and 1990, my impression was that there was a trend toward quarrying in the most accessible sectors like Mesa Chiquita and Cerrito de los Metates, and that less activity was occurring in the least accessible ones, like Mesa Grande, Cacalote, and Frente de Coyote (see Map 2).

Positing such trends can be deceiving because of several intervening factors. For one thing, historic patterns of private usufruct in communal quarry areas influenced activity, as did short-term stone yield; metateros' need for cash set an upper limit on the length of time a low-yielding quarry would be quarried. Some metateros had little or no interest in selling stone for construction purposes but were amenable to hauling unfinished metates back to the village by burro from relatively remote quarries, so long as the stone supply was stable and the products were selling well.

The process of determining precisely where to start a quarry in a new, promising area "to discover stone" (descubrir la piedra) was characterized by Luis Gutiérrez as a raffle (una rifa) full of uncertainty. Filomeno Gabriel described the process as probing bedrock with a barreta; when stone was found and split open, and determined to be clear of flaws, then a blast was set and the vein was exploited (Cook 1990, Tape 1554). The key to this process was to determine if the stone was suitable for making metates. Unsuitable stone was too hard to cut or too soft and crumbled when struck by the barreta (blanda y solo se desvorona). Whitish stone had less appeal in the market than green- or blue-tinted stone. Stone could be flawed by cracks (ventiadas), fissures (realices), or intruded imperfections or ribbons (cintas) and, therefore, be rejected by the metateros as unsuitable for metates and manos (Cook 1982, 187–190).

If stone was deemed suitable, several blasts typically occurred before a final decision was made to continue working a particular spot. The alternative was to relocate the process to another spot in the same quarry or to a different quarry in another sector.

Following a blast, loosened material was cleared away to expose bedrock that could be penetrated deeper with another blast. This was following the vein (seguir la veta). Blasted stone was sorted into use categories (i.e., metate, mano, millstone, construction) and set aside, and metateros continued working. If, on the other hand, several blasts failed to yield signs of suitable stone, workers simply had to start over in another spot that looked promising. This exploratory probing was a challenging phase for metateros because when it yielded a productive vein, "We earn money and livelihood," said Filomeno, whereas "we are always sad when we don't have suitable stone; we lose days and sometimes a week of work."

Changes in activity between different quarrying sectors were matched by fluidity in the formation and dispersal of work companies in accordance with perceived availability of workable stone or coworkers. Edmundo, who was working in a quarry in the Cerrito sector in 1990, explained that when coworkers failed to show up in a nearby quarry, he was invited to join a group in the quarry where he was then working, to help them blast and clear debris in the search for a promising vein of stone; after several days and several blasts, they hit pay dirt (Cook 1990, Tapes 1552–1553). Edmundo commented on the situation, noting that the stone has been suitable for metates since the vein was exposed, and waste stone could be sold either for construction or fill. Even so, Edmundo's coworker had less luck and had withdrawn to another quarry, leaving Edmundo to work alone. Subsequently, his friend Aniseto came to Edmundo after a blast and asked for a trozo to make a consigned metate. Edmundo gave it to him and invited him to stay on to work with him (le dije, "orale, hay chamba, no más trabajar unido y bonito"). Then another acquaintance showed up and asked for a job, and Edmundo gave him one. This supported his belief that it was better "to work together in a company (compañía) to avoid getting bored."

Regarding the sharing of stone in this quarry, Edmundo explained that at the end of a successful blast, each worker who participated was entitled to at least one trozo of more or less the same size to keep everybody happy. If a blast yield was deficient, then the worker who did not get a share, or who received a smaller share, was compensated in the next round.

Edmundo lived with his wife and six sons ranging in age from four to eighteen years (another son, aged twenty, was married and lived apart), and he also worked in agriculture; he had an ox team and a steel plow (arado de fierro). His work strategy involved working in agriculture as required seasonally but getting to the quarries as much as possible. Even during agricultural season, he came to the quarry by 3:00 p.m. after a full day of work in the fields.

On the day I interviewed Edmundo in the early afternoon in January 1990, he had just come to the quarry after cutting and loading fodder (zacate) for his oxen. His sons helped out by cutting alfalfa and grazing the oxen. Edmundo's strategy of working throughout the year in both agriculture and stone quarrying was greatly facilitated by the convenient location of his quarry in the Cerritos area in Sector I of the village lands (see Map 2) near agricultural fields, the main road, and the settlement itself.

Filomeno Gabriel Mateo (b. 1930, four children) grew up in a household of stoneworkers—his father and uncle made manos, and his two brothers were metateros. Yet, according to his account, "I grew up among metateros but I didn't know their work." After returning to San Sebastián following three years of military service (1949–1952), he decided to buy unfinished manos and finish them for sale and, in effect, initiated his career as a stoneworker. He admitted that, at first, he could not finish a mano in a day because he found the seated position required for using the handpick (pico) to be too uncomfortable. As time went by, he decided to overcome his discomfort and got to the point where he could finish five manos a day. He bought unfinished manos for 1 peso each and sold them finished for 5 pesos each.

Filomeno's mano business continued until 1954, when he entered the migratory labor stream as a bracero. Between then and 1964, when he spent five months working in California agriculture making 125 dollars every two weeks, he experienced five stints as a bracero in Arkansas, California, and Texas for a total of forty-two months. From 1961 to 1964, when not employed as a bracero, he worked in a soft drink bottling plant in Oaxaca City making 15 pesos daily. During this period, he also married twice, first with a daughter of Maximiano Hernández that ended in divorce, and then with the daughter of Fidel Martínez, a relatively prosperous molinero-campesino. He had four children from these marriages.

When I met him in 1965, Filomeno was dividing his time between quarry work, agriculture, and buying (and finishing) unfinished metates and manos for resale. He had also experimented with the corn business, which he abandoned because customers wanted corn in advance of payment, and with cutting and selling firewood or simply grazing animals or cutting fodder when the metate business lagged.

Filomeno had also worked seasonally in the extensive quarry area of Ixcotel, in the eastern periurban zone of Oaxaca City, where he acquired a great deal of knowledge about quarrying and stonecutting. In the 1970s, he displayed a penchant for carving designs on gift metates, which he sold on an encargo (special-order) basis, and also dabbled in carving figurines. For a time in the 1970s, he also sold stone figurines to a well-known tourist craft business in Oaxaca City. He estimated that over the years he had worked in ten or so different quarries in San Sebastián, including three located on Cerrito de los Metates, one of which was the private property of his father-in-law, who also worked for several years there cutting stone to make grindstones for use in his molino de *nixtamal* as well as for metates and house construction.

Filomeno had many bad experiences in the business of buying up un-finished metates and manos for resale, especially due to the expectation on the part of San Sebastián metateros that they be paid in advance, and their habit of failing to supply products as promised. He continued his business only by avoiding cash advances and by accumulating inventories during low-price months for resale during high-price months.[14]

When possible, starting in the 1960s, Filomeno invested saved earnings in land and animals, including burros, pigs, and oxen. In 1967, he had ten plots of arable land, mostly rented, encompassing a total of 5.4 hectares and with an estimated annual harvest of 2,000 kilograms of shelled corn (four carretas of mazorca), well above the 1,389-kilogram estimated harvest of twenty-one San Sebastianos that same year.[15]

During the 1990 Oaxaca Shoot, Filomeno took us to a section (tramo) of private land measuring 70 meters in width that he got through his wife when his father-in-law redistributed lands to his heirs prior to his death. Since San Sebastianos were accustomed to approaching their neighbors about pawning land, Filomeno identified a section next to the one inherited by his wife, which he held in pawn (empeñado). His brothers-in-law, seeing that he knew agricultural work, sought him out to work some of their lands as a sharecropper (a medias). This gave Filomeno access to a mix of seasonal (temporal, or rainfall-dependent) land: next to his plot that was held in pawn was another owned as private property; and beyond that were four separate plots, each with 14 furrows belonging to his four brothers-in-law, which he sharecropped.

During the January harvest when crops were picked and carted back to the village, tasks had to be done quickly to avoid damage by wind and graz-ing animals. Aside from corn, Filomeno planted chickpeas and squash. Also, dried cornstalks with ears (zacate con mazorca) were harvested. After this work was completed, Filomeno returned to the fields with an ox team to plow everything up and start the process all over again. That, he said, was the life of a peasant (así es la vida de un campesino).

Filomeno also had land in other parajes, Los Sauces and La Ciénaga, which were first-class lands with wells for irrigation, where he grew alfalfa, early corn, and other crops like broad beans. He emphasized that in years like 1990, with some rainfall from February to May but little afterward, there was a reduced harvest. In areas of seasonal land, it was customary to plant in June, so in 1990 they experienced crop failure. The sections he planted in April yielded a good harvest, but those planted in June yielded next to nothing (Cook 1990, Tape 1550, 1–8).

Filomeno's description of his particular land tenure and use situation underlined the complexities of land accessibility through a combination of relations mediated by cash, kinship and marriage, and product sharing. Like the quarries, uncultivated communal land (usually fourth class) may be cleared and planted by a ciudadano/contribuyente in good standing and provides an alternative to purchasing, renting, and sharecropping for such households. His description also emphasized that harvests from rainfall-dependent land were highly variable, placing a premium on irrigable land.

Filomeno's 1989–1990 harvest was adequate to meet his household consumption needs, but his concern was that it might barely last until the next early harvest. It probably would not be enough to feed his poultry or his burro, much less fatten pigs, as was the case in good harvest years, and meant less cash income from the sale of hens and pigs, and fewer eggs for own use. This highlighted the role of corn as the all-purpose crop, a staple food for household members and, when the supply was adequate, important also for fattening animals like pigs and chickens, and as an energy source for burros (and oxen) who consumed the entire unhusked ear as a sort of treat. This use of corn was considered to be an investment because it created commodity value that could be realized in the future, either by sale or consumption (Cook 1990, Tapes 1556 and 1560).

During the period of plowing and planting, the primary concern of peasant-artisans like Filomeno was to participate in agriculture on land that was owned, rented, or worked on a share basis so as to maximize subsistence crop output. Filomeno did not have enough irrigated land to overcome a poor harvest from seasonal land, hence a period of three or so months opened up for stoneworking. This earned him cash for household expenditures and was the main motivation for his involvement in the metate industry.

Filomeno and other metateros like him pursued a mixed work schedule that was more heavily weighted toward agriculture from when the rains began in May to the main harvest in November; and more heavily weighted toward stoneworking in the months after harvest and before the next plowing-planting period began in May. December through April was the period of greatest activity and highest returns in the metate business for all concerned. Even during the period of agriculture-heavy work, some portion of the workweek was still devoted to stoneworking in many metatero households.[16]

In summary, in San Sebastián, stoneworking fit nicely into the agricultural work schedule, which was seasonally determined. For households with access to mostly rainfall-dependent land, it was scheduled according to seasonal rainfall patterns. Only after the first spring rains could rainfall-dependent land be plowed.

During his career, Filomeno never failed to raise cash from some aspect of the metate business, whether making products from scratch and selling them or finishing and reselling semifinished products bought from others. This is what kept the metate industry going; it provided a reliable means for metateros to convert their labor power into cash, especially during periods of the year when the local agricultural labor market was stagnant.

Metate product pricing, for the producer-seller, was pegged to the going day wage for an agricultural worker (jornalero) or a construction laborer (peón de albañil). Filomeno explained that he priced metates on the basis of a wage equivalency for a full day's work. (Tiene que salir el dinero lo que equivale al día.) If it took two days, then the price had to cover two days of work. The fact that most metateros shared with Filomeno a labor market standard for determining the market value of their products remains for me a powerful indicator of how capitalist relations of production penetrated without transforming a peasant-artisan petty commodity industry in the twentieth-century Oaxaca Valley economy (Cook 1990, Tape 1556).

## CHAPTER 5

# San Lorenzo Albarradas,
# Xaagá, and the Hacienda Regime

The consolidation of Hacienda Xaagá was critical to the formation of the communities of San Lorenzo Albarradas and Xaagá. Local discourse identified the residents of Xaagá, together with those of San Lorenzo and Unión Zapata, as castellanos in a Zapotec region. This implied their common origin but provided no explanation of it.

It has been speculated that the Spanish-speaking populations in Mitla's neighborhood, including Xaagá and San Lorenzo Albarradas, were descendants of non-Zapotec speakers from the Mixteca or from another region of Mexico. According to this thesis, non-Zapotec speakers were imported into the greater Mitla region in the early 1520s by the Spaniards to weave palm or to provide military support in a campaign against the Mixe (Schmieder 1930, 23–24; Olivera and Romero 1973, 233–234).

One fact is certain: during the colonial period, the ancestors of twentieth-century castellanos in San Lorenzo and Xaagá became sharecropping tenants of a Spanish estate as it evolved from a sitio de ganado to estancia to hacienda. Documents in the Agrarian Reform archives (ASRA) show that tenants from Xaagá served the hacendado as armed wardens (guardamontes) who patrolled hacienda lands in its mountainous expanses surrounding San Lorenzo, whose inhabitants were also tenants.[1]

This chapter will focus on late nineteenth-century and early twentieth-century experiences of San Lorenzans (or "Lenchanos," as they refer to themselves and are referred to regionally) under the hacienda regime. They toiled as renters in agriculture and animal husbandry; and they were subjected to a surcharge system for the utilization of forest resources, including, most prominently, native stands of palm suitable for plaiting baskets (tenates) and mats (petates). Many San Lorenzans lost their lives during this period from aggressive actions by hacienda agents. Acts of retaliation and open resistance to hacienda rule did occur, but organized movement for change did not take hold until the 1910s under the impact of the revolutionary agrarian reform program. Formal petitions launched by 1918 culminated in the 1934 establishment of an ejido by dotación in accordance with the Agrarian Code (Código Agrario).

In the last century of Hacienda Xaagá's existence, the hacendados (the Guergué and Iñárritu families) used terrazgueros settled near the hacienda to police, intimidate, and terrorize San Lorenzans; they also cynically exploited and fomented divisions among San Lorenzans as an effective extrajudicial tactic to stall and sabotage agrarian reform.

The movement toward agrarian reform initiated by San Lorenzo triggered a process that would ultimately liberate the landless terrazgueros in Xaagá. In the 1950s and 1960s, the people of Xaagá, as ejidatarios, developed a treadle-loom weaving industry to stimulate material progress and release them from dependency on subsistence agriculture and animal husbandry.

## San Lorenzo's Origins and the Development of the Hacienda Regime

Since 1936, the pueblo of San Lorenzo possessed 10,356 hectares of mostly mountainous terrain, some 10 percent of which was estimated by government officials to be arable. Considering its entry into the twentieth century with a meager 190 hectares of land (fundo legal + zona urbanizada + pequeñas propiedades), the question may be raised as to how a meager land base in 1900 expanded by a factor of 55 in three decades. The answer lies in a tangled history of colonial and postcolonial relationships between San Lorenzo and two neighboring nonentailed estates, Xaagá and San Bartolo.[2]

Manuel Martínez Gracida (1883) placed the founding date of San Lorenzo as 1518. This appears unlikely, considering that it preceded the 1529 date for the founding of Antequera, which became the main base of Spain's colonial enterprise in the Oaxaca Valley and part of Hernán Cortés's marquesado (Chance 1978, 32–36). We know that San Lorenzo Albarradas Lachibixe in 1580 was one of eleven sujetos of the cabecera of Mitla, which had a secular priest dating from the 1550s (Gerhard 1993, 191). Spanish missionaries initiated their proselytizing activities in major native communities like Mitla and then incorporated outlying subordinate settlements into the cabecera-based parish (Gerhard 1993, 26–27). Outlying subordinate settlements incorporated into the Mitla parish, apart from San Lorenzo, included San Juan del Río Quelaa and San Miguel Albarradas Cunzeche. In the first list of corregidores for Oaxaca dating from the middle of the sixteenth century, within the corregimiento of Mitla were thirteen Zapotec-speaking sujetos, including Lachibixe (Olivera and Romero 1973, 260). The subjection of these settlements to Mitla's control suggests their possible Zapotec origin and identity.

If San Lorenzo was a new or congregated pueblo established by Spaniards in the sixteenth century for the purpose of plaiting palm, as Schmieder (1930) and others (see Parsons 1936, 54n46; and Taylor 1972, 23, 28) have asserted, it most likely would have been granted a fundo legal (town site) and a public grazing ground, or ejido. Even if it lacked the latter, the fundo legal could have been legally expanded later on to include some land for cultivation and grazing (Taylor 1972, 68–70). We simply do not know when or if San Lorenzo was ever "self-sustaining and held more than enough land to escape the paternalism and peonage of hacienda life" (ibid., 8).[3]

The settlement's early colonial presence as San Lorenzo Albarradas Lachibixe poses the possibility of a pre-Hispanic origin. Since San Lorenzo was already on record as a sujeto of the cabecera of Mitla by 1550, it is reasonable to assume that its Hispanicization went hand in hand with the despoliation that began in the early decades of the seventeenth century with the development and expansion of Haciendas Xaagá and San Bartolo.

The lack of colonial documentation of this process was confirmed by San Lorenzo's reliance on an outright grant (dotación) rather than restitution (restitución) in its original 1918 solicitation of ejido lands. The restitution alternative required early-colonial documentation, especially a título that typically included a map (croquis) of the boundaries of a given pueblo's common lands (terrenos comunales) surveyed and approved by representatives of the Spanish Crown (Whetten 1948, 129–136). The authorities of San Lorenzo had no such documentation, owing to a fire that destroyed its ayuntamiento and archive in 1918 (Mecinas 1955, 26). Martínez Gracida (1883) noted, regarding San Lorenzo, that "its titles were expedited in 1741," but none of them survived the fire.

Both haciendas originated in late sixteenth-century grants to Spaniards: Hacienda Xaagá in 1564 began as a sitio de ganado menor granted to María de la Cueva, who received mercedes for two more sitios in 1571 and 1583 (Taylor 1972, 219); and Hacienda San Bartolo began as an estancia de ganado mayor granted to Pedro de Espina in 1591 (Taylor 1972, 217). Hacienda San Bartolo remained under the ownership of the Espinas until the early 1690s, and in 1589 Pedro de Espina also acquired Hacienda Xaagá, which remained in the Espina family until 1728. The seventeenth-century ownership of these two haciendas by the same family was symptomatic of a wider trend toward land concentration in the hands of a few families in the Oaxaca Valley at the time (Taylor 1972, 133). In the realm of nonentailed estates, the Espinas were among the most notable landholders in the valley, with several estates, a trapiche in Cuilapan, and a mill with 200 acres near Magdalena Ocotlán (Taylor 1972, 134). It is also known that Gaspar de Espina Calderón gave a cash dowry to the convent of Santa Catalina de Sena when his daughter became a novice (Taylor 1972, 186–187), a fact indicative of his elite status. In short, the Espinas were among the most distinguished and powerful families in Antequera, with strong ties to the church, so they must have played an important role in the development and Hispanicization of Xaagá and San Lorenzo Albarradas Lachibixe.[4]

In addition to the above-mentioned trapiche near Cuilapan, the Espinas were also involved in sugarcane cultivation for some 150 years at Hacienda San Bartolo (Taylor 1972, 127). This hacienda in 1883 had 205 residents (119 males, 86 females) and was bordered on the north by San Miguel Albarradas, on the south by San Juan del Río, on the west by San Lorenzo, and on the east by Santa María Albarradas (Martínez Gracida 1883).

Both Hacienda Xaagá and Hacienda San Bartolo, from their beginnings and into the eighteenth century, proved no exception to the rule that "grazing livestock was a principal form of land use on Valley haciendas" (Taylor 1972, 128). They were on record throughout this period as raising cattle, horses, sheep, and goats in some combination.

Land available for free and unfettered use by the inhabitants of pueblos like San Lorenzo was minimal and subject to arbitrary invasion by the haciendas as occurred in the Zapotec community of Coyotepec, where a "shortage of arable land was aggravated in the 1640s, when Gaspar de Espina, the owner of a neighboring hacienda, took over a section of the community's best land and used it to graze his cattle" (Taylor 1972, 99). In 1815, Santa María Albarradas was awarded 600 varas of land (100 varas = 275 feet measured in each of the four cardinal directions) to compensate for lacking a fundo legal (Taylor 1972, 68, 70); it can be assumed that this land was repossessed from the nearby Hacienda San Bartolo. There is no evidence that San Lorenzo ever invaded hacienda land or destroyed boundary markers, as did Mitla vis-à-vis Hacienda Xaagá in 1792 (Taylor 1972, 87).

Hacienda Xaagá began as a sitio de ganado menor in 1564, and evolved to an estancia through the addition of mercedes for sitios in 1571 and 1585. During the first half of the seventeenth century, it became one of a handful of estates in the Oaxaca Valley that "approached the larger definition of hacienda" by obtaining political and religious control over the peasants within its domain, as well as by having a casa grande (big house) and cultivating crops in addition to raising livestock (Taylor 1972, 123, 219). By the late eighteenth century, Hacienda Xaagá encompassed seven estancias (Taylor 1972, 135). It was in the hands of the Dominican order from 1758 to the late 1840s, when it again reverted to private ownership, possibly in anticipation of disentailment laws that emerged in the 1856 Ley Lerdo (Bailón Corres 1999, 129–140). Hacienda Xaagá's expansion led periodically to conflicts with the neighboring Zapotec town of Mitla over boundaries and water rights (Taylor 1972, 87, 106).

José Joaquín Guergué became owner of Hacienda Xaagá in 1849 (1849 "Testimonio de Gratitud," OVSIP files), apparently buying it from the Dominican order (Taylor 1972, 219). Joaquín was the son of a Spanish merchant, José Antonio de Guergué, who came to Oaxaca in the mid-eighteenth century; he leased six sugar plantations in Tlaxiaco from Indian communities and built trapiches. His son, José Joaquín, first featured as one of three members of the Junta Provisional Gubernativa when Oaxaca proclaimed itself to be a "Free and Sovereign State" in mid-1823. In 1836, he became coproprietor of the Haciendas Marquesanas (with Esteban Maqueo) in the Isthmus of Tehuantepec; and in 1843 he became a senator in the National Congress. He then served as (liberal) Governor José Simeón Arteaga's vicegovernor in 1847 (Brian Hamnett, personal communication, October 2012).

According to Hamnett: "The Oaxaca repercussions of the Mexico City Polko insurrection of February 1847 led to Arteaga's resignation and to Guergué's (un-elected) de facto governorship from 15 February to 28 May 1847, coinciding with Santa Anna's return to power at the national level. The fall of Arteaga was not recognized by the Federal Congress (struggling against Santa Anna), which declared Guergué's administration illegitimate on 27 April. He resigned on 28 May 1847, deeply compromised by the support given him from conservatives and clericals" (cf. Rojas González 1949, 172; Reina 1988a, 259, 261).

The liberal opposition managed to regain control under the leadership of Benito Juárez, who was Constitutional Governor (officially elected) from mid-1847 to 1852 and again in 1856. The entire period from 1845 to 1857, the last year of Juárez's incumbency, involved internecine struggles between liberals and conservatives as evidenced by the fact that, in addition to Benito Juárez, fifteen other individuals were leaders of the state government, several like Juárez serving more than once in office, albeit provisionally and not constitutionally elected.[5]

After acquiring Hacienda Xaagá, Guergué subsequently leased a large tract of land from San Lorenzo for the purpose of grazing goats and sheep. For several years he paid rent according to the terms of the lease but, at some point, stopped making annual payments. Much to their consternation, the San Lorenzans were informed one day by Guergué that he was now paying taxes on the land directly to the state government and no longer had an obligation to do so to the village. San Lorenzo's inquiries and protests led nowhere, and Guergué simply added the lands that he had been renting to his Xaagá holdings (Mecinas 1955, 5).[6]

The consequence for San Lorenzo of Guergué's land grab was that all land to the south and west of the settlement remained under the ownership of the hacienda. To pour salt in the wounds of his politically sanctioned maneuver, Guergué set boundary markers (mojoneras) flush with the southern and western peripheries of San Lorenzo's settlement area (zona urbanizada or fundo legal) to demarcate the hacienda's land (Mecinas 1955, 5).

Guergué's post-1849 land grab and setting of new boundary markers initiated a period of hostile relations between the hacienda and San Lorenzo. Later in the century, José Joaquín Guergué's son, Joaquín María Guergué, assumed control of Hacienda Xaagá, as can be inferred from an official complaint he filed in 1886 "for assaults committed on lands of the Hacienda de Xaagá" (Esparza 1991, 184, citing AGEO Leg. 80, exp. 2, 4ff.). In 1898, San Lorenzo was again accused of "invasions of Xaagá" (Esparza 1991, 184, citing Leg. 80, exp. 3, 86ff.). At some point after 1886 but during this period of violence, Joaquín María Guergué sold Hacienda Xaagá to Silverio Iñárritu, who with his two sons, Francisco and Luis, proceeded to deal harshly with unruly tenants in San Lorenzo.[7]

## The Agrarian Struggle in the Late Nineteenth and Early Twentieth Centuries

Ironically, the first casualty in the continuing conflict between hacienda and pueblo turned out to be Don Silverio's eldest son, Francisco, who "disappeared mysteriously with his horse when he was cultivating land near Roaguía [an outlying ranchería of San Lorenzo Albarradas] with his peones" (Mecinas 1955, 5–6). This disappearance led to an investigation by the rural constabulary, which found no body, no horse, no remains, no evidence of any kind, nothing. Pursuant to the code of justice of the Porfiriato, several officials in the San Lorenzo government were summarily hanged without trial in retaliation for what everyone, including the San Lorenzans themselves, assumed to be Francisco Iñárritu's murder. These hangings were followed by additional vengeance killings—apparently on the direct orders of Don Silverio and his remaining son, Luis—of three Lenchanos working their fields in an area adjacent to where the murdered Francisco had been supervising work prior to his disappearance. These violent events were undated in Mecina's (1955) oral history, but the mention of the intervention of the Rurales suggested a post-1877 date during the Porfiriato (1876–1910).[8]

Following Silverio Iñárritu's death around this time, the reins of owner-

ship of Hacienda Xaagá passed to his remaining son, Luis, whom Lenchanos rightly considered to be their "number one enemy" (Mecinas 1955, 6);
and whom Mitleños viewed as a "feudal overlord who was destined to be
shot some day" (Parsons 1936, 19).

Luis Iñárritu was educated as a lawyer and predictably "stood in with
the state government against the Carranzistas, who sacked his hacienda"
(Parsons 1936, 19). He had the background and motivation to resist the
agrarianist movement both legally and otherwise to the bitter end. Iñárritu
was the apparent victim of an assassination attempt as he was making a
speech in Tlacolula a few years after his participation in the anti-Carranza
movement. He was shot in the face, the bullet passing from cheek to cheek;
locals mocked his official naming as colonel as a reward for his running
away and as general for being shot, both titles being considered appropriate,
since they were common names for dogs (Parsons 1936, 19n14).[9]

Luis Iñárritu was not only a victim of violence but perpetrated the same
against his tenants. He arrived unexpectedly in San Lorenzo on horseback
one day in 1916 leading a group of soldiers. In front of the municipal government building (municipio), he demanded that the municipal secretary,
Andrés Olivera, come outside. Iñárritu angrily reprimanded Olivera for
sending a letter with the theme "CONSTITUCION Y REFORMA" printed on it,
which had recently been replaced by the "CONSTITUCION Y PAZ" theme of the
most recently installed regime in Oaxaca City. According to eyewitnesses,
Iñárritu ordered Olivera's arrest and had him executed forthwith in front
of the ayuntamiento. Twenty Lenchanos who had assembled in support of
Olivera were jailed. They were eventually released but not before an armed
group of Lenchanos was defeated and disarmed by government soldiers
(Mecinas 1955, 7).

San Lorenzo's dotación document, dated November 9, 1923, emphasized
land scarcity as well as egregiously uneven distribution of land between
pueblo and hacienda. San Lorenzo had 359 inhabitants, with 124 family
heads and agriculturists who were essentially landless, and had only 38
hectares for its fundo legal with poor-quality seasonal lands suitable only
for corn and beans. Its neighboring haciendas, San Bartolo and Xaagá,
had 7,200 hectares and 18,000 hectares respectively (ASRA, exp. 955). The
Comisión Local Agraria cited a copy of San Lorenzo's 1918 dotación solicitation document, which referred to the two neighboring haciendas as surrounding the pueblo on all sides, confirming San Lorenzo's enclaved and
land-starved condition.

Mecinas's (1955, 10–12) testimonial history dramatically narrated San
Lorenzo's difficulties with Hacienda San Bartolo. Those difficulties revolved
around a Lenchano named Juan Pedro who was designated, at the hacen-

dado's request, as the pueblo's representative in "everything related to lands and surveying properties of one or the other, to eliminate motives for difficulties" (Mecinas 1955, 10). The hacendado (possibly Ignacio Monterrubio, who acquired the hacienda in 1778) promptly bribed Juan Pedro by giving him 30 pesos, for which sum he "betrayed his community." On the day cited for "the survey of the lands of San Bartolo and San Lorenzo Albarradas," Juan Pedro arrived at a place near the hacienda complex (casco) and was asked by the hacendado where he wanted boundary markers placed. He reportedly gave the same response repeatedly: "Continue forward, sir." The same question-and-response process continued until the group arrived in a paraje called San Nicolás, situated very close to the settlement, at which point Juan Pedro told the hacendado, "Place the markers here, sir." Mecinas (1955, 11) located the ruins of this boundary marker near the walls of a house where the hated guardamontes had made sure that no one who was not a terrazguero of the hacienda crossed the boundary to gather firewood, cut palm, wash clothes, or simply bathe or swim in the waters of the nearby arroyo. According to local oral history, those who were caught for these infractions were whipped like animals and, on occasion, hung from a nearby tree, which still existed in the 1950s.

The Monterrubio family controlled Hacienda San Bartolo from 1758 until the early twentieth century. As if to confirm their reputations among Lenchanos as "evil persons," all of them died violently. In 1906, Luis Monterrubio, the father, was murdered by one of his sharecroppers on the day he was returning to the hacienda after having taken his landowner's share of the harvest. Shortly thereafter, Luis Monterrubio, the son, known as "Luis Grande," was murdered on a street in San Lorenzo for having shot and wounded a young Lenchano; and "Luis Chiquito," the former's brother, considered the worst of all, was murdered by his cousin Rafael Ruiz as a family vendetta (Mecinas 1955, 11). Francisco Monterrubio, older brother of the two Luises, left to fight in the Mexican Revolution as a counterrevolutionary in northern Mexico, achieved the rank of colonel, but met his fate when he returned to Oaxaca with a supply of weapons. He was captured by soldiers from the Sierra Juárez under the command of General Isaac M. Ibarra and executed near Tlalixtac de Cabrera.

Doña Leandra, the mother of the ill-fated Monterrubio brothers, remained in charge of Hacienda San Bartolo and sought vengeance against those responsible for killing Luis Chiquito. She elicited the aide of none other than Luis Iñárritu, the hacendado of Xaagá, whose son married the daughter of Soledad Monterrubio and Victor Olivera (Parsons 1936, 18). She rewarded him with a horse and cash for his help. It was known that Rafael Ruiz, who was the family relative responsible for killing Luis Chiquito, had taken refuge in San Lorenzo together with his friend Ricardo Martínez. Iñárritu searched San Lorenzo but was unable to find them. He subsequently tricked these two individuals into coming to Hacienda Xaagá. Despite warnings from Lenchanos that a trap had been set, the two men went to the hacienda, were arrested, and, without a trial, were taken to the cemetery in Mitla. After being forced to dig their own graves, they were executed and buried as common criminals (Mecinas 1955, 12).

The wheels of the agrarian reform movement in San Lorenzo began turning not long after Andrés Olivera's murder in 1916. San Lorenzo's ASRA file (expediente 638) in Oaxaca City was replete with documents that traced the actions and counteractions of the agrarian authorities of San Lorenzo and the hacendado in the 1910s, 1920s, and 1930s during a politically charged and ever-changing land reform process that had to wind its way through state and federal agrarian reform bureaucracies and the Office of the Presidency. The 1918 dotación petition document described San Lorenzo's economy as based on goat raising, petate plaiting, and curing of deerskins to make rain capes (capulinas; ASRA: exp. 272, May 14, 1923, "Informe sobre los Trabajos de Topografía y Censales").

The initial phases of the process were hampered by the hacendado's armed intimidation of boundary survey operations, his legalistic maneuverings, a botched survey, and bureaucratic bungling. Following the provisional approval by state agrarian authorities of the 1918 petition, it was sent to the Comisión Nacional Agraria (CNA) in Mexico City, where it languished for several years and never became definitive. In response to San Lorenzo's reopening of the process and filing a new petition for an adjusted dotación de ejidos, Iñárritu sent a telegram to President Obregón (at the time on the presidential train in Cuernavaca) falsely claiming that San Lorenzo, with only eighty households, had neither requested nor needed ejidos, since he had given them more than 1,000 hectares, and requesting that all illegal and threatening land surveys of hacienda lands be immediately suspended (ASRA: exp. 272, March 22, 1923).

Iñárritu's complaint triggered a request by President Obregón to CNA-Oaxaca for more information about the case. This, in turn, elicited a detailed rebuttal to the content of Iñárritu's telegram by CNA-Oaxaca, stating specifically that its staff had no knowledge of Iñárritu's alleged gift of land, that the surveyor had been repeatedly threatened by the hacendado's armed men on horseback to suspend the survey, and that San Lorenzo was hesitant to cooperate with the process of granting provisional possession of its ejido due to being terrorized by the hacendado. The CNA-Oaxaca response also included the text of a telegram received from the surveyor, stating that his military escort on routine inspections of hacienda boundaries was fired upon with Mausers by hacienda personnel. The response closed by warning President Obregón "about the statements, false as false can be (falsas de toda falsedad) contained in the message of complaint from the owner of the Hacienda Xaagá."

The initial dotación process ended in December 1924, when its provisional status was changed to definitive: 1,488 hectares belonging to Leandra García of Hacienda San Bartolo and 372 hectares belonging to Luis Iñárritu Flores of Hacienda Xaagá were awarded to San Lorenzo without incident (ASRA: exp. 638, Dec. 13, 1924, Delegado CNA-Oaxaca to Sec. Gen. CNA-Mexico). The precedent rather than the actual result of the redistributive process motivated Iñárritu's resistance. He realized that the process had been flawed because of his intimidation tactics, and that the amount and quality of land approved for redistribution was inconsequential. Considering the instability in state government in those years, indicated by the fact that Oaxaca had twelve governors representing different political factions between 1915 and 1925, it is remarkable that even a flawed reform process was concluded (Bailón Corres 1999, 176).

Many landless Lenchanos did not participate in the 1918 agrarian census out of fear of retribution from the hacendado (Mecinas 1955, 14). A new surveyor sent to investigate the matter agreed with San Lorenzo that the dotación was inadequate due to low participation in the census and to land measurement errors. Also, it was recognized that the inadequate amount of land redistributed in the original dotación was of poor quality (puros pedregales completamente impropios a todo cultivo).

A new survey was undertaken to expand (ampliar) the ejido in 1924 (ASRA: exp. 272 and exp. 638). The surveyor complained to his superiors of the lack of safety; the hacendado's armed guardamontes intimidated Lenchanos who were in urgent need of harvesting crops planted on the lands provisionally granted. This report and several others led to the assignment of a military detachment to protect the survey party and Lenchanos from assaults by hacienda guardamontes, as occurred in 1925 when ten of them armed with .30–30 rifles and Mausers showed up in San Lorenzo's ejido where residents were cutting palm for petates. Bundles of palm fronds were burned, machetes and other items were confiscated, and a Lenchano named Cayetano Sibaja was tied up and taken to the hacienda as a prisoner.[10]

The official complaint from San Lorenzo to CNA-Oaxaca elicited a telegram from José A. Navarro, Procurador de Pueblos, CNA-Oaxaca, to the head CNA office in Mexico City (a copy of which was sent to the Office of the Presidency of the Republic; asra: exp. 638, doc. 515, March 4, 1925), describing the incident and requesting an order to absolutely disarm all "white guards" ("guardia blanca," or the hired guns of hacendados) existing in the state for being a serious threat to the tranquility of pueblos.

Iñárritu, in full prevaricating mode, replied by denying any knowledge of the incident, referred to the land in question as still belonging to his hacienda, and accused the Lenchanos of stealing his palm. This reply was countered by a report dated February 4, 1926, from San Lorenzo's Comité Administrativo Agrario of still another incident of harassment reported to CNA-Oaxaca, in which five ejidatarios complained that Iñárritu appropriated one-third of their wheat harvest at the threshing floors (eras) where they were at work threshing wheat on their ejido.

A similar complaint in 1926 by an agronomist to the CNA-Oaxaca office reported that Alberto Iñárritu, the hacendado's son, accompanied by two men (one of whom was identified as a wanted criminal), all armed with .30–30 rifles, approached a Lenchano who was threshing wheat and forcibly confiscated a third of his harvest, amounting to 2.5 fanegas, and smashed a boundary marker. In 1928, another incident in the same paraje involved the destruction of field crops (milpa, frijol y calabazas) with machetes by the hacendado's guardamontes.

The hacendado responded to all such complaints with a form letter stating that he had no knowledge of the situation described, that the hacienda cultivated wheat on its own property (which, by implication, included the provisional ejido of San Lorenzo), and that he personally had not had dealings of any kind with the inhabitants of San Lorenzo for a long time. The evidence is overwhelming that Iñárritu used terrazgueros from Xaagá to police and terrorize their castellano counterparts from San Lorenzo.

Iñárritu filed several complaints with officials in Tlacolula and Oaxaca City against the 1924 San Lorenzo ejido amplification petition on several grounds, including that the census of ejidatarios incorrectly listed nonresidents or ejidatarios who had already been given access to land; that ejidatarios who were too old to work had land allocated to them; and that the number of animals claimed by San Lorenzo Albarradas was too high. These alleged inaccuracies caused state agrarian officials to reduce the extent of the requested ampliación in 1935, but they were all rejected by the secretary general of the Agrarian Department in Mexico City in the official announcement of the definitive dotación (asra: exp. 638, August 28, 1936).

In retrospect, 1934 was not an ideal year for San Lorenzo's petition for an ampliación de ejidos to be successful. The odds were stacked against them regionally. Iñárritu was nothing less than a diputado in the Congreso

Local and a compadre of the governor (Mecinas 1955, 15). The comisariado ejidal in San Lorenzo had the assistance and support of several regional agrarianists, and the pueblo had the good fortune of being visited by Lázaro Cárdenas on his preelection tour (Mecinas 1955, 15) in 1934. A few months after this visit, when Cárdenas was president, two representatives of San Lorenzo's ejido, Marcos Olivera and Vicente García, went to Mexico City to ask for an acceleration of the reform process (a pedir la pronta tramitación del expediente; Mecinas 1955, 16). On their first day at the office of the president, they were recognized by a member of the presidential guard who had drunk beer with them during Cárdenas's visit to San Lorenzo. With his support, they were able to meet with President Cárdenas, who not only gave them a written order for the Agrarian Reform officials but also enough money to cover their trip back to Oaxaca. The result was that on October 22, 1936, San Lorenzo Albarradas received 7,556 hectares of land according to the procedure of ampliación. "On that memorable day for the sons of this suffering pueblo," Mecinas (1955, 16) wrote, "a small festival was held in which many compañeros ejidatarios from Xaagá, Loma Larga, Tlacolula, Mitla and San Baltazar Guelavila celebrated their happiness."

The Cárdenas administration distributed more land "than in all previous administrations put together" (Whetten 1948, 127). Nevertheless, without the Lenchanos' opportunistic trip to Mexico City to follow up on Cárdenas's fortuitous preelection visit to their pueblo, their petition would probably not have enjoyed a fast track to definitive resolution.[11]

Communications pertaining to the agrarian reform struggle between Hacienda Xaagá and San Lorenzo continued almost until the 1936 finalization of the dotación. Their content was repetitive: Iñárritu Flores denounced military and police authorities for having arbitrarily obligated his terceros (sharecroppers by thirds) in San Lorenzo to hand over to San Lorenzo's ejido authority (comisariado) crops harvested from what he considered to be his hacienda's land. Until official authorization occurred, by law a period of time was set for the landowner to harvest his crops prior to expropriation. In this particular case, the granting of provisional possession to San Lorenzo was only a few days away, so the Agrarian Department office in Oaxaca City reluctantly ordered officials to permit the hacendado to claim his harvest. There is no evidence that this order was respected.[12]

A cluttered and winding trail of documents provided proof of the Xaagá hacendado's unremitting determination to defend his estate through the decades of the late nineteenth and early twentieth centuries by any and all means available. This was to no avail and served merely to prolong the inevitable unfolding of the agrarian reform process for two decades. These documents suggested the existence of fractures within San Lorenzo owing to differential relations of Lenchanos with the hacendado, who cunningly treated some of his tenants better than others to sow discord among them. The hacendado's deployment of guardamontes from Xaagá to police San Lorenzans of the same "castellano" identity also sowed discord among them.

A great deal of credit in the entire prolonged and difficult land redistribution process belonged to the public servants in the agrarian bureaucracies who persisted against wealthy and powerful opponents to see that the revolution's goals of hacienda expropriation and redistribution to long-exploited and -oppressed peasant communities were realized.

## Xaagá: From Terrazgueros to Weavers

Elsie Clews Parsons, who worked in nearby Mitla on three separate stays between 1929 and 1933, labeled the tenants of Hacienda Xaagá as "Spanish-speaking Mixteca," identified the owner as Don Luis Iñárritu Flores, and reported that over two hundred tenants paid him half their ears of corn, one-third of their zacates, one-third of their wheat, twenty out of every hundred goats and sheep, and 1 peso a year to pasture a cow. He supplied seed in return for one week of labor (Parsons 1936, 19, 54; cf. Wolf 1967, 302). The 1900 census assigned the Xaagá community 221 inhabitants (Arellanes Meixueiro 1999, 39).[13]

Their condition of servitude limited the economic possibilities of Xaagá's peasants for generations. Xaagá's 1936 petition for an ejido grant declared their pressing need (apremiante necesidad) of ejido lands, given their complete dependence on tenant agriculture. Without land, they were obligated to hand over the greater part of the product of their annual harvests, without any payment, to the hacendado. "The finca where we find ourselves residing," the petition explained, "belongs to señor Luis Iñárritu Flores, who spends very little time among us and resides in Oaxaca City in a residence unknown to us (reside en la ciudad de Oaxaca, cuyo domicilio ignoramos)."

Until 1934, when legislation was passed facilitating filing of "piggy-back" petitions for land, resident hacienda peons like those of Xaagá were excluded from agrarian reform. This was remedied in August 1937 by a decree signed by President Cárdenas that made them officially eligible "to receive the same agrarian rights as other segments of the rural population" (Whetten 1948, 132).

About one year after initiating the dotación process, on September 11, 1937, the petition of the people of Xaagá was approved by the state governor with an allotment of 2,145 hectares as follows: 347 hectares was seasonal; 508 hectares of pasture with scattered portions cultivable; 508 hectares of

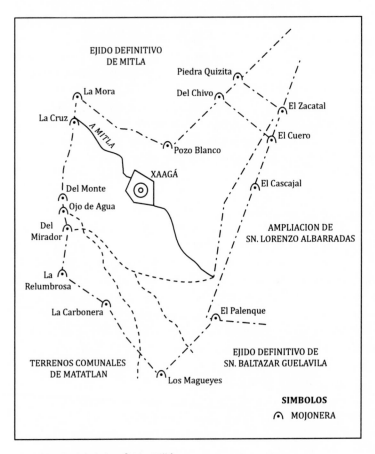

EJIDO DEFINITIVO
DE MITLA

Piedra Quizita

La Mora        Del Chivo

La Cruz                                El Zacatal

A MITLA                                El Cuero

Pozo Blanco

XAAGÁ

El Cascajal

Del Monte

Ojo de Agua

Del                                    AMPLIACION DE
Mirador                                SN. LORENZO ALBARRADAS

La
Relumbrosa

La Carbonera                      El Palenque

                                  EJIDO DEFINITIVO DE
TERRENOS COMUNALES                SN. BALTAZAR GUELAVILA
DE MATATLAN
                Los Magueyes

                                  **SIMBOLOS**
                                  ⌒ MOJONERA

MAP 3. **Territorial Limits of Xaagá Ejido**

pasture for grazing cattle; 773 hectares of high mountains; and 9 hectares comprising the urbanized zone (Map 3). This dotación was to benefit 105 campesinos. Ninety additional hectares, given initially to Mitla, were also earmarked to complete Xaagá's dotación (ASRA: exp. 955, Sept. 22, 1938).

The agrarian reform did not treat hacendado Luis Iñárritu kindly. Prior to its implementation, the Hacienda Xaagá had just under 9,100 hectares, including the habitation area (zona urbanizada) of 9.8 hectares. There were only 1.40 hectares of irrigated land, with the bulk of the land consisting of 3,992.40 hectares of mountainous terrain (cerril), 1,696.35 hectares of seasonally cultivable land, 2,711.80 hectares of high brushland (monte alto), and 689.15 hectares of pasture (agostadero).

A total of 8,366.80 hectares was expropriated from the hacienda for re-distribution as follows: San Lorenzo Albarradas (4,436 ha); the pueblo of Xaagá (2,145.60 ha); San Baltazar Guelavila (1,108 ha); and Mitla (677.20 ha). This reduced the ex-hacienda to a mere 717.35 hectares, including the buildings (casco), .4 hectares; irrigated land (tierra de riego), 1.4 hectares; seasonal arable land (tierra temporal laborable), 14.75 hectares; and high brushland (monte alto), 700.8 hectares. An official communication pro-vided a symbolic epitaph for the once-sprawling hacienda by officially con-firming that "no more land can be taken from what constitutes this small property (pequeña propiedad)" (ASRA: exp. 955, doc. 3933, Oct. 22, 1938). This undoubtedly did little to console the ex-hacendado, Iñárritu, for his losses. In short, Xaagá's movement from sitio de ganado menor to estancia to hacienda to pequeña propiedad had come full circle.

## CHAPTER 6

# "Castellanos" as

# Plaiters and Weavers:

# San Lorenzo Albarradas

# and Xaagá

As described in Chapter 5, San Lorenzo Albarradas and Xaagá may well have shared a common indigenous origin, but their shared identity as "castellanos" was forged from the sixteenth century into the twentieth century as subalterns of the same hacienda. They were divided in terms of settlement, means of material support, and specific relationship to the hacienda but were similarly subjected to exploitation and oppression by it. San Lorenzo evolved as a peasant-artisan community with some resources to produce subsistence staples and a modicum of palm products to sell, although its residents probably paid a surcharge for palm cut on hacienda land. The community of Xaagá, like San Antonio Buenavista, was landless and totally dependent on the hacienda. As sharecroppers, its population had no opportunity for independent household production, much less the possibility of developing craft commodity culture.

This chapter describes economic life in these communities in the twentieth century after their chances for improving material well-being were boosted by agrarian reform and the establishment of an ejido. Xaagá's deferred entry into weaving reflected its post-hacienda dependency on Mitla, where several merchant shops employed men and women from Xaagá as pieceworkers.

### The Palm Products Industry

San Lorenzo Albarradas is a municipio within the district of Tlacolula, located just off the Mitla–Ayutla road some ten miles east of Mitla. In 1980, the municipio included several other settlements: the ranchería of Santa Ana del Río was an agencia municipal; and several other rancherías, including

San Bartolo Albarradas (ex-hacienda), Roaguía, and Corral del Cerro were agencias de policía. All of these mountain settlements, contiguous with San Lorenzo, were exclusively Spanish speaking, as were Xaagá, ten miles to the south in the valley; Unión Zapata (also known as Loma Larga), just to the west of Xaagá; and the small mountain settlement of Santo Tomás de Arriba (ranchería and agencia municipal of San Dionisio Ocotepec).

It seems unlikely that the Spaniards imported Mixtec people to the region to plait palm simply because the native Zapotec were already doing so when the Spaniards arrived. In 1980, as in the 1920s when Schmieder did his fieldwork, palm plaiting was practiced in several Zapotec-speaking settlements in the San Lorenzo vicinity, specifically in the other Albarradas villages of Santa María, Santo Domingo, San Miguel, and Santa Catarina, as well as in San Baltazar Guelavila. Oral tradition in these Albarradas villages in 1980 was that palm plaiting had been practiced by their inhabitants for generations, and at least one of them, San Baltazar, had petate weavers in the colonial period (Taylor 1972, 103). It is unclear why Schmieder failed to observe this activity in San Lorenzo's neighboring Zapotec communities. Instead, he insisted categorically that palm plaiting was not practiced at all among the valley or mountain Zapotec. Incidentally, he also failed to mention that the community of Xaagá, right next door to his base in Mitla, shared a castellano identity with San Lorenzo (Schmieder 1930, 23–24).

In all likelihood, the original inhabitants of San Lorenzo, who probably knew how to plait, began to supply palm to native Zapotec plaiters of the region in the sixteenth or seventeenth century. The use of deer bone awls by Santo Domingo Albarradas plaiters in 1980, as well as cooperative plaiting known as golaneche, suggested an indigenous Zapotec palm-plaiting tradition.

The early sixteenth-century Spanish intrusion into Zapotec territory subordinate to Mitla, which included San Lorenzo Albarradas Lachibixe and San Miguel Albarradas Cunzeche as well as other Albarradas pueblos, probably did not deprive the native Zapotec of access to native stands of palm. Mixtec speakers (or Nahuatl speakers) used by the Spaniards in the Mixe campaign could have remained in the San Lorenzo area and gradually intermarried, allowing Spanish to gradually emerge as the lingua franca (Whitecotton 1977, 183; Cook 1983).

Although there is no direct evidence to support the thesis of early Spanish intervention in the palm trade to collect tribute or taxes, it is likely that hacendados levied an annual surcharge on their tenants for palm cut on the hacienda. Several Lenchanos in 1980 characterized the practice of collecting a municipal surcharge on cut palm fronds under the vigilance of local guardamontes as a carryover from the hacienda regime (Cook 1983, 49n9).

In 1980, all palm plaiters in surrounding Zapotec communities bought San Lorenzo palm. This included Santa Catarina Albarradas and San Miguel Albarradas, which were pre-Hispanic dependencies of Mitla (Taylor 1972, 107). In the early 1940s, the palm plaiters of Santo Domingo Albarradas also bought palm from San Lorenzo "at a price of 30 centavos per bundle (manojo)" (Alba and Cristerna 1949, 549). It is possible that in pre-Hispanic times palm was controlled by the Zapotec ancestors of the colonial settlement of Santa María Albarradas, which also had native stands of palm. In 1980, the Zapotec plaiters of San Miguel Albarradas and Santo Domingo Albarradas referred to the palm they plaited as "Palma de San Lorenzo" or "Palma de Castilla" (Cook 1983, 44n9). These terms evoked the enigmatic origins of San Lorenzo Albarradas Lachibixe (as San Lorenzo was called by Spanish missionaries in the sixteenth century [Gerhard 1993, 191]) and its involvement with palm.

Palm grows in varying degrees of density on mountain slopes with an eastern exposure; it is a genus of the family Phoenicaceae: the *Brahea dulcis*, or palma de abanico (*yagziyn* or *yagaxina* in Zapotec and *yutnu-nun* or *yucu-teyeye* in Mixtec; Standley 1920, 76; Pesman 1962, 162–163). Centuries of human occupation modified Oaxaca's southern highland forests. In limestone areas, a low fan palm (*Brahea*) invaded moribund oak forests as secondary forest cover, especially where excessive soil erosion exposed bare fluted bedrock (West 1964, 373).

Palm fronds, which were cut once a year for plaiting, rejuvenate rapidly. Within a few weeks after being cut, trees begin to show visible signs of new growth, and within a few months (into the rainy season), they grow a full display of fronds. Lenchanos did not cultivate palm and were concerned that they did not control its growth, even though there were no signs that it was becoming less prolific. Their only problem was caused by goats grazing in areas with palm stands; young, low palms were eaten by goats and made unfit for human use, so an effort was made to keep goats from grazing in areas of heavy palm growth.

Aside from a municipal government, San Lorenzo also had an ejido authority (comisariado ejidal) and a cultural mission (misión cultural) representing the Secretaría de Educación Pública (SEP) of the federal government. The list of 231 households initially used to draw a survey sample was compiled by the cultural mission in November 1979. Another list, acquired from the municipal president, included an additional 156 names, bringing the total population of household heads in San Lorenzo proper to 387.[1]

In 1976, an accord was reached in San Lorenzo stipulating that every male between the ages of fifteen and fifty, whether married or not, had to cooperate in paying taxes and giving municipal service. Female heads of household of the same age range had a similar obligation. This entailed an annual assessment of 50 pesos to the patron saint's festival fund and an additional 15 pesos to the school fund. Household heads who met this obligation became contribuyentes in good standing, and were thereby qualified to receive an allotment of palm from two sections of public land: the terrenos del santo and the ejido. The terrenos del santo were located within a section of the colonial fundo legal comprising some 2,700 hectares that had historically been recognized as belonging to the pueblo even after it became encapsulated within Hacienda Xaagá. In 1980, all of the privately owned parcels were located within this section.

Despite its history as a Spanish-speaking enclave in indigenous Zapotec territory, San Lorenzo had a long history of social and economic interaction with Zapotec and Mixe neighbors. It was the home base for several traders known as arrieros who traveled extensively through the adjacent Zapotec and Mixe mountain regions with strings of mules and burros carrying palm products and mezcal from San Lorenzo to sell and returning with coffee, avocados, and other products.

The local economy in 1980 combined agriculture, animal husbandry, quarrying (of marble and onyx), and crafts (palm and *ixtle*). Thanks to agrarian reform, only two of seventy-four households surveyed were landless; nine households held land as private property and did not report having ejido land. Eighty-seven percent of households had only one parcel of arable land ranging in size from .3 to 4 hectares. Twenty-three percent had .5 hectare or less, 35 percent had .6–1.0 hectare, and 42 percent had 1.1 or more hectares. About two-thirds of reporting households bought corn during five or more months each year; only one in five of these households did not buy corn every year. Average corn yield for the 1978–1979 harvest was 105 kilograms per household, which was substantially below the 250-kilogram median for Oaxaca Valley households (Cook and Binford 1990, 46).

Forty-three percent of households owned an ox team, but none owned carts. This was slightly higher than the average of Oaxaca Valley households (Cook and Binford 1990, 46). Burros, the favored beast of burden, were owned by 62 percent of households. Goats were more widely distributed than cows or pigs; 35 percent of households owned goats, and 25 percent owned herds ranging from six to more than twenty.

Cultivation was primarily by hoe (coa) and shovel (pala), although ox-driven plows were employed in some sectors. The principal subsistence crops were corn, beans, and wheat. There were some spring-fed, well-watered areas where plantains, tomatoes, avocados, and other garden crops were grown for own-household consumption. The main cash crop was maguey mezcalero, which flourished on arid mountain slopes and was harvested for sale to three local mezcal distillers (palenqueros). The palm products industry (petates and tenates made by women and brooms by men) was the most important nonagricultural economic activity; palm was cut annually from trees growing wild in several sectors of the municipal jurisdiction. During the dry season, many Lenchanos worked outside the community.

The most important commercial ties were with Mitla and Tlacolula, but there was some trade with Ayutla and with other Zapotec and Mixe communities. Relatively few Lenchanos made regular visits to Oaxaca City and rarely participated in the Oaxaca City market on Saturdays, opting instead to buy and sell in the Sunday market in Tlacolula. There were three privately owned trucks in the municipio: one belonged to a local storeowner, one to a palenquero who was the head of the ejido in 1980, and the other belonged to an ex-arriero and restaurant owner–trucker who resided in San Bartolo. Also, in the summer of 1980, the ayuntamiento/presidencia municipal acquired a government surplus pickup truck.

## THE ANNUAL PALM DISTRIBUTION AND HARVEST (DESTAJO DE LA PALMA)

Most of the lands of the municipio fell within the jurisdiction of the ejido, but there were also terrenos comunales and pequeñas propiedades corresponding to the original fundo legal. Natural stands of palm were about equally dispersed between the ejido and communal lands designated as terrenos del santo (lands of the patron saint). Ejidatarios and contribuyentes in good standing were assigned a section (tramo) by each of the respective authorities. Assignments were made or renewed annually in January on communal lands and in February on ejido lands. I observed this process in February 1980. At a meeting of all ejidatarios, the comisariado ejidal set the dates and announced them to the assembled group. On the day the process was scheduled to begin, members of the ejido's Comité de Vigilancia (Vigilance Committee) met with the four wardens (guardamontes) at a designated point in the ejido.

The group of ejidatarios, led by the two ejido officials, the president, and the secretary, who carried and compiled a palm list (lista de la palma), proceeded to walk through the palm stands to assign tramos that were physically marked by machete cuts at appropriate points. Each tramo was measured by paces, and an area was assigned according to its estimated yield of cut palm. No actual count was made of the number of trees within each tramo. Nevertheless, an effort was made to apportion trees equitably.

The ejido terrain containing the palm stands was generally open but did have some fenced areas known as potreros (pastures) for grazing animals; palm-cutting rights were assigned here as well. Open stretches were assigned either to members of the ejido authority or to ejidatarios who made late requests. The guardamontes moved through an area section by section, marking brush with machete strokes. If household representatives were not present at the marking, guardamontes showed them where their tramo was located later on. The period of allotment usually lasted for three days on the terrenos del santo and for four days on the ejido; the period for cutting lasted four to six weeks.

All Lenchanos who wanted to cut palm, and who were bonafide contribuyentes (with all fees paid), were qualified to get an allotment. Unmarried women or widows who were heads of household and had paid taxes and fees were also qualified to receive a destajo. Some households requested only one allotment when, as ejidatarios and comuneros, they had rights to two.

The key principle underlying allotment was that the person who put in time and labor to improve a piece of ejido or communal land by clearing brush and undergrowth, and who habitually cut palm on it, had annually renewable use rights. Minor disagreements arose regarding the precise location of the previous year's palm cutting. One ejidatario became quite indignant when it appeared that he was not going to be assigned a tramo that he had habitually worked. A few such cases were resolved through alternative allotments. Contribuyentes were not assigned tramos they preferred or requested. The most preferable tramos were those with the densest stands of palm on the most open and flat terrain; the more scattered the palms and the more steep or rough the terrain, the less desirable the tramo.

Following the allotment process, a period of three weeks was scheduled for cutting. This was done under the surveillance of four guardamontes who patrolled the palm stands and were required to verify the exact amount of palm that was cut per allotment. The ejidatario (or comunero in the case of communal palm) was required to pay a fee of 2 pesos per manojo (each manojo contained 100 fronds). The guardamontes reported the name of the cutters and the amount cut to the ejido treasurer, who recorded the information on the palm list. In 1980, the 2-peso-per-manojo fee had been in effect since 1969, when it was decided to increase it from 1 peso in order to help pay for the installation of electrical service in the village (84,000 pesos paid off over four years).

A preliminary examination of palm lists for 1978–1979 and 1979–1980 indicated that in the 1978–1979 season, a total of 10,698 manojos (1,069,800 fronds) were cut (plus about 300 additional manojos cut on private land). This averaged out to 7.72 manojos per comunero (communal lands divided by 645 names) and 9.08 manojos per ejidatario (ejido lands divided by 629 names). A comparison of the 1978 and 1979 lists for communal lands showed that a total of 645 persons cut palm in 1978, whereas only 540 did so in 1979. It was clear from a study of the lists that it was difficult to determine the amount of palm cut annually per household.

Persons listed tended to be heads of household, but this was not always the case. For two successive years on the communal palm list, Luis González Ramírez, a household head; his common-law wife, Felícitas González Ramírez; and his niece Irene Martínez, who resided in his household, were listed in order as buyers of palm—a total of 33 manojos in 1978 and 31.5 in 1979; these figures were considerably above the per capita average for both years. Households with the most allotments tended to cut the most palm.

Another characteristic of per capita annual palm distribution that emerged from these lists was its interannual variability; some tramos yielded more palm than others. The range of palm purchased from the terrenos del santo in 1979 was from 1 to 87 manojos compared to the 1978 range from 1.5 to 92 manojos. In both years, the largest number of manojos was purchased by the presidente municipal, illustrating one of the benefits of public office. By comparison, the ejido palm list for 1979 displayed a range from 3 to 57 manojos, with the largest number being purchased by a member of the comisariado but not by its head. One result of this variable distribution of palm was that households with a surplus sold it either to deficit households or to intermediaries who resold palm to buyers in Santo Domingo, San Miguel, and San Baltazar, where there were many palm plaiters but a scarcity of native palm.

Palm was cut exclusively by men, but both men and women collected and sorted cut palm. Cutting was said to be "too heavy, hard, and difficult for women" (trabajo pesado, fuerte y difícil para las mujeres). It was done with a machete on low, accessible fronds and with a special curved-blade knife (cuchillo palmero) attached to a bamboo pole for higher-up fronds. Depending on the height of the fronds from ground level, the cutter was able to reach them from the ground or would have to climb up the trunk until the fronds came within range. A typical division of labor was for one person to cut while another gathered and sorted the cut fronds.

In early February 1980, I accompanied Ubaldo Martínez García and one of his sons, Isaac Martínez Olivera, to their palm section. Isaac and Ubaldo left their residence lot in the village on foot leading four burros at 9:20 a.m. They arrived at their tramo at 9:50 a.m.; tethered the burros; and at 10:00 a.m., Isaac began cutting palm in one lower corner of their steeply sloped tramo; he cut his way across the tramo as he moved up the slope. Ubaldo gathered up the fronds and carried them up the slope to a flat area near where the burros were tethered and arranged them in piles (amontonar).

They both worked continuously, Isaac cutting and Ubaldo gathering, hauling, and piling, until they broke for lunch at 1:30 p.m.

During the 3 1/2-hour work period, Ubaldo, about sixty years of age,
made a dozen trips up the slope (cargando arriba) with a large bundle of
fronds on his back. He averaged about one trip every 17 minutes. The job
entailed stooping to pick up the fronds, carrying them to a staging area, tying them in a bundle with *ixtle* rope (mecate), hauling the bundle up the
slope, and depositing it in the sorting area. It was hard, physically demanding work; each bundle of palm weighed between 60 and 80 pounds. In this
3 1/2-hour period, all of the fronds within the tramo were cut, hauled to the
sorting area, and piled.

After the lunch break, work resumed at 2:10 p.m. The main task was
to sort (manojear) the fronds into two categories: (1) long and leafy, and
(2) shorter and less leafy. Ubaldo described this as separating good from
false palm (apartar la buena y la falsa) or setting aside palm that is frayed or
split from good palm (la palma que está reventada, se aparta). Next, fronds
were re-sorted into three different piles: new-growth fronds (cogollo), flawed
palm (palma falsa), and good palm (palma buena). The sorter picked up a
frond from the pile, examined it, and either tossed it into a reject pile or held
it in one hand until completing a handful (mano) consisting of five fronds.
These were then placed together in separate piles of 20 handfuls (manos)
of 100 fronds, making up one bundle (manojo), and then counted by manos
until reaching 20 to complete a manojo. Both Ubaldo and Isaac sorted and
tied manojos.

Narrow strips of palm were used to tie the manojos into bundles. This
task was referred to as "belting the palm" (hacer faja de la palma). At 3:15
p.m., Ubaldo continued sorting, while Isaac left the sorting area to look for
the guardamonte to verify the count of manojos. In one hour and five minutes, Ubaldo and Isaac worked continuously to sort a total of 13 1/2 manojos
of regular palm and 2 manojos of young palm (cogollo). Ubaldo continued
working alone until 3:30 p.m. to bundle and tie the sorted manojos.

The guardamonte mayor arrived on the scene, counted, and listed 15 1/2
manojos. Ubaldo and Isaac then started to load bundles of palm onto the
four burros, placing 3 manojos on each burro. Three additional manojos
were left in the sorting area to be picked up the next day. At 3:55 p.m., Ubaldo and Isaac headed back to the village, an uphill trek the entire way, where
they arrived at 4:45 p.m.

The entire work day lasted 405 minutes (or 810 minutes for two workers). Given the output of 15 manojos, this converts to an average of 54 minutes of social labor per manojo.

A few days later in February 1980, I talked briefly with the presidente municipal, Pascacio Olivera García, in his office, and then left for the campo with "Tío Alfonso." We passed by a drunk (borrachito) in front of the tienda near the municipio, and as we left the pueblo we ran into Isaías Olivera García leading a string of burros to the campo to cut palm.

We took a roundabout route to the palm-cutting area through private land (pequeña propiedad). We arrived first at a small plot near the village where Alfonso had planted tomatoes with irrigation and natural fertilizer (abono). The plants appeared to be growing well and were loaded with tomatoes. Farther down the hill, we came to an area with a substantial channel-irrigation (apparently a spring-fed reservoir, or presa) system with only one channel (zanja). We saw plantings of plantains (plátano), guava (guayaba), and chile. An adjacent large irrigated field was being plowed, and was to be planted in corn, beans, and squash.

When we arrived in the area where I had observed the destajo earlier that week, several members of the Comité de Vigilancia (from the comisariado ejidal) were already engaged in cutting their palm. I followed Isaías, who was cutting his destajo in a labor exchange (ayuda mutua) arrangement with his brother Santos.

They started cutting around 11:00 a.m. and by 2 p.m. were on their way back to the village with 7 manojos (plus another of cogollo and a bundle of low-quality palm for techos [thatched roofs]). Isaías's two young sons gathered the palm for bundling; Isaías and Santos cut off the ends and tied the palm into manojos of 100 fronds each. The tasks (tareas) involved were: cortar (cut), manojear (group into manos, or handfuls, of 5), juntar (gather together the manos), recortar (cut off ends), and amarrar (tie the manos into manojos, or bundles). Isaías and Santos loaded the bundles onto the four burros. Each burro got a load of two bundles. Before they left for the village, a guardamonte came and listed in his notebook the number of manojos that Isaías had cut.

Isaías said that he was not assigned a tramo to cut palma del santo simply because he did not have time to participate in the destajo when it was scheduled. He chose not to send a representative either. Given this failure, his wife would have to buy palm for petates when the manojos from that day's cutting ran out.

On my return from the palm area later that day, I stopped by the residence lot (solar) of Prisciliano, an escobero who was making brooms. He told me that he spent one day a week cutting four dozen broomsticks (varas) from a particular tree that grows wild. He also bought varas made of the interior of organ cactus stems from Totolapan sellers in the Tlacolula market.

He spent one additional day trimming and smoothing out varas to make them ready to use as broomsticks. He then spent two days to make four dozen brooms, by tying palm, unsuited for petates or tenates, to the stick with *ixtle* cord. He sold brooms for 10 pesos each in the Tlacolula market.

The palm-cutting and -sorting processes resulted in all of the cut palm fronds being bundled into two broad groupings: palma and cogollo. It is unclear what percentage of the 13 1/2 bundles classified as palma in the first report were, in fact, sorted as palma falsa (or reventada). Next, the cut palm was hauled back to the village for drying, further sorting, and preparation by the women of the household to be plaited. This postdrying phase was most critical in the plaiting of mats and baskets.

After green palm was unloaded at household residence lots, it was unbundled and spread out on the ground or roof to dry in the sun for six to eight weeks. Some households preferred to dry palm at the staging area of their tramo simply because it was much lighter after it dried and easier to haul back to the village.

The stage of drying (secamiento) was very important, since green palm shrank as it dried out. Plaiting with green palm resulted in inferior products. Lenchanos took a great deal of pride in the superior quality of their mats and baskets and used only well-dried palm.

When palm fronds were determined to be dry, they were cleaned and "fixed" (arregladas). This meant that defective palm (palma defectuosa) or palm that was not of good quality (no de calidad buena) for mats or baskets was eliminated, usually because it was too frayed or too short. Palm that had shorter, frayed leaves was used to make brooms (escobas), whisks (limpia-comales), and fans (sopladores); as roofing for houses; and as fireplace fuel (para lumbre del fogón). Shorter, tender palm referred to as "the heart of the palm" (el corazón de la palma, or cogollo) that was not frayed was used to plait small mats or baskets.

Once dried, palm hardened and had to be softened by soaking it in water to protect hands and fingers from pin-like pricks. Some women preferred to leave the palm outside at night to absorb moisture from dew (sereno) so that the next day it was moist and soft. Then they threw water on the ground in a shady spot on their patio, and spread out the dry palm so that it maintained its softness and moistness. Others put it out at night to absorb dew before retiring, sprinkled it with water early in the morning, wet down a shady spot on the patio, and then allowed the palm to soften for five or six hours. Only a supply of palm used in a given day's plaiting, typically 100 fronds, was processed in this way. Next, in a process called "rajar la palma" (cut the palm into strips), using a simple knife, plaiters removed softened leaves radiating off the central spine of the frond and cut them in half lengthwise along their spines to form individual strips of palm. Plaiting of mats was always done in pairs (pares) of palm strips.

The most desirable palm was the so-called white palm (palma blanca); also preferable was "long palm" (palma larga) because plaiting with it was faster, since fewer strips were added to complete a product. It was mostly used for medium to large baskets (tenates), since it was not necessary to add shorter-length strips to complete the basket (queda todo en una sola pieza). Palma blanca was not as common as palma verde (green palm), which even after drying maintained a yellowish-greenish tint rather than a whitish tint. The households that were able to cut long palm that dried white were considered to be very fortunate because products made from it brought a higher price in the market.

### PLAITING, MEASURING, AND MARKETING OF PETATES

Petates ranged in size from half of a single-bed size (used for cribs or small children as sleeping mats: 40 pares) to a queen- or king-bed size (100 pares); the most popular and common measure was a double-bed (cama matrimonial) or medium size (60 pares). Smaller sizes (20 or 30 pares, or petates chicos) were also plaited. The measurement "par" (pair) referred to the fact that plaiting was always done by interlacing two palm strips and was equivalent to the width of two strips (roughly two finger widths).

The largest sizes were usually made only by special order (encargo). They were made cooperatively by two plaiters according to an arrangement known as ayuda mutua in San Lorenzo and *golaneche* in Santo Domingo and other mountain Zapotec villages. Although a petate was plaited between two women working together, only one of them retained the finished product. The other partner kept the next finished petate. No money changed hands in this arrangement, only labor-time and palm were expended. Two plaiters finished a large petate in two weeks, working four hours daily; a lone plaiter typically made one large petate every four weeks. A medium petate, typically referred to as a "tapa carga" (or "basket top," since its main use was to cover large corn and bean storage baskets) took two four-hour days for two plaiters and three days for a plaiter working alone. The smallest petates required between one and a half or two hours for a lone plaiter.

The most experienced plaiters were more concerned with doing good work rather than fast work. They considered the petates they made to be extensions of themselves; accordingly, they used more palm and plaited it more tightly to assure a superior product.

The finishing stage in plaiting petates was "cleaning" (la limpieza). First, a knife was used to cut all the visible protruding points of the plaited palm strips from the petate; then it was washed with a wet rag to soften it. Once dried, the petate was ready for sale.

Petate (and tenate) prices varied by size and quality. The best months for sales were from November to April, the dry season, after harvest and before the next planting of rainfall-dependent crops. During the rainy season, when crops are planted, prices dropped. Plaiters explained that buyers for own use were engaged in agricultural work during the rainy season and used available cash to pay hired hands and buy seed. They also indicated that petates sold throughout the year, and that they rarely brought petates back to the village from the market.

The only women in San Lorenzo who did not know how to plait palm were those who married in from nonplaiting communities and did not want to learn the craft. In 1980, we counted about ten nonplaiting women in San Lorenzo. The daughters of these women were taught the oficio by female members of their father's family. Among native Lenchanas, the craft was traditionally passed down along maternal descent lines, mothers teaching daughters. It was taken for granted that this enculturation would occur in every village household as unquestioned tradition.

Daily time allocated by girls and women to the craft was variable within and between households. The most important consideration from the Lenchanas' perspective was the number and ages of females in a household. Next they considered size of the house and residence lot as important—the more space, the better—and whether or not the water supply was nearby. Seasonality was also mentioned as a factor determining work time allocated to plaiting: less was allocated during the rainy season when agricultural tasks such as planting or supplying food and drink to male workers were being performed by women.

Given the range of daily household chores for women, full-time craft work was not possible. Women with breast-feeding infants and preschool children had less time available for plaiting compared to those with older children. If the family was large and relatively young, women had to make more tortillas, cook more beans, and so on, giving them less time to plait. Women without daughters between the ages of eight and fifteen, who could help out with daily household duties, had less time available for plaiting than those who had such help. Girls began helping plait petates by the age of twelve. In short, daily household chores and care of the family took precedence in the lives of Lenchanas.

The relative lack of facilities influenced the performance of women's chores. All of them cooked with firewood and had to haul water from a street-corner spigot; tortillas were still prepared by hand on a metate, a daily task that typically required some three hours in the morning and two hours in the afternoon. This was true even though the community had molinos de *nixtamal* to grind masa; masa brought from the molino still had to be reground at home on the metate.

Despite all of the above demands on their labor-time, Lenchanas always managed to take some time every day to plait palm (un rato para el oficio), even if only two or three hours. These hours might be continuous but, more often, were broken up into discontinuous thirty- to forty-five-minute segments. The amount of time dedicated daily to the craft varied according to the female age composition of the household. Economic necessity was also a factor. When households had an urgent need for cash (unos centavitos para luego), women worked faster to finish sooner so they could take a finished petate to empleadoras (some of whom are also storeowners), either for cash or exchange for grocery items. "Here there isn't another craft occupation to earn money," one informant emphasized, "palm plaiting is the only one."

Several women in San Lorenzo were petate intermediaries known as empleadoras (employers). Most of these women were also plaiters but, in addition, bought palm products from other plaiters to resell in either Mitla, Tlacolula, or Ayutla markets. This business probably predated the twentieth century and certainly was thriving in the late 1920s and early 1930s before the final resolution of San Lorenzo's ejido. "Under the mountain fig tree at the crossroads," Parsons (1936, 368) observed a San Lorenzo party of "three women selling mats, brooms, and fire fans" to Mitla buyers.

In 1980, only two empleadoras sold in Ayutla and Mitla; none sold in Oaxaca City or to any government agency like FONART or FONAPAS. Most sold in the Sunday market in Tlacolula. Some of these empleadoras also operated small stores where credit was extended to petate plaiters. In effect, petates were priced in pesos, allowing the seller to buy groceries or pay a debt, often without cash changing hands.

Empleadoras bought at a fixed price year-round; prices only varied according to size. In 1980, the most popular medium-size petates were bought for 60 pesos each and sold in the Tlacolula market for 70 to 90 pesos. Particularly high-quality petates of this size were sometimes sold for as much as 100 pesos. By comparison, smaller petates were bought for 10 pesos and resold for 15 to 20 pesos each or bought for 25 to 30 pesos and resold for 40 to 50.

Some empleadoras paid cash in advance to plaiters who then brought

them finished petates as payment. Most preferred cash-on-the-spot transactions, but a few paid for petates with products from their small grocery
stores. One empleadora indirectly bartered (cash prices are put on all articles exchanged) lard (manteca), chile, soap (jabón), and school supplies
(materiales escolares) for petates, tenates, or sopladores.

Plaiters had favorite empleadoras, but if they were able to earn 5 or 10
pesos more, they would sell to the highest bidder. One plaiter who was also
an empleadora declared that they were not all the same. Some paid more
than others. Those who paid higher prices got more business than those
who paid less.

Empleadoras agreed that their goal was to earn at least 10 pesos on each
petate sold, but they always tried to get more. (Ni modo, así es el negocio,
nunca para perder.) If prices got too low, inventories were expanded until
prices rose again. One empleadora regularly traveled to Ayutla to sell. She
left San Lorenzo on the day before market day and spent two nights in
Ayutla. She had more sales at higher prices there than in Tlacolula. Her
explanation was: "The farther away the place, the higher the price."

When possible, plaiters sold their products themselves in the Tlacolula
market on Sundays, bought what they needed with their cash earnings, and
then returned to the village on the same day. This was the only option available to them traditionally. As thirty-eight-year-old Avelina explained: "When
I was fourteen years old (when she started learning to plait from her paternal grandmother), there were no empleadoras here. We went to Tlacolula
to sell. Now, it is different because there are empleadoras here. I buy up
petates to take to Tlacolula to resell; I don't do business in tenates. When
I was younger, we walked to Tlacolula to conduct our business; there was
no bus service or trucks. We got up at 3:00 a.m. to arrive by 4:00 p.m. We
followed a path from the Cumbre, and walked down to Mitla. We left on Saturday and spent the night in Tlacolula. We went to market on Sunday and
left Tlacolula, walking, by 3:00 or 4:00 in the afternoon to arrive in Mitla
by 6:00 or 7:00 in the evening. We spent the night in Mitla. We left Mitla
at 3:00 a.m. on Monday and by 6:00 or 7:00 p.m., we were back here again.
The whole trip lasted two days and two nights."

Long and arduous treks by sellers or traders of craft products were typical for Oaxacans until roads improved and transportation was motorized
during the second half of the twentieth century. Even so, in the 1960s in
Oaxaca City and market towns like Tlacolula and Ocotlán, there were still
inns (posadas) and storage places (bodegas) with corrals filled with burros
on the evenings before market day (día de plaza).

### The Treadle-Loom Weaving and Garment Industry of Xaagá

Following our frustrating attempt to survey weaving households in Mitla in August 1980, my assistants and I learned that weaving was also practiced in the ex-hacienda of Xaagá, a settlement located some four miles east of Mitla in the Oaxaca Valley. Several Mitla weavers complained about competition from Xaagá weavers, and they also told us that the Casa Brena from Oaxaca City had recently established a weaving workshop in Xaagá. As I later learned, the workshop was established by Félix Sibaja in 1949 and was long defunct by 1980, as explained below.

Through the tax office (Recaudación de Rentas) in Tlacolula we compiled a list of twelve weavers in Xaagá who paid business taxes to the state government. Toward the end of September 1980 we visited Xaagá to obtain a complete list of heads of household and to make some preliminary inquiries about its weaving industry. The director of the elementary school gave us a map of the community (see Map 4) together with a list of parents of school-age children; and the local government office (Agencia de Policía, Municipio de Mitla) also supplied a complete list of household heads from which we selected a 20 percent random sample for our household survey.[2]

After the 1937 hacienda expropriation, Xaagá was an ejido community and an agencia municipal of Mitla. It had no privately owned land and no communal land (see Map 3). Cultivable portions of the ejido were assigned to individual households according to the system outlined in Article 27 of the Mexican Constitution of 1917 and in agrarian laws (Código Agrario) first codified in 1934 (Whetten 1948, 116–123, 616–622; Mendieta y Núñez 1966, 235).

In 1980, about one-half of Xaagá's population belonged to the Seventh-Day Adventist religion. There was a small Catholic chapel, but the community had no patron saint and did not celebrate mayordomías. Several informants told us that in the past, Catholic worship was hosted by the hacienda located on the outskirts of the community (see "Casco" on Map 4). The hacienda was damaged, sacked, reduced in size, and redefined as a small private property (pequeña propiedad) by the agrarian reform. According to Catholics in Xaagá in 1980, at some point during the early twentieth-century agrarian struggle, the hacendado sold the image of the patron saint to the Mitla church, where it still resided. Therefore, the worship of the saints no longer existed in Xaagá, whose Catholics paid tithes to the Mitla church. Parsons (1936, 4) embellished this oral history about Xaagá and the church in Mitla: "Some of the tenants of the Hacienda de Xaagá, whose forbears are buried in the graveyard, or atrio, of the Mitla church, are expected to keep

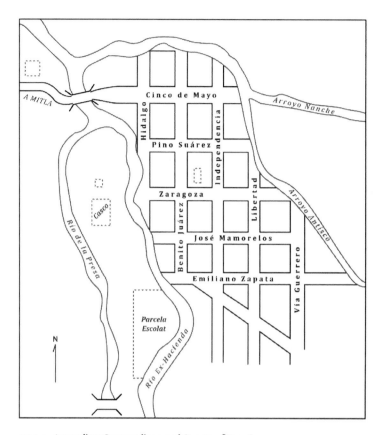

MAP 4. **Immediate Surroundings and Streets of Xaagá**

one half of the yard clean, the half between church and central cross; they also pay tithes to the priest."

A certain degree of mistrust, envy, and lack of conviviality existed between Adventists and Catholics in the community. But apart from a few disagreements regarding marriages, there had apparently been no real conflict between them.

The religious divide was paralleled by another within the occupational structure: everyone in the community whose principal occupation was weaving was Adventist, whereas the Catholics who wove considered themselves to be primarily agriculturists with weaving as a secondary occupation. Some full-time weavers felt that the part-timers tended to sell their products too cheaply, thus lowering the price (and earnings) structure of the entire industry. Although not supported by quantitative data, this attitude reflected the tension that existed between the two groups.

## FÉLIX SIBAJA AND THE ORIGIN OF WEAVING IN XAAGÁ

Xaagá was uniquely representative of Oaxaca Valley pueblos that were non-participants in craft commodity production during the pre-Hispanic or colonial periods and, in fact, did not begin craft involvement until the twentieth century. An explanation of this uniqueness can be found in a life-history sketch of Félix Sibaja Santos. Félix was born in 1914 in a small ranching community he identified as "Rancho de Guajes" (officially named San Antonio los Guajes) located in the municipality of San Carlos Yautepec. His father worked in agriculture and also made and sold deerskin capes (capulinas de cuero de piel de venado) on a special-order basis (por encargo). His father died shortly after Félix was born, and his mother was killed at the beginning of the Mexican Revolution. Félix moved from Rancho de Guajes to Tlacolula with an uncle and spent his next twenty years there.[3]

As an orphan in Tlacolula, Félix sold cigarettes and matches and began to realize "what life was all about." He did not like peddling, so he became a shawl finisher (tying up loose ends on woven shawls or rebozos) in the early days of the rebozo industry (al principio de la rebozería) in Tlacolula. This was during the revolution, which erupted in the region by 1913. His uncle was a peasant who also bought and sold cattle; he was persecuted for a time during the revolution for supporting Venustiano Carranza. Félix accompanied his uncle on trips and learned how to buy and sell cattle.

Félix worked five years finishing rebozos in Tlacolula for 1.50 pesos per dozen per day. He gave the money he earned to his aunt. In his early teens, he decided to try his hand at weaving. He never apprenticed himself to a weaver, but he bought a treadle loom from savings earned from finishing rebozos and wove rebozos at home. He sold rebozos wholesale in the Tlacolula market to merchants or shopowners and was successful enough to hire another weaver (operario) on a piecework basis. Félix supplied the thread and paid the weaver a wage. (Yo tenía un operario que tejía, y daba mantenimiento al operario en su material.)[4]

In 1938, Félix left Tlacolula and went to work as a loom operator (operario) at the Casa Brena, a well-known pottery and craft store in Oaxaca City with a mantelería (weaving workshop). He wove tablecloths (el tejido de mantel) for a wage of 35–40 pesos per piece. In Oaxaca City, he married Guadalupe Martínez Joaquín from Ocotlán; they had six children.

In 1944/1945, Félix signed a contract to be a bracero and spent six months in Salinas, California, working in beet (betabel) fields. He earned

5,000 pesos, which he deposited in a savings account (caja de ahorros) at Casa Brena, but in 1946 he went on another six-month stint as a bracero in Salinas.

With 10,000 pesos in total bracero earnings, Félix bought six looms and started his own workshop on Calle Guerrero in Oaxaca City, where he had as many as eleven employees. His main product was tablecloths with pre-Hispanic figures (manteles con ídolos), which he considered to be of "ordinary design" (diseño corriente). This business lasted three years until the industry suffered a strike and labor problems. Félix had been selling all of his products to Casa Cervantes, but they suspended their purchases due to the labor crisis. Eduardo Vasconcelos became governor but lasted only two months, and Félix kept his employees on payroll for as long as possible even though they were not weaving. (Yo mantenía a los empleados. Ellos no tejían, pero yo les prestaba dinero para mantenerse.)[5]

Félix finally closed his workshop in 1947 and moved to Xaagá, where his brother lived and worked as an associate of the owner of the ex-hacienda property. At that time, the main house of the hacienda still retained signs of the pretensions of its previous owners (Arellanes Meixueiro 1999, 48). Félix's brother found him a job in a charcoal business (la compra y venta de carbón) financed by his brother-in-law. The business consisted of buying product from charcoal makers in Xaagá, depositing it in a storeroom in the ex-hacienda, and hauling it by truck for sale in Oaxaca. Félix became assistant manager of the charcoal business.

In 1949, Félix moved nine looms from Oaxaca City to Xaagá after a falling-out with the owner of the charcoal business. He established a weaving workshop in the buildings of the ex-hacienda, working alone for about one year. Then he hired apprentices. With them and the help of the local authorities, he established a revolving credit cooperative in which his apprentices financed the activity of the workshop. They made tablecloths, cotton cloth (manta), bedspreads, pants, shirts, and jackets. Félix's wife was the seamstress. Every week he traveled to Ayutla by foot, hauling products on a burro. Félix paid his five apprentices a salary of 5 or 6 pesos weekly after they learned to weave.

The weaving cooperative lasted about a year before it shut down. The main reason for its closing was the intervention of authorities in Xaagá who accused Félix of becoming rich at his workers' expense. Several workers apparently complained to the authorities of being underpaid, and they stopped coming to work. Not one of the Xaagá weavers had the means to buy a loom and set up an independent shop.

After shutting down his weaving operation in the ex-hacienda, Félix turned full-time to agricultural work as a sharecropper, including handling an ox team. His wife also assisted in tasks like planting. They planted 24 almudes of corn and divided the harvest three ways: his brother, the land-owner, and themselves. The ex-hacienda also had medieros under the ad-ministration of Don Rafael Toro (encargado). The agricultural period in Félix's career at Xaagá also lasted for about one year.

Ervin R. Frissell, owner of the Hotel Sorpresa in Mitla, bought woven tablecloths and napkins for the hotel restaurant from Félix's cooperative. In 1953, Frissell came up with the idea of establishing a weaving school at the hotel, and he convinced Félix to move his looms there from the ex-hacienda. Frissell recruited apprentices from his hotel workers, all of them from Mitla, to become apprentice weavers in the school.

Félix remembered the names of Eliseo Reyes Soriano, Rufino Reyes, and Abel Santiago but could not remember three other names of his six appren-tices at the Hotel Sorpresa workshop. Félix emphasized that "there was no treadle-loom weaving in Mitla when those apprentices came to work there. There was only weaving by backstrap loom."

Félix worked for three years with Frissell in Mitla, the first four months without salary. He had to sell off some of his animals to support himself and his family until he was paid a salary. The rebozos were woven of cotton and wool; they also wove woolen sarapes with the famous Mitla "Greco" design. Félix remembered that he "copied designs from the Mitla ruins and trans-ferred them to the sarapes." According to him, the famous Mitla rebozo, made of fine white wool thread, was also "his own creation." He protested to Frissell that he was no longer willing to work without a salary, so Frissell agreed to pay him a salary of 14 pesos per day. In 1955/1956 Félix decided to move back to Oaxaca, and Frissell bought the six looms Félix had in Mitla for 1,500 pesos and continued to run the business for a time.

Félix started to work again in the Casa Brena in 1956, where he worked until 1961, earning a weekly salary of 150–200 pesos. "One day," he ex-plained, "I went out to have a few drinks and when I came back to work, they told me they were going to punish me with a one-month suspension. I was not disposed to suffer that punishment, so I quit." He eventually found another job as a weaver at Casa Acevedo, for a daily wage, where he was employed for a year or two. He quit working at Casa Acevedo around 1965 to go to work for his comadre Felipa Córdoba (on Calle Santos Degollado), who owned several looms and who paid "un poco más" than Casa Acevedo.

At the time I interviewed Félix in Oaxaca City in 1981, he was still work-ing for his comadre. I received a letter from him dated January 31, 1982, in which he lamented the decline of weaving in Oaxaca City: "What will become of my beloved craft that you became familiar with? I notice that cotton weaving workshops are disappearing in Oaxaca City, despite the fact that wool weaving is flourishing in Mitla. I am sorry about this but can do nothing about it." (¿Qué será de mi oficio tan bonito que usted lo conoce? Yo noto que se está acabando o desapareciendo en la ciudad de Oaxaca la mantelería, a pesar de que en Mitla está en flor la tejeduría en lana nada de hilaza. Lo siento, pero ¿qué le vamos a hacer?) Félix Sibaja went to his grave lamenting the fate of his craft in Oaxaca City but, although unexpressed, surely with some pride in his role in establishing and nurturing it in Mitla and Xaagá.

Beals's (1975, 258) summary account of the arrival of treadle-loom weaving to Mitla (based on field notes submitted by Miguel Ramírez) lacked details but confirmed the dating remembered by Félix. Beals also added some information lacking in Félix's narrative about Mitla: two of the apprentices (who were brothers) set up their own looms in the town of Mitla and continued to weave in the new manner. In time, others began to emulate them, although most could only afford small, improvised looms (colloquially, machetes).

Beals thought that increasing population pressure in land-poor Mitla gave impetus to the industry, and that the entrance of new money with braceros returning from the United States, together with the developing tourist market, provided additional means and opportunity. The aforementioned brothers who began as apprentices in Frissell's shop were the principal loom owners in Mitla. In the 1960s, each owned several looms and maintained a spacious shop with a show area. Owners of large looms numbered about one hundred and those with machetes about two hundred, but most owned from two to four looms. The most important loom owners employed at least one salaried weaver and a young apprentice (Beals 1975, 258–260).

Mitla experienced a sort of weaving boom in the aftermath of the Frissell workshop experiment based on treadle looms brought from Oaxaca City via Xaagá. The irony is that this boom was unrelated to an earlier weaver (not mentioned by Beals), Fachín Pérez of San Pablo barrio, who learned treadle-loom weaving in Teotitlán del Valle; or to the traditional backstrap-loom weavers of skirts and belts (Parsons 1936, 45).

A further irony is that Xaagá, where treadle looms were introduced in 1949 and operated into the early 1950s, did not have weaving again until the mid-1970s, by which time weavers from Xaagá had achieved at least an additional decade of experience in the post-Frissell workshops of Mitla. Dionisio Martínez, who got his first experience in treadle-loom weaving with Félix Sibaja in the ex-hacienda, worked afterward in Mitla before setting up his own loom in Xaagá. The son of Melquíades Olivera (who died shortly after

Félix closed up shop in the ex-hacienda) named Fausto Olivera Mendoza worked as a weaver in post-Frissell shops in Mitla and was among the first to set up a treadle loom at his home in Xaagá before Dionisio did so.

The two unnamed brothers mentioned in Beals's account were Eliseo and Rufino Reyes, who employed men from Xaagá as operarios (pieceworkers) in their Mitla weaving shops. Their employees included Efrén Ruiz Olivera, Odilón Olivera Díaz, and Luis Mecinas García, who, along with Fausto Olivera, became pioneer weavers in Xaagá. With saved earnings, these operarios from Xaagá purchased looms in Oaxaca City or in Mitla to set up independent shops in their home community.

### XAAGÁ AND ITS WEAVING INDUSTRY IN 1980

Unlike San Lorenzo Albarradas, where almost 100 percent of households participated in palm plaiting, Xaagá's households had craft participation rates varying from 36 percent in shawl finishing (tying the loose ends of a shawl after it has been woven), to 32 percent in treadle-loom weaving, and 20 percent in sewing. A close linkage existed between weaving and sewing: over 80 percent of households with seamstresses also had weavers. This pointed to the specialization of Xaagá's weaving industry in producing finished, ready-for-sale garments.

The Xaagá community's participation in agriculture was even more beholden to agrarian reform than San Lorenzo's. All agricultural land in Xaagá was controlled by the ejido; there was no private land and no communal land. A comparison between weaving and nonweaving households with respect to land cultivated disclosed a tendency for weaving households to cultivate less land (69.2 percent cultivated fewer than 2 hectares) than did nonweaving households (53.8 percent cultivated fewer than 2 hectares). Nevertheless, an equal percentage of weaving households and nonweaving households had more than 3 hectares of land cultivated; two weaving households had more than 5 hectares of land cultivated compared to only one nonweaving household.

A division existed among weaving households between those who considered weaving to be their principal occupation and those who considered it to be secondary. The former group of households tended to have less land under cultivation and cultivated it through sharecropping or wage labor, whereas the part-time weaving households had more land and cultivated it themselves. It turned out that the full-time weaving households were exclusively members of the Seventh-Day Adventist religion, and the part-timers were all Catholic.

In 1980, there were still some Xaagá weavers who worked in Mitla, but most of the weaver-employees in Xaagá worked at home. There were one or two cases in which a Xaagá weaver worked at home as a pieceworker for a Mitla merchant who was the loom proprietor. Even the weaver-employers in Xaagá, who were proprietors of looms and other necessary means of production, were still mostly dependent on Mitla merchants for the sale of their products and for the purchase of their raw materials (Cook and Binford 1990, 94–99).

Of twenty-six weaving households surveyed in Xaagá, the typical case was one weaver and one loom per household; only two households had more than one weaver (either two or three), and seven had more than one loom. In the five cases where there were more looms than weavers, households employed operators on a piecework basis at a rate of 3 to 6 pesos per meter of woven cloth. Reynaldo Olivera was the only resident weaver in his household in 1977 when he bought a used loom in Mitla to start weaving at home; but by 1979, he had acquired four additional looms that he operated with hired pieceworkers.

The Xaagá industry produced two types of cotton cloth, a loose weave (tela deshilada) and a tighter weave (tela tupida). The cloth was used to make pullover shirts, dresses, and shawls. Some weavers produced and sold only cloth, but most of them wove cloth that was then sewn into shirts, blouses, or dresses on their own premises, or was "put out" to seamstresses in other households who were employed on a piecework basis (4–7 pesos per shawl). The occupation of sewing, in other words, was completely integrated with weaving.

The typical production unit consisted of a loom operator (operario) plus a sewing machine operator (seamstress, or costurera). As Reynaldo's wife, Mauricia, expressed it: "My husband began to work here with his own loom and then asked me 'Who is going to make shirts?' and I told to him 'I will make the shirts.' He said that I didn't know how to make them; I told him that I could learn to make them and that is what I did. He bought me a sewing machine. Then we used our cloth to make shirts. I did this because he needed me to do it. My sister-in-law, who was the first one here to make shirts, had already learned to do it by taking apart finished shirts bought in Mitla to measure the parts, make patterns, and then make cutouts from whole bolts of cloth. Once she figured out how to make patterns and cut pieces of cloth to sew up shirts, she also taught me enough so that I could begin to work alone."

The labor process of weaving tela deshilada and of sewing shirts from the same material (which was the highest-volume product in the Xaagá industry) began with the acquisition of factory-made thread from Mitla merchants and ended with the sewing of buttons onto the shirts. The process involved bleaching of the skeins of thread (pintada o blanqueada del hilo; six steps), the preparation of the bleached thread for weaving (preparación del hilo para el telar; six steps prior to actual weaving), and cutting the cloth and sewing up (la costura; three steps) the shirts.

Labor-time estimates from several cases focused on the preparation and processing of two packages of 16/2 cotton thread (each package weighed 4 kilos and contained twenty skeins of thread). One package was used for the warp (trama) and the other for the filling, or weft (pie). The average amount of social labor-time required to manufacture eighty-five shirts (127.5 meters of loose-weave cloth, or tela deshilada) was 117.5 hours. In terms of individual labor-time, this required 1.38 hours per shirt for a return of 18 pesos per hour.

Weavers did not include their looms or other means of production as a cost of production, nor did they include the value of the labor-power expended by themselves or other family members. Only direct and immediate money costs were included in their calculations (e.g., thread, dyestuff, bleach, wage labor).

Shawl finishing (tejido de rebozos) was also fully integrated with the weaving industry, but, unlike machine sewers, the majority of finishers were not members of the weaving households. Weavers tended to employ outworkers to finish their shawls on a piecework basis at a rate of 4–7 pesos per shawl. It took a shawl finisher from 1 1/2 to 2 hours to knot both ends (tejer las puntas) of an unfinished shawl, and they spent an average of 2 1/2 hours daily at this job.

Weekly income of weavers was much higher than that of seamstresses or shawl finishers. The majority of the latter earned less than 50 pesos per week, whereas seamstresses earned between 50–99 pesos weekly. This compared to the average weekly earnings of weavers of more than 300 pesos (median = 350–399 pesos). These differential earnings implied a differential valorization of male and female labor-power; females earned much less per day than did males. Of course, the jobs were quite different; treadle-loom weaving was physically much more demanding, and punishing, than either of the other two jobs. Also, weaving was a full-time job, whereas the other two were strictly part-time. However, in terms of value added to the final product, the role of women's labor was of paramount importance (see Cook and Binford 1990, 94–99).

The Xaagá weaving/garment industry served as an example of petty capitalist development within the regional peasant-artisan economy, along with the weaving industry centered in Teotitlán del Valle and the handmade-brick industry in towns like Santa Lucía del Camino. It provided several examples of successful household enterprises that grew from a basis in family labor to employers of in-house and outsourced pieceworkers. These household enterprises in the Xaagá branch of the regional treadle-loom weaving industry were analyzed in-depth in a previous book (Cook and Binford 1990, 127–136).

## Conclusion

Lenchanos did not say directly that their long history as terrazgueros on the Hacienda Xaagá encompassed all of their relationships with the land, including the cutting and plaiting of palm. Several informants did attribute the practice of collecting a municipal surcharge per bundle of cut palm to a similar practice under the hacienda (Cook 1983, 45n9). During the hacendado's resistance to agrarian reform in the early 1900s, bundles of cut palm were burned by hacienda wardens in retaliation for Lenchanos' pursuit of an ejido. The entire process of palm allotment conducted in the 1970s under the watchful eye of ejido guardamontes probably replicated a process previously conducted under the supervision of hacienda guardamontes.

In the eighteenth and nineteenth centuries, Hacienda Xaagá occupied most of the land where palm grew and was harvested. Since the hacendado would most likely have been informed by his guardamontes regarding its systematic harvest and use by terrazgueros for commercial purposes, a system of apportionment and control of palm, including surcharges, was probably instituted at some point by the hacienda. It simply strains credulity to suppose that the hacienda's extreme defense of its economic interests during the Porfiriato and the early decades of the twentieth century was unaccompanied by a finely tuned system of exploitation of terrazguero labor and enterprise earlier in its history.

Schmieder's thesis regarding the Mixtec origin of San Lorenzo's population was based on the assumption of Dominican involvement in the palm industry. That priestly order's involvement in Oaxaca Valley craft industries like weaving in Teotitlán del Valle (Stephen 1991, 107) supports the thesis that some Spanish actors in the colonial Oaxaca economy had more than a passing interest in indigenous craft industries. Schmieder's thesis assumed that palm plaiting was not indigenous to the Albarradas area. This contradicts circumstantial evidence that palm plaiting among the mountain Zapotec was as indigenous as the palm itself.

Lenchanos were assailed from all sides by two aggressively and ruthlessly managed haciendas, San Bartolo and Xaagá, which employed every available legal and extra-legal means to keep them land-poor and dependent in a perpetual relationship of political subordination and tenancy. Lenchanos could not have toppled the hacienda system and transformed their lives without merging with a broader regional and national revolutionary and reform process during the second decade of the twentieth century, culminating in the mid-1930s under Cárdenas. Cadres of dedicated employees of the agrarian bureaucracy were indispensable in securing a successful outcome for the popular struggle waged at the community level by Lenchanos.

The terrazgueros who lived near the hacienda in Xaagá were used by the hacendado to oppress terrazgueros residing in San Lorenzo, but they were poor, landless, and equally exploited as tenants. Following the establishment of the Xaagá ejido, dependency on the hacienda was replaced by dependency on Mitla merchants and, for a period in the 1950s and 1960s, on Mitla weaving workshops. By the 1970s, Xaagá had a thriving weaving and garment industry ironically developed in a roundabout way from a 1949 origin in the casco of the ex-hacienda.

## CHAPTER 7

# The Jalieza Communities:

# Peasant-Artisans with

# Mixed Crafts

Santo Tomás, administrative center of the Jalieza cluster of villages, is located approximately 26 kilometers from Oaxaca City on the highway to the district town (cabecera de distrito) of Ocotlán de Morelos, 6 kilometers farther south. At least since the early 1940s, and in escalating fashion after 1960, Santo Tomás was on the tourist circuit out of Oaxaca City that typically included guided tours of black pottery–making workshops in San Bartolo Coyotepec; of the backstrap-loom weaver's market in Santo Tomás, conveniently located next to the highway at the entrance to the community; and of the bustling Friday market in Ocotlán.

Santo Tomás's location on the main road between Oaxaca City and Ocotlán made it a natural point of exit and entry for people living in the isolated mountain settlements of Santo Domingo and Santa Cecilia to the northeast. These two villages were connected to Santo Tomás historically by a path (vereda), which in 1965, when Welte's map of the Oaxaca Valley was first published, did not merit classification even as a "Camino Menor dudoso" ("doubtful passage" even for his Renault 4L; Welte 1965). This path was the most direct route from Santa Cecilia and Santo Domingo to Ocotlán, and also a trade route between the Tlacolula and Ocotlán arms of the Oaxaca Valley before truck and bus service from the hub of Oaxaca City was established, as indicated in Elsie Clews Parsons's map of truck routes (Parsons 1936, 568; cf. Cook 1969, 246–247). By 1891, Santo Tomás was a municipio in Ocotlán district; Santa Cecilia and Santo Domingo were its administrative dependencies as agencias.

This chapter begins with a review of archaeological findings about the "Greater Jalieza" area. It then reviews significant findings from 1978 household surveys, beginning with Santo Tomás; continuing with Santo Domingo, the most populous community of the cluster in the 1970s; and ending with Santa Cecilia, historically the most isolated and smallest Jalieza community.

## The Jalieza Communities in Prehistory

The ancient area of the Jalieza complex of communities, designated by archaeologists as "Greater Jalieza" (Finsten 1995, 3), is located in the southern part of the Oaxaca Valley on the mountain passes between the Tlacolula, Ocotlán, and northern Valle Grande subvalleys. It occupies an east-west ridge (Cerro Ticolute) joined on its eastern end by a north-south trending mountain chain (Cerro Piedra de Gavilán), both of which rise from the valley floor at 1,550 meters above sea level to over 1,900 m. In total area, Greater Jalieza is the largest archaeological site in the Valley of Oaxaca, although it was never all occupied at once.

The total site encompassed about 9 square kilometers, with its westernmost component "spilling down the slopes of a hill between the modern towns of Santo Tomás Jalieza and San Pedro Guegorexe," and its eastern component focused on the Cerro Piedra de Gavilán (which forms the divide separating the Tlacolula and Ocotlán Valleys) and spreading "over rolling hills, continuing almost as far as the modern town of Santo Domingo Jalieza" (Finsten 1995, 9).

This area hosted a series of terraced residential human settlements in the Early Classic phase, the Monte Albán IIIA phase, and the Early Postclassic phase, that is, from roughly AD 200–600 to AD 900–1200, albeit discontinuously in any one of its three components (Finsten 1995, 3). Perhaps the most relevant archaeological finding from Jalieza is that during the Postclassic (Monte Albán V or City-State) stage, "reuse and reoccupation" of sites was very widespread, indicating "short term and/or superficial use or habitation" (Finsten 1995, 81). There was a continuous occupation of a hilltop site in the westernmost component from the Early Classic through the Late Classic phases that ended in relocation to the east in the period from AD 900 to AD 1200.

Population estimates by phase are: Early Classic, 13,000; Monte Albán IIIA, 16,500; and Early Postclassic, 16,000. In the Early Postclassic (Monte Albán IV), Greater Jalieza was by far the Oaxaca Valley's most populous site (Finsten 1995, 3). According to the 1960 and 1970 censuses, the combined populations of the Jalieza communities plus San Pedro Guegorexe were 1,581 and 1,867 respectively. Both of these population numbers, for an area that approximates archaeologists' Greater Jalieza, are considerably below its estimated pre-Hispanic average of 15,166.[1]

The overall picture of the Jalieza subregion from the archaeological re-cord is one of unstable and shifting settlement patterns during the Urban and City-State stages (Winter 1995, 128), but of relatively dense populations viewed in the context of the Oaxaca Valley as a whole. Given the wide di-vergence between archaeological population estimates and historic census data, the demographic history of the subregion remains problematic.

Aside from settlement patterns and population estimates, archaeological research to date has yielded little of substance regarding the economic life of the Jalieza populations. This ranges from scant evidence for craft pro-duction (Finsten 1995, 85), which "probably was oriented predominantly toward local rather than regional markets" (ibid., 90) to inferences made from clay griddle (comal) remains that piedmont agriculture was in decline during the Early Postclassic (ibid.). The archaeological record tells us some-thing about ceramics and stoneworking, especially obsidian, but nothing about weaving, woodworking, plaiting, or other craft activities that do not leave durable remains.[2]

## The Jalieza Communities in the 1970s

In 1978, Santo Tomás had 100 households, Santo Domingo had 140, and Santa Cecilia had 57. These communities also presented interesting con-trasts in occupational structure. Santa Cecilia was more heavily agricultural than were Santo Domingo and Santo Tomás. Only one male head of house-hold in Santa Cecilia considered his principal occupation to be something other than "campesino" (peasant agriculturist), compared with only three (2 percent) in Santo Domingo and twenty-two (40 percent) in Santo Tomás. The reported amount of land cultivated per household corresponded to these responses to the principal-occupation question. The mean and median es-timates in hectares by village were as follows: SCJ, 2.64/2.62; SDJ, 2.05/1.75; STJ, 1.47/.97. This relationship also held for data regarding ownership of ox teams, a necessary means of agricultural production: SCJ, 81 percent; SDJ, 52 percent; STJ, 29 percent. In short, the occupation of peasant cultivator decreased significantly in importance from Santa Cecilia to Santo Domingo to Santo Tomás, where it had the least overall importance. To the outsider, a day's visit to these communities in 1980 gave the impression that their economic life was more or less the same. Likewise, the "multiple clusters of mounded architecture and public plazas, suggesting barrio organization like at Monte Alban" (Joyce 2010, 200) were invisible to the untrained eye.[3]

A tabulation of the occupations reported by household members in Santo Tomás (55 of a total of 110 households were surveyed) disclosed that 82 percent of them participated in backstrap-loom weaving with an average of two weavers per household. Of the total of 93 weavers in these households, 70 percent were females and 30 percent were males. The other reported occupations in Santo Tomás covered a wider range of work experience than those reported in Santo Domingo and Santa Cecilia. These included truck/bus driver (chofer), conductor (cobrador), mason (albañil), musician (músico), intermediary (regatón), miller (molinero), and storekeeper (tendero). The strong participation of Tomasinos in weaving, and the fact that fifteen male heads of household in the survey considered weaving to be their principal occupation, underscored the relative shortage of land and the relatively reduced role of agriculture in that community's economy.

### Santo Tomás Jalieza: Backstrap-Loom Weaving

Backstrap-loom weaving was practiced in Santo Tomás by both women and men, in Santo Domingo mostly by men, and marginally by men in Santa Cecilia. Tourists walking through the streets of Oaxaca City in the 1970s were targeted by itinerant merchants hawking weaving products from Santo Tomás and Mitla, but the woven goods could also be found in craft shops and marketplace stalls. By the 1970s, backstrap-loom weaving was increasingly commercialized for the export market and the local tourist trade. In some cases, like the Trique, the Huave, the Chinantec, and the coastal Mixtec (e.g., Pinotepa de Don Luis), weaving still provided traditional clothing for local populations, especially for women, but in Santo Tomás and Mitla by the 1970s, it was almost exclusively devoted to the export/tourist trade. During most of the 130-year period that weaving had been practiced in Santo Tomás, it was focused on finely woven fajas (sashes), which were sold locally and in the Sierra Zapoteca, the Mixteca, and elsewhere (Clements 1980, 116–126; 1987, 2).

Our survey (of 55 of the 110 households) identified forty-five weaving households (82 percent of the sample), making mostly fajas, bolsas (bags), tiras (strips or ties), tapetes (tapestries), and cotorinas (vests). These forty-five households had a total of 93 weavers, of which 71 percent were females. There were five females under ten, and no males in that age group, in the households censused. Seventy percent of all weavers, female and male, were between ten and thirty-nine years of age. All weavers employed backstrap looms (telares de cintura) that varied in width, but always consisted of a cord (cordel or mecate), a yoke (yugo), a comb (peine), a batten or shuttle (machete), one heddle and one heddle rod (dos palitos), and a backstrap (mecapal). As late as the 1950s, Tomasinos spun their own thread from a locally available variety of cotton growing on a tall bush (Clements 1980, 130).

Based on his field observations, Peter Bertocci (1964, 1) described back-strap-loom weaving as an arduous occupation, requiring long hours of kneeling while manipulating a primitive loom. The end of the piece being woven was hung from a hook in a tree or wall, and the weaver put the thread under tension by attaching the opposite end of the carefully mounted thread to a strap around his or her waist, the weight of his or her body pulling the thread tight. The manipulation of the thread to form designs was accomplished by using a thick, machete-shaped shuttle, with which the weaver tightened every stitch by a forceful thrust. The comb through which the thread passed was at its longest some 30 centimeters, used for the largest belts, and some 20 centimeters long for the smallest belts.

Of the weaving outfit described by Bertocci, the cord or rope, the comb, and some backstraps (those plaited of palm leaves or made of leather) were purchased and others were locally woven; the rest of the wooden components were homemade from locally available materials. The estimated cost of the purchased components varied from 37 to 118 pesos ($1.65 to $5.25); a day or a day and a half was required by a male household member to make the yugo, machete, and palitos. Weekly earnings were reported as less than 99 pesos ($4.40) by 47 percent of the household units; 22 percent reported weekly earnings of 300 pesos ($13.33) or more.

A few weavers also owned sewing machines to sew together the bolsas, *quechquemitl* (shawls or neckerchiefs), and cotorinas/chalecos (vests). Most, however, used the services of a few specialists in the village who charged 2.50–7.00 pesos per unit for sewing.[4]

All of the above products were made mostly from cotton thread (hilo de algodón) but also of wool (hilo de lana) and acrylic thread (acrilán). The large majority of weavers bought their own thread, although some of them were supplied by intermediaries. Cotton thread generally cost about 25–27 pesos per skein, according to color; hilo firme (colorfast thread) was more expensive than hilo corriente (common thread, uncolored/off-white); wool thread sold for 55 pesos per kilogram and acrylic thread for 60 pesos per kilogram. Wool thread was rewound to make it more resistant to weaving, a task that required 1–2 hours per half kilogram.

Thread was purchased in stores in Oaxaca City or in Santo Tomás. In Oaxaca City, the most important thread stores were Casa Fuerte (of Jorge Linares), Textil Lanera, and Productos Químicos. An intermediary in Santo Tomás, Bernardo Santos Mendoza, dyed, sold, and supplied thread to weavers, and also purchased finished products from them for resale. A study of

Santos's case provides insights into male involvement in backstrap-loom weaving, and about how and why specialization in dyeing occurred.[5]

Bernardo was forty years old at the time he was interviewed in October 1979, married, and had five children (two sons, ages fourteen and eleven, and three daughters, ages nine, three, and one). He was born in Santo Tomás and raised by his unmarried mother in his grandmother's extended household along with two brothers and a cousin. Bernardo was literate but had only three years of schooling. At the age of fourteen, he started working on his grandmother's and mother's land; his two younger brothers contributed to household expenses through agricultural wage labor. His grandmother and mother were weavers, so he was exposed to the craft early in life but did not start weaving seriously until 1968. This was around the time that he married Margarita Navarro, who was also a weaver. Not long afterward, and for several years during the 1970s, he served as the elected president of the community's Unión de Artesanos.

Bernardo emphasized that over the years he and his wife "always tried to make new things, to improve weaving, to bring out new products" (hemos tratado siempre de hacer algo nuevo, de mejorar el tejido, sacar alguna cosa nueva). He viewed this in the context of competition in the local cooperative using the introduction of the *quechquemitl* (women's triangular shawl) as an example: "When other people, in or out of the cooperative, see that a new product sells well, they also begin to make it. Those *quechquemes*, my wife was the first to make them as they are now, and we sold them very well. When other weavers began to weave that same kind of *quechqueme*, we began to make individual tapestries (tapetes individuales), which we still sell very well even though others began to make them too." This statement highlighted the problem of competition and envy among weavers. Bernardo added: "We do not ask ourselves why these people are making the same things that we make, but we have to accept the fact that people in our group do that."

It was in a general discussion of competition, product innovation, and thread price increases that Bernardo introduced the topic of how and why he learned to dye thread and how he eventually moved from tejedor to teñidor. Dyeing interested him because he knew that nobody in Santo Tomás had learned how to do it, even when prices of dyed thread were on the increase. Bernardo's first learning experience came in the early 1970s when a group of technicians visited the weavers' cooperative to provide instruction on how to dye thread. Everyone took careful notes, and demonstrations were given, but they were not provided with the necessary equipment, scales, timers, and thermometers to correctly measure water temperature and ingredients.

The end result of this program was that none of the weavers who stuck with it were able to successfully dye thread after it ended.

Bernardo retained his notes from the course, including recipes for mixing dyes, and persisted in his efforts to master the process. Subsequently, he was able to acquire more firsthand knowledge about dyeing through his contact with a thread salesman from a Mexico City company who visited Santo Tomás. The salesman offered a new type of uncolored thread at a favorable price and encouraged Bernardo to visit the factory to observe the details of the dyeing process to improve his understanding of it. He accepted the invitation, spent two days observing the process, and was given additional recipes by the factory experts in Mexico City.

When Bernardo applied his new knowledge back in Santo Tomás, he encountered problems and repeatedly ruined the thread he was dyeing. Sometimes the colors would be too strong and would burn the thread. Other times, some colors would leave spots. In frustration, he took a break and focused exclusively on weaving for a time. When he tried to dye again, he still failed. He went through a long trial-and-error process until he achieved better results by carefully noting what he had done wrong and by doing it differently the next time.

When he first began to weave, Bernardo liked it a lot, but when he experienced low earnings, his enthusiasm waned. He became interested in learning how to dye to supplement his income. Dyeing also took its toll by requiring work on Sundays and depriving him of rest and time with his family. He liked weaving and dyeing almost equally but focused more on dyeing because of fewer local competitors and greater income stability.

Bernardo recognized that agriculture enabled a household to supply food staples, but he also knew that it always entailed expenditures and that crop prices were low. He invidiously compared a peasant who carried heavy sacks of corn to sell for 500 or 600 pesos with a weaver who sold a much lighter bundle of woven products for 1,000 or 2,000 pesos. On one occasion, he bought some chickens in the hope of raising them as a supplementary source of cash, but they got sick and died. Bernardo recognized that even successful agricultural households needed additional income from weaving, and that the two occupations were complementary.

Bernardo owned .8 hectare of first-class agricultural land, had access to an additional .5 hectare owned by his mother, but lacked agricultural means of production (ox team, cart, plow). Agriculture, for him, was not a viable occupation. His household included three family workers—his wife and two children, all of whom worked either at weaving or dyeing thread. Weekly income was 360–400 pesos; weekly expenditures on the week previous to the interview amounted to 500 pesos, a higher than usual amount due to a festive expenditure. His reported weekly income placed Bernardo's household in the top twentieth percentile of weaving households in Santo Tomás.

In addition to his service as president of the cooperative, Bernardo, like all male members of the community, was required to serve in local civil-religious positions from time to time. His first service was when he was fourteen years old as topil de la iglesia; afterward he served as a mail carrier for the municipality, which required him to deliver official mail to Santo Tomás's municipal agencies, Santo Domingo, San Pedro, and Santa Cecilia. He also served five different times as a municipal policeman, was named secretario del alcalde in 1964, and in 1966–1968, secretario del presidente municipal. Later, he served as suplente del presidente municipal and, next, as vocal of the Comisión de Agua Potable. He viewed service in these cargos as a responsibility of local citizenship: "You cannot get out from under that matter of cargos because we are citizens and we have the obligation of serving our community. We cannot eliminate offices like presidente municipal, síndico, regidor, and all the other offices that the municipio needs."

Bernardo drew the line at mandatory sponsorship of mayordomías, a custom that he associated with poverty and backwardness. He had reached that conclusion through conversations with elders who lived when mayordomías were more widely practiced and expenses of sponsorship were very large. Sponsorship became voluntary, he insisted, because the earlier practice either led to or was associated with impoverishment. "Traditions are very nice," he admitted, "but for me they are against the progress of the community." In expressing these views, Bernardo was representative of many entrepreneurial artisans in Oaxaca Valley villages interviewed in the late 1970s.

We interviewed twenty-two male weavers in Santo Tomás, including Bernardo, who was the only teñidor (dyer) in the group. The range of ages was from twelve to fifty-nine. Fifteen of the twenty-two were household heads, the remainder being sons or grandsons of the household head; two resided in female-headed households. They worked an average of 6.75 hours per day, 5.3 days, and 35 hours per week. Seventeen informants considered weaving to be their full-time occupation (two each considered it to be seasonal or part-time). The twelve-year-old had been weaving for only four months at the time he was interviewed and worked only ten hours per week; he learned from his mother and helped her weave fajas. The others had been working as weavers for an average of nine years (range: 4–23). Thirteen male weavers learned to weave from their wives, six from their mothers, two from their sisters, and one from both his mother and wife. This suggested that despite male crossover into this traditionally female occupation, women remained dominant in the transmission of weaving culture.

Men appeared to make the same range of products as women, but in eight households where husbands and wives were both weavers, only one reported an overlap in products woven. The remainder had a gender division of labor with no overlap in products woven. In one of these households, the husband specialized in tapetes anchos and chalecos, whereas his wife wove bolsas chicas and tiras angostas; in another, the husband wove bolsas and tiras grandes, and the wife wove fajas chicas; in still another, the husband specialized in tapetes and his wife wove quechquemes, bolsas chicas, chalecos, and fajas.

There was also a division by age within the industry; children between eight and ten, who were mostly apprentices (aprendices), wove fajas chicas, first without designs and later with simple floral or animal designs. By contrast, the faja fina was made by females between twelve and fifteen years of age "porque ven mejor" (because they see better). Better vision was required because this product was made with fine, mercerized cotton thread or silk thread. It required a great deal of skill due to the fineness of the material and the small size of the loom used to weave it (Aranda Bezaury 1989, 83–85).

Taurino Pacheco Padilla, at fifty-nine the oldest weaver interviewed in Santo Tomás, had been weaving for six years in 1978 and learned by observing his wife, Agustina Mendoza. Taurino specialized in weaving fajas chicas, and his wife wove tiras anchas. They had a son, José, eighteen, and a daughter, Gloria, sixteen, both of whom still lived at home with their parents. After marrying, Taurino worked for thirty years as an agricultural wage laborer (jornalero) in Santo Tomás; he had been raised as the only child in a household with his father and mother. They were sharecroppers. Neither one of his parents was a weaver, but his father had a salary as a musician in a government-sponsored band. After retiring from agricultural work as a jornalero, Taurino was basically at home taking care of his children and performed chores like tending animals and gathering firewood. He owned only one agricultural plot of .6 hectare, not enough to justify ownership of an ox team or other agricultural instruments of production.

Even though Taurino took up weaving because he had nothing else to do, he still considered that agriculture yielded a return, albeit delayed, on one's labor. In his words: "When you begin to cultivate land, you don't earn a cent. From April to September, all those months you earn absolutely nothing. Not until harvesttime can you calculate the results of your work in money terms. You have to maintain yourself from one year to the next with leftover harvest. In those years of very abundant harvests, you can sell some of your crops for cash but not enough to have capital to invest because the land is really not of good quality."

As a member of the weavers' cooperative, Taurino was somewhat discouraged by the lack of orders in 1978, but emphasized that he was going to continue to support the cooperative in the future. He understood that prices weavers charged for their products had to cover costs of materials, labor, and time. Labor cost, for him, was synonymous with "the hours that you work, the days that it takes you to make the product." Lower prices might increase sales, but the first consideration was covering costs.

Rodolfo Santiago Muñoz was thirty-four in 1978, had been married to María Hernández for seventeen years, and had eight children—six sons and two daughters—ranging in age from one year to sixteen years. His principal occupation was talabartero (leather crafter); weaving was his secondary occupation. Rodolfo was only one of two leather workers in our twenty-village survey. Leather working was a spin-off from weaving, since leather straps and strips were used as components in finishing various woven products like bags and belts. He also made leather backstraps for weavers to attach looms around their waists.

Rodolfo estimated that he worked eighteen hours weekly in leather and the same in weaving. His wife and eldest daughter, Sofía, were also weavers. He had no agricultural land and earned income exclusively from his craft occupations. His estimated weekly income was 630 pesos, which included the contribution of his wife and daughter, who wove a combined average of six to eight hours weekly. Given his lack of land, he had to buy his supply of corn and other staples year-round. He owned twelve goats but no other farm animals. The estimated weekly household income was equivalent to weekly estimated expenditures, a situation that did not permit savings.

In 1985, Rodolfo complained about rising prices, noting that every two weeks he paid higher prices than the preceding two weeks. He also complained about inflation in staple food prices and the fact that prices increased over short periods of time. The same pattern applied to thread: they were forced to match increases in thread prices with increases in the prices of their woven products. (Conforme compramos más caro el hilo, pues aumentar un poquito para nivelarnos, para nivelar la compra y la venta.) Aside from making compensatory price adjustments, he admitted that they also worked a little harder and longer but that some of the burden on him and his wife was lessened because two of his sons were old enough to help out (Cook 1988, 61–67).

Rodolfo's marketing behavior changed between 1978 and 1985. In the late 1970s, he would only sell his products in the local craft market on Fridays when tourists came and occasionally sell products to craft shops in

Oaxaca City. In the 1980s, he and his wife took more trips to sell in distant places like San Miguel de Allende and Mexico City. He saw a village-wide trend in weaving represented by more intermediaries who traveled more extensively to sell their own products, as well as products purchased from other weavers who did not travel.

We interviewed fifteen female weavers in Santo Tomás. Their average age was forty (range: twenty-seven to sixty-one). All but one of these women was married; two were childless, but the rest had an average of four children each. They all started weaving between the ages of twelve and fifteen, although most of them started doing chores and helping out in the household when they were ten years old or younger.

Nicolasa Mendoza Gómez, age forty, lived in a household with her mother, Asunción Gómez, age seventy-seven, and two daughters, Angela, twelve, and Anastasia, fourteen. She learned to weave by age ten from her mother, and later on learned how to weave with a combination of colored threads (combinar colores) as a member of the cooperative. She bought a sewing machine in 1970 to finish bolsas and other products that required sewing. Her estimated weekly earnings of 500 pesos ($22.22) were among the highest in Santo Tomás. The total estimated gross value of her weekly output was 5,000 pesos ($222). Her two daughters helped with weaving. She sold her products in the village and in Oaxaca City.

Despite Nicolasa's relative success, and her admission that she preferred weaving to doing household chores, she was tired of doing it and continued only out of necessity (nada más por necesidad). She ranked agriculture as the best occupation in the village "because you harvest corn, beans, and chickpeas." She owned 3.8 hectares of cultivable land and an ox team, placing her in the upper quarter of households in the community, but she did not own a cart. She rented a tractor for plowing her land and paid for thirty days of agricultural wage labor during the year. Her estimated annual expenditures on renting agricultural means of production were 1,200 pesos ($53.33). Her last harvest yielded 600 kilograms of corn, but she still had to buy corn for four months that same year to meet household consumption needs.

Nicolasa was a member of the weavers' cooperative because it helped stimulate retail sales and higher returns (el beneficio es para venderle al menudeo, resulta más así). She had no trouble personally with the cooperative but admitted that "two or three members do not understand that when they do not sell, there is no reason to cast the blame on those who do sell."

Her explanation of product valuation and price setting showed her main consideration was covering costs of thread and labor-time; her selling price did not include a "ganancia," or profit, above and beyond these costs. The value of labor-time or "salario" mentioned by Nicolasa was 32.50 pesos per day. "The amount of thread that I use, the kind and amount of work I do," she explained, were all reflected in her price calculations. She summed up the valuation process in more formulaic terms: the price of a product had to cover the amount of thread used and the work time expended.

Nicolasa viewed the difference between relative wealth and poverty strictly in terms of degree of effort: "Those who work more benefit more. Some families are poor because they don't work; others are rich because they work hard like they are supposed to."

She recognized that resellers earned more from her products than she did, noting that she sold bolsas for 110 pesos to traders who resold them for 175 pesos. The only remedy for this inequity was simply to ask the buyer to pay higher prices for her products (diciéndole que se le aumente más el precio, que me pague más).

In 1985, the Mexican peso devaluation crisis was full-blown; the peso-to-dollar exchange rate had risen from 22.50/1 in 1978–1979 to 450/1. Nicolasa estimated her monthly net earnings at 7,750 pesos ($17.20), a drop of about twenty dollars monthly from 1978. Understandably, she complained that everything was more expensive and that she suffered from a lack of money. Her overall sales were down, but her earnings had gone up a little because one of her daughters had gotten married and moved out of the household, hence reducing her household expenses. (Han mermado las ventas, pero mis ganancias son un poquito más porque mis gastos son menos.) Still, the bottom line was that she could not buy as much as she used to because prices of consumer goods she bought had gone up while sales of her weavings had declined.

Francisca Navarro learned weaving from her grandmother who raised her; first she helped with spinning thread and then, by the age of twelve, she began to weave. She married at age eighteen and learned the specialized craft of making penachos (feather headdresses) from her husband. She referred to this craft as "el trabajo de las plumas." In 1980, Francisca was forty-nine years old and had been widowed for four years. She headed a household that included her son Teódulo; his wife, Clara; and their two children, Jesús, five, and Salomé, one.

When her husband was alive, he taught Francisca how to dye, stretch, dry out, select, and bunch together feathers (purchased locally) that he would use, along with tin crowns (coronas de lata) purchased in Zaachila for 1,800 pesos a dozen, to assemble penachos of different sizes. Penachos were purchased for ceremonial use by indigenous dance groups (danzantes) in several Oaxaca Valley villages, including Santo Tomás.

Francisca related with disappointment that in 1972, the government development bank (Fomento) had sponsored her and her husband's attendance at a craft festival in Guadalajara, where they sold only one large penacho for 400 pesos and did not sell any of twelve smaller penachos in their inventory (no se vendió ni uno). By contrast, in early 1980, she sold three penachos for 1,000 pesos each on a trip to Puebla. She also rented penachos as a regular part of her business.

Francisca said that "at times I have my corn ground by others because I work at home" or "I buy in the market because I am working" (a veces doy a moler porque trabajo en la casa o se compra algo en el mercado para que así esté uno trabajando). She also said that her daughter-in-law "did the kitchen chores" (hace el quehacer de la cocina). Her income from penacho sales and rentals was variable but averaged 430 pesos ($19) weekly. Francisca owned 3.5 hectares of arable land, which was cultivated by her son-in-law; two ox teams; two carts (carretas); eighteen goats; and two burros. She estimated her household's last annual corn harvest as 400 kilos, which translated into about one hundred days of the household's estimated daily consumption need of 4 kilos. Francisca's assets and income put her in the upper quarter of Santo Tomás households, but her household had to buy corn during several months of the year.

I interviewed Francisca in November 1985, after the peso devaluation and in the midst of a national economic crisis exacerbated by the catastrophic September 19 earthquake in Mexico City. From 1980 to 1985, the peso-to-dollar exchange rate dropped from 23/1 to 450/1. She estimated her income for the week preceding the interview as 2,000 pesos ($4.50), some 800 pesos ($1.80) less than her expenditures for that same week, which were elevated due to the Día de los Muertos celebration. She admitted that the 1985 economic crisis was difficult because everything was more expensive. She illustrated this by using the example of women's clothing: "Money doesn't go anywhere these days because everything is so expensive. We can't afford to buy ready-to-wear dresses but only bolts of cloth to make them, and even the cloth is expensive, the cheapest are about 1,200 pesos per bolt. That is where we spend the little we have."

She was pleasantly surprised that her penacho business was better than ever: "It has increased. There are more rentals lately. I don't understand why. It seems that there are more folkloric dances now." To underline the negative effects of the economic crisis, she related that several weavers from Santo Tomás had recently returned from a crafts fair (feria) in San Miguel de Allende and had experienced disappointing sales due to the drop in tourism in the aftermath of the earthquake.

### SUMMARY OF WEAVING IN SANTO TOMÁS

The highest-volume products woven in Santo Tomás were fajas (belts/sashes) and bolsas (shoulder bags/other bags); a smaller proportion of weavers made tiras (runners), tapetes (tapestries), manteles (tablecloths) and servilletas (napkins), *quechquemes* (neckerchiefs), and cotorinas/chalecos (vests). The greatest majority of products were sold to several intermediaries who lived in Santo Tomás or others who came to the village periodically. Apart from the intermediaries, the other sales alternative was to sell directly to tourists who came to the village—particularly on Fridays, or día de plaza in the nearby town of Ocotlán.

To facilitate this tourist trade, the weaving cooperative constructed some stalls in the main village plaza for its members to exhibit their products. Two or three weavers sold their products to shop owners (comerciantes de artesanías) in Oaxaca City, and one sold as an ambulatory street vendor there. Not a single weaver said that they sold to FONART or to other government agencies. It was not common for weavers to accept special orders for products; however, a few of the most skilled weavers—especially those dedicated to working in natural wools—did so for products like sashes, tablecloths, runners, and tapestries.

Some weavers occasionally were supplied with thread from intermediaries, but most weaving was done by independent, self-employed household units without ties to suppliers of thread or buyers. The weavers' group that was established in 1963 under the name of Sociedad de Tejedores (subsequently changed to Unión de Artesanos) had forty-five members in 1978. The board of directors of the group distributed orders received among members; prices were set at member meetings for products ordered as well as those sold in the village plaza. These set prices were generally greater than those paid by intermediaries. The organization did not have any control over sales by its members outside of the plaza (e.g., on their own resident lots), so that the largest proportion of sales were made at lower prices to intermediaries.[6]

### Santo Domingo Jalieza

Santo Domingo, in contrast to Santo Tomás, had only two male household heads in our survey whose principal occupation was weaving. Still, only five households reported receiving no income from craft activities: two of them had small stores, one lived exclusively from remittances from nonresident members, one was an elderly woman living alone who survived on the charity of her neighbors, and the final household generated all of its income from agriculture. Embroidery ranked first, with 81 percent of households reporting members that earned income from it; backstrap-loom weaving was next at 38 percent, followed by firewood or charcoal production at 27.5 percent, basket making at 17 percent, and broom making at 11.6 percent.

Embroidery was mainly a female activity, since only 2 out of 102 embroiderers were males. The rest of the craft industries were overwhelmingly masculine: only four women were weavers, and one woman earned income from firewood/charcoal; basket making and broom making were exclusively done by males. The unexpectedly low rate of female participation in backstrap-loom weaving, traditionally in Mexican indigenous culture a female occupation, was clearly related to their high participation in embroidery. The two principal crafts in Santo Domingo had been practiced there for only ten years prior to our survey. Weaving was borrowed from Santo Tomás, and embroidery was introduced by putting-out merchants.

The embroiderers of Santo Domingo worked with cloth and threads supplied by intermediaries and did not buy materials on their own. They received sets (juegos) consisting of pieces of cloth for a dress (vestido) or a blouse (blusa), precut and designed (cortado y dibujado), and tied together in a bundle with the threads needed to complete the embroidery. Women embroidered the designs by hand and were paid 70 to 110 pesos per finished set, depending on the style and quantity of embroidery the piece required. The embroiderers bought their own needles and hoops for 10 to 15 pesos. A few embroiderers also bought thread, but not frequently. The field team estimated that no more than two or three embroiderers in the village bought all of their materials.

Dresses and blouses embroidered in Santo Domingo were in the traditional floral design associated with San Antonino (Waterbury 1989). However, the majority of embroiderers worked for merchants from San Martín Tilcajete, whereas others worked for intermediaries from San Juan Chilateca or Ocotlán. There was one intermediary in Santo Domingo as well as a commission agent residing there who distributed embroidery sets for a San Juan Chilateca merchant. In most cases, embroiderers took their finished work to Ocotlán on Friday market day (día de plaza), delivered them to the intermediaries from various villages who gathered there, collected their salary, and picked up a new set to embroider.

Almost all of the embroiderers worked only one to two hours daily and finished one set every month or two. They did not have a precise notion of how much time they spent embroidering, and it was difficult to calculate the exact number of hours required to finish a set. They did not earn more than 1 or 2 pesos per hour, an income much lower than the average for other craft occupations. In Santo Domingo, for instance, agricultural day laborers (jornaleros) earned 40 pesos per day.

The intermediaries, aside from tracing and cutting designs on the cloth, also put together garments with sewing machines. They crocheted borders of sleeves and necks with a special stitch known as "hazme si puedes" (make me if you can), a type of gathered pleat (fruncido) on the front of the garment. They washed, ironed, and folded each finished garment prior to selling it.

In Santo Domingo, very few women were skilled enough to perform all of these operations; a majority only knew how to embroider the designs already drawn on the cloth. Aside from not being trained to cut and sew up garments (corte y confección), most of them did not have sewing machines. To become independent of intermediaries, they needed technical assistance in these tasks and in crochet and "hazme si puedes." Moreover, many of them did not have the money required to buy cloth and thread, much less sewing machines.

Twelve survey households participated in basket making as a secondary occupation in Santo Domingo compared to none in Santo Tomás and only two in Santa Cecilia. The baskets (canastas) made there tended to be classified as "finas," which meant plaited with finer strips of reed (carrizo) and with handles. Only one canastero had worked for more than three years in the craft. They bought reeds in bundles of fifty or one hundred strips for 1 peso per strip. Only one canastero harvested reeds on land that he possessed; the rest paid to harvest it. The price of the raw material constituted a variable part of the sales price of baskets because a fine basket with thinner strips sold for a higher price than a larger basket with thicker strips. Canasteros obtained higher income from making and selling canastas finas than from canastas grandes. They made large harvest baskets (piscadores) only for their own use or for local customers. The only tools that every canastero used were an inexpensive (30–80-peso) knife for cutting reed strips and a machete for cutting reeds.

Baskets were sold in Oaxaca City or Ocotlán to intermediaries or commercial buyers at prices ranging from 30 to 125 pesos ($1.30–$5.55) each. There were also intermediaries in Santo Domingo who bought baskets for resale. The median weekly income for canasteros was around 200 pesos ($8.90), and three reported earnings of 400 pesos ($17.77) or more weekly, compared to only one tejedor (weaver) and one escobero (broom maker). By contrast, the estimated weekly income for all but five of ninety-four embroiderers was 49 pesos ($2.17) or less; the median weekly income of thirty-nine weavers was between 150 and 199 pesos ($6.66–$8.84); and wood-cutters/charcoal makers were evenly divided between those who had weekly

TABLE 7.1. **Santo Tomás Jalieza and Santo Domingo Jalieza Weaving Industries Compared**

| Santo Tomás Jalieza | Santo Domingo Jalieza |
|---|---|
| Majority of weavers are women (71% vs. 29%, N = 93) | Almost all weavers are men |
| (90% vs. 10%, N = 41) | |
| Weave a wide variety of products | Weave only fajas and bolsas |
| Complicated designs | Simple designs |
| Buy best-quality colorfast thread @ 25–27 pesos per skein; also use wool thread | Buy cheaper-quality noncolorfast thread @ 15–17 pesos per skein, or plain thread is colored with noncolorfast dyes |
| Sell to intermediaries from the village or from Mexico City; also sell directly to tourists that come to the village | Sell to craft shops or market stalls in Oaxaca City; tourists never come to the village |
| Organized as a weavers' cooperative | No organization of weavers |
| Sell at high prices | Sell at low prices |

incomes of 149 pesos ($6.62) or less and those with weekly incomes of 150–249 pesos ($6.66–$11.06).

Broom making was less common than other crafts in Santo Domingo (only eight households of sixty-nine surveyed). The majority of the broom makers (escoberos) had long work histories in the craft, ranging from seven to thirty-eight years. They cut and fashioned the handles (mangos or varas) from locally available flora, including organ cactus, and bought palm leaves, paint, and nails in the Ocotlán market to put together the brooms. The costs of producing one dozen brooms were: palm, 20–28 pesos; cordel or mecate, 10–15 pesos; paint, 1.50 pesos; nails, 1.50 pesos, for a total of 33–46 pesos. The paint was used to color the cord or rope that binds the palm to the handle or broomstick. The only tools used in the fabrication process were a machete (35–50 pesos) for cutting the wood and an aguja de arrea (large needle with an angled point for 1.50 pesos each) for securing the cord binding. One half of the escoberos sold their brooms directly to clients in Ocotlán or Oaxaca City for 5–8 pesos per broom, whereas the others sold wholesale to businesses for 4–6 pesos each. There were no intermediaries in Santo Domingo who purchased brooms for resale.

The weavers of Santo Domingo made fajas and bolsas in the traditional style of Santo Tomás, a craft tradition that they acquired only in the early 1970s from the Tomasinos. Like the Santo Tomás weavers, they bought raw materials on their own account rather than receiving them from intermediaries. There were several differences between the two industries, as outlined in Table 7.1. Santo Domingo weavers were less skilled and wove products of lesser quality than those in Santo Tomás.

Fondo Nacional para el Fomento de las Artesanías (FONART) organized a group of weavers in Santo Domingo in the 1960s and provided them with credit to buy thread and other materials. The promoter recruited by FONART, a man from the neighboring village of San Martín Tilcajete, refused to buy the poor-quality fajas and bolsas made by Santo Domingo weavers and they remained unsold. This led to disillusionment with FONART, and in 1978 no Santo Domingo weaver sold products to that agency.

### Santa Cecilia Jalieza

The historical record of litigation and conflict surrounding Santa Cecilia Jalieza's land base and community identity, which is examined in detail in Chapter 8, highlighted the importance of agriculture in its economic survival. Wooden spoons have also been manufactured there at least since the eighteenth century (Taylor 1972, 103). Oral tradition in Santa Cecilia reinforced by ethnography suggests that its most unique product was decoratively carved stirring sticks (acahuetes), used since pre-Hispanic times for stirring hot chocolate (Parsons 1936, 35–36).

Parsons (1936, 37) presented six line drawings of "crudely carved stirring sticks" of unspecified origin. Her invidious comparison with stirring sticks of pre-Hispanic Aztec design implied that her drawings were of stirrers in use in Mitla at the time of her residency there. It is likely that Mitleños acquired the stirrers through the regional marketing system and that their provenience was Santa Cecilia Jalieza. My comparison of the designs of six stirrers made in Santa Cecilia in the late 1970s with those presented by Parsons indicated similarity with two she presented with stylized antlers. Other Santa Cecilia stirrers in my possession were more finely carved and had more detailed animal representations (including a bird, a rooster, and a turkey-cock) than those shown in Parsons's drawings.

Santa Cecilia wood-carvers made another implement traditionally associated with the preparation of hot chocolate, namely, a hand beater (molinillo), which, when spun between two hands, mixes the beverage until it has foam on top. Parsons did not mention this implement, but it might also have a pre-Hispanic origin, and during the twentieth century was probably more widely used in Oaxaca peasant households than the stirrer. In the 1970s, stirrers were mostly sold to tourists for use as bookmarks or letter openers and seemed to have declined in everyday use as hot chocolate stirrers among peasant households.

## LAND USE AND DISTRIBUTION

Land was critical to Santa Cecilians, not only for agricultural purposes, including livestock grazing, but also as a source of wood for carving. Centuries of boundary disputes with neighboring villages made it difficult to regularly cut wood in mountainous communal land, and by the 1970s, this problem was compounded by deforestation, compelling Santa Cecilia's wood-carvers to buy their wood supply from sellers in the Ocotlán market. Marciano García Vásquez, a leader of the wood-carvers and of the ejido, explained: "One can live from this occupation of wood carving if one goes into the mountains and leaves the village. That is how they lived in my grandfather's time. After the Day of the Dead festival, they put some belongings and food in a basket and headed for the mountains (sometimes as far away as the Sierra Juárez), slept and worked there for a week, and then went into the Oaxaca City market on Saturday to sell the products they had made. Then they would come back to the village, load up on tortillas, and take off for the mountains again. That is how our people sustained themselves before we got our ejido. They planted crops but did not harvest anything, not until 1924 when the ejido was granted. Even then, when they had a food supply on hand, they would be invaded. Then they were out of luck."

A total of thirty-four interviews were conducted with heads of household in Santa Cecilia between October 27 and November 25, 1978. Households were selected randomly (table of random numbers used to start with an even or odd number) at an interval of 50 percent, or every second case from an official list of heads of household supplied by village authorities (Cook and Binford 1990, 244). We experienced a relatively high rate (20–30 percent) of households unwilling to cooperate with the survey in its early phase when the survey crew involved as many as five interviewers; cooperation improved when the survey crew was reduced to only two interviewers, my wife and I. Households unwilling to cooperate were replaced by the next available uncensused household on the master list.

Santa Cecilia Jalieza had a reputation for being suspicious (desconfiados) of outsiders. In 1973, with the introduction of electricity and an improved road, the community was more accessible. It still had ongoing difficulties with the neighboring community of San Juan Teitipac regarding communal land boundaries, but internal factionalism and infighting was quiescent at the time the household survey was conducted. Reportedly, there were several homicides in the village during the peak years of family feuding in the 1950s–1960s. During the 1970s, conditions were relatively peaceful, and delegations from various government agencies occasionally visited the community. Contradicting its reputation as a closed community hostile toward outsiders was the fact that it had a significant number of exogamous marriages: seven of the thirty-four households (21 percent) in our survey reported that the wife of the male household head was from another village in the Ocotlán district. This compared with only 11 percent in Santo Domingo Jalieza and 16 percent in San Pedro Guegorexe, both of which share boundaries with Santa Cecilia.

Every household surveyed had arable land and participated in agriculture, and only three reported having no members with craft occupations. Of the three households without crafts, one consisted of a widow and her unmarried daughter who depended on charity and assistance from relatives to survive, and two that had more than 5 hectares of arable land and were full-time cultivators. The seventy-one-year-old head of one of these households had only recently retired from his secondary occupation as a wood-carver. The average amount of land cultivated per household was 2.64 hectares, 60 percent of which was ejido and 40 percent private (pequeña propiedad). This average exceeded those of the neighboring villages of Santo Domingo Jalieza and San Pedro Guegorexe by .59 and 1.05 hectares respectively. Most land was rainfall-dependent (temporal); only six households had irrigated land.

### EMBROIDERY AND THE FONART PROGRAM

The craft occupation with the highest rate of household participation in Santa Cecilia was embroidery, followed by wood carving, backstrap-loom weaving, brick making, and basketry. Embroidery had the highest household participation rate. It was introduced in the late 1960s by intermediaries from San Martín Tilcajete and San Juan Chilateca. Of fifty-four embroiderers in our sample, six were males but most were females between ten and thirty-nine years of age. Every fifteen days or monthly, they received materials (prepatterned cloth with a floral design precut into four pieces for dresses or blouses: capa, cajón, and mangas) and then delivered them finished to the putting-out merchants in the Ocotlán plaza on Fridays. The tendency was for embroidery work to be divided up by piece among family members. In some cases, merchants did not supply thread, so it had to be purchased by the embroiderer.

The embroiderers reported earning between 90 and 170 pesos per embroidered set (juego). The time required to complete a set ranged considerably, from two weeks to six months. One woman estimated that she earned 700 pesos every three to six weeks but earned more or less depending on her work schedule and pace. Income per embroiderer was the lowest of Santa Cecilia craft occupations at 0–49 pesos weekly; basket making was the highest at 400 pesos weekly. Embroiderers spent less time daily embroidering (2–3 hours) and typically did not finish a set in less than three weeks. Wood-carvers only averaged 6–8 hours per week carving but earned between 150–350 pesos weekly for their work.

A main reason women took up embroidery, despite its low return, was the ease with which they could integrate it into their daily work schedule "por ratos" (during spare time). In the words of Leonor Gabriel Vásquez: "When I finish making tortillas, grinding tejate, that's when I begin to embroider. Then the babies start screaming, and I have to breast-feed them and stop embroidering. Then when the two babies (girl and boy) go to sleep, I pick up the embroidery again. After I put the *nixtamal* on the fire to boil it, I also embroider."

Several embroiderers expressed discontent regarding their dependence on intermediaries, which was grounded in a sense that they were being exploited in their dealings with them. This was evident in statements like "They sell at high prices and pay me cheap wages" (venden caro y me pagan barato) or "I do the work and the intermediary gets the money" (Yo trabajo y el regatón se lleva los centavos). It was also implicit in expressed preferences to work independently: "It is better to work on your own account so that you can find clients who will pay you better than the merchants do" or "I earn more on my own account, since there are no discounts from the selling price. We get cloth from the merchants and they discount for it when they pay you for the work. They take some of our earnings." Another woman expressed the view that the best earnings go to embroiderers who can sew up finished garments, and she planned to get an iron and sewing machine so she could become independent of the merchants.

In 1978, a schoolteacher in Santa Cecilia noted that many women in the village worked in their spare time as embroiderers. Through conversations with them and noticing that the quality of their embroidery needed improvement, she went to the FONART office in Oaxaca City to investigate the possibility of obtaining assistance. Such an intervention coincided with the agenda of that agency and its capable director, Tito Cortés. By August 1, 1978, a cooperative group of sixteen women, ranging in age from thirteen to sixty (the majority unmarried, dependent teenagers), was formed in Santa Cecilia and a technical specialist (promotora) was sent there. A room was assigned to the group in the Agencia Municipal building, and two sewing machines were supplied by FONART in addition to cloth, thread, and other materials. The promoter stayed in Santa Cecilia during the week and held classes daily on patterning and cutting cloth, sewing machine operation, and embroidery techniques. The program lasted four months.

The promoter was available at the convenience of group members, but even so, it was difficult for many of them to attend classes on a regular basis; the period from August to November coincided with the harvest, when women had unusually heavy work burdens. Still, the program improved skills in patterning, cutting, and sewing garments and provided women with all of the necessary equipment and supplies to accomplish this at below-market prices. It also provided a means to pay costs over time (including the salary of the promoter) through discounts from finished garments returned to FONART, which sold them in its Oaxaca City store at an average price of 750 pesos each.

During the initial four-month period, many women were unable to master certain of the most difficult finishing tasks, such as using special needles to crochet intricately designed figures on the pleated front of blouses below the neck, the appropriately named "hazme si puedes." The agreement with FONART stipulated that when the period of apprenticeship ended, embroiderers would have the option of going independent.

Work histories of Santa Cecilia's embroiderers show participation in the household division of labor by the age of eight or nine by helping out with food and beverage preparation, carrying food and beverages to men working in the fields, and other household chores. All of them also performed tasks in the agricultural cycle, like planting, weeding, harvesting, and tending animals. Esperanza Pérez said that she started working when she was eight years old, "helping her mother with household chores and going with her father to the fields to plant, do weeding, and everything until the harvest ended." All of the embroiderers were also involved in tortilla preparation for household consumption, and six made tortillas for sale (usually selling on Friday market day in Ocotlán).

In response to the question as to which of their jobs was most rewarding (rinde más al trabajador), six of ten chose tortilla making because it paid the best (hay más ganancias), and the rest chose agriculture ("con el tiempo hay algo de comer" or "trabajo de campo porque de allí viene lo que se necesita para la casa"). It did not bode well for their future dedication to embroidery that none of them rated it highly in comparison to other jobs and that several mentioned it negatively as paying too little (se gana muy poco en eso) or was too time-consuming ("El bordado se hace muy despacio" or "El bordado, siempre tarda uno en eso").

Many of them acknowledged that embroidery was worth pursuing only in large households with several females where more time was available to embroider. According to María Ruiz, "There are those who earn more, like in my sister's house where she has two daughters who work hard." Virginia López Martínez said, "There are those households that earn more because there are more of them to work; those households that do more work earn more because some prepare meals while others do craft work." Finally, according to Juana Pérez, "There are households that earn more from embroidery because they spend more time at it. We don't have that much time, only spare time, to embroider."

## WOOD CARVING

Embroidery and wood carving represented two deeply contrasting ways in which the people of Santa Cecilia Jalieza participated in commodity production. Embroidery was recently introduced by external merchants opportunistically seeking to employ locally available labor, whereas wood carving represented a cultural legacy transmitted through many generations of families in a local and regional division of labor. (Viene de los abuelos y los bisabuelos.) The difference was between a putting-out system in which the household production unit was subordinated to an external enterprise, and a petty commodity system of independent household enterprises of self-employed craftspeople. Embroidery and wood carving shared participation in the tourist/urban markets. Wood carving, unlike embroidery, persisted by cleverly adapting its products to meet a tourist/urban aesthetic market and a rural utilitarian market. Stirrers were transformed into either letter openers or bookmarks, and combs were introduced for the tourist/urban markets; spoons, ladles, and beaters (molinillos) were made for regional rural households.

The principal raw materials for embroidery were factory made and supplied by merchants. The wood-carving industry evolved as wholly dependent on local resources. Five types of wood were cut by the carvers themselves in communal forested areas (los cerros comunales del pueblo): naranjo (orange), yagalán (tlaxistle, *Amelanchier denticulada*), saúz (willow), cedro (cedar), and palo de águila (Mexican alder, *Alnus jorullensis* Kunth). In the late 1970s, many wood-carvers complained about the scarcity of wood resources. Their situation was aggravated by conflict with San Juan Teitipac. This obliged them to buy much of their wood supply in the Ocotlán market or to seek arrangements to cut wood on mountainous communal lands belonging to other pueblos. At that time, there were still occasions during the postharvest season when carvers worked full-time in the craft and spent at least a full day in the mountainous area of their ejido to cut sufficient wood to supply four to five days of carving. Nevertheless, there was also a growing consensus that they would have to explore new sources of wood to sustain their craft in the future.

Specialization along product lines occurred among Santa Cecilia wood-carvers. Acahueteros carved agitadores or acahuetes sold mostly for festive use when chocolate was served; or modified as bookmarks (separadores) and letter openers ("abrecartas," which had curved rather than straight blades) sold as souvenirs to tourists. Cuchareros carved spoons or ladles (cucharas), and molinilleros carved molinillos. These were mostly utilitarian products used by regional peasant and working-class households.

A basic distinction was made between acahuetes finos (fine stirrers) and sencillos (simple), the former having the most detailed carving and a smoother finish. These were produced and sold as bookmarks or letter openers to tourists, whereas the acahuete sencillo was basically made for purchase and use by indigenous households. A handful of carvers also made combs (peines), thus earning them the appellation of peineros, or comb makers. There was some crossover in this division of labor, especially between carving of stirrers and spoons, but less so regarding combs and beaters. This was mostly a matter of personal preference, although comparatively less patience and skill were required to make spoons than the other products.

One day in 1979, I visited the residence lot (solar) of Marciano García Vásquez, then fifty years old, head of an extended household of nine members and one of the political leaders of the village. He was seated on a board placed on the stone floor of the front porch of his adobe house, working on separadores and abrecartas but also combs (peines). Seated nearby was his younger brother, Andrés, who was also working on the same products. Two years prior to my visit, at the suggestion of clients, Marciano and other acahueteros started converting the straight blade on the acahuete/separador to a half-curved blade for a letter opener (abrecarta). His brother added that some of them, also at the suggestion of clients, had begun to use a wood-burning tool to engrave each abrecarta/separador with "Oaxaca, Mexico."

These products were made by stripping bark from a piece of wood and cutting it into shorter lengths; each length was then cut into strips. These tasks were performed with a small hatchet. (Se raja con hacha y la deja destroncada donde el cuchillo puede entrar.) Next, a small knife was used to shave the resulting strips into a uniform thickness and to cut the figures into the handle. Once cutting was finished, the surface of the semifinished product was smoothed out with sand paper (lija). This was the only task (la pulida) regularly performed by women and children. The most adept carvers like Marciano made three dozen of the elaborately carved separadores/abrecartas per week, the same number of molinillos, or fifteen combs of different sizes.

Félix García Vásquez, another brother of Marciano, was seated and working on cucharas with his father, Pedro, on his resident lot next to Marciano's. They described spoon making as first involving a search for wood to cut in the mountains. They typically cut one-half of a burro load in a half day, which was a three days' supply. A full day of wood cutting in the cerro supplied enough wood for a full week's carving of spoons.

The next step was to chop (destrozar) long pieces of wood (vara de madera trozada) into shorter spoon-size lengths (trozos) using a hatchet (hacha), and then split the trozos in half lengthwise. The product of this task was a split trozo (un trozito rajado o partido). The small piece of wood was then gouged out with the same hatchet to make a roughed-out spoon (un trozito labrado o una cuchara labrada). The roughed-out spoon was smoothed out more with a hatchet (componer cuchara del trozito labrado con hacha), and was finished with a special tool called a spoon gouge (urbia). (Se usa una urbia para terminar o afinar el trabajo hecho con hacha.) The product at this stage was called an emptied-out trozito or simply a spoon (el producto se llama trozito vaciado o cuchara) and was considered to be finished and ready to sell.

Félix and Pedro worked as a team, dividing up the above tasks. They made a minimum of three dozen spoons per week, typically a dozen each of small, medium, and large sizes.

The output in Santa Cecilia's wood-carving industry fluctuated seasonally: it tended to increase during the dry season and decrease during the rainy season when there was more agricultural work. Output increased in anticipation of important celebrations on the festive calendar like All Saints' Day (Día de Todos los Santos). Output also varied according to family size and composition and amount of agricultural land cultivated. Depending on these and other factors, some households devoted more time to carving and thus regularly produced more products than others. Despite these differences, almost every household devoted some time to carving year-round. The tendency was for each household to manufacture and sell their products independently. Marciano García sometimes enlisted other households to complete an especially large order.

Constantino Ruiz López, thirty-three years old in 1985, headed a seven-person extended virilocal household that included his unmarried daughter, a married son who was a weaver, and his daughter-in-law. He had less than 1 hectare of arable land, owned an ox team, and had to rent or borrow a cart. His last annual corn harvest was estimated at 250 kilos, which met only sixty-two days' worth of estimated daily household consumption of 4 kilos. Constantino's wife, Esperanza Pérez, was an embroiderer, made tortillas for sale (tortillera), and also carved wooden spoons. She summed up reasons for occupational shifts in her household as follows: "I think I earn more from making and selling tortillas. Embroidery is slow work and tires out my brain. I tire out after doing only one section. I don't have good vision. I don't feel tired after making tortillas from a bucket full of dough (masa). Carving little wooden spoons gives good results, but there is a scarcity of wood. You have to go searching for wood in the mountains, but when you get back to the house and make the spoons, you can sell all of them. My husband wove fajas and so did my sons but without much success because they had to buy their thread, buy dyes to dye the thread, and then sit down to weave them. Then when you take them to sell, you have to pay money for more thread and dyes. So there is next to nothing left over in earnings. That is the advantage of making wooden spoons. You don't have to spend any money when you sell them. You just have to look for more wood, and all of the earnings are yours."

Esperanza's statement illustrates that Santa Cecilians were open to working in different activities to make a living, including those like embroidery and weaving that were new to them. Their different activities were constantly compared with a focus on real short-term costs and benefits. Those activities that fell short were substituted by other available activities without hesitation or regret. The principal motivating factor in all of their craft activity was to raise cash for necessary household expenditures.

Since 1980, when Esperanza had experimented with making tortillas for sale, she had switched back to embroidery for a time but had once again given it up. Consequently, she complained that they had no meat or bread to eat or chocolate to drink but only corn and beans because they were working mostly in agriculture now. She had less cash due to the decline in the embroidery business. Her statement emphasized the capriciousness of demand for embroidery but also that, under conditions of economic crisis, the last resort for peasant-artisan households was agriculture, especially the direct production of household staples, corn and beans. Fortunately, in the case of Santa Cecilians, thanks to their access to ejido land, agriculture was a viable refuge for most households.

Esperanza's husband, Constantino, elaborated on his wife's statement by observing that "in agriculture we don't earn money. We earn money from wood carving. Today I decided not to pick crops but to stay at home and carve wood. When I go to the agricultural fields, I work from sunrise to sunset there and have no time for wood carving. I reserve an entire day to do it." In other words, cash-earning activities were necessary complements to subsistence agriculture.

Constantino made additional points regarding the effects of the economic crisis on making and earning a livelihood, comparing 1980 and 1985. In 1980, they were able to accumulate some cash savings to use in case of illness or some other emergency. They were not able to do so in 1985. When an emergency arose, they had to sell animals for cash and reduce expenditures. Clothing or other durable items were deferred, and purchases were limited to items that were consumed daily and weekly. Wood carving provided enough cash to replenish this category of consumables.

The strategy of selling farm animals to raise cash was relied upon traditionally by many Oaxaca peasant-artisan households to meet expenses for medical emergencies, festive expenditures, or other situations not related to wider conditions of economic crisis when cash earnings and savings were low. However, general reduction of household expenditures and postponement of larger expenditures were among several strategies employed in response to inflation by households in Santa Cecilia and other villages (Cook 1988, 68–73; Cook and Binford 1990, 169–175).

## Conclusion

Two Jalieza communities, Santo Domingo and Santa Cecilia, together with the neighboring community of San Pedro Guegorexe, were categorized by our survey project as "mixed-craft," since they combined heavy involvement in embroidery with significant household involvement in several other craft industries (Cook and Binford 1990, 69–78). Santo Tomás, as a municipality, was the head community of this cluster, and its backstrap-loom weaving industry spread to the other communities but did not predominate in them as it did in Santo Tomás.

Known as Mecatepeque in the colonial period, Santo Tomás was politically dominant over its neighbors. That relationship still held in the second half of the twentieth century. Ironically, the craft commodity most likely to have pre-Hispanic origins in twentieth-century Jalieza was wood carving in Santa Cecilia, which was not only the smallest community in the cluster but also the one with the most documented history of settlement instability.

## CHAPTER 8

# Santa Cecilia Jalieza:

# Defending Homeland in

# Hostile Surroundings

From the sixteenth century and earlier, Santa Cecilia Jalieza experienced subjugation, conflict, invasion, and resettlement without loss of its identity or place in the regional landscape. The archaeological record shows that the greater Jalieza area had shifting settlements and fluctuating populations related to its location in a strategic zone of passage between the Tlacolula and Ocotlán branches of the Oaxaca Valley. This zone of passage was contested first between Zapotec cacicazgos (e.g., Zaachila versus Teitipac), and then among the Mixtec, Nahua, and Zapotec. During the colonial period, it was contested by competing Spanish jurisdictions and interests (e.g., caciques in Teitipac and Jalieza; alcalde mayor de Santa Catarina Minas versus alcalde mayor de Teozapotlán or Zaachila; Santo Tomás Mecatepeque versus Teitipac); and in the twentieth century, between caudillos in San Juan Guelavía (Juan Brito) and San Juan Chilateca (Angel Trápaga). The archival record for Santa Cecilia contains a host of references across the centuries to litigation, invasions, and combat with San Juan Teitipac and other Jalieza communities regarding ejidal and communal land boundaries and use.

This chapter reviews in detail archival land records to show the perseverance of Santa Cecilians in pursuing legitimation of their communal land boundaries and defense of their settlement against larger, predatory neighbors over centuries of violent discord and intermittent interventions by external authorities. It also picks up a thread of discussion introduced in Chapter 2 concerning the origin and development of Hacienda San Antonio Buenavista. That process had implications for Santa Cecilia, as recognized by the hacienda's late nineteenth-century owner Carlos Castro, and resulted in twentieth-century property dispositions related to the expropriation of hacienda land and Santa Cecilia's ejido endowment. Another discussion thread launched in Chapter 2, that regarding the implications for Santa Cecilia's past arising out of its location in a narrow corridor between Tlacolula and Ocotlán, is interwoven with the early twentieth-century saga of militias, banditry, raiding, abandonment, and boundary conflicts involving Santa Cecilia and San Juan Teitipac.

This case illustrates a determined, centuries-long struggle against all odds by a small peasant-artisan population using judicial and extrajudicial means to survive as a viable community. Santa Cecilia's settlement was vacated on several occasions during and after the colonial period, a pattern that also occurred during the preconquest period, only to be reoccupied when circumstances permitted. Despite these periodic interruptions in use and occupation of settlement and land over the centuries, Santa Cecilians managed to retain their core traditions of subsistence agriculture and carving of wooden utensils.

### The Foundational Title Document and Pre-1800 Surveys

The first paragraph of the oldest surviving colonial document in Santa Cecilia Jalieza's archive (dated 1620 but incorporating a 1592 document that was introduced in a hearing) contains the following lines that capture the essence of this pueblo's historic struggle for place and identity (AAMSCJ, 1): "Regarding the estancia of Santa Cecilia subject of the pueblo of Teozapotlán, its native people were congregated in the pueblo of Teozapotlán (ca. 1606) but have been returning little by little to the estancia which is (an) ancient pueblo. They were congregated without losing their ancient lands for cultivation and maintenance." This sixteenth-century record of the removal, congregation, and resettlement of the pueblo of Santa Cecilia is paralleled by a similar pattern in the pre-Hispanic period (Kowalewski et al. 1989). Santa Cecilia was invaded in 1620 by Santo Tomás (then Mecatepeque) and by its dependency, Santo Domingo, under the jurisdiction and sponsorship of alcaldes mayores based in Miahuatlán and Santa Catarina Minas de Chichicapan.[1]

During official hearings held in Antequera in 1620 regarding land disputes involving Santa Cecilia, a witness named Francisco de Cabrera testified that around 1600 he accompanied his brother, Fray Pedro de la Cueva, on a trip from Zaachila to Santa Cecilia for the purpose of "attending some festive celebrations" (AAMSCJ, 2). While walking through an arroyo near the church in Santa Cecilia, his brother told him a story about "a cacique and a cacica of the empire of Zaachila" who had engaged in some unspecified activity on a "large boulder" in the arroyo. The witness made reference to it as a way of demonstrating the antiquity of the pueblo of Santa Cecilia and its position of being subject to Zaachila, and then declared that "before they were congregated, there was a large population that I saw with my own eyes." He also observed that "the Indians of Santo Tomás Mecatepeque want to occupy the lands of Santa Cecilia Jalieza."

An invasion was triggered by a 1592 viceregal grant (merced) to Santo Tomás of a sitio de estancia de ganado menor (known as Quelaló in Zapotec) that bordered Santa Cecilia. During Santa Cecilia's period of congregation in Zaachila, the expansionist ambitions of Santo Tomás/Santo Domingo Mecatepeque were undoubtedly encouraged by the relative depopulation of Santa Cecilia and the tribute demands of Santa Catarina Minas de Chichicapan. According to a document dated May 6, 1620 (AAMSCJ, 9–11) and written by authorities in Zaachila, "The Indian Marcos de Aquino, of the estancia of Santa Cecilia, was robbed of 6 pounds of grana [cochinilla, or cochineal] that today is worth 5 pesos, as well as 6 pesos' worth of chili." The same robbers, who were not from Santa Cecilia, stole fifty calabazas, four woolen blankets (mantas de lana), three painted mats (petates), and a table; destroyed three houses and stole the beams. The invaders brought an image of San Juanito to Santa Cecilia for the purpose of erasing the given name of its chapel. They threw out the Indians who were there, knocked down their houses, and brought other Indians to settle there against their will. This represented a concerted effort on the part of the authorities in Mecatepeque and Santa Catarina Minas to remake Santa Cecilia as their own dependency (Taylor 1972, 26–27).

The fourteen-year struggle between Zaachila and Mecatepeque/Chichicapan over Santa Cecilia came to a head in 1634, when the case was presented to the alcalde mayor and juez de agravios in Antequera by the authorities of Teozapotlán (Zaachila). They expressed their alarm when the Indians of Santo Tomás Mecatepeque presented a title to certain lands that included those of Santa Cecilia, which it had occupied since preconquest times (AAMSCJ, 14–17). They also reported that Indians of Santo Tomás Mecatepeque, without cause or reason, took the alcalde mayor of Chichicapan to Santa Cecilia (their subject) accompanied by a force of Indians with trumpets blaring and flags raised (clarines y banderas enarboladas). They entered Santa Cecilia, made prisoners of five tribute-paying native Indians and neighbors, and took them away as prisoners to Santo Tomás Mecatepeque. They also took with them two ox teams, a horse, and two chairs. By force and with violence, the report ended, the Santa Cecilians were counted as tributaries.

Other documents (AAMSCJ, March 30, 1634, 16; April 20, 1634, 17–19) further described this incident by specifying that the prisoners were taken to work in the mines of Chichicapan. The matter seemed to have been resolved in an official document dated December 5, 1634, which recognized and legitimized the location and boundaries of Santa Cecilia, gave them legal protection (se le manda les haga amparo de las tierras), and declared that the Santa Cecilia Indians lived on the lands of their pueblo and could not be dispossessed of them.

As it turned out, that resolution proved illusory. In 1720 and 1721, the alcalde mayor of Antequera was involved in a judicial process to resolve boundary issues on communal lands between Santa Cecilia Jalieza and Zaachila, which was resolved in favor of Zaachila. A new stumbling block emerged that would keep Santa Cecilia's land base and population in jeopardy well into the twentieth century: San Juan Teitipac caused tumult on the land where the boundary inspection (vista de ojos) was under way in 1720–1721 (ASRA, Magdalena file copy of *Diario Oficial de los Estados Unidos Mexicanos* 149, No. 10 [Monday, May 12, 1945], 2–4). Despite San Juan's opposition, the inspection continued but left the dispute unresolved, since the judicial proceedings (diligencias) were considered to relate only to difficulties of Santa Cecilia with other neighboring communities.

The difficulties proved that land was the most critical resource for local economies, not only for its agricultural role, but also because of its potential for mining, quarrying, hunting and gathering, and wood cutting. Land categorized as unsuited for agriculture due to being hilly or mountainous, rocky or having poor soil, or covered with forest or scrub vegetation was still coveted and fought over by communities like San Juan and Santa Cecilia.

It is not surprising that little progress was made during the eighteenth century in resolving intercommunity land disputes, considering the increasing decay in the corregidor/alcalde mayor system of governance. This decay was exposed by José de Gálvez's Plan de Intendencias in 1768 to abolish those offices and replace them with a system of intendancies and subdelegations, in hopes of solving the endemic problems of violence and corruption (Hamnett 1971, 41–42).

The next phase of Santa Cecilia's struggle for land and settlement occurred under a regime supportive of the reform effort that was also favored by the clergy. These reforms were an official response to the decline of the cochineal trade (after its peak in 1769–1778), which was the economic engine of the alcalde mayor system (Hamnett 1971, 30–31, 48–51). Following a royal decree in 1786, the corregidor/alcalde mayor/repartimiento system was replaced by an intendancy/subdelegate system, launching a period of resistance and efforts at counterreform by actors who had profited from the prereform system, which essentially bound indigenous local economies to merchant capitalists in Mexico City through a network of agents and corrupted government functionaries in Oaxaca (Hamnett 1971, 92–95).

During the period of "destabilization and fragmentation" from 1770 to 1867 in Mexico, and particularly the period from 1810 to 1821 of criollo insurrection culminating in the final overthrow of the colonial state (Hamnett 1999, 133–143), the wheels of the agrarian judicial apparatus were still turning in the Oaxaca Valley. After 1770, land conflicts rose, reached a peak during the last decade of the century, and dropped significantly in the first two decades of the nineteenth century, from 60 to 41 to 37 conflicts (Reina 1988a, 206). Of these conflicts, 51 percent were between pueblos fighting to delimit their boundaries. This can be explained through the intertwining of several factors: the multitude of different ethnic groups (etnias) that populated Oaxacan territory, the permanence of indigenous cacicazgos, and the retention by the pueblos of the major part of their lands, which, with the change to the colonial property regime and the increase in population at the end of the eighteenth century, made boundaries unclear to everyone concerned (Reina 1988a, 207).

The signing of the Plan de Iguala in 1821 confirmed Mexico's independence from Spain and also initiated a counterrevolution under the guise of a liberal criollo nation-building project that "not only abandoned the social question of the Revolution of Independence, but excluded the indigenous population from the process," and sought to eradicate indígenas as a juridical category (Reina 1988a, 217). In the transition from colonial to independent Mexico, there was no clear continuity in the judicial organization reigning in the country.[2]

## Early Nineteenth-Century Surveys and Litigation

Toward the end of the colonial period, in 1798, a map of Santa Cecilia Jalieza and Santo Domingo Jalieza was drafted that clearly delimited community boundaries, including parajes and markers, and indicated the location of habitation areas and cultivated fields (see Taylor 1972, 76). The map showed Santo Domingo was a compact settlement, whereas Santa Cecilia had a more dispersed type of settlement with individual homesteads within or very close to cultivated fields. The area mapped was the core of Santa Cecilia's fundo legal since a 1776–1977 document in the Archivo General de la Nación (Tierras) listed it as one of thirty Oaxaca pueblos that possessed one (Méndez Martínez 1999, vol. 997, exp. 191, Oaxaca City). The extent of Santa Cecilia's landholdings at the time is unclear, but three areas of cultivation were shown: one was the zone of dispersed habitation itself, and two others were located on the north and south sides of the habitation area. The map showed that residents of San Juan planted cornfields only a few hundred meters northeast of Santa Cecilia, with the rest of the land between the towns used strictly for grazing (Taylor 1972, 105).

In 1777, Fr. Agustín de Aguilar observed that San Juan's cultivated lands extended from the front door of the convent a distance of one league (2.6 miles) to Santa Cecilia (Esparza 1994, 311). He also described the ravines (cañadas) that shaped the landscape historically contested by Santa Cecilia, Santo Domingo, and San Juan (ibid.; translation mine): "Once again in the center of Tectipac to take the half-day trip to the middle of the pueblo of Santa Cecilia, in a westerly direction a distance of one league on a flat road: here there is a cold and humid climate due to a river that crosses its fringe, coming down from Santo Domingo, and on the other side in rainy season producing a torrent of water toward Teitipac. The cañada that it has in its monte is large and has many types of wood that the Indians use for cutting. From Santa Cecilia to the pueblecillo of Santo Domingo, there is a quarter of a league in distance with difficult ravines, cold and humid in the extreme, due to the river that passes near it."

Late colonial-period judicial proceedings focused on Santa Cecilia's boundary disputes began under the authorization (Decreto de Comisión) of the corregidor intendente. Proceedings were conducted under the direction of a "comisionado" and a "teniente letrado," presumably an upgraded type of official compared to those excoriated by Gálvez in the corrupt and compromised justice system existing in 1768 (Hamnett 1971, 41). The commissioner was on site and actually ran the proceedings. The teniente letrado was a lawyer and military officer stationed in San Juan Teitipac. Both Santa Cecilia Jalieza and San Juan Teitipac were within the territory of the corregimiento. All costs pertaining to the judicial proceedings, as well as personal costs that included the maintenance of more than forty servants, were supposed to be borne by San Juan as the plaintiff (pueblo recusante; ASRA-SCJ, February 24, 1820).

The 1798 map was the product of a late colonial-period survey to definitively settle long-simmering disputes involving Santa Cecilia. It foreshadowed a renewal of judicial proceedings among San Juan Teitipac, Santa Cecilia Jalieza, Santo Domingo Jalieza, and Hacienda San Antonio Buenavista to resolve disputed boundaries and communal land use and ownership. The focus of the process was to determine the boundaries of Santa Cecilia's fundo legal, which originated as a royal grant. The fundo legal's northern boundary bordered sections of San Juan Teitipac's most coveted agricultural lands. Any and all surveys throughout the colonial period that placed those lands in potential jeopardy were contested or challenged (recusado) in the courts. It was San Juan's challenge to the survey that produced the 1798 map that resulted in a resurvey in 1820.

Documents dating from 1816 to 1831 anticipated or followed up on the resurvey conducted over a period of three days in February 1820. An official report described all events and activities related to the resurvey. A 1977 letter from the municipal authorities of Santa Cecilia to the Agrarian Reform office in Oaxaca referred to this 1820 report as representing "our primordial titles."

The process, as well as the terminology and references recorded in the resurvey report (e.g., "Excelentísimo Señor Virrey," "Your Majesty," "el Rey," "Repúblicas," the latter referring to the Zapotec communities), suggested that the institutions of the crisis-ridden viceregal government were still functioning regionally in 1820. The Spanish parliamentary and constitutional reforms between 1810 and 1812 included the abolition of colonial repúblicas de indios in favor of town councils and "had a lasting impact in nineteenth-century Mexico." By September 1820, after a six-year-long Absolutist spasm in Spain under Ferdinand VII, this new constitutional system was restored in New Spain (Hamnett 1999, 140).

The purpose of the 1820 resurvey was to determine the boundaries of Santa Cecilia Jalieza's fundo legal, the same purpose motivating the survey behind the 1798 map: to locate, verify, and set boundary markers (mojoneras) to separate lands under Santa Cecilia's jurisdiction from those under the jurisdictions of neighboring settlements and, particularly, from those belonging to its historic nemesis, San Juan Teitipac to the north. Santa Cecilia Jalieza's fundo legal, presumably delimited in the contested 1798 map, was recognized as originating in a royal grant (merced real).

The 1820 resurvey was also intended to promote a certain degree of agrarian reform. Agricultural specialists in the retinue were tasked with evaluating and classifying land enclosed by boundaries. The element of land need and use, made more urgent by population growth, was discussed at several points by village representatives and the hacendado of San Antonio Buenavista during the survey process. The process anticipated the procedural and policy concerns of late nineteenth- and early twentieth-century agrarian reform in Oaxaca.

The retinue (comitiva) for the 1820 resurvey included the commissioner (comisionado); two lawyers (abogados patronos) representing San Juan Teitipac and Santa Cecilia Jalieza respectively; the hacendado of San Antonio Buenavista (Don José Mariano Magro); an official agent representing Santo Domingo Jalieza; the head surveyor (perito agrimensor); another surveyor named by Teitipac; a third surveyor as arbitrator (perito tercero en discordia); and the scribe (escribano de la República) who took notes on the proceedings and wrote the final report (minutario). Five members of the retinue were "assistants" and also signatories of the minutes. Other members of the retinue did not sign minutes: three labradores (agricultural specialists to make estimates of land-use potential); a military commander (comandante de la partida de usares) who had three to six cavalrymen under his command daily; and an undetermined number of observers from the communities involved.

The group assembled in the parish priest's residence (casa cural) of Santa Cecilia, where most of them were fed and lodged during the proceedings. At the time, Santa Cecilia had a resident priest under the jurisdiction of the head parish church in San Juan Teitipac. Forty servants served retinue members.

The lawyer for San Juan Teitipac indicated agreement with the resurvey, since the district judge's decision already incorporated his clients' objections of not possessing "sufficient land for the more than three hundred individuals living there." He interpreted this to mean that the fundo legal of Santa Cecilia would have to include land from areas other than San Juan (por otros rumbos).

Santa Cecilia's lawyer countered that the delay in resolving the boundary dispute caused undue hardship to his clients, who were so economically pressed as to make it difficult for them to bear the costs of the proceedings. He reiterated that every effort should be made to investigate the veracity of the claim made by San Juan Teitipac of its inability to pay for the proceedings due to its alleged "notorious misery" caused by population increase that created a serious land shortage (ASRA-SCJ, February 24, 1820).

The survey began from the church and proceeded northward through a paraje named Pochutla. Measurements were taken, estimates of the cultivable area were made in terms of quantities of seed corn (fanegas and almudes), and the boundary marker named Chivaniza was located and confirmed. One of the elder members of the retinue suffered a fall and was replaced by an individual from San Miguel Tecomatlán, Jurisdicción de Yanhuitlán, who was Spanish and an agriculturist (labrador).

The retinue proceeded in a northwesterly direction toward the Hacienda San Antonio. Distances were measured up to a hill on the way, and the three agrarian experts were asked to describe the terrain in terms of its potential for agriculture; they agreed unanimously that the area in question could be planted in only 5 almudes of seed. Several blocks (cuadros) of land were surveyed, cultivability estimates were made, and activities were suspended, to be continued the following day. The report of that day's activities was signed by all twelve participants, including the escribano de la república (ASRA-SCJ, February 24, 1820).

On the morning of day two, the scribe observed that Indians were not obligated to attend Mass so as not to be burdened with expenses. After Mass, the retinue departed the village at 11:00 a.m. Measurements and crop-yield estimates were made, and the retinue returned to an area surveyed the previous day in the Pochutla paraje to the north and, in accordance with measurements taken, set in place the first marker to demarcate the boundary with San Juan Teitipac. After the marker (mojonera) was set, "stones were thrown and grass pulled" to confirm possession. The commissioner took the hand of Santa Cecilia's mayor and told him that from this day forward the paraje demarcated would be officially recognized by the king as a possession of Santa Cecilia and named the paraje San Ignacio Pochutla.

The retinue proceeded eastward to a place known as Chavaniza, where there was a boundary marker on an elevated masonry base that demarcated boundaries between San Juan Teitipac, Santa María Magdalena Teitipac, and Santa Cecilia. A new marker was placed to the left of the preexisting marker at 450 varas' distance; the paraje was officially named San Antonio Chivaniza and its possession granted to Santa Cecilia.

Afterward, the retinue proceeded south, arriving at the summit of a mountain next to the pueblo of Santa Cecilia where a cañada known as Santa María Quiesichi began. At that point, an official of San Juan Teitipac presented the commissioner with documents variously dated from 1714 to 1812 that appeared to grant possession of lands in the cañada, considered to belong to Santa Cecilia, to San Juan Teitipac for purposes of grazing livestock. A discussion ensued between the commissioner and the lawyer representing San Juan Teitipac that involved tortured explanations as to why the documents had been introduced to interrupt the survey rather than in previous court proceedings. The gist of these explanations was that Santa Cecilia's fundo legal should not be completed at San Juan's expense when other lands were available (e.g., Hacienda San Antonio Buenavista), especially since San Juan itself was short of land for cultivation and pasturage.

Don José Mariano Magro, owner of Hacienda San Antonio Buenavista, was present in the retinue and took apparent delight in responding to the statement of San Juan's lawyer. He confirmed that Sanjuaneros had planted on his lands but not due to lack of land, as they claimed, but rather due to a lack of ox teams (yuntas). He added that San Juan had several tracts of land that they did not cultivate, not because those lands were infertile, but either because they did not want to cultivate them or because they had an excess of cultivable land (expuso que es cierto que han ido a sembrar, pero no por falta de tierras sino por falta de yuntas, y que aún tienen varios pedazos de tierra que no siembran, no por infructuosos sino porque no quieren o porque les sobran).

Before the group reached the boundary marker with San Juan Teitipac, Santa Cecilia's lawyer asked the surveyors to measure the distance to the church in San Juan, which could be seen in the distance. This would make it possible for all concerned to see up close the large plots of cultivated land belonging to San Juan that were between their present position and the San Juan church. The distances were estimated to be between 1 1/2 to 2 leguas, or 6,500 varas. The lands seen in the distance were described as beautiful green plots under cultivation (tablones verdes, hermosos al parecer y sembrados, que se perciben a grande distancia). Magro, the San Antonio Buenavista hacendado, commented that the area of land in the distance that appeared to be black in color was, in fact, a swamp in the midst of San Juan's cultivated lands, which came to be in that condition due to their laziness (expuso que junto a ellos y lo que parece negro desde aquí, todo en ciénaga que dichos naturales han convertido en tal por indolencia).

The chief surveyor classified the cañada between San Juan and Santa Cecilia as having land useful for pasture as well as for cultivation in a proportion of 1 to 8 almudes of seed corn. The lawyer for San Juan, in an apparent attempt to goad the surveyor into overstepping his authority, asked for the number of fanegas calculated by the agrimensor that might be subjected to expropriation from San Juan. The surveyor's response was 49 fanegas plus 16 almudes, and that another amount would be taken from the Hacienda San Antonio Buenavista. He clarified that he had measured land between three markers—Guielopa, Calicanto, and Chivaniza—amounting to more than 3,000 varas, which would not be expropriated, since it was not a boundary (nada le puede tomar porque no linda por ninguna parte).

At the outset of the third day's proceedings, the lawyer for San Juan Teitipac demanded the prorrateo (proportional distribution of land) from the preceding day's survey, and was told by the surveyor that it was not ready in written form but only in terms of mathematical calculations (ASRA-SCJ, February 26, 1820). This was the response he anticipated and jibed neatly with the "overreach" elicited from the surveyor the day before.

The lawyer for San Juan conveyed to the commissioner his displeasure with the previous day's survey in the cañada, where there had been much "walking to and fro," with the surveyor saying that only land from Hacienda San Antonio Buenavista and San Juan would be taken for the fundo legal of Santa Cecilia, to the exclusion of land belonging to Santo Domingo Jalieza and Magdalena Teitipac. The commissioner reiterated that only he would make such determinations, since the surveyor's job was simply to take measurements, and that all of the contiguous settlements would be considered as possible donors to make up the fundo legal of Santa Cecilia. He noted, however, that Santo Domingo lacked its own fundo legal and that the contiguous land of Magdalena was already the object of litigation with San Juan.

The lawyer for San Juan reiterated his concern that the proceedings were stacked against the interests of his clients because the surveyor had displayed bias and was unfamiliar with Hacienda Buenavista's lands. The surveyor, upset by this accusation, interjected that a second surveyor should be recruited, along with an arbitrator (tercero en discordia), to evaluate if he did good or bad work. The commissioner deemed this to be impracticable, and the third and final day of the survey commenced.

As the retinue proceeded eastward from the center of Santa Cecilia to a point where the hills begin, they observed that all of the high grounds were filled with multitudes of people up in arms (nos constituimos por el rumbo del oriente hasta llegar al principio de una loma donde comenzamos a observar todas las alturas cubiertas de mucha gente en ademán de armas y tumulto). The commander of the cavalry unit assigned to the survey had been wary of the unusual tranquillity of days one and two. Nevertheless, on day three he initially sent out only six cavalrymen with the retinue to give additional rest to his remaining horses. He and the rest of the detachment later caught up with the retinue, and as they continued on their way, large numbers of people were seen occupying the summits of two mountains the retinue had to cross. The commander ordered his troops to disperse the crowds, identified as "indios" from San Juan Teitipac, from the retinue's path. A participating cavalryman reported that upon encountering the crowd blocking the path in front of him, an Indian threw rocks at him, so he whipped his horse toward the individual at a fast pace to dispatch him with his drawn sword.[3]

With the retinue at rest behind the troops, the lawyer for Santa Cecilia warned the commissioner that there was a man standing behind him carrying a knife. The retinue immediately returned to Santa Cecilia, and a hearing was held forthwith concerning the incident. The knife wielder's name was José de la Cruz, an Indian, a widower, born and raised in San Juan Teitipac, and a butcher and cook by occupation. He claimed to be carrying the knife in order to cut grapefruit to quench his thirst during the survey and in no way to disrupt the proceedings or to cause injury to anyone. Despite his testimony, he was jailed.

The commissioner resumed the survey westward to a paraje named Tanichi, then turned and proceeded through "infertile land" to arrive in another paraje named Coronilla that was renamed San Luis Yanizada Coronilla and was given in possession to Santa Cecilia. Next, the retinue proceeded westward for 1,250 varas to a paraje named Lechiguego, which, according to the representatives of Santo Domingo Jalieza, belonged to the Rancho de Guelaviate. The chief surveyor placed a mojonera and renamed the place San Juan de Dios Lechiguego and recognized it as belonging to Santa Cecilia. The retinue moved 1,000 varas to the west to a paraje named El Portillo where another marker was placed, renamed La Magdalena del Portillo, and recognized as belonging to Santa Cecilia.

From El Portillo, the retinue proceeded northward 634 varas, after having passed through several plots of cultivated land. The surveyor placed another mojonera, named the place San Francisco and, addressing the alcalde, recognized it as a possession of Santa Cecilia. Following this boundary line to the summit of Yaniche, the "cuadro" that separated Santa Cecilia and the Hacienda San Antonio was completed. Having completed the survey, except for the boundary with San Juan Teitipac, the retinue returned to the rectory in Santa Cecilia.

The lawyer representing Santa Cecilia was furious about Teitipac's egregious disruption of the survey and demanded that they be criminally prosecuted and compelled to pay all of the expenses for the entire undertaking. He acknowledged that the commissioner, confronted with San Juan's sabotage of the proceedings, was obliged to suspend the boundary survey with San Juan in order to avoid bloodshed, which would have occurred if the cavalry had been ordered to use force to dislodge them from the heights they occupied and punish them for their interference. He argued that the survey should still be completed, markers set, and possession granted to Santa Cecilia on the boundary with Hacienda San Antonio, and farther to the west, despite San Juan's challenge.

The lawyer representing San Juan Teitipac, apologetic to the court, expressed his extreme displeasure over the fact that despite measures he had taken to assure that Sanjuaneros stayed within the limits of the pueblo, except for the two authorized to accompany the surveyors, a group of them went out to observe and harass the survey party, with one of them being caught carrying a knife. Recognizing that what was done could not be undone, he said that in the event that the superior court judge decided to continue the survey, it should be kept in mind that "Indians do not think and, due to their rustic nature, commit many errors" (los indios no reflexionan e incurren por su rusticidad en muchas faltas).

Predictably, the result of the post-incident deliberations was that it would be "very costly to continue at the pleasure of those from Teitipac" but that they were obliged to "pay the onerous costs of the delay on top of everything else for which they have been condemned." The commissioner then ordered the suspension of the survey.

The San Antonio Buenavista hacendado, Magro, asked for a copy of the proceedings, since he found his interests to be severely prejudiced by the survey conducted in the area of his hacienda and had been required to pay the cost for same. The surveyors agreed that the hacienda land involved amounted to 4 fanegas of land under cultivation and two hills with pastures.

The report was read and the representatives of Santa Cecilia reiterated that the survey had conformed to the court order and that the chief surveyor "was not going to take even one vara of cultivated land to the north that belonged to San Juan Teitipac but only from the cañada de Yaniche that was located to the West." Santa Cecilia's representative also entered into the record that a portion of that land had been purchased for 500 pesos by Santa Cecilia and requested that the land title be shown to all of the presiding officials; he also insisted on placing in the official record that the distance from the church in Santa Cecilia to the pueblo of Teitipac, as well as the distance from the center of Teitipac to the southernmost boundary marker, was shown on the surveyor's map to be 1 league and 1.5 leagues, respectively. This was to assure that everyone could clearly see the extensive amount of land enjoyed by San Juan.[4]

## Agrarian Reform, the Ejido, and Persisting Conflict

The 1820 survey did not result in a definitive official resolution of Santa Cecilia's boundary disputes with contiguous settlements. It did, however, provide substantial official documentation to support an eventual resolution favoring Santa Cecilia. In 1882, Santa Cecilia filed a formal complaint with agrarian authorities regarding an alleged "land invasion by Teitipac" (Esparza 1991a, 186, citing AGEO, Leg. 81, exp. 7, 34ff.), and another in 1906 (ibid., citing AGEO, Leg. 81, exp. 9, 25ff.). Indeed, between 1900 and 1915, more than four hundred pages of documents were accumulated in a file addressing the boundaries of "the pueblos of Jalieza of the District of Ocotlán and Teitipac of the District of Tlacolula" (Esparza 1991b, 163, citing AGEO file Jalieza, Leg. 71, exp. 14 with 2 maps). This served as background to the subsequent legal and extralegal struggle that would be waged between Santa Cecilia Jalieza and San Juan Teitipac after 1915.

The early decades of the twentieth century were plagued by outbreaks of violence between Santa Cecilia and its old nemesis, San Juan Teitipac. The following narrative is contained in ASRA: exp. 7, March 21, 1927: "According to the people of Santa Cecilia, in 1910 and 1916 people from San Juan have devastated the pueblo of Jalieza, pillaging the population and burning down many houses, forcing them to emigrate to the neighboring pueblo of Santo

Domingo Jalieza, for the reason that they did not have sufficient guarantees of safety in the place where they live where there are not more than sixty men whereas San Juan has more than six hundred." One of the ironies here is that in the 1700s, Santa Cecilia and Santo Domingo were at odds due to their dependent status in competing jurisdictions, namely Zaachila and Santo Tomás Mecatepeque/Chichicapan, only to find Santa Cecilians taking refuge in Santo Domingo in the 1900s to escape the depredations of San Juan Teitipac. This illustrates the old rule of diplomacy: the enemy of my enemy is my friend.

The long history of hostile relations between Santa Cecilia and San Juan Teitipac regarding land and territorial boundaries was exacerbated by the agrarian revolution that would bring into play the land of a third party: Hacienda San Antonio Buenavista. The ASRA file for Santa Cecilia began with an official communication (oficio) dated November 20, 1916, acknowledging that on that date it solicited through the office of the delegado of the CNA (Comisión Nacional Agraria) in Oaxaca "the restitution of lands that the pueblo of Teitipac took away from them" (ASRA: exp. 7, Nov. 20, 1916).

In 1923, Inspector Sotomayor was assigned Santa Cecilia's case for the purpose of examining the possibility of a dotación (not of a restitución) of a fraction of land measuring 567 hectares belonging to Hacienda San Antonio Buenavista, since it was the only hacienda bordering the pueblo. At that time, Santa Cecilia had 213 inhabitants dispersed among seventy or so households. Sotomayor's report incorporated a detailed account of the annual cycle of variable precipitation that was so critical for seasonal cultivation of corn, beans, and chickpeas; and it accurately characterized Santa Cecilia's land as uneven and mountainous, full of limestone and rocks, with some hills and mountains with heavy vegetation (ASRA: exp. 7, July 31, 1923).

On August 6, 1923, Sotomayor recorded that forty-eight heads of household in Santa Cecilia possessed lands within the perimeter of the ejido, which consisted of a total of 330 hectares, of which 46 hectares was residential, 60 hectares was cultivated, and 224 hectares was hilly (lomerio) and unsuitable for cultivation. All of the cultivated land was worked directly by possessor households (posesionarios) and not through rent or sharecropping arrangements. An undisclosed number of households provided seasonal workers (peones temporeros) at the going rate of 50 centavos per day to the adjacent Hacienda San Antonio Buenavista. It was also recorded that Santa Cecilia's principal nonagricultural industries at the time were the manufacture of spoons and beaters made of wood and production of charcoal (ASRA: exp. 7, Aug. 6, 1923).

On June 2, 1926, Santa Cecilia was awarded definitive possession of 628 hectares from the adjacent Hacienda San Antonio Buenavista owned by

Carlos Castro, thus justifying Castro's special concern about Santa Cecilia reported in Chapter 2. Shortly thereafter, Santa Cecilia ceded 67 hectares of mountainous land (terreno montañoso) to San Bartolo Coyotepec, and Lic. Castro ceded to Santa Cecilia 74 hectares in exchange for access to two dams that were included in the dotación. After the expropriation, the hacienda retained approximately 1,355 hectares. These transactions all occurred peacefully, but the peace was short-lived (ASRA: exp. 7, June 2, 1926).

A report dated March 21, 1927, submitted to the CNA delegate in Oaxaca City by the surveyor commissioned to locate the places where boundary markers were lacking in the ejido of Santa Cecilia, described difficulties with the pueblo of San Juan Teitipac that resulted in murder and mayhem. It disclosed that people from San Juan Teitipac, on Monday, March 7, brutally assaulted an individual from Jalieza and were presumed to be responsible for the disappearance of two others feared to have been the victims of murder. Because of a long history of such incidents, there was fear in Santa Cecilia that they would not be able to cultivate the ejido ceded to them. During the investigating official's stay in Santa Cecilia, news was received that San Juan intended to invade and depopulate the community.

The official, obviously intimidated by the threat of recurring violence, requested support from the Oaxaca City CNA office, indicating that the people of Santa Cecilia desired an agreement over the question of territorial limits so they could dedicate themselves to their ejido and to acquiring animals and the equipment necessary to cultivate the land without fear of imminent attack by San Juan (ASRA: exp. 7, March 21, 1927).

Arellanes Meixueiro (1988, 53–54), on the basis of additional documentation from the Archivo General del Estado de Oaxaca (AGEO), wrote a vivid account of San Juan's March 1927 attack on Santa Cecilia. The incident involved two hundred armed Sanjuaneros and a platoon of twenty soldiers from an encampment near Abasolo, who fired at will, shooting and selectively burning and looting houses in a search for Santa Cecilia's municipal and agrarian authorities. The attack resulted in eight dead and five wounded; surviving Santa Cecilians fled to the mountains and surrounding communities. Sanjuaneros claimed that the army's help had been requested as backup for an attempt to reclaim property that had previously been stolen from them by Santa Cecilians.

Two months later, Sanjuaneros again invaded Santa Cecilia's ejido, burned their pastures, and set loose animals to destroy crops and plantations of reeds (carrizal) for constructing their houses. The following month, with the intervention of the governor and the chief of military operations, both pueblos signed an agreement to respect the land in dispute, but soon afterward San Juan invaded again. One year later, there was yet another assault of Santa Cecilia by San Juan that resulted in cattle being stolen. Santa Cecilians were unable to defend themselves against 125 well-armed men.

A connection undoubtedly existed between the events described by Arellanes Meixueiro and the period of the "defensas sociales" under the direction of Juan M. Brito from San Juan Guelavía, which involved a network of armed groups in San Antonio Buenavista, San Sebastián Teitipac, and San Juan Teitipac, as described in Chapter 2. The testimonial record is uneven, but there is sufficient circumstantial evidence to suggest the involvement of the Sumano gang. This gang originated in Rancho Guelaviate, but its members resided in San Juan Teitipac before 1920, and they participated in the running battle between Santa Cecilia and San Juan in the 1920s and 1930s.

Although the defensas sociales, first organized in 1928, were disbanded and presumably disarmed in 1934, the culture of regional "peace by force" and local gangsterism institutionalized under Juan Brito continued. In 1935, there was a renewed outbreak of aggression by the Sanjuaneros, causing, yet again, the abandonment of Santa Cecilia, forcing its residents to take refuge in the neighboring community of Santo Domingo for a year and abandon their ejido. According to a report (ASRA: exp. 7, June 23, 1935) by the agrarian reform case officer, the incursion was due to "a running battle from time immemorial for the possession of certain communal lands." The report went on to declare that Santa Cecilians were part of the defensa social under the command of Sr. Angel Trápaga until October 1934, the date when they withdrew from that militia and were disarmed. Until that date, they worked regularly on their ejido, since they had guns to defend themselves from constant attacks from San Juan Teitipac. As a consequence of the disarmament of the ejidatarios of Santa Cecilia, the Sanjuaneros immediately invaded the communal lands and left Santa Cecilia in complete ruins.

The case officer ended his report dramatically by noting that complete misery reigned among the ejidatarios of Santa Cecilia, owing to the fact that they had not been able to cultivate their ejido's seasonal lands. The few parcels of land that they were able to cultivate were located in the mountains. If it were not for the hospitality of the neighboring pueblo of Santo Domingo Jalieza, which gave them space and materials helpful to their subsistence, Santa Cecilians would have had to disband and abandon their settlement and land.

The militia headed by Ángel Trápaga in San Juan Chilateca was decommissioned in 1934, as was the one under the command of Brito in San Juan Guelavía. According to regional oral tradition, the passage route from the Tlacolula arm to the Ocotlán arm of the Oaxaca Valley went directly through the Teitipac and the Jalieza communities, with Santa Cecilia strategically and historically positioned in the middle of this zone. During the period in question, it served as a northern outpost of control from the Ocotlán side (based in San Juan Chilateca and controlled by the Trápaga family).

Divided loyalties in Santa Cecilia pulled some Santa Cecilians into the orbit of San Juan Teitipac and Guelavía, and others into the orbit of San Juan Chilateca and the Ocotlán side. Like Brito himself, who was assassinated in Guelavía in 1936 by unknown assailants, Juan Sumano reportedly met a violent death sometime later. Running through a scattering of conversations I had with informants in Santa Cecilia in the 1970s was a current of rumor, innuendo, and allusions that suggested connections between the violent deaths of Juan Brito and Juan Sumano, vengeance for the reign of terror experienced by Santa Cecilians during the 1920s and 1930s, and fallout from competition between Brito in Guelavía and Trápaga in Chilateca. This is certainly a thought-provoking, if investigatively challenging, scenario that might justify further inquiry.

The 1940s saw violence erupt yet again between San Juan Teitipac and Santa Cecilia Jalieza over the boundaries of their terrenos comunales, triggered this time by a 1942 petition filed by Santa Cecilia to reclaim 2,213 hectares of mountainous grazing land and brushland (terrenos de agostadero cerril y monte) from San Juan Teitipac. It was determined at the time that Santa Cecilia had 220 inhabitants with 68 adult males capable of cultivating 220 hectares of terrenos comunales and 628 hectares of ejido, 20 percent of which was agostadero and the rest temporal. By contrast, San Juan Teitipac had 2,427 inhabitants with 738 adult males capable of working their land "without being able to get an ejido endowment for its lack of access to land adjacent to it that could be expropriated (por carencia absoluta de tierras afectables), and with the settlement having only 2,563 hectares, in addition to 2,212 hectares that have been under dispute with Santa Cecilia" (ASRA: exp. 7, May 6, 1942; Dec. 3, 1945).

The report further declared that "dividing the land areas enjoyed by both settlements by the total number of qualified household heads results in households in Santa Cecilia Jalieza having at their disposal a land parcel of better quality and greater area than corresponds to each head of household in San Juan Teitipac." On that basis, it was decided in 1943 to allow the ejido endowment to San Juan to stand, while confirming Santa Cecilia's rights to only 340 hectares "that it has quietly and peacefully enjoyed since time immemorial."

The final paragraph of the presidential resolution signed June 14, 1944, by President Manuel Ávila Camacho proclaimed "that the conflict existing over the limits of communal lands between the settlements of Santa Cecilia Jalieza and San Juan Teitipac has been solved" and that "the 340 hectares of communal land that has belonged to Santa Cecilia Jalieza will remain under the control of that settlement" (ASRA: exp. 28, June 14, 1944, copy of article from *Diario Oficial de los Estados Unidos Mexicanos* 149, no. 10 [Monday, March 12, 1945]: 2–4).

Despite the June 1944 presidential resolution's rhetoric of finality, the matter was not solved, as was foreseen in a March 6, 1943, telegram from the Delegación Agraria in Oaxaca to the Departamento Agrario in Mexico City that reported "serious emerging difficulties that can lead to a bloody outcome." This proved to be a self-fulfilling prophecy. A written report submitted on December 3, 1945, by José Martínez, agente municipal of Santa Cecilia Jalieza, to the jefe de la Delegación Agraria in Oaxaca, complained that "the difficulty that we have with the neighboring pueblo of San Juan Teitipac is still not resolved," as demonstrated by the fact that "recently the neighbors of San Juan Teitipac killed our comisariado ejidal, Sr. Marcelino Antonio, whose murder is now in the hands of the proper judicial authorities." It elaborated: "We have complained on several occasions about invasions of our communal land, the most recent on November 17, and now we are attempting to harvest our ejido lands but cannot do so due to constant threats by armed men from San Juan Teitipac," and requested the intervention of the Departamento Agrario so that the "neighbors of San Juan Teitipac will allow us to harvest our crops, consisting of beans, corn and zacate, on our ejidal land" (ASRA: exp. 7, Dec. 3, 1945). These communications were dated subsequent to the June 14, 1944, signing by President Ávila Camacho of the document that was supposed to definitively resolve the land and boundary disputes between San Juan and Santa Cecilia (*Diario Oficial de los Estados Unidos Mexicanos* 149, no. 10 [Monday, March 12, 1945]: 2–4).

In the month of January 1948, another survey was undertaken of the San Juan Teitipac–Santa Cecilia Jalieza boundary by the Departamento Agrario under the protection of soldiers from the third and fourth military sectors (Sectores Militares) of the 28th military zone in Oaxaca City, as well as by the Procuraduría General de Justicia del Estado. The presiding surveyor acknowledged that "the neighbors of San Juan Teitipac were those who did not respect" the ejido of Santa Cecilia and "arbitrarily invaded their lands"; he verified this through a field inspection confirming that the Sanjuaneros "have destroyed the boundary marker named 'el Calicanto' that served historically to demarcate the boundary between lands of the Hacienda de San Antonio Buenavista that was affected by the ejido endowment to Santa Cecilia Jalieza and the communal lands of San Juan Teitipac" (ASRA: exp. 7, Jan. 15, 1948; ASRA-SCJ-Terrenos Comunales: exp. 28, Jan. 15, 1948).

This surveyor, Ing. Iruegas Chávez, reconfirmed the boundary line between San Juan and Santa Cecilia to be the one shown in the official map delineated in several previous surveys; it ran in a southeastward direction from the Calicanto marker to the Yaniche marker located on the mountain of the same name. In referring to the Sanjuaneros, he noted that "these neighboring invaders had to recognize the destroyed boundary marker as being the real one" instead of the remains of "small diversion dams for the waters of Arroyo de San Antonio." To leave no lingering doubts about the proper boundary, the surveyor proceeded to set three new intermediate markers between Calicanto and Yaniche (ASRA-SCJ, Jan. 15, 1948, Informe del Ing. Iruegas Chávez).

Iruegas Chávez's judgment was that the recent conflicts between San Juan and Santa Cecilia revolved around the use of water from the Arroyo de San Antonio, which was within the Santa Cecilia ejido and near the Yaniche marker. Cattle from San Juan would drink water from this arroyo and, in the process, damage crops planted by the Santa Cecilians. He admitted, however, that the alleged need for Sanjuaneros to water their cattle on land belonging to Santa Cecilia might simply be a pretext to continue hostilities. In any case, an agreement was drawn up and signed by representatives of both pueblos that permitted San Juan access to arroyo water for purposes of watering their cattle. As might have been predicted at the time, this agreement did not end the boundary conflict, which erupted again in 1952, 1969, 1970, and 1977 (ASRA: exp. 7).

As if the chronic conflict with San Juan Teitipac was not sufficient to disrupt the daily routines of Santa Cecilians, the 1960s witnessed the emergence of a rather unanticipated source of conflict from another neighboring pueblo, which a few decades earlier had provided refuge to Santa Cecilians fleeing San Juan invaders, Santo Domingo Jalieza. Several documents submitted by Santa Cecilia to agrarian reform officials in Oaxaca City in the 1960s described or implied the existence of internal factionalism in addition to conflict with a neighboring village or, at least, suggested the possibility that factionalism and boundary disputes fed upon each other.

This was made explicit in a remarkable letter dated June 18, 1964, from agrarian officials in Santa Cecilia Jalieza to the Secretaría de la Reforma Agraria (SRA) office in Oaxaca City, explaining that a group of thugs there, headed by C. Guadalupe Morales, were terrorizing the community and relied upon the assistance of thugs from neighboring Teitipac. The Teitipac group was headed by Lorenzo Grijalba, an individual alleged to have a history of several pending counts of criminal behavior. In their consideration, the situation was related to the fact that individuals from Teitipac invaded Santa Cecilia's ejidos in collaboration with thugs from their own community.

A letter to the state governor dated August 3, 1964, signed by twenty-three Santa Cecilia women as possessors of fractions of communal land, reported several attacks by people from Santo Domingo Jalieza that interrupted their agricultural work, during both cultivation and harvest, and claimed that their complaints to justice officials in Ocotlán and Oaxaca City went unheeded. This letter was followed up by another on February 28, 1966, from the presidente del comisariado ejidal of Santa Cecilia to the jefe de zona, requesting a resurvey of ejido boundaries to avoid conflicts with Santo Domingo Jalieza and San Pedro Guegorexe, since it had never been done and no one knew what the true boundaries were between these neighboring pueblos (ASRA: exp. 7, Aug. 3, 1964, and Feb. 28, 1966).

On June 1, 1966, a letter signed by all of the existing authorities in Santa Cecilia (agente municipal, comisariado ejidal, representante de bienes comunales, and alcalde) was submitted to the state governor, Lic. Brena Torres, and explained that on May 31 at 8 a.m., members of their ejido who were working in the fields were shot at by a group of thugs headed by Porfirio Vásquez Morales. The aggressors came to the outskirts of the community, shot at houses, and committed robberies of a number of cows and goats, which they took to Santo Domingo. These perpetrators were allegedly tied to another group of thugs residing in Santo Domingo, headed by Ángel Martínez y Palemón Salas, who had thirty armed men who allegedly committed constant outrages in Santa Cecilia (ASRA: exp. 7, June 1, 1966).

A letter to the governor, dated June 4, urgently requested a detachment of state police for Santa Cecilia to provide protection so that they could work on their ejido during a forthcoming planting of crops. It alleged victimization by a group of armed thugs led by Porfirio Vásquez Morales, now identified as having left Santa Cecilia to seek refuge in Santo Domingo (ASRA: exp. 7, June 4, 1966).

In an official roster of household heads for 1978, Porfirio Vásquez Morales was listed as a resident of Santa Cecilia; Ángel Martínez did not appear on either list, but Palemón Salas was listed as a resident of Santo Domingo. Salas was included in our household census of that community. He was fifty years old, born in Santo Domingo, married; had six household members and two years of elementary schooling; and was bilingual in Spanish and Zapotec. His principal occupation was campesino, and his secondary occupation was canastero; he possessed 3.7 hectares of arable land, 1.4 of which were privately owned. In short, a fairly typical peasant-artisan profile. Coincidentally, Porfirio Vásquez Morales, Salas's alleged associate, was also a canastero. As it turned out, both of them learned basket making as prisoners in the district jail in Ocotlán, where they were incarcerated for the 1960s banditry incidents described above (OVSIP archive).

The allegations made in the 1964 and 1966 documents reviewed above reinforced the thesis that land conflicts between these communities had internal ramifications. Santa Cecilia clearly had inhabitants with divided loyalties to factions either in San Juan Teitipac or in Santo Domingo Jalieza. During the period of local militias, apparently some Santa Cecilians were loyal to the cacique in San Juan Chilateca on the Ocotlán side of their corridor, and others were loyal to the Brito-Sumano nexus in the two other San Juans, Teitipac and Guelavía, on the Tlacolula side.

Land invasions and boundary conflicts plagued Santa Cecilia Jalieza during almost every decade of the twentieth century through the 1970s. This clearly contradicted a communication from an official of the Agrarian Reform office in Oaxaca City dated February 7, 1970, reminding Santa Cecilia authorities that their boundary problem with San Juan Teitipac had, in fact, been definitively resolved by the proceedings of 1943–1944, which found that "San Juan Teitipac had greater need for land and a larger number of household heads and that on the other hand, Santa Cecilia Jalieza already had been endowed with 620 hectares and had better-quality land available, and for that reason only 340 hectares were confirmed as indicated in the presidential resolution" (ASRA: exp. 7, Feb. 7, 1970).

This reminder fell on deaf ears, as demonstrated by a series of official correspondences from Santa Cecilia to Oaxaca City reporting "a conflict over boundaries with the neighbors of Santo Domingo Jalieza" (8/17/71); another citing "an attack with a firearm suffered by C. Pantaleón Martínez García and others by people from San Juan Teitipac" (4/15/77); still another reporting that grazing livestock from San Juan "constantly cause damage to their planted fields and other lands belonging to their ejido" (1/2/78); and, lastly, a report of "an invasion of the ejidos of Santa Cecilia by people from San Juan Teitipac" (9/15/78). The last document in Santa Cecilia's ASRA file was dated 10/1/79, and rather than conforming to the pattern of complaints regarding land invasions, it showed that the wheels of agrarian reform were still operative by confirming the distribution of "Certificados de Derechos Agrarios" in the ejido to twenty persons (ASRA: exp. 7).

## Conclusion: Defensas Sociales, Pistoleros, and Desmadre

Alan Knight (1999) has written provocatively about the postrevolutionary political culture of rural Mexico in the 1920s and 1930s as follows:

> Throughout the country, local "defence" forces (defensas sociales) proliferated. Formed in order to protect communities from "bandit" attack, which they sometimes did, the defensas sociales became key institutions of political socialization, promotion and struggle. Impres-

sive political careers . . . began in the rank of the defensas . . . Durable cacicazgos . . . similarly depended on control of the local defensa social, whose members were sometimes indistinguishable from the broader population of pistoleros (political hired guns) who surrounded local caciques. Not surprisingly, protagonists of this form of political domination were . . . rough, tough, political pachyderms. Allegations of illiteracy, brutality and immorality were legion. At the grassroots they practised a kind of hardball politics, política cochina. Local hardball involved recurrent use of force and intimidation: murders, ambushes and "punitive expeditions."[5]

In the Oaxaca Valley, one of the consequences of revolutionary activity initiated after 1910 was the dismantling of the jefe político system that operated from Mexico City to the state capital in Oaxaca City through district cabeceras like Tlacolula and Ocotlán and then down to local communities. This system was authoritarian and encompassed political, administrative, judicial, and police-military affairs. It took decades for central governmental authority to reemerge under the auspices of the Partido Revolucionario Institucional (PRI) after 1940. Until then, and even lingering into subsequent decades, a political culture of disorder (descontrol) prevailed that nurtured the rise to power of violent men whose schooling came from either prerevolutionary banditry or the agrarian revolution itself.

Intervillage land and boundary conflicts and intravillage feuds and factionalism (Dennis 1987), which in many cases like San Juan Teitipac and Santa Cecilia Jalieza had deep historical roots, were hijacked and reinvigorated by the policies and activities of a series of strongmen, or valientes, and their followers ("gentes" or "allegados"). The latter were, in effect, hired guns specialized in intimidation and extortion as well as theft (especially of farm animals and implements, crops, or anything of value that was portable). The seeds of dissension, mistrust, hatred, and law-by-vengeance sown during this period were still bearing fruit during the second half of the twentieth century in the districts of Tlacolula and Ocotlán—especially in the case of Santa Cecilia, San Juan, and the descendants of the peones/terrazgueros who worked for the Hacienda San Antonio Buenavista (some of whom either lived in or took up residence in San Sebastián Teitipac and San Juan Teitipac).

This process involved a temporary shift in the locus of de facto district political power away from the traditional cabeceras (which became ex-distritos) to surrogate towns: San Juan Guelavía in the case of Tlacolula, and San Juan Chilateca in the case of Ocotlán. Between 1928 and 1935 in the Tlacolula arm of the valley, this de facto power system operated around an ex-revolutionary general, Juan M. Brito, who settled in San Juan Guelavía after spending time in prison in Mexico City for counterrevolutionary activities. Through the mechanism of a central government–promulgated program of so-called rural or social defense, this ex-general established a series of alliances with valientes in several localities, including San Sebastián Teitipac, San Juan Teitipac, and Santa Cruz Papalutla; weapons were provided to participants in local militias, apparently through the military establishment but for a cash payment by participating villagers. The counterpart to this in the Ocotlán arm of the valley operated around Ángel Trápaga in San Juan Chilateca.

These two militias, together with another headed by Luis Pacheco in San Bartolo Coyotepec (see online *Enciclopedia de los municipios de México, Estado de Oaxaca, San Bartolo Coyotepec* under "Personajes Ilustres"), policed and contested each other for control of the corridor between the two valley arms that passed directly through Santa Cecilia Jalieza. The 1935 report quoted above indicated that Santa Cecilia belonged to the militias commanded by Ángel Trápaga, and my conversations with Marciano García Vásquez and others in Santa Cecilia confirmed this.

Based on fieldwork conducted in 1940 in the Oaxaca Valley, Bronislaw Malinowski and Julio De la Fuente made the following observations regarding the Tlacolula-Ocotlán corridor, including what they considered to be "perhaps the most sensational discovery we made during our research" (Drucker-Brown 1982, 93–94; cf. Malinowski and De la Fuente 1957, 58):

> The Cerro de Mantecón is interesting because it has the reputation—well deserved—of being a suitable place in which to ambush travellers. Only a year or two ago, a large herd of cattle driven from Ocotlán to Oaxaca was captured, the drivers beaten and sent home. Later on some of the stolen animals were found in a neighboring village—two in the house of the municipal president, one with the local judge, and three with the head of the Social Defense League, an organization for the maintenance of safety in the villages. Near that same village, local robbers engaged in a mutual vendetta. Several people were wounded, a woman killed. The killer then was run down, executed, his heart taken out and eaten with tortillas. (This was perhaps the most sensational discovery we made during our research. We will not analyse legal aspects of the case, or inquire whether the eating of the heart was a "survival" of some old sacrifice.)
>
> In general, safety on the roads in the whole district is a problem that still has to be solved by the authorities and the inhabitants. The region between Tlacolula and Ocotlán—and it was in this region

that the incidents mentioned here occurred—is regarded as one of the most enterprising in robbery, murder and vendettas. Some of the roads are "guarded" by members of the local Social Defense League (Defensa Social). This means that the brave local defenders, like medieval robber barons, hold up the travelers or merchants and exact a small tribute.

Malinowski and De la Fuente observed that "cattle magnate" Don Taurino Barriga, "even with several herdsmen, was unable to protect his property" from being stolen on the trek from Ocotlán as the herd passed near Cerro Mantecón. What Malinowski and De la Fuente may not have known, or at least did not write about, was that just a few kilometers to the east of that cerro was Hacienda San Antonio Buenavista, owned by Barriga at the time of the cattle-rustling incident, and the notoriously conflictive area of Rancho Guelaviate, San Juan Teitipac, and Santa Cecilia Jalieza from which Barriga recruited henchmen and ranch hands like the Sumanos to work for him and "protect" his interests. Although the defensas sociales had been officially disarmed and disbanded by the time the Cerro Mantecón incident occurred, it is clear that armed violence continued to plague people living in communities east of Cerro Mantecón or passing northward or southward through the corridors connecting the Tlacolula and Ocotlán arms of the Oaxaca Valley.[6]

## CHAPTER 9

# Magdalena Ocotlán:

# From Terrazgueros to

# Artisanal Ejidatarios

Magdalena Ocotlán qualifies for the dubious distinction of being among a handful of Zapotec communities in the Oaxaca Valley that failed to preserve their territorial integrity and economic independence throughout the colonial period (Taylor 1972, 8), with the proviso that its preconquest and early colonial history is murky. It was among thirty pueblos in the Oaxaca Valley mentioned in a 1776–1777 document as having a fundo legal (Méndez Martínez 1983, 96). Oral history suggests that it originated in the colonial period as a congregation of Coatecans. Whatever its origin, the pueblo fell victim to the consolidation of the region's largest hacienda complex, San José La Garzona–El Vergel, at the end of the eighteenth century, relegating most Magdalenans to the status of landless terrazgueros (sharecroppers/tenant cultivators).[1]

Magdalena entered the twentieth century as a municipio with a council of five members, one of whom was designated as president and the others as regidores and síndicos. These officials were elected yearly by male voters twenty-one years of age and older (eighteen years of age or older if married). This was in accordance with the liberal Constitution of 1857; after 1863, the office of alcalde was also added.

Magdalena emerged relatively unaffected by the disentailment laws of 1857 formulated to privatize communal land and redistribute private land, since it had already been reduced to the boundaries of its fundo legal by the expansion of Hacienda San José (Bailón Corres 1999, 129–140, 144–145). As of 1910, surrounded on all sides by the Hacienda San José, Magdalena still had a small degree of autonomy exercised through its local government and grounded in private and communal landholdings adjacent to its habitation area (see Bailón Corres 1999, 155). This autonomy had relatively little effect on the landless majority of Magdalenans who were sharecroppers on hacienda land.

The agrarian reform and the establishment of the ejido in the 1920s and 1930s transformed and complicated Magdalena's civil-religious organization, and set in place an institutional basis for conflict between the relatively few small private landowners (pequeños propietarios) who controlled local affairs through the community council (ayuntamiento) during the Porfiriato. To a significant extent, their influence carried over into the new ejido regime. Most, if not all, local private landowners and merchants also became ejidatarios and became more prosperous through the inequitable ejido allotment process.

The influence of the landowning class fraction was dampened by the empowerment of the previously landless majority of ex-terrazgueros, many of whom for the first time were given access to land to cultivate without being shackled to an externally imposed and confiscatory sharecropping system. Since the ejido was directly connected to the central government in Mexico City, albeit through a regional bureaucracy, and had a privileged place in the postrevolutionary rural development program of the federal government, it opened new channels of political relations and communication in communities like Magdalena. This diluted the authority of the municipal government because there was a new competitive local player, namely, the comisariado (commissariat or the local ejido authority).[2]

In the pre-ejido period, land conflicts were between Madgalena's pequeños propietarios, or between Magdalenans (as pequeños propietarios and comuneros) and non-Magdalenans, including the behemoth Hacienda San José. Such conflicts were resolved by local municipal authorities, sometimes aided by district political authorities. In the post-ejido period, by contrast, land conflicts were between ejidatarios and pequeños propietarios, or between Magdalena's ejidatarios and those of neighboring communities, and were resolved at the local and regional levels mainly through the ejido system.

When an internal dispute occurred between a pequeño propietario and an ejidatario, both sets of community authorities were involved in its resolution. Also, damages to crops by animals owned by Magdalenans, regardless of whether the lands involved were ejido or pequeña propiedad, were handled by municipal authorities (presidente municipal, alcalde, and síndico). In short, whereas the majority of Magdalena's households were empowered and benefited economically by the ejido, their lives were also complicated by new obligations as ejidatarios, including new rules and regulations for economic conduct, superimposed upon persisting "usos y costumbres" or traditional modes of community service (Cook 2004, 187–188).

Life for Magdalenans as ejidatarios was immeasurably better than it had been when they were terrazgueros under the hacienda regime. As ejidatarios, regulated individual usufruct of ejido land made it possible for them to cultivate crops for their own use and to participate in the market system with cash crops as well as with products of their work in stone quarries. It also provided them with the means to participate more fully in civil and religious activities associated with the rights and duties of community citizenship, including posts in local government, sponsorship of mayordomías and other festive celebrations, and membership in cofradías. Low-asset households sometimes suffered financial setbacks or worse in their struggle to participate according to the local rules of civility and ejido governance.

At the level of intercommunity relations, the ejido system seemed to function well to resolve conflicts with neighboring ejido communities. This was in marked contrast to the situation in communities like San Sebastián and San Juan Teitipac where communal and private land tenure regimes and non-ejido governing organizations predominated, and where peace-keeping required the intervention of state or federal authorities.

Through the ejido system, Magdalenans were able to get help in constructing a dam and irrigation canals to irrigate a portion of their ejido. Most households included ejidatarios who had allotments of irrigated land, but allotments were unequally distributed among ejidatarios. Agricultural credit was also available through ejidal banks but, again, with uneven results and with a relatively low degree of meeting repayment schedules. Unquestionably, the most successful ejidatarios were those who astutely managed crop selection and market participation and who fared better in the land-allotment process. In short, this chapter provides real-life evidence of the struggle for economic well-being and civility in an ejido community.

## An Excursion through the Past

The earliest historical reference to Magdalena was in a 1695 document addressing a land dispute between the community of San Pedro Apóstol and Hacienda El Vergel in which it was alleged that Don Pedro de la Vega, the hacendado, attempted to take over a sitio known as Romanolópez, "between the settlement of San Pedro and Magdalena" (AGNT: vol. 1901, exp. 11, fol. 2v). Vega, an alférez (lieutenant), built two jacales, grazed cattle, and prevented Indians from grazing their cattle on that site. In a 1737 document addressing the same dispute, it was alleged that Vega built jacales on Lachiasoo (a paraje that became La Chilana, on the northern boundary of Magdalena) that delimited boundaries along the camino real from Magdalena to San Martín de los Cansecos. It was also noted that the "hacienda de San Joseph" was on the eastern boundary and that the boundary of Magdalena became higher along the dividing line (la línea divisora) between its lands and those of Hacienda San José (AGNT: vol. 1901, exp. 11, fol. 14).

The corregidor de Antequera made an invidious comparison between this case and another in Etla to express his bias against Indian witnesses. The Etla case had twelve witnesses, the majority of whom were Indians, whereas the case brought by San Pedro Apóstol against Don Pedro de la Vega had one mulato and "nine Spaniards, men of quality," who "have a clearer and firmer knowledge of the disputed lands because several of them are owners of the said San Joseph and El Vergel haciendas, others are their overseers and administrators, and others rent or live on or near these lands." Since most of the Spaniards were "well known as men of truth, integrity, and esteem," the corregidor reasoned, the evidence in this case, in comparison with the Etla case with a majority of Indian witnesses, was "better and more worthy of credit" (AGNT: vol. 1901, exp. 11, fol. 58v–59r; cf. Taylor 1972, 109). San Pedro Apóstol was among the largest landholding Indian communities in the southern arm of the Oaxaca Valley (ibid., 98). Even though San Pedro may have had an indigenous majority, at some point it fell under the control of resident Spaniards, including members of the Santibáñez family who were prominent there in the nineteenth and twentieth centuries.[3]

In the 1746 *Relación de Antequera*, "La Magdalena" is referred to as a "subaltern settlement" (pueblo subalterno) of San Pedro Apóstol, which was a "cabecera de doctrina" (parish headquarters) with a resident priest ("un Cura Religioso Domínico"; Welte 1973, 13, 14). Francisco Cosme, presidente municipal, summarized the local oral history version of Magdalena's origin without reference to the preconquest period. The settlement was founded as a "congregación" of Zapotec-speaking people who lived originally in the Coatecas region in the mountains to the south of Hacienda San José. The congregation grew up around a church. Cosme's account is quite plausible, considering the pre-1615 origin of the hacienda (license issued for Mass to be said in the hacienda chapel by 1616; Taylor 1972, 214) and given the location of the Coatecas region only 20 or so kilometers directly to the south of the hacienda.[4]

Hacienda San José, according to Cosme, originated as two sitios de ganado mayor that expanded their landholdings and operations at the expense of the congregation of Magdalena. The hacendados of San José invaded and expropriated communal lands that were located east of the pueblo. These lands were never legally acquired by the hacienda. Lands to the south and west of Magdalena were legally acquired by Hacienda El Vergel of Ejutla. They extended up to San Matías Chilazoa and La Chilana to the north of

Magdalena, as well as to La Noria and Monte de Toro to the south. All of the ejido lands expropriated from Hacienda San José by the twentieth-century agrarian reform were located across the Ocotlán–Ejutla road to the east of Magdalena's residential area (see Map 5).

Hacienda San José originated as two sitios de ganado mayor held by the cacique of Ocotlán in 1615 and grew through a process of sale, resale, and consolidation. There were a total of eleven separate transactions prior to its acquisition by a secular priest, Gerónimo Morales Sigala, who already owned the Hacienda El Vergel and one other, in 1738. The "priestly hacendado" sold Hacienda San José in 1742, and it was sold three more times until purchased in 1766 by José Mariano de Mimiaga (Taylor 1972, 192, 214–215).

Already one of the largest estates in the Oaxaca Valley in 1766, San José encompassed seven estancias de ganado mayor y menor and two small agricultural estates (labores) equivalent to 20,000–30,000 acres. It became the largest estate after the Mimiaga family consolidated it with Hacienda El Vergel, which apparently had been rented out for a period after 1740 (Taylor 1972, 123, 162). As it turned out, the Mimiaga family retained ownership of Hacienda San José La Garzona until the agrarian reform process redistributed much of it to its terrazgueros, including those in Magdalena.

In 1798 and 1799, the Mimiaga family asked the Real Audiencia "for the reconstruction of the boundary markers which had been destroyed and which had delimited the boundaries between their land and those of Magdalena Ocotlán" (ASRA: doc. 28:2). It may be that Magdalena lost its communal lands over time through underhanded sales or legally sanctioned confiscation before the Mimiaga family's ownership began in 1766. If not, it surely did so as a result of the process culminating in the Mimiaga-sponsored judicial initiative.

By 1850, Magdalena was not a closed community, given its location on the main road between Oaxaca City and Ejutla/Miahuatlán at the junction of the road to Hacienda San José Progreso and its mines. The first accurate map of Oaxaca's central valleys region, published in 1848, showed that the main road bypassed Ocotlán and, instead, went through Santa Ana Zegache, San Pedro Apóstol, Magdalena, and San Martín de los Cansecos (Ortega 1848). The same map also showed a spur road from Magdalena to Ocotlán de Morelos.

Its proximity to a mining hacienda, a main road, and a railway lent Magdalena a greater degree of accessibility and openness than more isolated Zapotec-speaking communities like San Sebastián Teitipac and San Juan Teitipac, and the Jalieza communities of Santo Domingo and Santa Cecilia. This was reflected in landownership patterns where nonresidents, mostly residents of contiguous ranchos like La Chilana and Rancho Los Vásquez, owned several hectares of private land in Magdalena. At least since 1880 when Nabor Martínez, a metatero from San Juan Teitipac, moved in with a widow in Magdalena, the community had some nonnative residents, both men and women, either from nearby communities like San Pedro Apóstol, San José Progreso, and Asunción or more distant communities like Coatecas Altas. In the 1960s, however, only one of every six households surveyed had either a household head or a spouse in this category; and our 1979 random sample survey of thirty-seven households found only four.

In 1885, the struggle of Magdalena against the hacienda regime entered the public record in litigation filed by the hacendado Manuel María Mimiaga y Camacho regarding boundaries with Magdalena (Esparza 1991a, 165, citing AGEO 1885, Leg. 72, exp. 16, 70ff.). Also, in 1905 a dispute arose between San Pedro Apóstol and Magdalena when San Pedro tried to expropriate land in Santa Magdalena in order to obtain a source of water (un manantial de agua; Esparza 1991a, 165, citing a one-page AGEO document, "San Pedro Apóstol, 1905," Leg. 72, exp. 17).

This was followed by 1912 litigation initiated by Magdalena against Hacienda San José complaining that the hacendado had not only dispossessed them of their lands but impeded their access to pastures for their animals, to the montes to cut wood, and to quarries to extract stone for metates that they manufactured. Mimiaga was notorious as a supporter of heavy-handed tactics (mano dura) to deal with assertive terrazgueros, and he prescribed either expulsion from hacienda lands or forced conscription into the army. Mimiaga's punishments included the hanging of one of his San José terrazgueros from a tree on that property (Ruiz Cervantes 1988, 353, citing documents in AGEO, Secretaría de Gobierno, Abusos de autoridad, "Ocotlán, 1912," leg. 45, exp. 21, 5 fojas).

The 1910 census included the 150 residents of two ranching communities, La Chilana and Los Vásquez, within the Magdalena population, and they were lumped together with Magdalenans on the original petition for restitution, an error that was corrected in the second petition for a grant (dotación; ASRA, exp. 14, doc. 28:5). Also, a resident of San José Progreso had a total of six teams of oxen rented out to Magdalenans on an "a maíz" basis, and received 4 fanegas of corn from each harvest per team. This suggested that several ex-terrazgueros in Magdalena, more than forty years after becoming ejidatarios, were still unable to break dependency relations emanating from the ex-hacienda.

The main highway south from Oaxaca City did not bypass San Pedro Apóstol until the early 1940s, when it was rerouted to pass directly from Ocotlán to Magdalena. There was also a railroad line (El Ferrocarril Mexicano del Sur) from Oaxaca City to Ejutla that passed through Ocotlán and

Magdalena during the late nineteenth century, but it was apparently abandoned during the revolution (Museo del Ferrocarril Mexicano del Sur,
Oaxaca, www.paginasprodigy.com). For miners and others working in San
José, Magdalena was strategically positioned as the nearest settlement to the
gates of Hacienda San José. Several Magdalena merchants took advantage of
this and operated businesses catering to people on the move.

José María Santiago, born in 1899, shared some vivid memories of life
and work in Magdalena during early transitional decades of the twentieth
century, which, among other themes, highlighted the commercial relationship with Hacienda San José. His uncle operated a store that did business
with San José mine workers. He slaughtered beef and hogs, made sausage,
baked bread, and sold mezcal, tepache, pulque, and beer. Travelers going
to Miahuatlán and Oaxaca were also customers there, since it was near the
main road. According to José María, fifty to sixty wagons (carretas) pulled
up to the store every day and bought fodder (zacate) along with other items.
The store had a cantina that operated all night long. People would come
there to have breakfast, lunch, and dinner. There was a corral for burros,
oxen, and horses, and travelers could also get lodging there.

José María claimed that the hacendado, Don Manuel Mimiaga, did not
allow people living and working at the hacienda to buy or sell liquor. Consequently, every Sunday a lot of mine workers from San José came to Magdalena to drink in one of seven taverns and cantinas.

This bustling commerce came to a halt during the Mexican Revolution.
One of the early violent encounters between Magdalenans and the hacendado's wardens involved women working in the fields who wielded machetes
and sticks to resist wardens' aggressions. José María explained that the ensuing dispute between Magdalena and San José led to the shutdown of the
mine. Everything came to a halt, and people no longer came to Magdalena.
Bullets started flying. More than one hundred Zapatistas came to Magdalena in 1912 and proclaimed that they were going to finish off the haciendas.
Magdalenans joined the Zapatistas and took out their weapons, but they
didn't have enough. Don Manuel and his guardamontes had more weapons
and they won.

Afterward, since Don Manuel was a member of the legislature (diputado)
in Oaxaca, fifty soldiers were sent to punish Magdalenans for the uprising.
Many were forced to abandon the pueblo and ended up in Pluma Hidalgo.
They were eventually rounded up and imprisoned in Oaxaca City. One of
José María's uncles was presidente municipal in 1912 and was jailed for
taking up arms. When Carranza took power, many Magdalenas left to fight
for him. José María's mother died when he was seven years old and his father left Magdalena after her death, so he was orphaned and raised by rela-

tives. His father, a soldier who had fought with Pancho Villa and later joined Carranza, came back to Magdalena with the Carrancistas from Pochutla in 1916.

## The Agrarian Struggle

Between 1911 and 1915, Magdalenans were at war with the hacendado and his guardamontes (wardens). After one failed attack on the hacienda, many Magdalenans took refuge in San Vicente Coatlán but were apprehended by the authorities and imprisoned in Ocotlán. Magdalenans were among an early wave of dispossessed pueblos to file petitions for restitution of their ancestral lands with the Comisión Local Agraria just three months after its establishment by the state government (Ruiz Cervantes 1988, 390). Complaints filed in 1912 were successfully contested by the hacendado and rejected by the Agrarian Commission. The 1912 initiative set a precedent for Magdalena's filing of a land restitution petition dated November 6, 1916, demanding a return (reivindicación) of their ejido land that had been taken by Hacienda San José La Garzona prior to 1791. They sought a restoration of boundaries to conform with their property titles, extending to a point bordering San Pedro Mártir, to the north; Haciendas El Vergel and San José La Garzona, to the south; Hacienda San José, to the east; and Rancho San Matías, to the west. The 1916 petition was also unsuccessful.

In 1919, Magdalena changed tactics and solicited restitution of land from the hacienda San José La Garzona in accordance with the law of January 6, 1915, but the "antiguos terrazgueros" saw themselves in conflict with Magdalena, which did not want to give them lands (Esparza 1991a, 165, citing AGEO file "Magdalena, 1919," Leg. 72, exp. 18, 12ff.). This protest from the "antiguos terrazgueros" caused a reduction in the definitive dotación, signed by President Álvaro Obregón on February 3, 1921, by moving the boundaries of Magdalena's land back from the main gate in a westerly direction. The 1919 sketch map by a government surveyor (Map 5) outlined the ejido as originally proposed, an irregular quadrangular footprint (large broken line) that nearly touches the hacienda at boundary marker 18 (Ojo de Agua) and included some land to the east of the main Ocotlán–Ejutla road, and also drew the alternative positioning (small dotted lines), a rectangular footprint to the northwest of the hacienda proper and mostly west of the Ocotlán–Ejutla road. The final dotación footprint, shown in Map 6, was a compromise of the 1919 sketches, with the eastern boundary angled to avoid passing through the yard of the hacienda casco but still including land east of the Ocotlán–Ejutla highway.

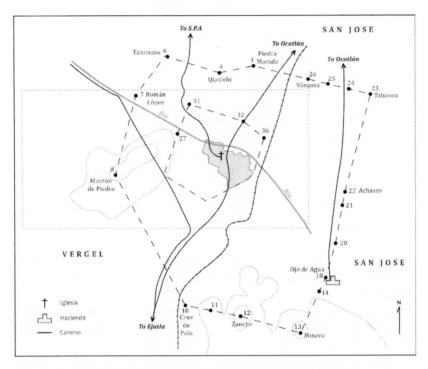

MAP 5. **Pre-dotación (1919) Surveyor's Sketch Map of Magdalena Ocotlán Ejido**

Prior to the implementation of agrarian reform, Hacienda San José had 5,500 hectares, 1,500 of which were planted mostly in corn with some alverja (peas), frijol, and garbanzo, and 4,000 were in pasture. According to the Solicitud de Dotación document (ASRA: exp. 14, doc. 15:7), the system of exploitation was sharecropping (aparcería), arranged under contracts that were very unfavorable to the worker, who paid out all kind of expenses and had to hand over, according to the class of land cultivated, one-third, one-fourth, or one-fifth of the harvest, in the form of dehusked ears of corn, placed in the granaries of the hacienda. The sharecropper was permitted to plant only white corn, and was prohibited from planting beans and squash together with corn.

The classification of land to set share percentages was done by the hacienda foreman (mandador) without the participation of sharecroppers. This practice resulted in the poorest-quality land parcels being cultivated by sharecroppers at the highest customary rate of 50 percent (el medio) and the best-quality parcels being cultivated at lower rates of 20 percent (el partido) or 33 percent (el tercio). Therefore, the hacendado's total share of harvests was maximized: 50 percent shares on the most productive parcels and either 80 percent or 67 percent shares on the least productive parcels assured this outcome. Sharecroppers probably considered themselves to be better off as medieros (halves sharers) than as tercieros (thirds sharers) or sharers al partido (fifths sharers). Nevertheless, the quantity and quality of the sharecroppers' shares of a harvest was always considerably below those of the hacendados (cf. Chassen-López 2004, 107). Sharecroppers lived in their native pueblos, or in five or six ranchos on the land of the hacienda. They were obliged to pay rent for their housing (piso). Given the fact that Magdalenans had possession of their fundo legal, which included arable and communal land, they were certainly better off than sharecropping rancheros residing on hacienda land.

Bordering Magdalena to the west, was Hacienda El Vergel, owned at the time of the agrarian reform by two Spaniards, the brothers Rogelio and Celestino Gómez. The casco of the hacienda itself, and much of its land, was within the jurisdiction of the district of Ejutla; it had 11,000 hectares prior to the agrarian reform expropriations that began in 1918. More than half of El Vergel's land was either pasture or uncultivated (eriazo), and the same crops were cultivated there as at San José.

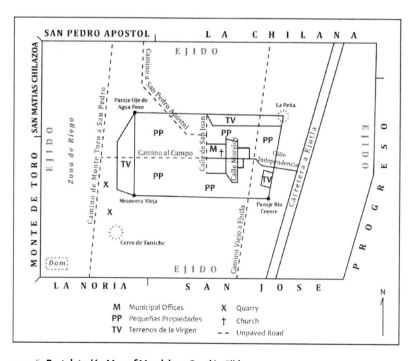

MAP 6. **Post-dotación Map of Magdalena Ocotlán Ejido**

Magdalena's dotación document contended that working conditions at El Vergel were somewhat less unfavorable for the workers than they were at San José. This may have been true before the agrarian reform movement took hold but was patently untrue afterward, as demonstrated by a shocking record of systematic violence—including lynchings, pillage, rape, and arson—perpetrated by the Gómez brothers for over a decade against the seven communities bordering it on its Ocotlán side who petitioned for dotaciones, the so-called Los Ocotes, which included Magdalena (Arellanes Meixueiro 1999, 35–39). An official communication of March 1931, addressed to multiple governmental authorities and signed with the thumbprints of eighty-one ejidatarios representing these communities, dramatically protested against the hacendados' terror campaign (ibid., 39).

Magdalena was the third of the petitioning communities to receive the benefits of their agrarian reform initiative; in 1921, it was granted 534 hectares from Hacienda San José La Garzona and 566 hectares from El Vergel for a total of 1,100 hectares. This was in addition to 287 hectares belonging to Magdalena prior to the agrarian reform: 50 hectares was occupied by the caserío, or habitation area; 60 hectares was cultivable land available to all households (this may have been the fundo legal); and 177 hectares was owned by eleven "pequeños terratenientes," which suggested that Magdalena was by no means strictly a poverty-stricken and egalitarian community of terrazgueros at the onset of the revolution there in 1912.

In 1921, Magdalena had a total of 641 inhabitants, 140 households, and 173 peasant cultivators. The Censo Agrario taken in September 1917 that served as a basis for the presidential resolution of endowment (la Resolución Presidencial Dotatoria) of February 3, 1921, listed 140 names, including seventeen women who were either widows (seven) or single. Only nine persons in the census, all males, were listed as married. A church wedding with an accompanying fandango entailed expenditures beyond the means of most households. Most of the ejidatarios whose civil status was designated single (soltero or soltera) were likely involved in a consensual conjugal relationship (unión libre).

According to estimates made by the Local Agrarian Commission (Comisión Local Agraria), which matched subsistence needs to average yields of shelled corn, the ejido's 94 hectares of first-class land was enough for 31 ejidatarios; 379 hectares of second-class land was enough for 76 ejidatarios; and the remaining 402 hectares of third-class land, combined with the 60 hectares of land from the prereform period, was sufficient for 66 additional ejidatarios. The remaining ejido allotment of 208 hectares was classified as nonagricultural communal land (ASRA: 1920, exp. 14).

A 1922 questionnaire (ASRA: doc. 35) signed by the presiding president of the Comité Particular Administrativo, Jacinto Hernández, classified the 1,100 hectares of ejido somewhat differently: 152 hectares, de humedad (meaning in normal rainfall years, no irrigation required); 47 hectares, second class; 351 hectares, third class; 300 hectares, uncultivated pasture (pastal sin cultivo); and 250 hectares, uncultivated (eriazo). He estimated that the average amount of seed corn required per hectare was 15 liters costing 23 pesos, and that the anticipated annual yield for all ejido land under cultivation was 20,000 liters of hulled corn with a market price of 4 centavos per liter.

Unfortunately, Magdalena's agrarian records lacked information regarding the actual process of land allotment to ejidatarios. I did not find any censuses from the period 1921 to 1962 that contained information about each household, specifying the amount of allotment land planted and corresponding corn yields. Such censuses were available for 1964 and 1966, but they lacked specific data regarding the location and class of parcels under cultivation by the listed ejidatarios.

Some thirteen Magdalenans at the time of the revolution owned all of the private lands within the fundo legal of the community, which also included the habitation area and three parcels of communal land referred to as "terrenos de la Virgen." Some of these individuals also had businesses such as stores, cantinas, and a molino de *nixtamal*. There is no basis for considering any of them to have been terrazgueros of the Hacienda San José. The two most prominent members of this elite group, Pedro González and José María Sánchez, did participate in the agrarian reform movement to the extent that they were listed in the Censo Agrario of 1917, which served as a basis for the grant made in 1921. In other words, they became founding members of the ejido and, therefore, as ejidatarios, were eligible to receive allotments from the land expropriated from the two contiguous haciendas, El Vergel and San José. Most of the other small landowners followed the same pattern and also received ejido allotments.

Despite incomplete records for the 1920s and 1930s, the allotment process in Magdalena experienced problems like those reported in the neighboring community of San Pedro Apóstol. The Comité Agrario was accused of assigning to themselves the best and largest land parcels (Arellanes Meixueiro 1999, 231). It was quite common for ejidos in the Oaxaca Valley to have internal conflicts due to inequitable and arbitrary distribution of parcels (ibid.).

Francisco Cosme said that Magdalena's "título" had caused a lot of bloodshed after it mysteriously disappeared from the municipal archive in 1930. An outgoing municipal president was accused of stealing it, causing the community to split into two factions. One faction was headed by José María

Sánchez, who by 1930 controlled a substantial share of the 177 hectares of pequeñas propiedades that only a decade earlier were distributed among eleven "pequeños terratenientes." According to Cosme, Sánchez had an annual harvest of more than 100 carretas of corn and owned several lots in the pueblo and two houses in Ocotlán.

The other faction was headed by Pedro González, who also acquired several parcels of private land from an absentee owner. This was not to Sánchez's liking, so when Sánchez's father-in-law was municipal president, he accused González of having orchestrated the disappearance of the land title, presumably to open up the possibility of acquiring additional land. At the time, a clairvoyant (suarín) was imported from Miahuatlán in a desperate attempt to find the lost title, needless to say without success. Sánchez and González were included in the Censo Agrario of 1917, which was used as a basis for the 1921 Resolución Presidencial Dotatoria; Pedro González was a twenty-four-year-old soltero, and José María Sánchez, also a soltero, was forty-six years old.[5]

González was subsequently murdered, which unleashed a cycle of vengeance killings between factions that resulted in a decline of Magdalena's population through a combination of homicide and emigration. Among the victims of the feud was González's son. Resolution of the feud required the intervention of external authorities, with each faction having a court-appointed representative who was held accountable for any misbehavior by his constituency. As it turned out, the Sánchez faction emerged less damaged by the feud, as reflected in the fact that in 1967, Elías Sánchez Cosme, José María's surviving son, retained a sizable portion of his father's landholdings, amounting to 15 hectares that yielded an annual harvest of 60 almudes on a sharecrop basis. Elías also became the owner of the community's only molino de *nixtamal*.[6]

In 1967, Elías lodged a formal complaint with agrarian authorities over a survey of the boundaries between the ejido and private parcels (pequeñas propiedades), including one measuring 420 x 110 x 100 x 126 meters that he acquired in 1944 from his father, José María (ASRA, exp. 14, March 6). The complaint alleged that surveyors had damaged a planting of plantains and that the survey itself incorrectly resulted in a reduction in the size of Elías's parcel (me despojaron de una faja de terreno). An investigation of the complaint, led by the jefe de zona, found that the alleged damages had, in fact, occurred before the survey began and were caused by grazing animals. On-site investigation also confirmed that a portion of Sánchez's parcel measuring approximately .25 hectare was within the boundaries of the ejido (está enclavada dentro del ejido), and should be reclaimed as such (ASRA, exp. 14, Acta de Investigación, April 5).

Eliseo Méndez, head of the ejido authority, proposed that Sánchez's possession of the disputed parcel be respected on the condition that he recognize that the land in question legally belonged to the ejido, and that, as an ejidatario, he would be subject to all the regulations of the prevailing agrarian code. Sánchez responded that he was not interested in being an ejidatario, since he purchased the land fair and square as confirmed by the bill of sale. He appealed the decision with the intent of retaining ownership of the entire parcel.

Elías Sánchez's father, José María, was on the list of dotación petitioners and, therefore, eligible to receive allotments as an ejidatario, but I found no evidence that he actually received any. Elías, who was entitled to inherit use rights over allotments made to his father, was not listed in ejidatario rolls in 1944 or in those in the 1960s, so he was never officially an ejidatario.

## The Ejido, Land Use, and Agriculture in the 1960s and 1970s

Map 6 of the territorial jurisdiction of the municipality in 1967 gives a bird's-eye view of how the agrarian reform transformed the fundo legal of "La Magdalena" from a terrazguero community enclaved within contiguous haciendas into an ejidatario community surrounded on all sides by ejido tracts. The ejido tracts to the north and east, covering 534 hectares, which were expropriated from Hacienda San José, combined with those to the south and west that were expropriated from Hacienda El Vergel, dwarf the 287 hectares of the fundo legal (caserío plus pequeñas propiedades plus terrenos del santo).

Map 6 and Map 7 also show Magdalena's habitation area very close to the highway and laid out along a main street (Calle Independencia) running east to west in an elongated block pattern, with the plaza containing the church, school, and government buildings located at its western terminus, differing markedly from the classic grid pattern of settlement. A section of the habitation area known as Detrás del Río is located north of Arroyo Santa Rosa (see Map 7). Even though separated from the rest of the habitation area by an arroyo and on somewhat higher ground, this neighborhood was part of the original fundo legal and pequeñas propiedades.

Detrás del Río had a higher water table than the rest of the community, which allowed every solar in this section to have its own well (pozo), whereas this was relatively uncommon in the main part of the village where households drew their water from one of three public wells. Some wells in the Detrás del Río section were used for pot irrigation, and several households cultivated portions of their residence lots that tended to be quite large.

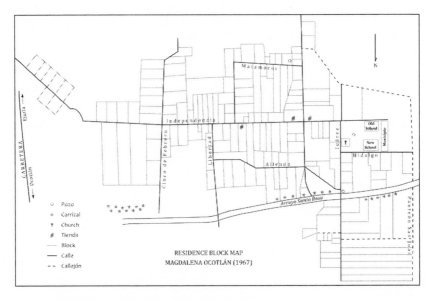

MAP 7.  **1967 Block and Street Map of Magdalena Ocotlán**

The frequency distribution of land cultivated by household in Magdalena, according to our 1979 survey, had a bimodal pattern: 48.6 percent of households fell within the range of 1.1–3.0 hectares of land worked, whereas 37.1 percent were in the range of 4.1 hectares and higher.

A 1966 government survey of 175 ejidatarios of land cultivated presented a somewhat more equal distribution slightly skewed toward the 1.1–2.0 range (32.3 percent), but the combined ranges of 2.1–3.0 (22.7 percent) and 3.1–4.0 (22.1 percent) accounted for nearly half of all households. This more equal distribution among ejidatarios was probably reflective of the fact that our 1979 survey included private landholdings as well as ejido holdings, whereas the 1966 census was limited to ejido holdings. It is noteworthy that Magdalena ranked first among ten communities surveyed in the district of Ocotlán in amount of land cultivated per household (mean 3.22 hectares, median 3.00 hectares).[7]

Estimates for variables like availability of cultivable land and land under cultivation per household can be misleading due to the underlying dependence of agriculture in Magdalena on rainfall—especially before the mid-1960s when a government irrigation project was completed. A September 1962 report from community authorities to the state governor highlighted the pitfalls of its agricultural sector caused by lack of rainfall or sporadic rainfall and resulting in crop losses. The purpose of this report (Informe de la Pérdida de Cosecha de Maíz y Frijol) was to request a suspension or reduction in land taxes (contribuciones prediales) for that year.

The most striking pattern regarding land use in Magdalena's ejido was that even in parajes that appeared to have predominantly cultivable land and uniform topsoil, there were fallow areas and areas still covered with brush (monte). The latter areas were usually baldío or land still not assigned to particular ejidatarios, whereas fallow land was possessed by an ejidatario who did not necessarily plant crops every year. Some third-class land that would have been suitable for planting seasonally remained uncleared.

One day in 1968, I accompanied Fernando Rosario to one of his plots located in an area of irrigation just north of the dam; he pointed across a nearby arroyo in a westerly direction and explained that Magdalenans only a few years ago began clearing a large tract of their ejido there to prevent the neighboring communities of La Noria and San Matías from seeking to lay claim to it with district ejido officials. My impression in the 1960s was that there was no absolute land scarcity in Magdalena, but there was inequality in ownership and access.

The paraje system described in Chapter 1 for San Sebastián Teitipac was also part of Magdalena's culture. The three quarry areas were in parajes denominated Piedra de Canoa, Piedra de la Cruz, and Mina del Santo, which were all located in the area north of Cerro de Taniche and west of Mojonera Vieja designated by "X" on Map 6. Four prominent parajes are located at the corners demarcating the fundo legal and ejido from pequeña propiedad: La Peña (NE corner), Río Coyote (SE corner), Mojonera Vieja (SW corner), and Ojo de Agua (NW corner; see Map 6). The large agricultural paraje on ejido lands lying to the northwest of the pueblo was known as La Chilana. Reeds (carrizo), corn, beans, squash, sugarcane, and alfalfa were growing in this paraje in August 1967. Many ejido lands lying across the highway to the east of the pueblo were in a paraje called La Raya de San José. Several parajes were named after prevailing geographic features like Arroyo Largo, Bajo de Tierra Salitrosa, Las Charcas, and Loma de San Juan, and others after human-made features like Detrás de la Presa, La Pila, and La Estación. Several parajes were named after native trees: Nogal de la Carretera, Debajo del Higo, Los Nogales, Monte de Higo, and Huamuche Arriba.

In late January 1968, I spoke with Benigno Aquino on his plot in La Chilana, where he had sugarcane planted on one-half of his plot and corn on the other. He commented that he planned to dig a well on one corner of his plot the next month to plant alfalfa where he had planted corn before. The plot measured 130 x 18 meters. In 1960, Benigno planted half of the plot (65 x 18 meters) in sugarcane (17 rows); he planted corn every year on the other half (34 rows). His average annual yield was 6 meters of cane (measured according to oxcart capacity of 1 cubic meter) and 2 fanegas (50 almudes) of shelled corn. In 1967, he sold his cane for 50 pesos per meter and also harvested 100 manojos of zacate worth 50 centavos each and 100 manojos of cogollo worth 25 centavos each. This gave him gross earnings of 375 pesos. The other half of his plot yielded 2 fanegas of corn valued at 100 pesos each, plus 30 tercios of zacate (50 centavos each) and 10 pesos' worth of *totomoxtle*, giving him gross earnings of 270 pesos. He spent 75 pesos on corn cultivation (rayar, sembrada, deshierbo, pisca), and 80 pesos on cane (cutting and hauling only). His lower return on corn cultivation convinced him to change to alfalfa, which he would use to fatten cattle and hogs. His well would be dug to a depth of 4–6 meters, since this land had a relatively high water table. He would also replant sugarcane and would use the new well to irrigate both crops.

Agricultural work that could not be done by household members unassisted was usually performed by hired workers rather than through reciprocal labor. Our 1979 survey did not find one household that participated in agricultural work on a reciprocal basis, but 19 percent participated in wage labor, both as employers and employees, during the previous annual agricultural cycle. Three households worked more than 98 days on that basis, one more than 72 days, and three worked for between 15 and 24 days on a wage basis.

There were occasions, however, when reciprocal labor was used during the agricultural cycle. On August 31, 1967, I accompanied Atanasio Hernández to the residence lot of his father-in-law, Simón Sánchez, to go with them to their fields for the corn harvest. Atanasio's wife, Eulalia, had gone to her father's solar earlier to help prepare the breakfast that was eaten prior to their departure for the fields. Atanasio's brother-in-law, Germán Rosario, who lived in a separate household on Simón's solar, was also included in the work group. As it turned out, the picking was done mostly by Atanasio and Germán; Simón was nearby but spent as much time pasturing the oxen as he did picking. Atanasio considered this as a *guelaguetza* arrangement between him, his father-in-law, and his brother-in-law, since it was understood that they would help Atanasio harvest his own field during that same harvest season. Atanasio noted that his father-in-law would probably reciprocate by allowing him to use his yunta and carreta.

If reciprocal labor was relatively uncommon in Magdalena agriculture, communal or tequio labor was the order of the day on the school parcel (parcela escolar) and the church parcel (terrenos del santo). The school parcel covered 2 hectares that were planted in corn and beans. It had soil classified as third class and thin, which, under conditions of normal rainfall, yielded 500 to 600 kilos of shelled corn and half that in low-rainfall years. In December 1967, the school parcel, which had 100 furrows, was harvested with a yield of 2 3/4 cartloads of mazorca and 250 bundles of zacate.

Work on the school parcel was performed through a tequio, with workers being mobilized through the cooperative effort of the School Parents Society (Sociedad de Padres de Familia) and both community authorities. Work assignments were made from the list of ejidatarios, eighty-five of whom had yuntas, by the four members of the Sociedad for the entire production cycle. Six almudes of corn were planted, entailing three half-days of work for one yunta. Ten yunteros with yuntas were assigned ten furrows to plant, one furrow each. The completion of the assigned task satisfied the yuntero's tequio obligation. Other ejidatarios with yuntas were assigned other tasks like secondary furrowing, weeding, and hauling. Ejidatarios without yuntas were assigned such tasks as planting, picking, husking, and degraining.

During the week of January 9, 1968, harvested corn was being husked; each ejidatario was responsible for husking three baskets (piscadores) each. The following week, the husked ears (mazorca deshojada) were shelled (desgranado). The resulting shelled corn was stored in a bodega adjacent to the head teacher's residence, where it was handled at the discretion of the Sociedad (of which the teacher was a member).

Another example of the use of tequio labor was brought to my attention when I accompanied Germán Rosario to his plot in La Chilana where he was harvesting corn. We came to a deeply rutted and nearly impassable spot along the road where, according to Germán, he and several others had come close to turning over their ox carts on several occasions. The road used to pass through the ejido plot of a Magdalenan who decided to block it off and prepare it for cultivation; the road was detoured and became rutted. A community assembly decided to organize a tequio, after the harvest was over, to repair the road.

There were two types of irrigation (riego) in Magdalena's agriculture: de pozo, with water from a well being applied to furrows with a pump and hose or with a clay pot (cántaro); and de presa y zanja, from a channel or ditch with water flowing from a reservoir created by a dam. The first type of irrigation occurred mostly within the pequeñas propiedades. On August 31, 1967, on the way to La Chilana paraje, I passed several plots with well irrigation: one was recently planted with frijoles, where the owner was watering with a cántaro; and another, located in Ojo de Agua paraje, was planted in alfalfa, where the well had brick walls built up around it—called a pozo de construcción—on a plot owned by Mariano Amador, a resident of nearby Rancho Los Vásquez. A third well was on a plot cultivated with sugarcane. Along an arroyo known as Gueoglach (Río de la Chilana), I passed a brick-constructed sluiceway that was used to dam water flow during the rainy season, similar to one I had seen in San Sebastián Teitipac where boards are inserted in slots and mud was packed in between the boards to break the flow of water. In 1967, the arroyo was bone dry, but in previous years of good rainfall, it had water. This dam, however, was no longer used.

Magdalena's new dam (presa) was of earthen construction, with the gate and portions of the main canal of cement and stone construction. It was built in the late 1950s by government engineers through the ejido program, and was located in the southwestern corner of the ejido (see Map 6) with the neighboring rancho of La Noria in full view to the south of the dam. The reservoir was stocked with fish. In dry years, the water level dropped below the flow-control gate to make irrigation impossible. When the water level was higher, water flowed through the main gate into a main ditch and then into a series of small ditches cut into the fields where water was fed, furrow by furrow, through shoveling. The "zona de riego" referred to all ejido lands directly to the west of the pueblo lying beyond the road between Monte del Toro and San Pedro that cut across Magdalena's ejido.

An ejido official known as the juez del agua (or juez de la llave) was in charge of allocating water for irrigation. In 1967, the officeholder was Ricardo Ruiz. He carried a large key that fit the mechanism for opening and closing the gate of the dam. He opened the gate early in the morning and returned each afternoon to close it. He carried with him a list of ejidatarios with irrigable land and a schedule of the days on which they were signed up to irrigate their fields. The ejido fields were called tablones. They varied in size and quality, but each ejidatario was entitled to be assigned possession of only one.

In early September 1967, I met Fernando Rosario on his irrigated plot, where he was using an ox team to plow furrows to plant garbanzos. His plot was 15 meters wide and about 200 meters long. According to him, all of the plots near his were exactly the same size. Immediately below the dam, I encountered Delfino Aquino (then holding the office of síndico) and his son, who were irrigating Delfino's tablón that measured 100 meters by 200 meters. It had heavy black topsoil, and the crops of corn, squash, and beans planted on July 20 were in excellent condition. The milpa was in tassel and some small ears were already visible. The flow of water through the channels was strong, and about one-third of the surcos had been watered (three at a time) since 7:00 a.m. (I arrived at 10:30 a.m.). According to Delfino, the plot required watering every three to four weeks, depending on rainfall patterns. When his scheduled turn to access irrigation water arrived, he was able to water his entire field, usually a one-day process. He said that the dam system then in operation had a larger capacity than the earlier system, which retained water in a reservoir by damming up a nearby arroyo with stones and releasing water by cutting ditches into nearby fields.

Magdalenans cultivated six varieties of beans (frijol, or zaw): blanco (zaw na kiych); amarillo; colorado; negro (zaw na gawtz); bichi (zaw biych); and bisagú. Types 1–5 were lumped together as "frijol chivo" and required about seven months to mature. The bisagú variety required only two and a half months to mature. All were planted either as tempranero (early) or temporal between April and August. The bisagú variety was planted at medio paso (every half step) between corn plantings, whereas the others were planted together with corn in the furrow.

Other crops grown in Magdalena were field peas (alverja or chícharo), chickpeas (garbanzo), castor beans (higuerilla), and sugarcane (caña). Field peas and chickpeas were planted in September and October, either on the same plot where "tempranero" corn was harvested, or on another fallow plot. They matured in three to four months. The early corn crop was planted in April and was consequently known as abrileño. It was harvested in late August for dried ears (mazorca) and cañuela (dried stalk), unless the ears were picked when green (as elotes). The task of using a sickle to cut cañuela was referred to as "rozar." The seasonal corn crop was planted in June and was usually harvested in October or November. In late August 1967, corn planted in June was still "tierna" (young), and some plants had small green ears (elotes), but others had only tassels. In low-rainfall years, crop harvests were destined to be subpar.

Castor beans were planted as tempranero or temporal at medio paso with corn. They matured in four to six months and were harvested plant by plant. Each plant (mata) was cut off at the trunk after the first harvest and left to mature more fully for a second harvest. After the second harvest, the plant was pulled out and the cycle begun again (although on a different plot, since fallowing is required).

Some of the different agricultural tasks performed by Magdalenans during the rainy season were recorded in my field notes of August 23, 1967. I encountered Martiniano Méndez leaving the village with his ox team and plow on his way to "echar orejera" (secondary furrowing). Beto Sánchez, carrying a machete and a sickle (hoz), was proceeding from the village to the campo to "cortar cañuelas para la yunta." I also encountered J. C. Méndez, carrying a machete and sickle, leaving the pueblo on his way to cut (rozar) alfalfa. Farther along the way to the quarry, I met José Cruz Rosario's young son carrying water to his father, whom we found in his field "echando orejera." I also observed several people weeding fields where milpa was planted. They referred to this activity variously as "arrancar yerba," "desherbar," or "desenyerbar." Other people were observed plowing ("rayar" or "arar") furrows with ox teams to plant either frijol or garbanzo.

Alfalfa was relatively scarce in Magdalena in comparison to San Sebastián Teitipac. It was grown on a few irrigated plots but was poor in quality. Nopal was preferred to alfalfa as the main fodder for oxen. When tender, nopal was also harvested for cooking and human consumption as nopalito. Nopal was cultivated extensively, especially on privately owned plots near the habitation area. Many vacant resident lots, in fact, were devoted to nopal cultivation. Unlike alfalfa, nopal did not require irrigation and it did not have to be stored for a time after being cut prior to feeding it to animals. Fresh alfalfa could not be properly digested by oxen.

A nopal leaf (penca), when planted with the cut end in the ground, gave birth to a new plant (mata). A mata of nopal attained full size two years after planting, and its total life span was from six to eight years, depending on how it was tended. Each plant was cut every two years, but continued to grow new pencas. A normal-size mata yielded one basket of pencas, which provided sufficient fodder for one feeding of two oxen. Oxen were usually fed zacate along with nopal. Many households did not grow enough nopal to meet their needs, so it was sold by growers with a surplus. Usually it was sold by row in a nopalera (plot with several rows of nopal), for a price ranging from 30 to 50 pesos, depending on the length of the row and the size of the matas. Cochineal (cochinilla), an insect used as dyestuff that thrived on nopal, was no longer cultivated in Magdalena in the 1960s, but several elderly informants claim that it was produced in abundance at one time. It was, of course, a major tribute and cash crop in the colonial period (Dahlgren de Jordán 1963; Hamnett 1971).

In April 1968, I talked with Erasto Rosario in his nopalera, which was located directly west of the ayuntamiento. He was cutting a row of nopal to feed his yunta (using a short machete to cut each penca into several bite-size pieces). Since I had previously seen Antonio Rosario cutting nopal in this same field, I asked Erasto who owned it. He said that he was the owner, and that Antonio, his brother, was a mediero: he planted the parcel with an agreement that he could harvest every second row of nopal planted. Erasto said that the field had belonged to his paternal uncle, but that after his uncle's death, it had been purchased by Benigno Aquino. As a boy, Erasto lived and worked in Benigno's house for five years, and in compensation for his work he was given food, lodging, clothing, and the title to his uncle's plot. Erasto lamented that "this damn piece of land cost me five years of work." (Este chingado pedazo de terreno me costó cinco años de trabajo.)

Not all fodder was cultivated like alfalfa or nopal, as I learned early one morning as I was visiting the household of Atanasio Hernández. His twelve-year-old son, Leovijildo, came into the solar carrying a machete and a bundle of branches from a large-leafed plant that they identified as acagual. It grew wild and was used as fodder for pigs. Leovijildo had spent about 45 minutes in the campo to cut the acagual before heading to school by 8:30 a.m. He performed such tasks regularly. On another morning he was sent out to one of his father's plots to collect squash blossoms (ghía, or "flor de calabaza"), used in cooking; he returned with a sackful in time to go to school.

Animal husbandry, especially focused on goats and sheep, was fairly widespread in Magdalena, as attested by a 1964 census of 130 ejidatarios showing that 26 owned herds of one or the other or both, and that 22 had an average of 12 kids (cría) each (range from 3 to 30). The largest combined herd was 80 (50 goats, 30 sheep); one ejidatario had a herd of 85 goats. The fact that cows were owned by 34 households, or 26 percent (mean of 2.5 per ejidatario; range from 1 to 10), indicated the presence of a small dairy industry that produced milk and cheese for sale in San Pedro Apóstol and Ocotlán.

A comparison of these data with the results of our 1979 survey suggested an increase in the percentage of Magdalena households involved in goat and sheep raising, from 20 percent in 1964 to 27 percent in 1979. Our survey, however, did not report herds as large as those listed in the 1964 ejido census; the largest had only 31 goats and sheep, and there were three others with between 20 and 25 goats. The percentage of households owning cows increased from 26 percent in 1966 to 39 percent in 1979, but in the latter year, no household reported owning more than two cows.

There was a liability for households owning cattle that must be grazed. This was demonstrated during my visit to the ejido office in October 1967, where the six-member Comité de Vigilancia was handling a complaint by one ejidatario against another for allowing cattle to graze on his land and destroy corn ready for harvest. The committee members personally went to the field in question and found that 300 corn plants (milpas) had been destroyed by the grazing animals; the responsible party was fined 3 almudes of shelled corn per 100 plants or a total of 9 almudes. Such cases were quite common as evidenced by the fact that, during my visit to the office, a sack of shelled corn holding 12 to 15 almudes was hauled in to pay for a separate pending case of crop damage that involved straying cattle. When the perpetrators were from contiguous communities like Rancho La Chilana, these cases sometimes led to serious intercommunity litigation or conflict.

In 1968, Simón Aquino had 52 goats and 21 kids, compared to Pedro Méndez, who had 84 goats and about 30 kids and 15 sheep. Both of these herds included animals held through a share (a medias) arrangement, according to which kids born from an owner's herd were divided equally with the mediero. Simón had animals from several different owners, whereas Pedro had an arrangement with only one owner. As a mediero, Pedro was entitled to take possession of half of the kids born in the herd. In his words: "If 30 kids are born, the owner will get 15 and I will get 15." He also had the right to milk the female goats, either to sell or to make cheese. It was understood that he had to keep the entire herd of goats and sheep in a corral on his residence lot and take them to pasture daily. Simón, who had raised goats since 1964, said that his herd had not become larger over that time period because he had to sell goats to buy corn to meet household needs. Pedro also was accustomed to the practice of selling goats to meet household expenses, and said that the average market price for an adult male goat hovered around 90 pesos. Only three households in our 1979 survey reported keeping goats or sheep on a share basis.

Turkeys were also kept by just over half the households we surveyed; they averaged 2.6 turkeys per household (range between 1 and 6). One day in May 1968, I was talking with Atanasio Hernández in his solar when an elderly woman arrived carrying a turkey. She spoke to Atanasio and his wife in Zapotec and then walked to their corral with the turkey. I asked Atanasio if the woman was a *guelaguetza* partner, and he replied "no" and explained that she was bringing her female turkey for a breeding visit with his guajolote, a practice that is referred to as "cruzar guajolotes." The woman was Atanasio's confirmation godmother (madrina de confirmación), and they had a standing agreement to exchange the breeding services of guajolotes. In 1967, Atanasio took a turkey hen to breed with his madrina's gobbler. He described this practice at that time as a form of *guelaguetza*. In these cases, the *guelaguetza* partner seeking to breed a turkey is entitled to all of the chicks, in contrast to the share arrangement regarding goats and sheep.

Turkeys were especially valued for their suitability in festive dishes (moles) and, consequently, were listed in every *guelaguetza* account book as either owed to a donor or given and, therefore, reclaimable in the future from the recipient household. Turkey eggs were also highly prized. Consequently, turkeys were in the category with shelled corn as the ultimate fungible commodity. As such, they had an important role in the ceremonial reciprocity system.

I passed by Atanasio Hernández's residence lot in August 1967 and saw him in his fenced corral grabbing a turkey. I entered and found that he was with a woman he identified as Juvenal Sánchez's mother. Atanasio had the turkey in his grasp and was proceeding to weigh it on a hand scale. The turkey weighed 5 1/2 kilos (verified by his wife, Eulalia). He gave the turkey

to Señora Sánchez, exchanged a few words with her in Zapotec, and she left
the solar with the turkey. No money changed hands.

Afterward, I asked Atanasio how much the turkey was worth and he replied "50 pesos." I asked him if Señora Sánchez had already paid him for the
turkey or would pay later. He replied, "Soy persona legal." (I am a trustwor-
thy person.) I asked him what he meant, and he replied that he would get a
turkey later in return for the one he had just given, and that the transaction
I had just witnessed was a "*guelaguetza.*"

Señora Sánchez, it turned out, had come the preceding afternoon and
spoken to Atanasio's wife about getting a turkey, and his wife talked it over
with him when he arrived from the campo. They jointly agreed to enter
into a *guelaguetza* agreement (trato de *guelaguetza*) with the señora. Señora
Sánchez had come the next morning to find out what their decision was
and to get the turkey if possible. Atanasio's wife kept a *guelaguetza* account
book and made an entry for the turkey. They did not owe *guelaguetzas* to the
Sánchez family, so this was a new trato or convenio (agreement) between
the two households. The turkey was used in a festive dish (mole) prepared
for a baptism celebration.

The 1964 ejido census showed that only 15 ejidatarios (11.5 percent) had
burros, compared with 87 (67 percent) that had two or more oxen (14, or 11
percent, had between four and eight). Our 1979 household survey found
that a slightly larger percentage, 14 percent, owned one burro each and that
62 percent owned oxen (none with more than two). These data suggested
that ox teams and carts had largely displaced burros as beasts of burden, in
addition to giving Magdalena a relatively high proportion of landed households that also owned ox teams.

It is possible that between 1964 and 1979 the use of oxen as agricultural
means of production was reduced by the greater availability and use of tractors. This may explain why there was no household randomly surveyed in
1979 with more than two oxen; perhaps it had become less rewarding to
own multiple ox teams for rental purposes. This inference was reinforced
by our survey's finding that in 1979 only 24 percent of Magdalena households owned both ox carts and ox teams, which was about four points lower
than the average for all Oaxaca Valley households surveyed with comparable
amounts of land cultivated (Cook and Binford 1990, 44).

The same survey found that only four of thirty-seven households (10.8
percent) surveyed did not rent or borrow agricultural means of production.
Of the 89.2 percent that did so, eleven (29.7 percent) rented tractors and
carts; seven (18.9 percent) rented only tractors; five (13.5 percent) rented
tractors, carts, and ox teams; two (5.4 percent) rented ox teams and tractors;

and one rented tractors and water pumps. There were no households that rented only ox teams, three (8.1 percent) that rented ox teams and carts, and four (10.8 percent) that rented only carts. In one sense, the drop in owner-ship of ox teams could be interpreted as complicating the scheduling of household agricultural activity and as pressuring households to either raise cash or seek reciprocity arrangements to access the means of production they lacked (cf. Cook and Binford 1990, 45). Alternatively, the relatively high rate of tractor rental combined with the relatively low rate of ox team rental in 1979 could also be interpreted as an indicator of "modernization" or, at least, of cost-benefit calculations that favored tractor rental over ownership of ox teams.

## Sugarcane Cultivation and Processing

Magdalena was among a select group of communities, mostly in the south-ern arms of the Oaxaca Valley, that cultivated sugarcane as an industrial crop, owing to the presence of twenty trapiches and panela factories in the nearby community of San Pedro Apóstol. All cane grown in the irrigated portion of Magdalena's ejido was sold there or in San Matías Chilazoa, where the ejido also operated a trapiche. Sugarcane was planted only in low ground with a high water table and moist soil. It was harvested once in Janu-ary, and each plant lasted about ten years. After each harvest, the fields were burned. Weeding was done at the beginning of the rainy season.

On January 18, 1968, I spent most of the day in the Bajo de Chilazoa paraje and talked with the following individuals as they worked: Margarito García, Juan Méndez, Severiano Vásquez, and Epifanio Méndez. Margarito and Juan were planting sugarcane, Severiano (with Genaro, his mozo) was "zacateando" (stripping the leaves for use as zacate) caña, and Epifanio was supervising the plowing of his plot by a tractor he rented in San Pedro. I was impressed by two things: first, the extent to which well irrigation was utilized in this paraje; and second, the careful calculations and informed decisions that these growers made regarding their agricultural activity.

Juan Méndez first planted cane in 1967 on one corner of his plot on a trial basis, and was planning to use his 1968 harvest to plant another sec-tion of his plot. The previous year's crop had grown extremely well, and his yield was about 2.5 meters; he attributed this to the fact that he planted relatively deeply to enhance the effect of the natural moisture of the land. Half of Juan's plot will still be planted in corn; he will do two plantings—one in February that will be harvested in June, and another in July that will be harvested in November or December. Juan has a well on this plot that he used to irrigate cane.

Severiano was the largest of some twenty cane planters in Magdalena; his annual yield was between 18 and 20 meters, compared to an average yield of 4.4 meters for fourteen other planters for whom data was available. He also claimed to be the first Magdalenan to grow cane. He was experimenting with tomatoes on this plot, having planted one row of fifty plants, and expressed satisfaction with their progress to date.

A man on horseback rode up as I was talking with Severiano. He was the manager of the trapiche in San Matías Chilazoa, run by four ejidatarios with financing from the Banco Ejidal, who was interested in buying Severiano's cane harvest. They bargained for about fifteen minutes; Severiano insisted on a price of 80 pesos per meter and the manager offered a final price of 77.50. No sales agreement was made, but Severiano said that he was inclined to accept the offer, since the going market price in San Pedro was 75 pesos, and the San Matías trapiche was closer to his field, which meant a shorter trip. He would still harvest his cane on the following Monday, after finishing his zacate harvest (zacateo).

During the bargaining process, Severiano made repeated references to the fact that San Pedro trapicheros were paying 80 pesos per meter, while the San Matías trapichero (trapiche owner) argued that the particular strain of cane that Severiano planted yielded less panela and more off-colored panela than that grown on sandier soil. Severiano explained that the price of sugarcane had appreciated steadily for several years. About four years earlier, there had been a buyers' market because the trapicheros claimed that their inventories of panela were too large. Accordingly, they paid only 30 pesos per meter. But the price had increased steadily ever since: to 40 pesos, then 50 pesos, 60 pesos the year before, and 75–80 pesos in 1968.

Epifanio, by contrast, was considering cultivating cane on his plot (which does not have a well but is tierra húmeda) but was discouraged by fluctuations in the cane market over the years. He rented a tractor from one of four tractoristas in San Pedro Apóstol to plow his field, and then rented a yunta to make furrows (pintar surcos). He had already spent 209 pesos that year for a tractor to plow his 1.75 hectares, and on the day I was there, he spent 54 pesos for the yunta. (I spoke to the tractorista, whose name was Antonio Hernández; he bought his tractor from earnings as a bracero in the U.S., and his father owned a trapiche in San Pedro.) Half of Epifanio's plot had been previously cultivated and was plowed the year before by Antonio for only 25 pesos (the standard rate was 125 pesos per hectare). But Epifanio decided to start planting a previously uncultivated section in 1968. It was tierra pesada (heavy and moist due to a high water table). The new section measured (with a tape by Antonio) 15 x 38 meters, and Antonio charged Epifanio 29 pesos to plow it with his tractor. Epifanio had experimented with various crops. In the previous year, he planted cantaloupe (melón), but the crop failed and he lost 200 pesos. He recognized the potential advantages of crop diversification and was a willing innovator (as were many Magdalenans) but was handicapped by a lack of technical knowledge. On a plot adjoining Epifanio's, his father, Eliseo Méndez, then serving as president of the ejido, had successfully cultivated peas (chícharos).

Earlier that January, I conversed in the field with Abelardo García and Paulino Cosme. They used five different terms to describe different parts of the cane plant: "cogollo" referred to the top leafy portion of the plant, including the upper green portion of the stalk, which is cut separately and used as animal fodder; "caña" or "tronco de caña" referred to the stripped cane stalk; "zacate de caña" referred to the leaves stripped from the cane stalk, which are dried and used in jacal construction as roofing material; "camote" referred to the root of the cane plant; and "pelío" referred to the young cane plant in the early stages of the annual growth cycle. Cane plants had a life span of from seven to ten years. Their normal growth cycle, after harvest, was one year from the time they began to sprout until they reached full growth, that is, from pelío to caña. After the cane plant was cut during the annual harvest, "el camote se retoña" (sprouts up again on its own). At the end of their life span, cane plants were uprooted and a new planting undertaken. Stripped cane stalks, just like those used to make panela but with some buds, were laid out end to end in two rows in a furrow about two feet deep, then covered with soil to start the growth process.

The sugarcane cultivation cycle began with planting (siembra); it was planted only on terrenos de humedad but during the first year was pot-irrigated from wells. Afterward, pot irrigation was considered unnecessary. Planting occurred in late December and January. Previously planted cane was harvested (el corte) in January and February, after which refuse on the fields was burned (la quemada). After the burn, soil between furrows was plowed (barbecho), followed by a first weeding (limpia) in July and a second weeding in August. The zacateo or deshoja (stripping leaves from the plant) occurred in December.

Abelardo planted cane on his .25 hectare parcel (10 meters wide) in 1964 when his padrino (godfather) gave him some seed cane (camotes). Previously, Abelardo had cultivated only corn on his parcel (1 almud de sembradura). Since 1964, his harvest record was as follows: 1965, 5 meters @ 40 pesos per meter; 1966, 12 meters @ 60 pesos per meter; 1967, 9 meters @ 59 pesos per meter; and 1968, 7 meters @ 75 pesos per meter. In addition to cane, each harvest yielded cogollo and zacate. The 1968 harvest (completed on the day I was present) yielded 175 manojos (bundles) of zacate valued at 50 centavos each and 50 manojos of cogollo valued at 25 centavos each. Abelardo did his own cost accounting of production costs (echar lápiz al trabajo a ver come sale) for the 1968 harvest as follows: barbecho (1 half day, 1 man with yunta), 12 pesos; first weeding (with mozos, 7 man-days @ 10 pesos per day), 70 pesos; second weeding (with mozos, 3 man-days), 30 pesos; zacateo (with mozos, 7 man-days), 70 pesos; corte (with mozos, 7 man-days), 70 pesos; carretero (seven trips to San Pedro, 1 metro per trip @ 9 pesos per trip), 63 pesos. This amounted to a total expenditure of 315 pesos. Abelardo earned 525 pesos from the sale of 7 meters of cane at a price of 75 pesos per meter, thus, giving him net earnings of 210 pesos. Although this was comparable to what he could earn from a good harvest of 3 fanegas of shelled corn plus 30 bundles of zacate on the same plot of land, he had earned more from past cane harvests. Cane harvests and prices fluctuated from year to year, but Abelardo had never been confronted with total loss in bad crop years as he had been with corn. In short, he was satisfied with his decision to plant cane rather than corn.

Delfino Aquino, by contrast, had been a cane planter (cañero) for twenty years when I talked to him in late January 1968, but in 1966, he decided to pull up most of his cane in order to plant corn and chickpeas. This decision was motivated by his disgust with the instability and unpredictability of the cane market from year to year. During the twenty years that he grew cane, his annual yield varied from a minimum of 18 meters to a maximum of 30. In 1966, the price bottomed out at 25 pesos per meter, and, for him, this was the straw that broke the camel's back. He had to hire carts at 10 pesos per trip from the fields to the trapiches, as well as provide food and drink for a substantial number of mozos. In short, he lost money.

Delfino attributed the interannual variability in the price of cane to a disconnect between supply and demand. In a high-price season like 1968 (75 pesos per meter), cane growers were motivated to plant more cane and noncane growers decide to move from other crops to cane. The result was oversupply, with a drop in price in subsequent years. He also took issue with the behavior of San Pedro's trapicheros, whom he referred to disparagingly as "those feeble rich guys" (esos canijos ricos). He alleged that they held periodic meetings to fix prices, a practice that he (and all Magdalenan growers) viewed as unfair. He also complained about their arbitrary behavior at the time of purchase, when they lowered their offer if a cart had a few centimeters less than one meter of cane or if the cane was too thin or the wrong color. They also tended to measure loads only at the corners of the cart, since they were aware that a load of cane tends to bulge in the middle.

Growers like him, said Delfino, were penalized for being truthful with the trapicheros. He cited as an example one occasion when a buyer to whom he had previously sold several cartloads at an agreed price suddenly and arbitrarily refused to pay the same price for the next load. In frustration, Delfino drove his cart to another trapichero, who asked him if he had sold to other trapicheros that season. He truthfully responded yes, and after hearing his response, the trapichero told Delfino that he would not do business with him because he was simply trying to dump his "garbage" (basura) on him, and he should take his cartload back to the other trapiche.

In view of his negative experiences over the years as a cane grower, Delfino resowed all of his cane fields with corn and chickpeas, and insisted that he would not replant cane in the future.

Severiano Vásquez's experience with cane cultivation had been favorable enough to justify his dedication to it for several years. He had two parcels where cane could be grown, and in 1968 was growing maize on one of them. The parcel in cane measured 30 x 60 meters and had 22 furrows; he had 3 meters of cane planted there, 1.5 planted early in 1968 and 1.5 planted in 1965. The paraje is known as Arroyo San Pableño and is located within a larger area known as the Bajo de Chilazoa, an area of well irrigation and some channel irrigation and with "tierra de humedad." His January harvest yielded 18 meters of cane that he sold to a San Pedro trapichero named Facundo for an arranged price of 80 pesos per meter for a total of 1,440 pesos. He calculated his labor costs as 300 pesos, 260 pesos for ox teams and carts, and another 320 pesos for a tractor, leaving him with earnings (ganancia) of 560 pesos. Some of these earnings were reduced by the cost of feeding all of his workers twice, in the morning before leaving for the fields (desayuno) and again in the afternoon after returning from the fields (comida). In addition, he was obliged to provide all of his workers with an early afternoon beverage (tejate) with tortillas and salsa.

The bottom line in the local sugar industry was summed up by Maximino Pérez, who was hired by Severiano to haul cane to the trapiche in his oxcart: "The real profit in the sugarcane industry goes to the trapicheros, not to the growers." Maximino was especially knowledgeable about the industry, since he was one of several Magdalenans who had worked in the San Pedro trapiches. According to him, 1 meter of sugarcane yielded 1 banco of panela equivalent to 117 trozos (cuadritos or marquetitas); at the 1968 market price of 75 pesos per meter for raw cane, and excluding all other costs, this translated into a 6 centavo cost per trozo of panela. The typical trapiche produced about 15 bancos of panela daily (per eight-hour shift). In 1968, panela sold for between 90 centavos and 1.20 pesos per trozo, which seemed to leave a substantial profit margin for the trapichero even after labor, marketing, and fixed capital depreciation costs were deducted.

During the last week of January and early February 1968, I devoted several days to observing the cane harvest, loading and hauling cane to the trapiches in San Pedro, and the processing of raw cane into panela (brown sugar cakes). As a result of unseasonal late-afternoon rains during the last week in January, the trapiches were forced to temporarily shut down because the reeds (carrizo) and bagasse they used to fuel their boilers, stored in the open, were soaked and would not burn. As a result, all of the trapiches had full inventories of cane to be processed. Also, rain muddied the cane fields and made it difficult for loaded oxcarts to move from field to road. Consequently, the Magdalena growers had to postpone their harvest for a week.

Before the rains started that season, I observed the harvest on Amos Aquino's plot, where he had planted only 1 1/2 furrows of cane that yielded two cartloads (2 meters). He and a mozo cut and loaded a cartload of cane in about two hours, and we headed to San Pedro's newest trapiche, owned by Bonifacio Sánchez, conveniently located on the south edge of town on the road to Magdalena. Amos already knew that the going market price for cane was 75 pesos. Although he used the phrase "echando competencia" (competitive) to refer to relations among the trapicheros, he admitted that typically they all offered the same price, so he was predisposed to sell to Bonifacio at a price close to 75 pesos.

When we arrived at the trapiche, Bonifacio came out to examine the load and offered Amos 70 pesos. He claimed that he could not pay more because the cane was not "deshojada" (stripped of leaves). According to him, cane that is stripped of its leaves and exposed to the sun for three to four weeks prior to cutting gives a higher yield of guarapo (cane juice) from which panela was made (essentially, panela was cooked and hardened guarapo). Bonifacio said that cane prices in 1968 were high and in previous years had been in the 40- to 50-peso-per-meter range; he noted that cane prices were dictated by the price of panela. Amos accepted Bonifacio's offer to save himself the trouble of visiting other trapiches where the price would be more or less the same. He said that Magdalena growers were aware of the trapicheros' preference for caña deshojada but that their preference was to strip leaves from cane at the time they cut it; he attributed this to "flojera" (laziness).

The trapiche was located on a large adobe-walled and reed-fenced lot with an open-air cane unloading area near the street entrance, next to an open-air cane storage area, both of which were on one side of the main building, which had adobe walls, a pitched tile roof supported by large columns of brick and heavy wooden beams, and, most notably, a chimney constructed of a combination of adobe and fired brick measuring about 5 feet square and about 15 feet high. On another side of the building, directly across from a sunken fire-stoking area under the roofed structure, was an open area for drying and storing bagasse (bagaso) and reeds used as fuel. Bonifacio conservatively estimated the value of his trapiche at 50,000 pesos.

After the cane was unloaded and stored, the four-step production of panela commenced. First, raw cane was manually fed into a motor-driven belt conveyor and press (John Deere) to extract cane juice that was piped into heating vats; the cane pulp or bagasse was carted away to the drying and storage area. Next, the heated cane juice was piped into a series of cooking vats in controlled quantities, where it was cooked until it became thick and syrupy. It was then ladled out of the vats into large wooden cooling tubs on wheels. After cooling, it was transferred to wooden molds to harden into panela. The most complex and labor-intensive series of tasks, involving about fifteen workers, occurred in the heating and cooking area. The key man in this operation was the maestro panelero, who controlled panela cooking, decided when it was properly cooked, and ladled the hot liquid from the cooking vats into the cooling tubs. This activity required considerable skill and dexterity in manipulating the six-foot-long wooden ladle.

### Nonagricultural Activities and the Household Economy

Embroidery was not practiced in Magdalena in the 1960s, but it was introduced and grew in subsequent decades. Our 1979 household survey (37 households sampled from a total of 168) found a total of 31 embroiderers, all females, distributed among 20 households; 9 (29 percent) of the 31 embroiderers were under the age of twenty. This placed Magdalena exactly at the median of nine communities we surveyed in the district of Ocotlán. Santa Cecilia Jalieza had the highest level of participation, with nearly 42 percent of households surveyed having embroiderers.

Thirteen women in Magdalena also worked in a chicken-raising facility funded through the Banco de Crédito Rural del Istmo, especially widows, and around eight women (mostly "puras mujeres solas") also made tortillas for local sale (muelen de la gente). I was talking with Abdón Aquino in his tienda during the evening of October 17, 1967, when a woman walked in and waited while Abdón's wife measured out 3 kilos of shelled corn, which she gave to the woman, who then left. In response to my query, Abdón explained that the woman was a molendera who made tortillas daily for consumption by his family, since his wife tended the store and was pressed for time. The molendera got 3 kilos of corn daily and delivered 50 tortillas. She was also paid an additional 1.40 pesos in cash, presumably to cover the local milling charge. According to Abdón, 3 kilos of corn yielded 80 tortillas, so the molendera kept 30 tortillas as her compensation. The molenderas had to cover the cost of grinding corn in the local molino de *nixtamal*, which charged 10 centavos per kilo, and in the case of Abdón's molendera, she earned 1 peso daily in addition to 30 tortillas. My observations at the local mill indicated that shelled corn and eggs were also accepted as payment in lieu of cash.

## Conclusion

The main purpose of this chapter was to explore the process through which the community of Magdalena, from its early colonial origins as a congregation, lost most of its communal lands by the end of the eighteenth century through the expansion of Hacienda San José La Garzona, and spent the next century or so under its domination. Like San Lorenzo Albarradas, which retained a fundo legal, and despite being squeezed on every side by two predatory haciendas, Xaagá and San Bartolo, Magdalena was able to maintain its separate identity as a pueblo. Due to the presence of a few landed households with mercantile interests, as well as its location along the main road from the district town of Ocotlán de Morelos to Miahuatlán and the Pacific coast and near the mines at San José, Magdalena was able to develop a modicum of economic independence from the hacienda's sharecropping regime and openness to the wider economy and society.

The combination of factors outlined above converged in the early period of the agrarian revolution that began in the second decade of the twentieth century to make Magdalena a relatively precocious participant in the struggle for land restitution/endowment. Its participation in the revolutionary process set in motion land reform and economic development that enabled Magdalenans in subsequent decades of the twentieth century to pursue new and reinvigorated forms and standards of economic well-being and civility.

## CHAPTER 10

# Magdalena's Metateros:

## Servants of the Saints

## and the Market

Magdalena exemplifies the thesis that occupational structures in Oaxaca Valley indigenous communities are subject to abrupt change. This was illustrated in Chapter 9 with the case of embroidery that was first introduced in the 1970s but also by the case of stoneworking. In 1880, Magdalena did not have a resident metatero, yet in 1901 a prominent Oaxaca writer specifically cited it (and no others) as one of the communities in the state where "the indígenas are dedicated to making metates, manos de metates, and mortars and pestles (tejolotes), indispensable artifacts in our pueblos . . . that serve to grind corn and make dough (masa) for tortillas" (Belmar 1901, 120). In the early 1940s, Magdalena was the only metate-making community mentioned in the classic monograph *Los zapotecos* (Mendieta y Núñez 1949). This is impressive coverage for an occupation that was first introduced to Magdalena by a metatero from San Juan Teitipac in the early 1880s.

This chapter traces the origins and development of the metate industry and examines contradictions in the process of securing economic well-being and civility in the daily lives of Magdalena's ejidatarios. Friction and difficulties occurred due to a combination of inflexible, sometimes heavy-handed ejido policies and administration, and the recalcitrance of some ejidatarios in complying with a tax/surcharge system in addition to their traditional tequio obligations. Ironically, these problems were dramatically experienced in the Martínez family, whose progenitor, Nabor, founded the metate industry around 1880, and one of whose mid-twentieth-century members, Guillermo, was expelled from the community owing to his difficulties in meeting obligations of citizenship there. Despite this, Guillermo's son, Juan, carried on with the oficio introduced by his grandfather in the company of many other Magdalenans who, in the last decade of the twentieth century, continued to make a living from manufacturing and selling this seemingly anachronistic commodity.

## Origin and Development of the Metate Industry

Nabor Martínez, a metatero from San Juan Teitipac, moved in with a Magdalena woman who would become the mother of Pánfilo Martínez and the grandmother of Guillermo Martínez. In 1966, Guillermo was living with his wife, Enedina Francisco; a daughter, Otilia, fourteen; and a son, Juan, eleven, on the same residence lot where his grandparents had lived. He was born in 1924 and began working as a metatero by the age of fifteen; he learned the craft from his maternal uncles, Manuel Macario Sánchez and Norberto Vásquez Sánchez. His paternal grandfather, Nabor, died around 1912, and his father, Pánfilo, who was listed on the Censo Agrario of 1917 as a thirty-three-year-old soltero, died when Guillermo was four.

There is no mention in oral history that Nabor arrived in Magdalena with a son. Given Pánfilo's 1886 birth date, it seems reasonable to infer that Nabor migrated from San Juan Teitipac around 1880. Simón Sánchez, who was born in 1904 and who became a metatero at the age of twenty, repeated the oral history that he heard as a child. Nabor Martínez, from San Juan Teitipac, came to Magdalena to work and asked people if there was stone to make metates. No one could answer because they knew nothing about that craft. They walked around the outskirts of the community, especially near the mountain, looking for a deposit of stone. Nabor found a spot and said to everyone present, "Let's dig a quarry here." They started digging for stone until Nabor saw that there was a vein of good stone. This oral history was independently repeated by José María Santiago, who was five years older than Simón and who, like Simón, never met Nabor Martínez, but knew that he came to Magdalena before his own childhood in the second decade of the twentieth century.

Simón also said that Nabor and a few Magdalenans interested in learning the craft started quarrying on the lower east side of Taniche Mountain (Cerro de Taniche; see Map 6), which was owned by Hacienda San José. The hacienda's guardamontes forced them off hacienda land, but, fortunately, Magdalenans found stone nearby in the southwest corner of their communal lands (terrenos del santo), and quarrying continued there. After the establishment of the ejido, Magdalenans reoccupied the original quarry called Piedra de Canoa (Yeg Cánóa in Zapotec; see Map 6 for the approximate locations of the main quarries).

Melquíades Sánchez, sixty-three years of age in 1966, started working when he was a teenager in a quarry belonging to Locadio Vásquez, who taught him how to work and eventually sold him the quarry for 25 pesos without papers but as an "agreement between us." His memory of what he was told about the beginnings of the metate industry in Magdalena differed in some details from the version of Simón and José María. According to his version, some men of the community went in search of a source of stone to use in the installation of a door for the church. They started a quarry for that purpose. After Nabor came to Magdalena, he found the stone from that quarry to be suitable for metates and began to work there and to teach others the craft.

According to Melquíades, Nabor Martínez was a maestro metatero who taught people by example how to make metates, manos, and chimoleras (mortars). He showed them how to set blasts, how to bore holes in rock with steel bars (barrenos), how to cut stone using a hammer and wedges, and how to mark large stones to make cuts. He ended up teaching more than half the pueblo—a total of fifty metateros, more than there were in 1967. According to Melquíades, after the ejido was established, the population of metateros shrank (comenzó a mermar).

Aside from Locadio Vásquez who taught him the craft, Melquíades mentioned Hermenejildo Aquino, Pioquinto Vásquez, Tiburcio Pérez, Juan Méndez, Tomás Vásquez, and Pánfilo Martínez as Magdalenans who worked with the founder, Nabor Martínez, and learned the craft from him. He singled out Tomás and Pánfilo as being "maestros" who assumed that role in the post-Nabor generation.

### The Metate Business in the First Half of the Twentieth Century

There is no definitive way to determine if Magdalena's metatero population was reduced as a result of agrarian reform and the introduction of the ejido, as Melquíades claimed. Since Hacienda San José prohibited access to an important quarry area on the slopes of Cerro de Taniche, forcing quarrying to be done on communal or private lands belonging to the pueblo, the ejido opened Magdalenans' access to land for quarrying stone as well as for cultivation. Its overall effect was to promote agriculture, so the metatero population composed of ex-terrazgueros and jornaleros could have been reduced in the 1920s and 1930s by virtue of their unprecedented access to land for agriculture. There was, however, seasonal complementarity between agriculture and metate making, reinforced by the fact that neither occupation required a year-around, full-time commitment.

Despite violence locally and regionally, including banditry targeting traveling merchants, José María Santiago launched a lifelong career as a trader (regatón) in 1916 when he was only seventeen years old. He did so at the suggestion of his uncle, whom he had asked for a 5-peso loan to spend on a Todos los Santos celebration. Instead of giving him a loan, his uncle invited him to work in his business, helping haul pottery and metates from Oaxaca City to Ejutla every two weeks. Between 1919 and 1922, the business expanded to include Miahuatlán, where José María sold onions, green chiles, and green tomatoes, purchased in Ocotlán, and metates purchased in Magdalena. He was the first metate trader in Magdalena and, in 1967, was still the only one. He explained that he traveled to Miahuatlán for four years, always with burros. One burro carried two small metates; another burro carried onions, green chiles, garlic, and tomatoes, which he sold in the market. For the return trip he would buy hens, pigs, turkeys, beans, and seasonal fruits like peaches and bananas. He would sell those products in Ocotlán and then buy other products to resell in Miahuatlán.

José María's business earnings enabled him to buy an ox team and eight cows, but these were stolen, at which point he contemplated working as a day laborer (jornalero) in agriculture. Again, his uncle came to the rescue, reminding him that he could only earn 37 centavos a day as a jornalero, and he convinced him to go on a long-distance business trip to the Isthmus of Tehuantepec. He traveled to Huatulco by way of Pochutla with two burros, one loaded with two metates, the other with a dozen manos. He bought small metates in Magdalena for 1.25 pesos each and sold them in Huatulco for 15 pesos each. In Huatulco he bought a team of oxen and took nine days to travel back to Magdalena. He paid 12 pesos for the ox team, and sold it in Ocotlán for 30 pesos.

In view of the success of his trip to Huatulco, José María decided in 1924 to embark on another trip to Tehuantepec and Ixtepec. He walked for eight days with two burros loaded with onions and garlic purchased in Ocotlán for 4 pesos per thousand. In Tehuantepec, he was unable to sell anything, so he left his burros in a corral and took a train to Ixtepec, where he had better luck; he sold his onions and garlic for 60 pesos per thousand. He returned to Tehuantepec for eight days; bought two dozen coconuts for his family; and, on the advice of his traveling companion, also bought four bull hides for 6 pesos each.

José María trekked back to Ejutla with his two burros and his load of hides. In Ejutla, he sold the hides for 40 pesos each, his burros for 10 pesos each, and bought an ox team (to replace the one that had been stolen) for 60 pesos and a cart for another 60 pesos. He swore to himself that he would not make any more long-distance business trips; and from then on began to cultivate land.

It was around this time that José María initiated his career of expenditures (gastos) in the civil-religious hierarchy and fiesta system, serving as regidor in 1929, so his earnings were quickly depleted. He noted that "I had to spend on four occasions during that year. I had to sell my ox team to raise money for the expenses, and later worked to buy a smaller pair of oxen (yuntita chiquita)." After that, his festive sponsorship expenditures began with mayordomías, then service as alcalde, and fandangos when his son and daughter married. In 1945, he volunteered to sponsor the mayordomía of the Santa Patrona de Magdalena, which cost him 7,000 pesos, paid for by the sale of 12 cartloads of corn. In 1956 he was mayordomo of the Virgen del Rosario and spent 9,000 pesos. José María clearly had an active and expensive cargo and festive sponsorship career: two major civil posts, regidor and alcalde; four mayordomía sponsorships, two of which were major, Santa María Magdalena and the Virgen del Rosario; and two fandangos.

He kept his word for many years regarding long-distance trading but continued to buy metates and manos on a small scale in Magdalena for resale in the Ejutla plaza. He left Magdalena at 2:00 a.m. with burros, typically in the company of eight or ten Magdalenans who traveled together to defend themselves from bandits. He hauled two metates and a dozen manos every week. Also, on occasion he bought zacate in Magdalena to resell in Ejutla during Lent.

From the mid-1920s until around 1930, José María worked as a hauler (fletero) for the San José mine. Initially he used his own oxcart to haul stone for construction, but later he became "boss of the cart drivers (carreteros)" and began to haul scrap metal from the mine to Ocotlán. He rounded up twenty Magdalenans with oxcarts to work with him; each cart held one ton of metal and they were paid 6 pesos a ton plus a fee for the use of the cart and ox team. The hauling was only on Mondays. José María earned 5 pesos per haul above and beyond the fee for the rented cart and his payment of a mozo who drove his own cart. He earned enough from this job to buy his house and residence lot for 350 pesos in 1927.

In the 1950s and 1960s, once the highway from Oaxaca City to Miahuatlán and points south was completed, José María occasionally traveled south on business trips, especially to Pochutla, where he had an uncle. He would sell onions, garlic, and peanuts purchased in Ocotlán and metates and manos from Magdalena. Since he found very little to buy in Ejutla for resale in the pueblo or in Ocotlán, he went there only about five or so times. In

1957, he made one other trip to Huatulco and to Candelaria, where he sold ten metates for 50 pesos each but lost money because travel costs exceeded earnings.

In comparing his various economic activities, and especially his regular business as a buyer and reseller of metates and manos, with agriculture, José María expressed a strong preference for "el negocio del campo." "With two, three, or four cartloads of corn," he said, "I have enough for my household needs." Some of his corn harvest was used to fatten hogs. In August 1968, he sold two hogs for 700 pesos each and bought a small ox for 900 pesos. His wife encouraged him to buy an ox because otherwise he would go on a drinking binge and waste all his money. At the time, he owned two cows, three steers (toros capados), and a team of oxen. He had only one small parcel of land, enough to plant 2 almudes of seed corn that yielded about a cartful of ears of corn.

In addition to one privately owned plot, ejido records showed that in 1964 and 1966 José María cultivated 3 hectares of ejido land for a harvest of 400 kilos in 1964 and 425 kilos in 1966. His 3 hectares of ejido land were at the mean for 176 ejidatarios, as was his harvest. His cultivation of an extra plot of private land placed him slightly above the mean on both counts among Magdalena's ejidatarios.

Simón Sánchez started working as a "resident jornalero" in the house of José María Sánchez, where he spent one year until he paid off his debt, then continued working for a time as an agricultural day laborer (jornalero) before heading to the quarries.[1] (Cuando ya yo me di cuenta que hay ese oficio, me enfadé con el trabajo de jornalero, de ir a las casas de la gente, y empecé a hacer metate.) He learned by observing. (Vi como trabajaban y aprendí también.) He used a barreta to rough-cut metates and manos, and a hand pick to finish them. His first experience was in a quarry worked by his elder brother, Andrés; when Andrés moved to another quarry on the slopes of Taniche Mountain, which had been within the boundaries of Hacienda San José, Simón continued working the Piedra de Canoa quarry. By the 1960s, he had turned this quarry over to his two sons-in-law, Germán Rosario and Atanasio Hernández. Simón admitted that he worked a long time as a metatero and wore out three barretas. From the beginning, most Magdalenans worked only with two steel tools, a barreta (bar) and a pico (hand pick), although Nabor also introduced them to the hammer-and-chisel technique; they used shovels and reed baskets (canastas) to clear away debris (descombrar).

From the time Simón started working as a metatero in the 1920s until near the end of the 1930s, there was not much sales activity in Ocotlán, so he hauled his products on a burro to Ejutla, where he sold metates for

1.50 pesos and manos for 37 centavos. Simón made two business trips each to Miahuatlán and to Candelaria but by 1935 stopped selling in Ejutla and started selling exclusively in Ocotlán, still making the trip to the plaza with burros. This change occurred because the advent of corn-grinding mills (molinos de *nixtamal*) reduced demand for metates and the interest of intermediaries in buying metates for resale. The market in Ejutla and Ocotlán was reduced to buyers for own use, and it was less costly for him to sell in the closest marketplace.

Buried on one page of the classic 1949 monograph *Los zapotecos* (Mendieta y Núñez 1949, 560), in a section on "Zapotec Industries" written by Carlos H. Alba and Jesús Cristerna under the heading "Metates," is the first twentieth-century social scientific description of that industry among the Oaxaca Valley Zapotec. Derived from fieldwork conducted in 1941 by a research team from the Instituto de Investigaciones Sociales at UNAM directed by Lucio Mendieta y Núñez, the essay focused exclusively on the derivative branch of that industry in Magdalena Ocotlán without mention of its San Juan Teitipac origin.

One discrepancy between this source and the account given by Simón Sánchez, who was an active metatero in 1941 when the UNAM study data were collected, is the description of the tool kit that specified "marro y seis cuñas" (hammer and six wedges) in addition to the barreta. Simón, like most Magdalena metateros, worked exclusively with a barreta to rough-cut metates from trozos, and a pico to smooth out (labrar) rough-surfaced metates and manos. The use of the hammer-and-chisel (marro-y-cincel) technique in lieu of the barreta to rough-cut metates and manos from larger stone blocks (trozos) was most popular among San Juan metateros; it was less seldom used in San Sebastián and minimally, if at all, in Magdalena. By the 1950s, all metateros employed the combination of a large sledgehammer (weighing 6 or 7 pounds) and wedges (cuñas) to split large slabs (planchas) of stone into smaller blocks (trozos).

Alba and Cristerna did not mention the hand pick (pico) as the indispensable smoothing-out tool, which was also part of the Magdalena metatero tool kit in the early 1940s that also included one or more of the steel bars (i.e., pulseta and barreno) that were used in the 1960s to perforate holes for installation of powder charges in the preparation of blasts (Cook 1982, 185–187).

Ejutla was not the exclusive market outlet for metateros in 1941, as Alba and Cristerna stated. At that time, a transition was already under way with a definite trend toward Ocotlán displacing Ejutla. During the 1950s, after the highway was opened from Oaxaca City to Miahuatlán, passing through Ocotlán and Magdalena, economic life in Magdalena revolved much more heavily around the Friday market in Ocotlán than the Thursday market in Ejutla.

Whereas metateros might not have considered cost of transport as a cost of production, they most certainly did consider it a factor in market pricing, contrary to Alba and Cristerna's contention. Time spent traveling to and from the market, as well as costs of food and fodder for themselves and their burros, was considered in their price negotiations and passed on to the buyer whenever possible.

Like the metateros of San Sebastián Teitipac, the Magdalenans could not predict the trozo (metate-size stone block) yield of a given blast. Typically, a blast would yield several usable trozos for both metates and manos, but a quantity as high as twelve trozos for metates would certainly be at the upper limit of possible outcomes. Variable outcomes at this stage had direct implications for output and earnings. Alba and Cristerna's estimate of an output of five metates per month was not out of line for the Magdalena industry in 1941, but price and output variability, rather than stability, were characteristic of the industry then and later (Cook 1982, Ch. 7).

Finally, Alba and Cristerna were misleading in their assertion that stone was "obtained free of charge" by the metateros. The Yeg Cánoá (Piedra de Canoa) quarry was within the ejido and therefore subject to the rules and regulations of the prevailing agrarian code and, more importantly, governed according to the traditional understanding of rights and duties of every community ciudadano/contribuyente that bound community resource use to tequio obligations. That is, in return for the right to extract stone for the fabrication of income-generating commodities, metateros were obliged to respond to community needs for stone for public works projects. This was in addition to the fee they paid to cultivate ejido land and their provision of tequio labor.

## Metateros as Ejidatarios in the 1960s and 1970s

As ejidatarios, all metateros were bound by governmental and community rules, regulations, and customs, but everyday work in the quarries was conducted by unwritten codes and understandings among the metateros themselves, as well as in response to the exigencies of quarrying. Access to quarries was one thing, but extracting stone from them was quite another. With few exceptions, extraction required cooperation.

One morning in April 1968, I accompanied Atanasio Hernández, Juvenal Sánchez, and Martiniano Méndez on a walk to the Piedra de Canoa quarry, where we arrived at 11:00 a.m. Germán Rosario was already at work with a mozo (who was paid 5 pesos with meals) clearing stone out of his quarry and moving a large block of stone from the quarry floor up onto the work patio. Martiniano worked alone in an adjacent quarry, and Atanasio worked in one section (tramo) of the same quarry where Germán was working. Juvenal, with his brother Victorino, who shortly arrived on the scene, worked a section of the quarry adjacent to Germán's and Atanasio's sections.

Shortly after our arrival in the quarry area, Martiniano asked Juvenal and Germán for assistance with a large slab of stone that had been dislodged by a blast from a wall of the quarry; it was still stuck and needed to be pried loose so that it would fall to the quarry floor. Both Juvenal and Germán went to the aid of Martiniano and, after about ten minutes of unfruitful work, were joined by Victorino. About five to ten minutes later, all four used barretas, strategically inserted in cracks between the quarry wall and the slab, as levers to "palanquear," or pry loose, the slab from surrounding bedrock. They succeeded, and the enormous slab tumbled to the floor of the quarry. Martiniano, using a sledgehammer and steel wedges (cuñas), proceeded to cut the slab into smaller blocks (trozos) suitable for metates. Juvenal, Germán, and Victorino returned to their own quarries and work.

I asked Martiniano if the slab was for his own use, and he replied "yes." I then asked him if any of the workers who had helped him pry the slab loose were entitled to any compensation, and he replied "no." He explained that their help was a case of lend-a-hand (dar mano) reciprocity (guelaguetza), according to which metateros informally exchanged labor. Martiniano was obligated to lend a hand to any of his fellow workers when they requested his help. Beyond that future commitment, the arrangement did not involve payment in kind or cash.

Pedro Vásquez worked on a product-share basis (a medias) with his elder brother and his father in his father's quarry until the latter's death in 1961. All the stone they quarried was divided into equal shares among the three. Pedro's father did not work in the quarry but simply made metates from his share of the trozos. This quarry was one of several deep quarries in Magdalena that lacked drainage and tended to fill with water after heavy downpours during the rainy season. It made little sense to rent a pump to remove the water until the end of the rainy season. So until that time, Pedro and his brother worked through share arrangements with other metateros in quarries that had better drainage and did not flood.

After his father's death and the division of his father's quarry between him and his brother, Pedro developed a new strategy to solve the rainy-season problem. Rather than immediately making metates from available trozos, he accumulated an inventory of trozos to tide him over the rainy-season months when the quarry became unworkable. He planned his quarrying activity in accordance with the patterns of rainfall (según como va pintando la lluvia). Each year he selected a month prior to the onset of rains to work exclusively on expanding his inventory of trozos.

In 1965, he put aside thirty trozos; in 1966, twenty-two trozos; and in 1967, twenty trozos. In the latter year, the quarry was flooded from June through December, and was pumped dry in January 1968. Pedro's trozo inventory lasted him until October 1967; when his supply ran out, he went to work on a share basis with Germán Rosario until he had the water pumped out of his own quarry in January 1968.

When not confronted with undue pressure to raise cash from metate sales, Pedro preferred to keep his inventory of trozos out of production during the low-price market of the rainy season until the onset of higher prices in the dry season. The best way he could accomplish this was to occasionally raise cash by selling a sheep or goat from his small herd of fifteen or, alternatively, sell castor beans (higuerilla), which he grew as a cash crop.

Starting in 1963, a controversy over the use of ejido lands for purposes other than cultivation emerged between two types of use: animal grazing and stone quarrying. All ejidatarios paid an annual fee to the treasury of the local ejido for agricultural parcels, and the ejido treasury paid taxes to the state treasury; for 1961, 1962, and 1963 this amounted to a total of 2,100 pesos (or about 16 pesos per ejidatario). An initiative for levying additional fees for grazing and quarrying stone originated with district ejido authorities, who pressured local authorities to enforce relevant articles in the federal agrarian code (e.g., Article 138 and Article 206, fraction 1).

According to a letter from the delegado de asuntos agrarios in Oaxaca City to the ejido president in Magdalena, the above-cited clauses meant that the product of pastures and the stone to make metates should provide income to the comisariado and the ejido treasury to help increase and develop cattle raising and construction of public works for collective benefit (ASRA, Magdalena file). In a response to the Oaxaca City office, the jefe de zona based in Ocotlán reported that the proposition was soundly defeated by vote in an assembly of eighty-one Magdalena ejidatarios. They already paid a substantial amount of taxes and fees monthly to the municipality. The jefe de zona attempted to convince Magdalenans that a fee should be paid to the ejido treasury for stone quarried on ejido property that was used to make metates; but that idea was rejected because they already paid such a fee to the municipal government.

The effort to charge an extra fee for grazing on ejido land was rejected by ejidatarios on the specific grounds that only one of them had more than fifty head of livestock, and that the majority of them had fewer animals than listed in the last census due to forced sales to raise cash to compensate for a bad harvest. Metateros, as peasant cultivators, contributed 420 pesos in annual taxes to the ejido treasury; furthermore, in 1963 they cooperated with the ejido by contributing 200 pesos' worth of stone for the construction of a patio in front of the local ejido office.

In 1969, the dispute was renewed by a request from local ejido authorities to the metateros to supply stone for the construction of a wall around the ejido office. Each of twenty metateros was required to supply two wagonloads of stone from the quarry for the project. The metateros met with ejido officials to negotiate a release from their annual tequio obligation of one day's labor if they complied with the request to supply stone. A meeting was held of all ejidatarios on January 25 to discuss the matter. A majority voted that metateros had to satisfy the new request for stone and also meet their annual tequio obligation, rejecting the metateros' request to waive the annual tequio obligation.

On the day scheduled for selected ejidatarios to come to the quarries with their carts to load stone, several metateros insisted that only stone could be loaded that was not suited for making metates and manos. The ejidatarios on tequio duty insisted that metateros had no right to prevent the removal of stone, since the quarry belonged to the ejido. The metateros picked up rocks and threatened to throw them at anyone who started loading stone that was not selected and approved by them. The forty ejidatarios and eighteen ox-carts retreated and did not load any stone. Predictably, this defiance of local authority ended badly for the recalcitrant metateros.

On February 11, hearing rumors of their imminent arrest, three of the involved metateros left for Oaxaca City to seek legal protection (amparo) from arrest. On February 12, a general assembly attended by more than one hundred ejidatarios voted to indefinitely suspend the quarry-use privileges of the three Magdalena-born metateros who had sought legal protection in Oaxaca City and to permanently expel from the community the other defiant metatero, Antonio Rosario, who was born in Rancho La Chilana of a Magdalenan mother. This decision was sanctioned by the ejido bureaucracy in Ocotlán and Oaxaca City (Cook 1982, 230–233).

The four metateros ignored the vote and were at work in the quarry on February 14 when they were arrested by Magdalena police and jailed overnight in Ocotlán. They were released the next day after each one paid a 100-peso fine. On February 25, another assembly of ejidatarios was held in Magdalena with ejido officials from Ocotlán and Oaxaca City. A vote was again taken to permanently expel Antonio Rosario from Magdalena, even though he was officially recognized as an ejidatario and listed on the 1966 list of ejidatarios as cultivating a 1-hectare parcel. The other three metateros were permitted to return to work if they agreed in writing to pay an annual fee of 500 pesos. The fee was considered fair, since they sold metates for 150 to 200 pesos each and could afford to pay it. The metateros protested that they could not pay such an unreasonable fee. Despite their protest, an act was drawn up obliging them to pay the fee if they wanted to maintain their rights to quarry use and avoid a jail sentence.

The end result was the permanent destruction of Antonio Rosario's mode of livelihood, and several years of disruption for the other three metateros, until they were able to come to terms with a new set of ejido authorities. All three metateros were back at work during 1979–1980.

This description of the ejido tenure enforcement reinforces the thesis, established in Chapter 4 regarding the communal tenure enforcement in San Sebastián Teitipac, that relations between metateros and non-metateros for stone extraction from quarries located on public land were prone to conflict. In both communities, there was a majority view that metateros used communal resources to generate private income and therefore had an obligation, above and beyond their status as regular tequio givers, to provide stone to public works when requested to do so. Magdalena's more codified and bureaucratized ejido tenure regime was more inflexible than San Sebastián's communal tenure regime, as the case of Antonio Rosario and his colleagues illustrated.

All of Magdalena's quarries were on ejido property, so the assignment of use rights was made by the comisariado ejidal. It was common for quarry-use rights to be bought and sold among metateros, just as it was among agriculturists for ejido plots. Many metateros considered themselves to be owners of the quarries where they worked, and they either paid another metatero for use rights or had sold use rights to quarries that had previously had different owners. It was understood that ultimate proprietorship belonged to the ejido, and that inheritance problems and disputes over quarry boundaries fell within the jurisdiction of the comisariado just as they did with regard to agricultural land.

An apprentice or newcomer had to gain access to an ejido quarry by permission from the recognized owner either by cash purchase of use rights or by an arrangement with the owner to exchange labor for stone. For example, in April 1968, Antonio Sánchez began making metates for the first time in his life in the quarry of Rufino Sánchez by paying for powder and fuses for blasting operations and receiving in return one-half of the usable stone for metates secured in the blast.

Severiano Vásquez's experience as head of the local ejido gave him a unique perspective on ejido policies and operation. He was not without blemishes on his record of community service. He was accused of illegally trafficking in ejido lands and water from the new dam and reservoir system during his period in office: he was accused of "illicit and illegal acts that consisted of arbitrary and excessive trafficking of irrigable ejido parcels belonging to the deceased Francisco Santiago and of the supply of water from our dam known as El Guayabo" (ASRA: exp. 14, Feb. 22, 1964).

An ejido assembly approved the redistribution of the deceased ejidatario's parcel of undisclosed size to one of three different ejidatarios on a waiting list, and Severiano on his own initiative (and in direct violation of the agrarian code that prohibited the sale of ejido parcels) proceeded to accept separate unreceipted cash payments from each of the three ejidatarios on the waiting list; this was after he previously conducted a separate transaction for the same parcel by accepting a cash down payment from a widow not on the approved list. One of the involved ejidatarios proceeded to hire a tractor to begin plowing the parcel in question. The plowing was halted by the intervention of a brother of the widow. They were on the verge of physical combat when the alcalde and police arrived on the scene. Severiano was removed from office in 1964 and paid an undisclosed cash fine.

Perhaps part of Severiano's punishment for his indiscretions as comisariado was his election as regidor in 1965. If not, then his indiscretions seemed not to have diminished his status in the eyes of his co-citizens, who considered trafficking in ejido parcels to be par for the course.

Severiano did not acknowledge that ejido land had been apportioned unfairly or inequitably but instead emphasized that the real difference in the ejido was between lazy and industrious ejidatarios. "There are some ejidatarios who obtain land parcels and don't take care of them and don't completely cultivate them," he declared, "they are citizens who plant only late crops and never get good results." He viewed the presence of "people who don't want to cultivate crops properly, planting both early and late in the season," as being "a drag on the growth of the pueblo who do not benefit the pueblo."

Severiano acknowledged that ejido land was not cultivated equally in Magdalena; this caused impoverishment of some ejidatarios and their failure to meet costs and expectations of community service. Citing again the case of Guillermo Martínez, Severiano alleged that he "didn't have one furrow planted on his ejido parcels" and was considered to be lazy and untrustworthy, eventually resulting in his loss of ejido use rights.

In sum, the cases of Guillermo and Severiano, each in its own way, exposed the hard realities of life in an ejido community like Magdalena in transition from a traditional "usos y costumbres" culture in the 1960s. They were symptomatic of a need for major reforms in the system of ejido tenure and governance initiated by the Salinas regime in the 1990s.[2]

## Metateros in the Civil-Religious Hierarchy

By the 1960s, Magdalena's council had grown to ten members: five incumbents (propietarios)—the presidente; the síndico; and first, second, and third regidores—and five suplentes (replacements). A lingering ladder system loosely operated in both the civil and religious spheres. The top-tier posts included the president and síndico in the ayuntamiento, president in the church, and president of the Comité Ejidal in the ejidal authority. Other high-level posts, though of somewhat lesser prestige, were alcalde and committee members in the municipio, the tesorero and fiscal in the church, and the jefe de vigilancia and the juez del agua in the ejido.

The top post in the second tier of municipal offices was regidor, followed in descending order by jefe de sección, teniente de policía, and mayor del alcalde (police and jailer posts). The mid-level tier of religious posts consisted of the mayordomo de pólvora and topil de la iglesia, both of which, held in succession, were necessary entryways to higher positions in the municipio, the iglesia, and the ejido. The mayordomo de pólvora had specific duties during the fiesta de Magdalena (early July) and the fiesta of Corpus Christi.

Serving in one of the second-tier committee or council positions in the ejido (consejo de vigilancia ejidal, consejo de administración ejidal, and secretario del comisariado) typically, but not necessarily, preceded service in executive ejido posts. The topil de la iglesia was essentially a caretaker of the two principal saints: la patrona (Santa María Magdalena) and the Virgin of the Rosary.

Low-level posts in the municipio (mayor del presidente, mayor del teniente, and policía/guardia) were all involved with policing the community; in the church, the low-level posts (topil del fiscal, campanero, second sacristan of the week, first sacristan of the week, and major sacristan) covered activities from door opening, to bell ringing, to servicing Masses, tending to church paraphernalia, and so on. Candidates for these posts were named prior to the celebration of the All Saints' Day Mass (misa de Todos los Santos).

Naming and election of officeholders was either every year or, in the case of regidor, alcalde, síndico, and presidente, every three years. The naming was by voice in a public meeting; votes were taken for the persons named, and offices were assigned according to the number of votes in the popular secret ballot. Ayuntamiento posts were not alternated during the three-year period of incumbency. On each New Year's Day, the entire ayuntamiento sponsored a fair (feria) for the community. Regidores were obliged to sponsor a Mass and provide food and drink (for guests and family members) on each All Saints' Day. The propietario spent alone on one year, the suplente spent alone on the next year, and both were required to spend on the third and final year's celebration.

The president of the church held office for five years and was responsible for managing the planting and harvest of the terrenos del santo (or for renting or sharecropping them). This position was always held by a respected elder citizen with service in high civil posts. Although some of the higher civil posts required expenditures in association with the largest mayordomías, especially the post of regidor, the rest did not. Mayordomía sponsorships were voluntary, and it was widely understood that only households that could afford sponsorship would volunteer. When major mayordomías had no voluntary sponsors, as was the case for the patron saint's celebration in 1967, then each head of household was levied a fee of 3 pesos by the ayuntamiento to pay for the celebration.

Many Magdalenans in their lifetime never moved beyond service in low-level cargos. Others who made it into mid-level cargos never progressed beyond regidor. A minority who served in high-level posts typically did so in more than one of them in different sectors. Manuel Aquino, for example, was serving as presidente de la iglesia in 1967 and had previously served as regidor, síndico, and comisariado. After completing his service in that post and enjoying a period of no service, he would be a prime candidate to be named alcalde or presidente municipal.

Individual cargo careers followed different trajectories in terms of specific posts held after passing through the second-level gateway sequence of topil de la iglesia (Santa Patrona) and mayordomo de pólvora. Simón Sánchez entered community service when he was fourteen years old and served as topil del presidente municipal, then as topil del teniente and mayor del teniente before entering service in the church as topil de la virgen and mayordomo de pólvora when he was twenty and twenty-one years old, respectively. Next he served as mayor del alcalde, teniente de policía, and finally, regidor in the municipal hierarchy. Afterward, his career entered a hiatus until 1955, when he served voluntarily as mayordomo de la Virgen de Juquila; then he was elected to a series of committee posts: tesorero of the Comité Escolar in 1957, fiscal de la virgen in 1959, and tesorero de la virgen in 1963. In 1966, he served in the municipal sector as suplente del alcalde for a second time in his career, and he was serving as cobrador del proyecto de agua potable (charged with collecting fees for the potable water system) in 1967. At that time, he was considered to be a prime candidate for an executive post as alcalde, síndico, or presidente, but he doubted this would happen on account of his illiteracy.

The most burdensome aspect of civil-religious service, aside from time commitment, was the expense it entailed. Fernando Rosario, who served as regidor from 1963 to 1965, was qualified to be named to a top-level post by 1967–1968. He spent more than 3,000 pesos in 1965 as regidor in celebrating the fiesta of Corpus Christi on December 22, and had to sell his yunta to meet expenses and avoid indebtedness. In addition, he spent 1,000 pesos in earnings from metate sales and made substantial use of the *guelaguetza* system. He admitted that he fared better than many others who did not have a yunta or other animals to sell to raise cash for this expenditure.

Fernando expressed doubts regarding the viability of a cargo system that obligated incumbents to make festive expenditures under threat of public censure, noting that "one makes those expenditures under duress, not because he wants to." Some households that did not have the means had to go into debt. He emphasized that he did not borrow money to serve as regidor but, instead, sold his ox team and used earnings from metate sales to meet expenditures.

Guillermo Martínez, a metatero and grandson of Nabor Martínez who was the founder of Magdalena's metate industry, had more difficulty than Fernando. He had neither the means nor the inclination to meet his obligations as regidor, an office he held in 1967 after having previously served as mayor del alcalde, mayordomo de pólvora, topil de la iglesia, major sacristan, first sacristan of the week, second sacristan of the week, and bellman. Despite this record of service, he was marginalized for not complying with the customary expectations of the office of regidor and, in 1968, left Magdalena and moved to San Pedro Apóstol, which was his wife's natal community. As far as I know, he never returned to Magdalena to live. Nevertheless, Guillermo's son, Juan Martínez Francisco, inherited his father's house (and presumably his ejido allotments) and was working as a metatero in 1980.

Severiano Vásquez in July 1968 was just finishing a three-year term as regidor. His first community service was in 1945 as topil de policía or, as he described it, "a year on the beat" (un año en la ronda). In 1947, he served as mayor de policía, then as mayor de teniente and topil de la iglesia, before being named in 1963 to serve as president of the Comité Ejidal (comisariado) for a three-year term that would prove to be cut short. He estimated that his expenses in these posts ranged from 25 pesos (policía, for cigarettes) to 1,000 pesos as a member of the comisariado (either for work time lost or for direct cash contributions to the ejido budget from personal corn sales) and as regidor (festive obligations).

Severiano had very strong opinions regarding the responsibilities of incumbency in community service posts. If you were not in agreement and did not spend, he warned, things did not work out well. In town assemblies, the attitude was that if you had money, you should spend it by following community customs (va siguiendo la costumbre del pueblo). He reiterated that "I am in agreement with the custom of spending when you hold office because if I do so, I am treated well and respected, and if I don't, I am considered a bad neighbor and friend."

Severiano referred to Guillermo Martínez, who failed to meet expenses of his service as regidor and suffered disrespect in community assemblies because he "didn't know how to respect others when he was in office." Severiano insisted that, unlike Guillermo, he knew how to respect others because he spent what he could to assure that his voice was respected in the community. When a man was voted into office as regidor, he was the choice of the people to serve the community, and if any officeholder failed to fulfill his duties, he would lose respect.

## Metatero Organization and Participation in Cofradías

Metateros had a titular head of their craft, the encargado de los metateros, who was expected to deal with internal disputes and serve as a liaison between the metateros and community authorities. In 1967–1968, Andrés Sánchez, the eldest metatero, held the honorific office. He explained that he had been named to this position by an assembly vote soon after the ejido was established. The office was entirely for the purpose of assisting ejido officials in managing the use of the quarries and, particularly, for resolving disputes between metateros regarding quarry boundaries, use rights, and tequio obligations.

Juvenal Sánchez gave an example of how Andrés intervened to resolve a problem in the quarry of Pedro Vásquez. The encargado decided that Pedro's mother was entitled to a part of the quarry, and the son of Pedro's deceased brother, to another part. Pedro essentially confirmed Juvenal's explanation of the role of the encargado but offered further details about his own case, explaining that the dispute centered on the fact that he did not know exactly where his father had worked in the quarry. So, to straighten out the matter, his mother sought the help of the encargado, who supposedly knew where his father had worked.

In 1968, Pedro was working in a quarry that was previously worked by his father, who died in 1961. When his father died, the quarry was divided between Pedro and his older brother, who died suddenly in 1966. Pedro's brother's share of the quarry was passed on to his fifteen-year-old son, who was not working it as of 1968. Pedro's mother was, in effect, concerned about getting some income from her deceased husband's share of the quarry. This really ended up as a matter of family duty, since Pedro's elderly mother either would be helped by her male relatives or not, despite any judgment made by the encargado about ownership.

Metateros recognized the practical need for a social control system in the quarries mediated by an encargado of their choosing, together with ejido and municipal authorities. Metateros did not like paying fees, taxes, or tequios, and they did so grudgingly only because it was obligatory for everyone. If anyone held out on these payment obligations, they felt that they also had a right to do so, yet slackers were resented. They also realized that failure to cooperate would bring punishment from the authorities and loss of social standing in the community. Some metateros considered Andrés Sánchez to be too old and out of touch with the quarries to be useful in settling boundary disputes, emphasizing that a proper encargado had to know exactly where one metatero's section in a quarry began and ended. They considered the intervention of ejido authorities necessary to resolve such matters. There was consensus that since disputes occurred, it really did not matter if the encargado could or could not resolve them, since either ejido authorities or, as a last resort, municipal authorities would do so.

Starting around 1940, Magdalena metateros participated in a unique civil-religious organization focused around the cult of Nuestro Señor de las Peñas, celebrated every fifth Friday of Lent (Cuaresma). It was sanctioned by civil and religious authorities and operated through a committee elected by the metateros. This committee had a sort of titular head known as the man-in-charge (encargado) of the Señor de las Peñas, a position best described as a steward of the saint's image rather than the supervisor or sponsor of the annual festival itself. This position was held by José María Santiago because he was reportedly involved, along with a priest from San Pedro Apóstol, in the original acquisition of the saint's image in Oaxaca City and its installation in the Magdalena church. In the eyes of some Magdalena metateros, José María's involvement with the acquisition of the image of the saint for the local church gave him exclusive trading privileges with the metateros, which he in fact enjoyed until the late 1970s.

Antonio Rosario, mayordomo of the fiesta in 1966, had an alternative explanation of the history of the celebration that attributed the arrival of the saint's image to a priest of San Pedro Apóstol. The priest would reclaim the image if the metateros failed to sponsor a festival on the saint's behalf every year.

The "Peñas" celebration was, in effect, a combination cofradía-mayordomía. Its annual sponsorship rotated among a three-man committee elected during a special assembly of the metateros held every three years. The assembly held a vote at the end of each three-year cycle: the top vote getter became president, the second-highest became secretary (secretario or rayador), and the third-highest became treasurer (tesorero or cobrador). Posts rotated annually during each three-year period. For the period 1967–1969, the incumbents were Pedro Vásquez, Arturo Vásquez, and Atanasio Hernández: Pedro was president in 1967, Arturo in 1968, and Atanasio was to be president in 1969 after serving as treasurer in 1968 and secretary in 1967.

This organization closely resembled that of Magdalena's only other co-fradía ("archiocofradía," or confraternity) of the Virgen del Carmen. The difference between them was one of degree: the Virgen del Carmen cofradía accumulated more paraphernalia (candles, vases, incense holders, etc.) cared for by the committee in charge.

The treasurer for the Peñas cofradía collected fees from metateros, which the secretary (rayador) recorded on a membership list. Fees paid mainly for fireworks, flowers, and candles. The president, at his discretion, could offer a meal to the members of the church committee who cooperated with the Peñas celebration. He emphasized that the fiesta involved "cooperation among all of us." Service in the Peñas celebration, said Fernando Rosario, was "obligatory for a metatero; one is obligated to do it because he is named, it's not that he wants to do it."

After Atanasio's service in 1969, the metateros assembled to name a new committee for the next three-year cycle. The president was the main sponsor of the two-day mayordomía-like celebration. He was exempt from paying the 20-peso fee agreed to by metateros in the assembly but was responsible for financing the costs of two days of expenditures: day one, when the curtains of the saint's image in the church were renewed and a vesper service (víspera) was held; and day two, when the procession and Mass occurred. During these two days, the president fed the members of the church who participated. Following the two-day celebration, a ceremony was held in the church in which the president-to-be received from the incumbent president the image of the saint, the candeleros (candleholders), floreros (vases), and any leftover candles or other materials.[3]

In May 1968, not long after his service as president of the Peñas celebration in March, Arturo Vásquez's records showed that his sponsorship of the fiesta as the designated president in March required additional expenditures both in cash and guelaguetzas. He admitted that it was becoming harder to get everyone to pay fees, despite the fact that they got stone out of the same quarries. It was unfair for some to pay and for others to refuse to pay, and if there were metateros who refused to pay their assigned fee, the matter should be resolved by the municipal president. Fiesta sponsorship, for Arturo, was done to solicit a saint's help and to show that God was first in all things.

The agreement to have a patron saint of the quarries, in Arturo's view, was an ancestral legacy celebrated annually with a Mass on the fifth Friday of Lent. The celebration should continue because Señor de las Peñas can help one out in his work, for example, when stone was lacking to make metates and manos. He stressed that the quarry helped him to go to market every Friday with metates and manos to sell for cash. "That is why we have to continue to celebrate the fiesta," he concluded.

Arturo showed me his *guelaguetza* account book pertaining to sponsorship of the Peñas fiesta, his first major community cargo, and explained: "I took out these *guelaguetzas* for the purpose of the fiesta de las Peñas. As is our custom, corn is supplied to those who agree to give us tortillas. There are several women on the list who will give us an almud of tortillas each." The earliest entries were *guelaguetzas* that he owed. The first entry was Tomasa Aquino, who, Arturo explained, was not family but was given corn to grind for making tortillas that she would give back to them as a *guelaguetza*. When she in turn sponsored a fiesta, she had an obligation to donate corn for tortillas; tortillas would be given back to her to compensate the work (mano de obra) she contributed previously. There were nine additional entries in this category, seven for 1 almud of tortillas and two for 2 almudes each.[4]

A second category of entries in Arturo's notebook was for *guelaguetzas* of soft drinks, mezcal, and cigarettes that families brought to his house on the fifth Friday. This list was divided into two groups: eleven described as "pure family, coparents and godparents and brothers," were invited guests who came to his house on the day of the Mass; and seven others who donated but were not invited to his house. Only one of these persons returned a previous donation of a case of soft drinks made by Arturo for a wedding celebration.

The remaining donations listed were solicited by Arturo's wife and included eight cases of soft drinks, one bottle of mezcal, one jug (medida) of mezcal, nine boxes of cigarettes, 5 almudes of tortillas, two turkeys (weighing 5.5 kilos and 3.5 kilos), and two dozen eggs.

Arturo estimated his cash expenditures amounted to 750 pesos for 1.5 fanegas of maíz, bread, two turkeys, 3 kilos of cacao, 16 kilos of azúcar, three medidas of mezcal. He bought most of these goods in a store in nearby San Pedro Apóstol where he had an account.

Germán Rosario, who had not yet served on the Señor de las Peñas committee or, for that matter, in any appointed or elected cargo except policía (but did volunteer in the church as sacristán del campanero), expressed a sort of grudging acceptance of community service and the celebration of the Peñas fiesta: "You have to do it because the community named you; you have to give service there in the church. If you don't spend anything, then people will start speaking badly about you (hay hablada de la gente). They will say that you don't want to spend your money."

After serving as topil, he explained, you are obligated to move on to be regidor; you are forced to (a la fuerza). The fiesta de las Peñas was the same. If you made metates, you had to sponsor that fiesta sooner or later. He repeated the history of the old encargado bringing the saint, noting that metateros agreed to hold the celebration to promote better luck in quarrying (vamos a dar la fiesta para que la piedra nos ayude más). He did not want to spend his money on fiesta sponsorship but did so anyway to avoid pressure from community authorities. (Quisiera yo no dar, pero andan detrás de uno porque uno es metatero.) He was aware that some metateros, most notably Antonio Rosario, did not cooperate, but noted that the encargado kept a list of those who gave and those who did not.

Germán, like many of his companions, had second thoughts regarding compliance with festive expenditures as a civic duty of metateros. But he was not willing to subject himself to gossip and disdain by failing to meet customary expectations of compliance.

Rufino Sánchez, like Germán, had served only as topil de policía, and he expressed disagreement with the obligatory cargo system because "they spend more than they have to spend, and mostly for mezcal." He admitted, however, that he might voluntarily serve as a mayordomo in the future because "it is a matter of one's devotion. And according to our elders, that is what they did. That is the reason why we have an obligation to the church, to celebrate the Mass. It is an honor for the entire community." He clarified that the only celebration for which he paid an assessment voluntarily was the Señor de las Peñas because it was about a belief that you had about the saint to help you make a living from stone. He was not confident that the celebration would continue for lack of willing fee contributors.

Fernando Rosario, who served as mayordomo de las Peñas in the early 1960s, rationalized support of the celebration "so that they don't charge us for using the quarries in the municipal budget. We get relief because we sponsor the fiesta, so with our sponsorship expenses we are actually paying what we owe to the municipal budget." This explanation exposed a collusive policy between civil and religious sectors in community affairs to effectively promote and perpetuate the "usos y costumbres" system. Metateros, in effect, were put between a rock and a hard place regarding how they managed to meet the community standard of civility—either by paying a surcharge on one side or a tax on the other. From their perspective, this amounted to double taxation on the civil side, since, as ejidatarios, they had already paid a surcharge for the use of ejido land—although not specifically for use of the quarries. Fernando agreed that it was preferable to pay the annual fee for sponsorship of what he termed the "casi mayordomía" (almost mayordomía), which amounted to a charge of 20 or 30 pesos, than to pay a tax to the municipio for the use of the quarries.

Fernando Rosario's position regarding the rationale behind metateros' continued support of the Peñas celebration was echoed by Pedro Vásquez. Pedro was troubled by the lack of clarity regarding the issue of a tax paid directly to local government as an alternative to annual dues (cuota) for the fiesta: "We all have to be in agreement. There are those who are in favor of celebrating the fiesta because they are uncertain about how, when, or how much they would have to pay in taxes to the municipio."

Antonio Rosario, who grudgingly accepted having to serve as mayordomo of the fiesta de las Peñas in 1966, justified it in similar terms as an occupational duty. "It is a vow (promesa) for us, the metateros, to have our fiesta del Señor year after year." Antonio estimated his cash expenditures for the sponsorship at 500 pesos, which he earned from metate sales. He insisted that he did not seek help from others through the *guelaguetza* system. His practice was to not ask for or give *guelaguetzas* to avoid problems with households that offer pretexts for not reciprocating when the time came to do so. When he needed something, he got wage work and then bought what he needed. It was probably this pragmatic, yet rather antisocial attitude of Antonio's that contributed to his marginal status and apparently led to his expulsion from the ejido in 1969 for his resistance to tequio obligations (and apparently also for not paying any additional surcharges for the Señor de las Peñas celebration after his service in 1966).

Atanasio Hernández, who was a member of the Peñas sponsorship committee in 1967–1969, was also the 1967 secretary of the archiocofradía de la Virgen del Carmen, an organization founded in Magdalena in 1943. Atanasio was one of only five male members, since it was founded essentially as a women's organization. The purpose of the cofradía was to serve as caretaker of the image of the Virgin in the local church, sponsor the annual Mass and celebration for the saint on July 16, and manage the finances and paraphernalia related to the celebration. The main difference between this cofradía and the metateros' Peña organization was its substantially larger inventory of ritual paraphernalia and an annual budget that regularly yielded a surplus, which then served as a source of small loans for its forty or so members.

Atanasio explained his membership in this cofradía through a "promesa" as a matter of one's own choice. If one believed in an image (imagen), then he (or she) could ask to become a member of a saint's organization. Doing so would facilitate invoking the help of that saint or virgin. When he got sick in 1950, he was on the verge of death and couldn't even walk. A lot of people asked him the question, "Don't you have a saint or a virgin that you are devoted to?" and he told them he didn't. They encouraged him to pray to a saint that he was devoted to in order to get relief from his illness. He decided to invoke the help of the Virgen del Carmen to ask for a cure of his illness (que me de un remedio que mata esta enfermedad que tengo). He promised then that if God extended his life, he would become a member of the archiocofradía. He recovered from his illness and joined the cofradía. Since then, he claimed to feel happiness on the dawn of the day when you hear the music announcing the arrival of the procession to celebrate Carmen's Mass. The celebration brought him happiness, and that is why he paid his annual dues to the cofradía.

In sum, most metateros viewed community service through a trifocal lens of material interest, social duty, and religious conviction.[5]

## Metateros in the Market System

The best and most accessible measures of the pulse of the metate industry in the Oaxaca Valley were marketplace inventories and sales transactions in the home districts of the metateros, namely, Ocotlán de Morelos on Fridays in the case of Magdalena, and Tlacolula de Matamoros on Sundays in the case of the Teitipac villages. Although it is true that in the 1960s the Teitipac metateros still participated heavily in direct sales in the Oaxaca City marketplace on Saturdays, intermediaries were increasingly displacing producer-sellers in the Oaxaca City market. Spatial reorganization of the Oaxaca City market in the 1970s further complicated the marketing situation for producer-sellers and anthropologists alike, making sustained, systematic data collection increasingly difficult.

A complete set of data for San Sebastián metateros in the Oaxaca City marketplace was collected over a 101-week period from August 1966 through July 1968, and also for the Magdalena metateros in the Ocotlán marketplace over a 47-week period from August 1967 to July 1968 (Cook 1982, esp. Chs. 6 and 7). In both cases, field assistants helped record inventory and transactional data: Filomeno Gabriel Mateo in San Sebastián and Oaxaca City, and Atanasio Hernández Pérez in Magdalena and Ocotlán. In the Ocotlán case, pricing and information on the provenience of buyers (Cook 1982, 250–288) and intended metate use were given priority.

Overall, time series data provided strong empirical support for a correspondence between key economic variables (price, income, output), the agricultural cycle, and the fiesta cycle. Supply and demand in the metate industry moved in harmony through a bifurcated year—relatively high and brisk in the postharvest dry season when most major festivals occurred, and relatively low and sluggish in the rainy season when agricultural work intensified and the festive cycle was less active (Cook 1970; 1982, Ch. 7).

The survey project presented an opportunity to collect another complete data set for the Magdalena metateros in the Ocotlán marketplace over a forty-seven-week period from October 19, 1979, through September 12, 1980 (see Table 10.1). Data were recorded in a notebook on Friday market days by Atanasio Hernández and included date, full names of the sellers, number of metates brought for sale, approximate time of sale (or storage), final selling price (if sold), and place of origin of the buyer. A spreadsheet analysis of these 1979–1980 data yielded interesting comparisons with data previously collected for 1967–1968.[6]

In 1979–1980, over a period of forty-seven market days, twenty-eight different sellers came to market for an average of sixteen times each to sell a total of 506 metates (average sales of eleven metates per market day). This compared to a period of forty-three market days in 1967–1968 with fifteen different sellers who came to market for an average of twenty-four times each to sell a total of 330 metates (average sales of seven metates per market day).

The first obvious difference is that the Magdalena industry expanded over the twelve-year period as indicated by a greater number of sellers (30 vs. 15) and a higher number of metates sold (506 vs. 330). Another is pricing: the average price per metate sold in 1967–1968 was just under 60 pesos (1 dollar = 12.50 pesos) compared to 774 pesos in 1979–1980 (1 dollar = 23 pesos). This means that a standard-size metate sold for the equivalent of 5 dollars in 1967–1968 and 34 dollars in 1978–1979—a striking appreciation in market price that reflected unremitting, steep inflation and growth in the wider regional and Mexican economies that, in fact, was documented (Cook 1982, 322).

Even more striking is a comparison between a six-week period in June–July 1978 (Cook 1982, 323) and June–July 1980 that shows a remarkable difference in activity: 29 sellers sold 35 metates for an average price of 308 pesos in 1978, whereas 24 sellers sold 64 metates for an average price of 659 pesos in 1980. Changes of this magnitude in output and price over a two-year period in the Magdalena metate industry cannot be accounted for simply as responses to increasing inflation in the wider economy. They also reflected the influence of factors that operated countercyclically to intensify metate production in the short run. In the summer of 1980, unusually irregular rainfall patterns disrupted the seasonal agricultural cycle and promoted a reallocation of labor from agriculture to metate production, thereby increasing weekly metate output per capita.

TABLE 10.1. **Magdalena Metates Sold and Average Prices in Ocotlán Plaza on 47 Trading Days in 1979–1980 (prices in pesos @ 23 per US$)**

| Month and Day | Number of Metates Sold | Average Selling Price per Week* | Average Selling Price per Month* |
|---|---|---|---|
| October 19 | 10 | 604 | |
| 26 | 13 | 700 | |
| 31 | 1 | 400 | 644 (N = 20) |
| November 9 | 7 | 538 | |
| 16 | 7 | 736 | |
| 23 | 12 | 839 | |
| 30 | 11 | 794 | 757 (N = 28) |
| December 7 | 9 | 800 | |
| 14 | 9 | 839 | |
| 21 | 5 | 830 | |
| 28 | 11 | 865 | 836 (N = 33) |
| January 4 | 8 | 786 | |
| 11 | 4 | 940 | |
| 18 | 12 | 1046 | |
| 25 | 15 | 909 | 899 (N = 34) |
| February 1 | 16 | 838 | |
| 8 | 17 | 904 | |
| 15 | 7 | 838 | |
| 22 | 9 | 792 | |
| 29 | 9 | 864 | 832 (N = 48) |
| March 7 | 14 | 800 | |
| 14 | 17 | 832 | |
| 21 | 12 | 803 | |
| 28 | 11 | 956 | 839 (N = 49) |
| April 4 | 10 | 975 | |
| 11 | 14 | 804 | |
| 18 | 11 | 779 | |
| 25 | 11 | 1023 | 874 (N = 38) |
| May 2 | 13 | 841 | |
| 9 | 8 | 875 | |
| 16 | 12 | 886 | |
| 23 | 11 | 650 | |
| 30 | 10 | 829 | 827 (N = 45) |

TABLE 10.1. **continued**

| Month and Day | Number of Metates Sold | Average Selling Price per Week* | Average Selling Price per Month* |
|---|---|---|---|
| June 6 | 12 | 706 | |
| 13 | -- | -- | |
| 20 | 11 | 754 | |
| 27 | 15 | 582 | 678 (N = 37) |
| July 4 | 14 | 620 | |
| 11 | 13 | 631 | |
| 18 | 9 | 723 | |
| 25 | 4 | 838 | 677 (N = 33) |
| August 1 | 6 | 714 | |
| 8 | 14 | 694 | |
| 15 | 11 | 628 | |
| 22 | 6 | 647 | |
| 29 | 10 | 694 | 676 (N = 37) |
| September 5 | 12 | 663 | |
| 12 | 12 | 550 | 590 (N = 21) |

* Totals in both columns were calculated as the sum of recorded selling prices divided by the number of available prices (indicated as N = 20, etc.). Prices were not recorded for all metates sold on a given market day, thus pricing data were recorded for only a sample of metates sold

Obviously, the jump in the average price level over the two-year period reflected broader inflationary conditions that affected both sellers and buyers. By contrast, the January–February periods in 1967–1968 and 1979–1980 corresponded with highest average price levels matched by highest average outputs; and the periods from mid-May through mid-September also corresponded with declining average price levels and lower outputs (although with more below-average output weeks in 1967–1968 than in 1979–1980).

Antonio Rosario emphasized that people did not have much interest in buying metates in May but did so in September, November, December, January, February, March, and April. By November, people had their harvest in and could sell some corn to buy metates and manos. They had a need for metates, he reasoned, since the festive season was starting and lots of people became godparents and gave metates as gifts to brides. "By April and May everyone is basically in ruin," he explained, "they are short on cash because corn is scarce, there is a shortage of fodder for animals, and everyone is engaged in cultivating their land. They cannot buy metates then, their possibilities are limited."

In short, there was a tight correspondence between the agricultural cycle, the fiesta cycle, and the metate market that metateros like Antonio understood and embraced as a modus operandi in the practice of their craft.

The number of different communities participating as buyers of Magdalena's metates in 1979–1980 increased to 80 from 68 in 1967–1968. The sales percentages grouped by district were as follows: Ocotlán (43 percent, 34 communities); Ejutla (27 percent, 21 communities); Zimatlán (16 percent, 13 communities); Miahuatlán (5 percent, 4 communities); other districts (9 percent, 7 localities). This contrasted markedly with numbers from 1967–1968, when Ocotlán accounted for 64 percent of all sales, Zimatlán for 20 percent, and Ejutla for only 4 percent. In terms of total sales percentages, the district of Ocotlán declined, Zimatlán and Ejutla reversed positions, and Ejutla's relative market participation increased strikingly by a factor of seven. Most of that growth was in the participation of communities (18) that bought four or fewer metates in 1979–1980, with the exception of the cabecera Ejutla de Crespo and San Martín de los Cansecos that bought six each, and Coatecas Alta that purchased fifteen. This increasing participation of communities from the district of Ejutla in the Ocotlán metate market apparently reflected the withdrawal from the Ejutla market of big-lot buyers who purchased metates in Oaxaca City and Ocotlán for resale in Ejutla. Buyers from small, remote indigenous communities who were accustomed to purchasing metates from these intermediaries in Ejutla in 1967–1968 had to do so in Ocotlán in 1979–1980.

In 1967–1968, five Ocotlán communities were the biggest buyers of Magdalena metates: San Miguel Tilquiapan, Ocotlán de Morelos (cabecera), Santiago Apóstol, Asunción, and San Baltazar Chichicapan (Cook 1982, 250–251). They remained so in 1979–1980, collectively accounting for 25 percent of total sales. San Miguel Tilquiapan remained in the lead (29), followed in descending order by Asunción (26), Santiago Apóstol (24), San Baltazar Chichicapan (19), and Ocotlán de Morelos (19). San Pablo Huistepec (Zimatlán), a major buyer in 1967–1968, bought only two Magdalena metates in 1979–1980. This probably reflected a change in marketing patterns rather than a drop in demand for metates. Since Huistepec had a secondary market on Sundays, Teitipac metates would occasionally be available there, but Huistepecanos also had the option of buying metates on Saturdays in the Oaxaca City market.

Other differences between the two marketing periods are noteworthy. First, in 1979–1980, Inocencio Morales, the expatriate Sanjuanero based in Tlacolula, came to Ocotlán a few times and purchased eleven Magdalena metates for resale in the Tlacolula market. Also, aside from the old-timer José María Santiago, who brought metates to market on only three occasions in 1979–1980, there were three new intermediaries buying up metates in Magdalena for resale in Ocotlán on a regular basis: Luisa Colmenares, Josefina Méndez, and Olivia Aquino Quero, who was the widow of Antonio Rosario, the expelled metatero/ejidatario (who was deceased by 1979–1980). Finally, there were several occasional metate buyers from Mexico City, the Isthmus of Tehuantepec, Tuxtepec, Candelaria, Juquila, and Nochistlán, who accounted for a total of fourteen metates sold in 1979–1980; there were no buyers from any of these locations in 1967–1968. This suggests that over the twelve-year period Magdalena sellers in the Ocotlán plaza had picked up some metate sales that traditionally went to sellers in Oaxaca City.

Of the twenty-seven producer-sellers participating in the Magdalena metate industry in 1978–1979, only eight, or 33 percent, were participants in 1967–1968. Of the ten who produced and sold more than twenty metates each, half were newcomers, including Pedro Cosme Méndez, who was the production leader (35 metates) among this group. Also among the newcomers was Juan Martínez Francisco (born in 1955), the great-grandson of the industry's founder, Nabor Martínez. The most prolific producer-seller, Juvenal Sánchez, with thirty-seven metates produced and sold, was born in 1935 and began in the industry in 1956. The remaining seven veterans in descending order of output were: Germán Rosario (27); Arturo Vásquez (24); Atanasio Hernández (22); Jacinto Cosme (20), the older brother of Pedro; Fernando Rosario (20); Rufino Sánchez (14); and Martiniano Méndez (14) (cf. Cook 1982, 320). During 1967–1968, all of these veterans were interviewed except Jacinto Cosme. They continued to make and sell metates year after year because, like their forerunners, they derived material benefits from doing so.

Magdalenans' economic alternatives were more restricted under the hacienda regime than they were after agrarian reform. In the last quarter of the nineteenth century, Magdalenans were not legally obliged to work as sharecroppers for the hacienda, but with little or no land, they confronted an economic imperative to do so, either for the hacienda or for local pequeños propietarios or for local rancheros. Under those conditions, the availability of a new cash-earning opportunity like metate making must have been appealing to many.

From the perspective of the individual worker in the latter half of the twentieth century, there were relative advantages and disadvantages to working for others in agriculture on a wage or share basis and working as a metatero, assuming that the worker in question was prepared and capable of working in either branch of production. If the goal was to get access to an ox team, the best alternative was to work as a hired hand for an ox-team owner in exchange for a future claim on use of the ox team. Ox teams could be rented on a cash basis, with cash raised through wage labor or by making and selling metates (or, as a last resort, selling crops on reserve for future subsistence), but there was no guarantee that one would be available to rent at the time it was needed, and the rental price could be higher than the value of a day's labor. If the worker's goal was to convert labor power into cash for the purpose of buying subsistence goods in the market, then it made sense to pursue the metate-making alternative by going to work in the quarries early in the week to obtain sufficient stone for making as many metates or manos as possible to take to market in Ocotlán on Friday.

For individual metateros, the great advantage of allocating labor to metate production and sale, rather than to agricultural wage labor, was the real possibility of realizing a higher than equivalent return per labor day (i.e., above and beyond the going wage rate). In spite of market variability, this route would probably yield workers a higher return on labor and, therefore, result in a larger bundle of subsistence goods. "We go to market on Fridays," said Antonio Rosario, "to buy staples that maintain us: corn, beans, other staples that we need to keep on working. On Friday afternoons, after selling metates and manos, you come back home with corn, beans, tomatoes, onions, chile peppers, lard, soap—all the things required to eat, to cook, to wash, everything." This was as true in the late 1800s and 1930s as it was in the 1960s and 1970s.

The bottom line was that metate production easily fit into a multi-occupational work schedule, not only seasonally as with agriculture, but interseasonally as with other part-time occupations and tasks. Fernando Rosario is an example of someone who was versatile in the occupational sense. In 1967, he worked part-time as a blacksmith (only one of two in Magdalena), as a metatero, as an aradero (plow maker), and as a campesino (he owned a yunta). Previously, he also worked as a baker (panadero) and a basket maker (canastero). He liked blacksmithing and metate making because he could adjust his work schedule in those occupations to the tillage cycle. As a blacksmith, he could sharpen and maintain his own tools as well as those of other metateros, for which he charged a small fee. Metate making had the added advantage of enabling him to take his animals to pasture on the way to the quarry and tend them while he worked there. Also, to meet his periodic costs for charcoal, Fernando used metate sales revenues.

Regarding labor cost, however, there was a difference in Fernando's reasoning in these different occupations. In agriculture and blacksmithing, he tended to view his labor simply as a means available to him to make a living for his household, not as a cost that had to be offset by revenue. Metate making was a different matter, since it was a market-oriented occupation. Fernando calculated the value of metates according to days worked in clearing the quarry, in blasting and cutting stone, and in making products. Expenses were calculated, more or less, by using a rate of 10 pesos per day for labor. A metate was sold for a price that compensated the days of work put into its production (que salgan los días de trabajo) plus the cost of forging tools and of transporting it to the marketplace. In 1968, Fernando priced regular-size metates around 35 pesos; asked 90 pesos in the marketplace; and, after negotiation, sold them for 70 pesos for a profit (ganancia) of 35 pesos each.

It was the possibility of profiting from their work through the process of haggling with buyers in the marketplace that was a strong motivator for metateros to produce and bring their metates to market. The data show that many of them were successful with this strategy, at least in the postharvest months of relatively strong demand (Cook 1982, Ch. 7). When profit realization was not possible, the bottom line for metateros was to sell at a price that enabled them to convert their labor-time into cash at a rate approximating the prevailing wage for day labor, which in Fernando's case, was estimated at 10 pesos per day.[7]

## Conclusion

Although its early history is poorly documented, Magdalena Ocotlán emerged from the colonial period with only a fundo legal and memories of additional communal land that had been lost in the process of expansion and consolidation of neighboring haciendas—San José and El Vergel—that completely encapsulated it. Like San Lorenzo Albarradas, and in marked contrast to Xaagá and San Antonio Buenavista, Magdalena, although an enclave with most of its population reduced to the status of landless tenant sharecroppers, had within its fundo legal sectors of private and communal property that supported a separate community identity. Like San Lorenzo, it was located on a main, well-traveled road that facilitated a certain degree of openness not found in more isolated communities like San Sebastián and San Juan Teitipac and Santa Cecilia and Santo Domingo Jalieza.

Since Magdalena was located on the main road from Oaxaca City to Miahuatlán and was close to the mining center of San José Progreso, opportunities for commercial activity were realized in the form of stores, cantinas, and rest stops catering to travelers and mine workers. It was open to outside influences and was involved in the revolutionary currents circulating in the region particularly after 1910, as shown by its conflicts with the San José hacienda starting in 1885 and culminating in a 1916 petition for land restitution.

Magdalena's location and relative openness surely were factors in the arrival sometime after 1880 of a migrant metatero from San Juan Teitipac, Nabor Martínez, who introduced his craft there and launched a new industry that thrived in conjunction with agriculture facilitated by a definitive ejido endowment in 1921. This combination of economic pursuits enabled Magdalenans, for the remainder of the twentieth century, to engage in usos y costumbres on their own terms, if not without obstacles and pitfalls in their pursuit of civility as circumstances dictated.

# Conclusion

This book's purpose is to promote understanding of a complex historical process of struggle for land, livelihood, and civility in the Oaxaca Valley. It was organized to achieve this through a series of community studies, by allowing subjects to speak for themselves, and by expanding the voice of selected subjects who were especially representative of particular communities and occupations, or were witnesses to particular events. Four haciendas—San Bartolo, Xaagá, San Antonio Buenavista, and San José La Garzona—affected the livelihoods and sociocultural life of several communities in different subregions of the valley and its mountain hinterland. The approach and mode of presentation of subject matter was designed to immerse the reader in historical or ethnographic detail, filtered and organized to avoid undue repetition and loss of narrative threads, but of sufficient substance to convey behavioral complexity and contextual meanings. The point was to produce a study that overcame the pitfalls of analytical detachment by populating it with real human subjects who were actually living history and reconstructing it from their memory banks, rather than with subjects located in abstract processes as exemplars of agency.

A broad theme is central throughout this book: the ramifications of the struggle for civility (meeting the requirements of local citizenship) by individual citizens in collectivities that establish and administer both customary and legal rules of the game. Community service through tequios, festive expenditures, or political office was reconciled in the lives of individual citizens with their pursuit of household and family welfare through hard work, enterprise, and market participation.

The attempts by individual citizens in households to meet standards of civility in their communities were sometimes at odds with their struggle for material well-being: land or the means of production to cultivate it had to be surrendered, or cash earnings from the sale of crops or crafts had to be spent to meet social or fiscal obligations. Labor or products had to be provided to meet tequio requirements. Trade-offs forced upon households to deal with conflicting obligations were arguably more onerous in Zapotec-speaking communities, where individual mayordomía sponsorship and festive expenditures linked to public office were more pervasive than in the mestizo communities of San Lorenzo Albarradas and Xaagá. The negative consequences of civility were most pronounced among households in the lower half of the socioeconomic structure even though large festive sponsorships were beyond their purview (Cook and Joo 1995, 45).

Among the questions that remain only partially answered regarding the collaborative role of the colonial viceregal government and the Catholic Church in Oaxaca Valley history is the extent and transformative effect of the policy to relocate and congregate indigenous populations during the sixteenth century and afterward. There was sufficient, if incomplete, evidence to suggest the constitutive effects of that policy on four of the nine communities studied: San Sebastián Teitipac, Santa Cecilia Jalieza, San Lorenzo Albarradas, and Magdalena Ocotlán. The possibility remains that the policy was more widespread in the Oaxaca Valley and its hinterland than has previously been supposed.

Another question specifically regarding the role of the Church derives from more recent history and revolves around the promotion of religious sodalities (cofradías, hermandades, sociedades) associated with the cult of the saints in the postrevolutionary period. This question was raised in my rereading of a classic 1957 study of San Juan Guelavía in which the authors noted that several of the community's religious societies, including la Señora del Carmen and el Señor de las Peñas, were introduced around the time the ejido was established there in 1937 (Martínez Ríos and Luna Méndez 1960, 297). This struck a chord with me because the same two societies were established in Magdalena Ocotlán within the same time frame, although the ejido was established there in 1921, earlier than in Guelavía. Was this religious development coincidental, or did it represent official Church policy in the postrevolutionary period in ejido communities?

A final question, raised by the Guelavía study and also worthy of further research, concerns the proactive role of a prominent member of the valley elite, Lic. Jorge Meixueiro, in that community's postrevolutionary agrarian politics. In the late 1910s and early 1920s, the role of Guelavía's largest landowning family, the Lópezes, was on the wane, and ex-general Juan Brito's fortunes were on the rise. Brito had married into the community, operated a general store there, and headed a regional militia (defensas sociales) in the late 1920s and early 1930s. But the complications and ramifications of

Brito's career were made even more enigmatic and demanding of explanation by another event.

On March 18, 1936, a total of 354 landless peasants from Guelavía, against the wishes of ecclesiastical authorities, the widow of the landlord W. T. López, and a group of her sharecroppers, officially filed a petition for an ejido endowment. Nine days later, on March 27, Juan Brito was assassinated in his Guelavía store. Licenciado Jorge Meixueiro, who came to Guelavía during this period, was instrumental in motivating and paving the way for the ejido endowment petition. Was coincidence at play here or power politics? It is frustrating (and inexplicable) that Martínez Ríos and Luna Méndez (1960, 240–244), in their account of the postrevolutionary agrarian history of Guelavía, made no mention whatsoever of Juan Brito, thus precluding any deeper understanding of that personage's role in regional agrarian political history. My sense is that this topic merits further scholarly scrutiny.[1]

## Archaeology, History, and Ethnography

Archaeologists and ethnohistorians have made Oaxaca's prehistory more intelligible through erudite and imaginative excursions into language, symbolism, religion, politics, militarism, and economy. Short of finding a method for incarnating and interrogating skeletal remains, it is hard to conceive of how future knowledge production will fundamentally alter our current understanding of change in Oaxaca's civilizational process from, say, the fourteenth and fifteenth centuries in a Mesoamerican matrix through conquest and colonization by Spain in the sixteenth and seventeenth centuries. It would be naïve, however, to think that knowledge production regarding this topic will stagnate and that newer, more refined understanding of it will not emerge.

The most impressive contribution of archaeology toward understanding the development of Oaxaca civilization was unraveling the complexities of the transition from the lithic to the village stages. That transition involved a unique interplay between seasonality and scheduling of labor-time associated with the changing mix of hunting, gathering, and plant domestication. It involved the emergence of a corn + beans + squash complex, and the subsequent fine-tuning of agriculture, which facilitated fundamental demographic, social, and political transformations (Flannery et al. 1968; Flannery 1968).

More recent archaeological research has shed light on settlement pattern instability and shifting elite-nonelite political relations engendered by the urban center–hinterland community dynamic (Blanton et al. 1999; Joyce

2010, 294), as well as trade patterns and craft production of lapidary and ceramic commodities (Feinman and Nicholas 2004). Archaeologists have even managed to extract information from pictographic writing and imagery regarding ancient Zapotec cognition, including "cosmology, religion, ideology, and other products of the ancient mind" (Marcus and Flannery 1996, 19), without interrogating living subjects with *pèe* (ancient Zapotec for "vital force") but through inferences from inanimate objects. The synthesis of archaeological research findings focused on the development of urban society among the Zapotec in the Oaxaca Valley is truly impressive (Marcus and Flannery 1996).

Nevertheless, the archaeological claim of "continuities in belief and practice" that bridge periods of great prehistoric transformations and postconquest history remains a hypothesis awaiting empirical demonstration (Joyce 2010, 295). This will be a challenging undertaking, given the depth and reach of the process of creative destruction set in motion by the Spanish Conquest. It is precisely that process that wreaks havoc on bridging arguments for continuity between preconquest and postconquest Zapotec life in the Oaxaca Valley (Marcus and Flannery 1996, 32).

There is much to be said for the potential of ethnoarchaeology to stimulate more involvement of communities themselves in projects on their own turf. Locals are necessarily involved as a labor force in archaeological excavations, and archaeologists have realized the advantage and educational value of supporting the establishment of museums in several Oaxaca Valley communities with excavated preconquest sites. The potential influence on popular historical consciousness of the archaeology–local community connection is illustrated by the serendipitous encounter of Rosendo Carranza with the tomb of metatero predecessors in a quarry of San Juan Teitipac, and the effect it had on his thinking about his own identity. Imagine how that effect could have been multiplied locally and regionally by the intervention of the INAH (Instituto Nacional de Antropología e Historia) archaeology program and the establishment of a community museum.

The ethnographer seeking to link understandings of the past with those of the present confronts a formidable challenge: the farther the time perspective moves backward from living generations, whether in the presence of monumental architecture in spectacular places or more humdrum residential remains, the more remote become the lives of ancient human subjects and their cultures. The double alienation, temporal and cultural, of trying to scientifically understand or imagine what life was like in colonial Oaxaca from a basis in twentieth-century ethnography is somewhat less daunting than doing so vis-à-vis the pre-Hispanic record. The process of Spanish conquest and colonization itself forced Mesoamericans, including the indigenous people of Oaxaca, into European life and culture. By virtue of the imperialistic, theocratic, authoritarian, and racist Spanish project, Mesoamerican indigenous "others" inevitably became less a product of "otherness," if not less distinctive, from the perspective of Euro-American ethnography.

Between 1500 and 1700, the Mesoamerican peoples were demographically decimated and their remnant populations were politically, economically, and culturally subjugated. As European colonial subjects, they were not uniformly acculturated but became less alien as Euro-American anthropological subjects. In sum, the discontinuities between the archaeological record of Mesoamerican civilization and the historical record of provincial New Spain inevitably loom larger than the continuities.[2]

There is no question that studies focused on colonial land tenure and use, social and political relations, and intercommunity conflicts involving land issues are more directly consequential for ethnography than archaeological studies. This is because of a more substantial and systematic documentary database about specific communities and a shorter time perspective. Significant continuity or mutual reinforcement can be found in historical and ethnographic data regarding economic specialization, landlord-peasant relations, the existence of cacique-like politics, and intercommunity conflict, as exemplified in the Teitipac–Jalieza–San Antonio Buenavista cluster.

When addressing problems involving behavior and cultural content, however, it is challenging to bridge ethnohistorical and ethnographic knowledge bases, many of which are fragmentary or incomplete. The so-called Teitipac rebellion comes to mind. Was it, in fact, a rebellion or simply a regional incident in Spain's spiritual conquest of Mexico? Historians emphasize the discovery by resident Dominican friars of the celebration of pagan rites under the leadership of an idolatrous Indian priest, but the oral history regarding Pablo Rojas was explicit in imagining something more akin to an uprising in referring to "'the priest of the devil' . . . who formed an army, started an armed uprising and went around killing people until there was a war." This would surely merit classification as a "rebellion" (Taylor 1979, 113–151), but earlier historians, mostly men of the cloth, viewed resistance to Catholic indoctrination itself as both irrational and, as a rejection of their authority, rebellious. In any case, the incident provided a classic example of terroristic oppression of indigenous people by the Spanish colonial regime.

There was another face to the role of Catholic proselytization in colonial Oaxaca that left a legacy in modern Oaxaca: the cult of the saints and the burdensome festive expenditures engendered by it. In the case of San Sebastián Teitipac, this involved a sort of miraculous vision of the kind associated with Juan Diego on Tepeyac Hill in the greater Mexico City area in 1531 that gave birth to the shrine of Guadalupe (Wolf 2001). In San Sebastián, the visitation of the Holy Mother was represented as the Virgin of Juquila.

In Oaxaca Valley communities, supplicant actions to honor particular representations of the Marian image occurred through promesas (vows) made to evoke problem-resolving divine intervention. These were, in one case, a "miraculous" cure of illness (Atanasio Hernández in Magdalena Ocotlán) by Nuestra Señora del Carmen and, in another, a "miraculous" escape from a violent crime-in-progress (Agustín Martínez in San Sebastián) involving the Virgin of Juquila. These examples reinforce Taylor's (2010, 8) insight regarding how in Oaxaca, "Guadalupan devotion was overshadowed by local and regional shrines to other images of Mary . . . ," as well as his finding from analyzing eight hundred Mexican miracle stories that most were cures or narrow escapes from life-threatening situations (2011, 12).

More mundane, less dramatic motives were at work in a host of other cases of mayordomía sponsorship. These ranged from compliance with local codes of civility, as in the cases of Magdalena metateros with the Señor de las Peñas celebration or of Inocencio Morales in Tlacolula, to opportunistic negotiation of a career path through the local cargo system, as in the case of Saúl Gutiérrez in San Sebastián Teitipac.

Years of imaginative and painstaking research—with bundles of mildewed and decaying documents lining dust-ridden shelves—by many dedicated historians have yielded richly detailed studies that breathe life into deceased generations of community dwellers and their circumstances. These have produced knowledge of broader and deeper reach than has been produced by those of us who have concentrated on research with and about living subjects. Studies like those by Taylor (1972), Chance (1978), and Olivera and Romero (1973) facilitate, even invite, ethnographers to undertake projects in retrospection to connect historical pasts with later "ethnographic presents" in specific communities.

The contribution of historians is not diminished by the fact that their studies depended on compulsive, exhaustive, and institutionalized record keeping by Spanish colonial bureaucrats. This process regularly involved on-site visitations and surveys of local communities. The postcolonial Mexican state deserves equal credit for preserving these records and making them accessible to the public, as well as for continuing and enhancing the record-keeping process.

The lack of definitive resolution of many intercommunity conflicts over boundaries, ownership, and use of communal lands that were the focus of so much litigation, surveying, and resurveying during the colonial period and afterward contrasts markedly with the relative success of post-1915 efforts to achieve either restitución or dotación through expropriation of land historically appropriated by haciendas from local communities. Certainly from the perspective of Haciendas Xaagá, San Bartolo, San Antonio Buenavista, and San José La Garzona and the communities influenced by them, agrarian land redistribution was creatively destructive. Inefficient and exploitative enterprises, mostly formed and consolidated by questionable means, were delegitimized, disassembled, and replaced by a mix of small private landholdings, communal lands, and ejidos. These elements provided a more promising and equitable basis for improvement of the general welfare of the rural population than those of the prerevolutionary regime. The relative speed with which these goals of the agrarian revolution were achieved in the 1920s and 1930s against the deeply entrenched, powerful oligarchy known as the Vallistocracia (including families like Iñárritu, Monterrubio, Mimiaga, and Castro) was remarkable. It exposed and inscribed the anachronistic, economically unviable, and socially repugnant nature of the hacienda regime.

The historical economic record shows that Oaxaca Valley haciendas were unstable enterprises, more often failing than succeeding as businesses, that represented barriers to local community and regional economic progress. Documentary and oral history records expose the inherent social justice of the land redistribution process realized through Article 27 of the Constitution of 1917 (Mendieta y Núñez 1966, 183–190; *Constitución Política* 2002, 22–31) and the establishment of the ejido system through the 1920 Ley de Ejidos (Mendieta y Núñez 1966, 191–197). Nevertheless, these same records also show a general rise in the level of social and economic welfare of rural communities in the postreform period. The case of Magdalena Ocotlán illustrated imperfections in the allotment process administered by local agrarian committees, as well as in ejido governance. Still, life for ejidatarios after agrarian reform was much better than it was for their predecessors.

The historical intervention of the Mexican state regarding intercommunity land boundaries and use of commons was much less successful than its role in agrarian reform, but not due to inattention. This mixed record is well illustrated by the case of Santa Cecilia Jalieza, which throughout the colonial and most of the postcolonial periods was assailed by outsiders, mostly in contiguous communities but also by private interests in mining, agriculture, and animal husbandry. Repeated interventions by colonial authorities, including hearings and on-site land surveys, took a significant toll in time and treasure that yielded positive cartographic and legal results in the short run but no definitive long-term solutions of the underlying problem, especially the conflict with San Juan Teitipac.

Failures of the colonial administration reflected to some degree faulty surveying and cartography (Aguilar-Robledo 2009). The utter recalcitrance of some communities like San Juan Teitipac to obey or respect external authority, as shown by rock-throwing protests against survey parties, also sabotaged the process (Taylor 1979, 136).

Santa Cecilia Jalieza's postreform land problems were exacerbated by being conjoined with intercommunity conflict, banditry, and factionalism that led to episodes of population displacement and considerable loss of life. This makes sympathetic outsiders more appreciative of the incredible perseverance, stamina, grit, determination, and ingenuity Santa Cecilians displayed over the centuries to maintain their culture, identity, and livelihood intact. The role of intelligent and strong leaders like Marciano García, a peasant wood-carver in the tradition of his ancestors who served as keepers of foundational documents (títulos), also must be acknowledged.

Inequalities and conflicts within and between San Sebastián Teitipac, San Juan Teitipac, and Santa Cecilia Jalieza had a precedent in pre-Hispanic cacicazgos and, most significantly, early Spanish colonial policy that was accommodative of the interests of indigenous nobility and allowed them to meld into the new colonial social order. It may not be overly speculative to see a connection between pre-Hispanic Zapotec rulers in Teitipac, Baaloo and Baalachi; Juan López and Lucas de Grijalva, both seventeenth-century caciques in Teitipac communities; and Matías Marcial, the jefe político in Teitipac during the Porfiriato. Intercommunity raiding and violence seem to have been a part of Oaxaca Valley culture even before it was "commemorated in monuments" by 150 BC (Blanton et al. 1999, 2). Perhaps the differences are of degree, not kind.

Official documentation is a product of state-local community interaction, a process that was present in the Oaxaca Valley from at least the ninth century AD when the Zapotec state had arisen at Monte Albán and recorded aspects of its history in various written forms of expression, including engravings on stone or inscriptions on deerskin or bark paper (Romero Frizzi 2003a, 25–26). The close relationship between the use of writing and governing power existed, with interruptions and invasions by the Mixtec and Tenochca, from that point until the early colonial period when a transformation began through the introduction of the alphabet to the native nobility by the Spanish priests. "Indigenous nobility desired to appropriate the new symbols of power: the alphabet of the conqueror" (Romero Frizzi 2003a, 39), but by the eighteenth century the many concerns of the Zapotec elite had been reduced to one predominant concern: defense of their territory. To paraphrase the words of Romero Frizzi (2003a, 48): There no longer were iconographic registers with their complications; there were maps with images of mountains, bridges, houses, settlements, and roads that formed part of extensive judicial files in defense of their lands. This is precisely the focal point of interaction between state power, its bureaucracy, and the leadership of indigenous communities, which in many cases was either descended from or was in the tradition of the cacicazgo.

The whole interactive process was fueled by intercommunity boundary disputes related to ownership and access to communal land suited to agriculture or other forms of economic activity; the income potential for all involved parties, including fees for bureaucrats and technicians; and the shared quest for violence reduction and peace maintenance. It is hard to disagree with Philip Dennis's (1987, esp. Ch. 6) thesis that the repetitive, intergenerational role of central governmental authority in arbitrating intercommunity boundary and land disputes in the Oaxaca Valley legitimized and relegitimized the state and its administrative bureaucracy.

The community studies in this book also suggest that intercommunity conflict was associated with intracommunity inequality in ownership and access to land and agricultural means of production. Whether in the colonial period of lingering cacicazgo relations or during the postcolonial period of caciquismo, the focus on neighboring communities as the source of agrarian problems served to distract attention from the class-based inequalities within many of the contesting communities themselves. This is most evident and empirically documented in the case of San Sebastián Teitipac but surely applied as well to its neighbor San Juan. Even the postrevolutionary agrarian reform process that targeted the hacienda as the source of agrarian inequality, as illustrated by the case of Magdalena Ocotlán, was only partially successful in reducing prerevolutionary inequality within the community.

## Differential Reactions of Subaltern Communities to Haciendas

San Lorenzo Albarradas, Xaagá, San Antonio Buenavista, and Magdalena Ocotlán had different reactions to their subaltern status vis-à-vis haciendas. San Antonio Buenavista and Xaagá, where terrazgueros had no fundo legal or land of their own of any type, even for housing, approximated Ronald Waterbury's (1975) notion of "non-revolutionary peasants" who did not openly rebel against hacendados in the second decade of the twentieth century and, in some cases, even defended haciendas against incursions by revolutionaries (cf. Ruiz Cervantes 1988, 355–357). By contrast, San Lorenzo and Magdalena, which had fundos legales that included land for purposes of residence and cultivation, were relatively early participants in the agrarian reform process. In the last quarter of the nineteenth century, San Lorenzans retaliated for violence perpetrated against them by Hacienda Xaagá, and Magdalenans did likewise vis-à-vis Hacienda San José in 1885. These two examples undermine the docility thesis regarding Oaxaca Valley peasants and the hacienda regime during the late nineteenth and early twentieth centuries (e.g., Waterbury 1975; Whitecotton 1977, 226).

One factor that might explain the different responses of these communities to oppression and exploitation by hacendados was that, unlike Congregación Buenavista (but not Xaagá), they were more distant from the hacienda's control center, the casco or caserío. This was especially so in the case of San Lorenzo. As in San Lorenzo, Magdalena's fundo legal had a limited amount of arable land. Unlike Congregación Buenavista, which was located on the hacendado's doorstep without any land of its own and relatively isolated in a corner of the Tlacolula arm of the valley, Magdalena and San Lorenzo were located on main roads leading elsewhere. Lenchanos could travel up the road to the Mixería and beyond, or down the road to Mitla, Tlacolula, and Oaxaca City; Magdalenans could travel south to Ejutla, Miahuatlán, Pochutla, and the Pacific coast, or north to Ocotlán and Oaxaca City.

It is probable, as the case of Xaagá suggests, that proximity to larger communities like Mitla and to the road to Tlacolula and Oaxaca City was less important in explaining its failure to rebel against the hacienda regime than was total dependence on the hacendado for livelihood, a condition it shared with San Antonio Buenavista. This supports Eric Wolf's (1969, 290) thesis that poor peasants or landless laborers who depended on landlords for the largest part of their livelihood, or the totality of it, were completely within the power domain of their employers. Without sufficient resources of their own to use in the power struggle, such subalterns were unlikely to pursue the course of rebellion unless they were able to rely on some external power to challenge the power that constrained them.

In the last analysis, none of these subaltern peasant communities achieved their liberation from the hacienda regime and access to land by rebellion. They ultimately got these only through their insertion in complicated and contested postinsurrectional processes led by evolving federal and state agrarian reform bureaucracies and functionaries. This cadre knew the laws and how to manipulate them, and cooperative peasant petitioners benefited accordingly (Arellanes Meixueiro 1999, 6–7).

## Land, Agriculture, and Craft Production

In the Oaxaca Valley, the historical struggle of rural communities to defend or obtain land was driven by the fact that agriculture was the engine of the economy and the sustainer of populations and their social life. Without land, no agriculture; without agriculture, no population, social life, or civility. Historically, nonagricultural commodity production in these local economies was undertaken either to directly supply agriculture with needed tools and equipment (e.g., plows, wagons, ox yokes, harnesses, baskets) or to supplement household income in off-season or low-task periods for agriculture. Consequently, 57 percent of the households in our survey of twenty communities (all selected because of known participation in craft production) were classified as "peasant-artisan," which meant that they cultivated land of their own in addition to having some members who worked full- or part-time, permanently or seasonally, in craft industries; 38 percent were evenly divided between full-time artisans and full-time agriculturists; and 5 percent were involved in neither own-agriculture nor own-craft production and were essentially full-time employees (Cook and Binford 1990, 42).

Of the 1,008 rural households surveyed between 1978 and 1980, 24 percent did not have land to cultivate. The amount of annual household labor-time allocated to nonagricultural commodity production was highly correlated with access to land and agricultural means of production: lower standing with regard to these variables made higher involvement in nonagricultural commodity production more likely.

The level of participation in nonagricultural commodity production among the communities examined in this book went from a high of nearly 100 percent in the palm products industry of San Lorenzo Albarradas to a low of 25 percent in the treadle-loom weaving community of Xaagá. The rest of the communities, all of which had several craft industries, had rates of participation falling somewhere between these two extremes. In Santo Domingo Jalieza, which had five craft industries, the rate of household participation was 81 percent in embroidery, 38 percent in backstrap-loom weaving, 27 percent in charcoal making, and 17 percent in basket making. In Santa Cecilia Jalieza, 90 percent of households participated in embroidery, 73 percent in wood carving, 17 percent in backstrap-loom weaving, 10 percent in brick making, and 7 percent in basketry. Magdalena, by contrast, had 54 percent household participation in craft production.

In the entire gamut of household participation in craft industries, only the treadle-loom weaving/cotton garment industry in Xaagá (and the handmade brick industry of Santa Lucía del Camino and vicinity) provided realistic opportunities for sustained capital accumulation, and even there the most successful household enterprises sharecropped their ejido allotments to contribute to their subsistence. Craft production could be rewarding but, as a general rule, did not lead to upward mobility (Cook and Binford 1990, Chs. 3 and 4).

With regard to household participation in crafts, the rationale cannot be reduced strictly to economic reward but is by no means explained by locally used catchphrases like "from the ancestors" (desde los antepasados). No craft culture was automatically transmitted intact from one generation of community members to another. Every generation of households negotiated its relationship to the craft cultures of prior generations: some rejected them; others adopted them with modifications; and still others adopted them unchanged. Each generation confronted new material and cultural conditions that created new aspirations and expectations. The relationship between artesano and oficio was susceptible to change.

The extreme examples are from Magdalena Ocotlán and Santa Cecilia Jalieza, where totally new crafts were introduced centuries after their founding. Magdalena became a metate-producing community in the last quarter of the nineteenth century thanks to an immigrant from San Juan Teitipac, and both communities became involved in embroidery in the 1970s owing to the expansion of merchant-centered putting-out systems located mainly in San Juan Chilateca and San Antonino del Castillo. In Santa Cecilia, the ancient utensil-carving industry experienced innovations in product design (chocolate stirrers, or acahuetes, to letter openers, or abrecartas), new products (decorative combs, or peines), new commercial relationships (selling abrecartas to San Antonio Arrazola, where they are decorated with painted designs for resale) (Hernández-Díaz and Zafra 2005, 191), and new sources of wood.

Metate culture was also diffused by the migration of metateros from San Juan Teitipac to Tlacolula during the second half of the twentieth century, as the cases of Inocencio Morales and others illustrated. Tlacolula did have a local quarry industry and also, in the 1960s, one remaining native metatero (Cook 1969, 318), but by that time, expatriate Sanjuaneros dominated the craft there, specializing in large, expensive ceremonial metates produced in a mixed workshop–putting-out system. Unlike the San Juan/Magdalena case, which led to the establishment of a new industry, there are at least two reasons why the Tlacolula branch of the metate industry will not survive: already by the 1960s urbanization was forcing a shutdown of local quarrying, and San Juan metateros were increasingly hard pressed to practice their craft in Tlacolula. Tlacolula's transitory involvement with metate making also characterized its earlier involvement with treadle-loom weaving.

The most improbable and complicated story of craft origins in the Oaxaca Valley pertained to treadle-loom weaving in Mitla and Xaagá by way of a peripatetic artisan named Félix Sibaja Santos, who was born in Rancho de Guajes, San Carlos Yautepec; orphaned; and went to live in Tlacolula with a paternal uncle, where he worked as an amarrador (knotter) in the local rebozo industry. By the time he was a teenager, he had earned enough to purchase a loom to weave rebozos for sale in the Tlacolula market. In 1938, he moved to Oaxaca City to work for Casa Brena, a well-known mantelería, as a treadle-loom weaver (operario), married, and started a family. Between 1944 and 1946, he worked as a bracero in California and, with his 10,000 pesos in savings, established his own six-loom mantelería in Oaxaca City. An economic downturn forced him to close his business and relocate to Xaagá, where his brother was a business partner of the administrator of the ex-hacienda, and found Félix a job in the charcoal business. In 1949, he decided to bring the looms that he had stored in Oaxaca to the ex-hacienda, where he established a new mantelería with five apprentices as a cooperative in collaboration with ejido authorities. This lasted a year, after which the arrangement broke down due to a dispute over revenues, and Félix resorted to cultivating land still belonging to the ex-hacienda as a yuntero and mediero. Then, in 1953, Félix once again moved his looms, this time to the Frissell hotel in Mitla where the owner and founder, Ervin R. Frissell, wanted to establish a mantelería (Beals 1975, 258).

It was in this setting that he became the teacher of several weavers who would later establish independent mantelerías in Mitla, specializing in a line of products Félix pioneered, including the famous white wool rebozo (rebozo de lana fina y blanca). By 1956, Félix sold his looms to Frissell and moved back to Oaxaca City, working again as an operario for Casa Brena and, subsequently, Casa Acevedo, before going to work in a smaller mantelería on Calle Santos Degollado owned by his comadre, where he was still working when I interviewed him in 1981. Ironically, the post-Frissell Mitla mantelerías were instant successes and became employers of loom operators from Xaagá, some of whom by 1970 had established their own mantelerías in Xaagá (Cook and Binford 1990, 94–99). It is hard to imagine a more convoluted history of craft development.

## The Metate as a Bridging Commodity between Economy and Culture

Special people and communities, and their relationships to land in the process of making and earning a living and meeting civil obligations, were the focus of this study. Inescapably, commodities were identified and discussed but in a subdued way. One very special commodity, however, merits some further consideration before the last word is written; it is a pre-Hispanic survivor in a twenty-first-century economy increasingly in the thrall of capitalist consumerism. I refer to the metate, "the life-giving stone" (Searcy 2011).

On the basis of conversations with Maya people in highland Guatemalan communities who consistently claimed that "without the metate, there would be no food," Michael Searcy (2011, 90–96) painstakingly documented the physical characteristics and entire lifespan of these artifacts, including their use in the household, their longevity, and even their fate when broken, worn out, and discarded. He also examined what the Maya say and think about them with implications for gender relations.

Searcy (2011, 149) contends that metates in Guatemalan Maya communities "are not markers of female gender exclusively," a thesis he supports by noting that metates are gifted to newlyweds as a couple, not to brides alone (ibid., 72–74). In the Oaxaca Valley, metates are also ritually gifted to brides and to the conjugal pair, by the bride's baptismal godfather to her, and by the groom's confirmation godfather, who is also expected to give a storage chest (baúl) to the newlyweds (Martínez Ríos and Luna Méndez 1960, 223). The ability to pay comes into play here, and the groom's confirmation godfather may not be able to make both gifts to the newlyweds. Then again, these godparents or others may be more generous. Accordingly, I saw (and photographed) wedding-gift arrays with a minimum of one to a maximum of five metates—and never saw one without a metate.

Among the Oaxaca Valley Zapotec, the cultural emphasis was biased toward the connection between bride and metate, whereas among the highland Maya, Searcy (2011, 143) emphasizes the connection between metate and the conjugal unit. As he expresses it: "Men rely on women to process food, just as women rely on men to produce the food they process. Their metates are a material manifestation of gender complementarity, produced, owned, and used by both sexes." He also admits (ibid., 139), somewhat paradoxically, that "assigning female biological traits to a metate, which most Mayas consider a woman's tool, is a significant instance of gendered anthropomorphization." Overall, Searcy builds a strong case empirically for his interpretation, and it may well stand as definitive for the highland Maya of Guatemala.

Valley Zapotec women exclusively used metates, but in production, men quarried and cut stone, whereas women contributed to finishing roughed-out products, decorating them, and selling them in the marketplace. Gender complementarity was partially modified by gender crossover. This was also the case with agriculture, where land preparation and any task requiring the use of traction animals, plows, and wagons was exclusively performed by males, whereas other agricultural tasks like planting, harvesting, and crop processing involved gender cooperation. Gender complementarity was an inherent part of the division of labor. It may merit empirical scrutiny and measurement, but it hardly merits emphasis as anything out of the ordinary (Searcy 2011, 3).

Searcy (2011, 149) does not deviate from the canon in the Mesoamerican archaeological literature that avoids conceptualizing artifacts as commodities, as if to do so might yield more theoretically relevant explanations about "grinding stone collections from excavations of pre-Hispanic sites." To his credit, he does raise the issue of the fate of grinding stones in Maya culture and economy but can do no better than offer an undertheorized, one-dimensional prognosis: "The Maya, given their diminishing use and production of manos and metates, are likely to abandon these tools within the next ten years" (ibid., 149). As far as it goes, this might prove to be true, but then again, it seems to ignore the cultural content and symbolic ramifications of these artifacts that Searcy systematically observed along with their obvious humdrum utilitarian features.

The production of metates and manos in the Oaxaca Valley was haunted by the same specter of diminishing utility grounded in the long association there, dating at least from a few centuries BC, between female labor, the comal, the metate/mano, and the tortilla as a food staple for household members around the hearth or in the fields (Feinman 1986, 365; Isaac 1986, 15–17; Searcy 2011, 89–90). This connection probably reached its peak early in the twentieth century prior to the introduction of mechanization in corn grinding (molinos de *nixtamal*) and tortilla making (tortillerías) and then began to decline. The role of metates/manos in gifting, specifically by baptismal godparents to brides, contributes to the demand for them and for their status as "a fitting symbol of wifely duties," since most ingredients used in cooking were ground by women on the metate (Drucker-Brown 1982, photo 27; Cook 2004, 229–234; 2006, 190–191).[3]

There is no systematic empirical evidence to support a twentieth-century decline in metate output and sales corresponding to a hypothetically reasonable decline in metate use in the Oaxaca Valley. The time-series data available for Magdalena metates sold in the Ocotlán market belie the decline hypothesis, since there was a demonstrated increase in metate inventory and sales there between 1967–1968 and 1979–1980. My visits with metateros in their villages and marketplaces in 1990 and 2004 did not provide any evidence of decline. On the contrary, I was surprised to see evidence of increasing rather than diminishing activity.

There are several reasons why diminished use of metates for food processing does not translate into diminished demand. First, diminished use does not equate to no use; metates continue to be used to regrind masa and to grind foodstuffs other than corn. This may result in a reduction in replacement demand but not necessarily overall demand. Second, metates are culturally significant in gifting and gender relations. Third, demographic growth in indigenous communities creates new demand for metates.

The demise of metates in the Oaxaca Valley economy, though inevitable, will be prolonged by its deep embeddedness in the usos y costumbres of indigenous communities. The fiesta system, marriage, and the almost exclusive involvement of women in grinding, regrinding, and preparing ingredients for food staples like tortillas are usages and customs that delay the metate's demise. The relation between female and metate transcends the "wifely duties" role mentioned by Malinowski and De la Fuente symbolized by the metate in the context of gifting, as well as the indispensable role of women in the household division of labor, and enters into the process of identity formation of women.

Older molenderas always emphasized that metate work was synonymous with being a woman. It was not until one day in 1990 in San Sebastián Teitipac, when I encountered Filomeno Gabriel's teenage daughter, Hilda, observing her mother on her knees next to the hearth regrinding *nixtamal* on a metate and slapping the dough onto a comal to make tortillas, that the real truth was driven home to me. Out of hearing distance of her mother, I asked Hilda if she would follow in her mother's footsteps and work as hard as she did with the metate; she replied without hesitation: "Yes, because that is what will make me a woman." I had experienced similar, if less explicit, responses from women and teenage girls previously in San Sebastián and Magdalena but with less impact on my thinking (Cook 2004, 232–233).

The metate is more than just a persistent, indispensable Mesoamerican utilitarian artifact. It is a bridging commodity between pre-Hispanic Mesoamerica and contemporary Mexico, between the utilitarian order of food processing and the gender division of labor, and between the economy and ritual/symbolic dimensions of indigenous society and culture. When and if metates are no longer produced and used in the transformed cultures of Mesoamerica, ethnoarchaeologists of the future will undoubtedly find plenty of used ones in the region's households as heirlooms through female lines of descent.

In April 2013, I attended a concert by Lila Downs at the Long Center in Austin, Texas. Among the songs she performed was a moving folk hymn of her own composition ("Palomo del Comalito") dedicated to the "molenderas" of Oaxaca, the women who use metates and manos to grind *nixtamal* to make tortillas for use and sale. Their words and images scrolled across a giant screen perfectly synchronized with Downs's masterfully sung lyrics and choreographed movements around the stage. Defining the front cover of her concert album entitled *Pecados y Milagros* (2011 Sony Music Latin) is the same image I had seen previously in a *New York Times* advertisement (Friday, October 21, 2011, c2) for a forthcoming Carnegie Hall concert: an attractive, bare-shouldered, jewelry-adorned woman with a flowing skirt in seated position, eyes forward, holding a mano lying on a metate positioned in front of her. Lila Downs's performances and presentation of herself through such striking images clearly reflect her Oaxaca roots and her identity as a woman of indigenous ancestry. Along with her innovative music, they also convey to the world her advocacy for Oaxaca's indigenous women and her deep understanding and appreciation of their work and lives.

## Citizenship, Civility, and Indigenous Identity

It is fitting to conclude with a statement of how the emphasis placed on citizenship and civility in the nine communities examined in this book relates to what is arguably a new evolutionary trajectory for the Mexican state, dating from the 1990s, that is based on cultural and national diversity rather than homogeneity. The possibility of such transformative change at the macrohistorical and macrosociological level was envisioned by Ángel Palerm (1970, 304–306) in his response to Gonzalo Aguirre Beltrán in a momentous gathering held in Xicotepec de Juárez, Puebla, in January 1970 to address the theme "Indigenismo en México: Confrontación de problemas."

Aguirre Beltrán, as the leading indigenista of his generation, made a provocative and scholarly defense of that policy in the decades following the 1857 constitutional reforms representing the ascendancy of mestizo liberalism led by Benito Juárez. Aguirre claimed that during the postrevolution decades of the twentieth century, even more progress was made in the process of nation building. This involved Mexicanizing or assimilating what had been, at the beginning of the independence period, a majority indigenous population. Aguirre admitted that this nation-building process extinguished regional indigenous cultures in those aspects that were "incompatible with coexistence" (Aguirre Beltrán 1970, 288–290). Paradoxically, he concluded by declaring his acceptance of "the reality of Indian cultures and the need for their preservation" to "enrich national identity and culture," thus leaving open the door to a basic revision of the role of anthropology in official assimilationist policy (ibid., 294).

For his part, Palerm (1970, 305) rejected Aguirre Beltrán's thesis that nation building necessarily involved extinguishing regional indigenous cultures and cited the examples of countries like Spain as nation-states with national and cultural plurality, implying that this was a possible model for Mexico to pursue in future revisions of its "política indigenista." Arturo Warman (2003, 33) seemed to have the same model in mind when his retrospective critique of twentieth-century indigenista policy led him to conclude that "the conception of a mestizo nation had a limitation that impeded it from reaching its full development in not associating mestizaje with plurality" (la concepción de la nación mestiza tuvo una limitación que le impidió alcanzar su pleno desarrollo al no asociar mestizaje con pluralidad).

Although Palerm did not live to experience it, the 1995 Chiapas uprising led by the Ejército Zapatista de Liberación Nacional (EZLN) caused important modifications of the Mexican constitution: first, to recognize the pluricultural nature of the nation represented originally by pueblos indígenas; second, to guarantee the protection and development of indigenous languages, cultures, usages, customs, resources, and forms of social organization; and, finally, to guarantee effective access to the jurisdiction of the state, including the consideration of indigenous legal customs and practices in agrarian cases. By 2001, according to Warman (2003, 291), "the reform took to its limits the possibility of consecrating particular rights to indígenas without breaking or annulling the constitutional order."[4]

Whatever their pre-Hispanic status or origins, the nine Oaxaca Valley communities examined in this book emerged from the colonial period with collective identities defined by local community nativity and membership, mostly forged in the cauldron of intercommunity conflict or conflict between community and hacienda rather than by ethnocultural affiliation (cf. Cook and Joo 1995, 37n2). Curiously, only the people of San Lorenzo and Xaagá articulated a specific notion of collective identity as "Castellanos"— which in their case was not exclusionary and included San Lorenzo, Xaagá, Unión Zapata (Maguey Largo), and one or two other smaller ranch communities.

Zapotec-speaking communities like San Sebastián Teitipac, Santa Cecilia Jalieza, and Magdalena Ocotlán did not have collective identities other than those defined by local community citizenship, combined with a vague notion of descendancy from "gentiles," or ancient speakers of their language (el idioma). In three cases, this notion of ancient descendancy was also related to the practice of particular craft traditions: Santa Cecilia Jalieza re wood carving and San Juan and San Sebastián Teitipac re metate making. Arguably, these cases could be construed as constituting a sense of indigenous identity, albeit not expressed as a specifically "Zapotec" identity.

Although my research never incorporated systematic polling of community members regarding identity or citizenship, my impression was that all of them had a clear sense of being citizens, not only of their particular communities, but also of the state of Oaxaca and the nation of Mexico. After all, the males in these communities had experienced obligatory military service, and many of them had migratory labor experience in the United States, plus an overwhelming majority of men and women had at least three years of formal schooling, where notions of Mexican and Oaxacan, not Zapotec, citizenship and history were regularly presented to them. Many generations of their ancestors from the sixteenth century onward had multiple identity-shaping experiences, not the least of which were reduction and congregation policies, forced Christianization, epidemic disease, merciless exploitation by encomienda and repartimiento practices, and then by hacienda and restored cacicazgo regimes—all culminating in the "constellation of many armed social and political movements" recognized as constituting the Mexican Revolution of 1910–1920 (Warman 2003, 30).

Through twentieth-century agrarian reform, "the indígenas received land as social property" (Warman 2003, 32). Aguirre Beltrán (1970, 288–289) interpreted agrarian reform as restoring to peasant Indians (campesinos indios) "the economic base necessary for them to acquire a new status, more human and dignified, in the country's social structure." He described the ejido as the destroyer of the old institution of the hacienda, which through peonage had served to integrate ancient Indian comuneros as proletarians into national society and economy. Finally, and paradoxically, Aguirre lauded the institution of the hacienda, not the ejido, for "succeeding to integrate into (Mexican) nationality (integrar en la nacionalidad) the great majority of peasant Indians."

On the basis of case studies of Magdalena Ocotlán and San Lorenzo Albarradas, the ejido, not the hacienda, must be credited for performing the integrative role highlighted by Aguirre and for instilling in ejidatarios a deep awareness of the benefits of national citizenship. Wage labor was surely experienced by Lenchanos and Magdalenans in the colonial period, but participation in command types of ad hoc wage labor in postindependence haciendas or cacicazgos was not nationally integrative in an assimilationist way as Aguirre contended.

The 1990s saw fundamental change in the Oaxaca polity represented by a focus on the quaint concept of "usos y costumbres," which was essentially unused and unknown in pre-1990s anthropology. The resuscitation of this nebulous concept from sixteenth-century Spanish colonial vocabulary was among the consequences of a grassroots autonomy movement among indigenous communities to reposition themselves as citizens within the wider polity through legislative and constitutional reform. Since 1995, a majority of Oaxaca's municipalities have held elections according to the common law system (ley consuetudinaria) of usos y costumbres, whereas a minority have continued with the party system that is standard throughout the rest of Mexico.[5]

This juxtaposition of systems opened up a Pandora's box of political, legal, and constitutional issues about pluricultural societies, not the least of which pits individual rights against those of collective identities that evoke the "aspiration of constructing more democratic, less unequal societies while at the same time respecting the right to be different by those who claim membership in particular groups" (Hernández-Díaz 2007b, 36). At the municipal level in Oaxaca, the politics of collective identity immediately generated problems of exclusion of minorities like newcomers, women, and Protestants, among others, whose rights were presumably protected under the electoral regime of the party system (but less so in the common law system) that is backed by state and federal constitutional law.

It is uncertain what the brave new world of "differential citizenships" (Hernández-Díaz 2007a) holds in store for the Oaxacans portrayed in this book and their descendants, but whatever may come in their future, I consider myself fortunate and privileged to have spent several years trying their patience and disturbing their daily routines as I attempted to learn from them regarding the hows and whys of making and earning a living, and of life in general, in their respective communities. I hope through my previous writings, and through the words and images in this book, that I have successfully communicated something of value regarding the question of how they are like all other people, like some other people, and like no other people.

# Photo Essay

{TOP}
**Metateros from San Sebastián Teitipac in Oaxaca City market, ca. 1950 (Postcard series Oaxaca Típico #205)**

{BOTTOM LEFT}
**Presidente municipal and regidores, San Juan Teitipac, 1967**

{BOTTOM RIGHT}
**Inocencio Morales in his metate workshop, Tlacolula, 1967**

{TOP}
**Ruins of Hacienda Buenavista
capilla and belltower, San
Antonio Buenavista**

{BOTTOM}
**Rosendo Carranza at ancient
grave site with recovered
hammerstones, San Juan
Teitipac, 1966**

(TOP)
**Emilio Alvarado and quarrymen (canteros) in Tlacolula quarry, 1967**

(CENTER)
**Emilio Alvarado and sons finishing metates with hand picks, Tlacolula, 1967**

(BOTTOM LEFT)
**Customer trying out a metate while husband bargains with San Juan seller in Tlacolula plaza, 1967**

(BOTTOM RIGHT)
**Luis Gutiérrez using a barreta to "vaciar" a trozo to form legs of a metate, San Sebastián Teitipac, 1966**

(TOP LEFT)
**Luis Gutiérrez and Ramón Ramírez using sledgehammer and barreno to perforate a hole, San Sebastián Teitipac, 1966**

(TOP RIGHT)
**Metateros moving a large block of stone from quarry to work patio, San Sebastián Teitipac, 1966**

(CENTER)
**Luis Gutiérrez working with improvised forge to temper points on barreta, San Sebastián Teitipac, 1966**

(BOTTOM)
**Aurelio Martínez, with son at bellows, tempering a barreta point, San Sebastián Teitipac, 1967**

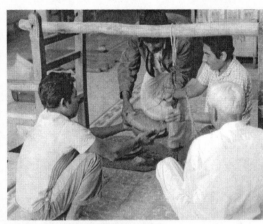

Gutiérrez family
compound with father
and sons finishing
(labrando) products, San
Sebastián Teitipac, 1966

Velero (candle maker)
pouring molten wax over
wick to form candles
(sirios), San Sebastián
Teitipac, 1967

Saúl Gutiérrez weighing
candle wax during
mayordomía ceremony,
San Sebastián Teitipac,
1967

Patron saint's
mayordomía procession
in San Juan Teitipac,
1967

Candle bearers kneeling
at station during
mayordomía procession,
San Juan Teitipac, 1967

Disfrazados (costumed
people) in carnival
procession, San
Sebastián Teitipac, 1967

Street-corner card
games, San Sebastián
Teitipac, 1967

Street-corner dice game, with Luis Gutiérrez throwing dice, San Sebastián Teitipac, 1967

Harvest by tequio on terrenos del santo, San Sebastián Teitipac, 1967

Filomeno Gabriel and friend standing at main irrigation gate and channel, San Sebastián Teitipac, 1967

Wedding party with bridal gift array, San Sebastián Teitipac, 1967

Panoramic view of quarries (lower left) and prime agricultural fields (center) in San Juan Teitipac, looking south toward Santa Cecilia Jalieza

Woman washing and bathing, men cutting alfalfa and irrigating, San Sebastián Teitipac, 1966

Unloading communal corn harvest from terrenos del santo in churchyard, San Juan Teitipac, 1967

(TOP)
**Cutting palm fronds with blade attached to bamboo pole, San Lorenzo Albarradas, 1978**

(CENTER)
**Ubaldo Martínez and son, Isaac, sorting palm fronds, San Lorenzo Albarradas, 1978**

(BOTTOM)
**Unloading bundles of cut palm, San Lorenzo Albarradas, 1978**

{TOP}
**Plaiting a tenate with dried palm strips (fan and whisks in background), San Lorenzo Albarradas, 1978**

{CENTER}
**Petate seller from San Lorenzo Albarradas and customers in Tlacolula plaza, 1978**

{BOTTOM}
**Rolling up an aligned warp of cotton thread in the solar of Reynaldo Olivera's workshop in Xaagá, 1980**

(FACING PAGE, TOP)
Operario at work on loom in
Reynaldo Olivera's workshop,
Xaagá, 1978

(FACING PAGE, BOTTOM LEFT)
Félix Sibaja Santos operating a
treadle loom in the Oaxaca City
mantelería, 1981

(FACING PAGE, BOTTOM RIGHT)
Tying the ends of a loose-weave
cotton shawl, Xaagá, 1979

(TOP LEFT)
Embroiderer and hen, San Isidro
Zegache, 1979

(TOP RIGHT)
Embroiderer and his seamstress
wife displaying an embroidered
dress, San Isidro Zegache, 1979

(BOTTOM)
Marciano García Vásquez using
hatchet (hacha) to prepare wood
strips for letter openers, Santa
Cecilia Jalieza, 1979

**Cart from Magdalena Ocotlán unloading sugarcane in midst of piles of bagasse (bagaso) at trapiche in San Pedro Apóstol, 1968**

**Bonifacio Sánchez, trapiche owner, in front of his cane-crushing machinery, San Pedro Apóstol, 1968**

**Workers and panelero in Sánchez trapiche (showing filled panela molds stacked in background), San Pedro Apóstol, 1968**

**Family at graveside altar during Day of the Dead celebration (cigarette used to light candles), Magdalena Ocotlán, 1967**

(TOP)
**Grandmother and granddaughter at graveside altar on Day of the Dead, Magdalena Ocotlán, 1967**

(CENTER)
**Vidal Méndez "vaciando" a trozo to shape the legs (patas) of a metate during rainy season, Magdalena Ocotlán, 1968**

(BOTTOM)
**José María Santiago, regatón (standing on right), with Magdalena metates bought for resale in Ocotlán plaza, 1967**

Spanish terms are not italicized in the book due to their frequency of use, but those not found in an English dictionary *are* italicized in the glossary. Zapotec and Nahuatl terms are italicized throughout.

Acta de Conformidad. An agreement drawn up by local officials to resolve a dispute between two parties.

*afuereño/afuerano.* Nonnative-born members of a community considered to be outsiders.

*agencia municipal.* Agency or small local governmental unit subordinate to a larger municipality (*municipio*).

*agostadero.* Grazing land.

*agrimensor.* Land surveyor.

*alcalde mayor.* Spanish colonial official in charge of a district.

*almud.* Unit of dry measure: one-twelfth of a *fanega.*

*al partido.* Share raising of animals.

*a medias.* A one-half (50 percent) share arrangement.

*ampliación.* According to the laws deriving from the 1917 agrarian reform, amplification was a procedure to expand the size of an original ejido established by *dotación* or *restitución.*

*archiocofradía;* also *cofradía.* Sodality; a lay brotherhood responsible for sponsoring and financing the care and worship of a particular community saint, as well as operating a *tanda,* or rotating credit association, for members.

*arriero.* Long–distance trader who transports merchandise by a string of mules or burros.

Audiencia. Court and governing body under the colonial viceroy in New Spain, or the area of its jurisdiction.

*aviador.* Financier, commodities speculator, money lender in colonial period.

*ayuntamiento.* Meeting place of local community governing council.

*baldío.* Uncultivated or unused land.

*barreno.* Steel tool with oval tip for stonecutting or boring holes in stone.

*barreta.* Steel tool with pointed tip for stonecutting.

*barretear.* To cut quarry stone with a pointed bar (*barreta*).

barrio. Neighborhood in an indigenous community.

bodega. Storage place.

*bolsa.* General term for bag made of any material.

*caballería.* Unit of agricultural land in colonial Mexico measuring about 105 acres.

*cabecera de distrito.* Political–administrative district headquarters town.

*cabecera de doctrina.* Parish headquarters town.

*cabildo.* Town council during colonial period.

*cacicazgo.* Estate of a cacique or *cacica.*

cacique. Indigenous male political leader (female = *cacica*)

*campo.* In rural communities, that portion of the landscape within their territorial jurisdiction that lies beyond the habitation area proper.

*canastero.* Basket maker.

*cañero.* Sugarcane planter.

*cantero.* Quarryman.

*cañuela.* Forage in the form of dried cornstalks without ears and leaves.

*capulina.* Rain cape made of deerskin.

*cargo.* Post or office in the civil-religious hierarchy.

Carrancista. Supporter of Venustiano Carranza during the Mexican Revolution.

*casa cural.* Parish priest's residence.

*casco.* Central building complex of an hacienda; also the central administrative area of a settlement.

*caserío.* House and outbuildings of a hacienda.

*chimolera* (also *molcajete*). Stone mortar for grinding chiles and other foodstuffs.

*ciudadano.* Citizen.

*cochinilla.* Cochineal, a reddish dyestuff made of insects harvested from the nopal cactus.

*cofradía.* Religious sodality or brotherhood. See *archiocofradía.*

*cogollo.* Top leafy portion of sugarcane stalk used as fodder; also young fronds at the heart of a palm tree.

*colindante.* Contiguous neighbor with land abutting one's property.

*comisariado ejidal.* The head official of a local *ejido* authority.

*comitiva.* Retinue of officials and citizens typically involved in colonial land surveys.

*comunero.* Citizen–taxpayer with the right to access communal land and the duty to provide labor on communal projects.

*congregación.* Removal, relocation, and consolidation of discrete indigenous populations into one settlement; also the name of the resulting settlement.

*contribuyente.* Citizen–taxpayer.

*corregidor.* Spanish colonial official in charge of a province in New Spain prior to the Bourbon Reforms.

*corregidor-intendente.* Spanish colonial official in charge of a province in New Spain during the period of Bourbon Reforms (late eighteenth to early nineteenth century).

*corregimiento.* Jurisdiction of a *corregidor.*

criollo. Person born in Mexico of presumed Spanish ancestry.

*croquis.* Map; typically refers to maps of colonial origin that show a settlement's location and lands within its territorial jurisdiction.

*cuadro.* Street block; also framed picture or painting.

*cuota.* Fee or surcharge.

*defensa social.* Armed militia organized at the local community level but under regional command.

*desamortización.* Disentailment as part of the 1857 Laws of Reform.

*desmadre.* Slang expression meaning "fucking mess."

*destajo.* Piece rate or piecework.

*día de plaza.* Market day, usually on an established day of the week for each town.

*diligencia.* Act by which a judicial ruling is carried out.

*doctrina.* Parochial jurisdiction or its administrative center.

*dotación.* In accordance with the agrarian reform of 1917, a grant of land to a community as an *ejido*, usually involving expropriation and redistribution of land from a privately owned hacienda.

*echar orejera.* Secondary furrowing to place soil around sprouted plants.

*ejidatario.* An individual community member who is a beneficiary of an allotment of land in accordance with the agrarian laws promulgated in 1917 and amended thereafter.

*ejido.* An agrarian community that received and continues to hold land, as an outright grant or by restitution, in accordance with the agrarian laws first promulgated in the Constitution of 1917. Also, land granted to agrarian communities that also have communal or private landholdings.

*encomienda.* A stewardship entitling the steward to tribute from an indigenous community.

*eriazo.* Land classified as uncultivatable.

*escobero.* Broom maker.

*escribano.* Scribe.

estancia. Ranch.

*expediente.* File.

*faja.* Woven belt or waistband.

*fandango.* Wedding feast and party.

*fanega.* Unit of dry measure equivalent to about 1.5 bushels.

*fiscal.* The office of treasurer in the civil-religious hierarchy; also a civil prosecutor.

*fletero.* Hauler, by truck or cart, for hire.

FONAPAS. Fondo Nacional para Actividades Sociales.

FONART. Fondo Nacional para el Fomento de las Artesanías.

*fundo legal.* Settlement site, usually including communal land, to which every community in New Spain was entitled.

*ganado mayor.* Cattle, horses, burros.

*ganado menor.* Goats, sheep, pigs.

*ganancia.* Profit or gain from a business endeavor.

*golaneche* (Zapotec). Cooperative (by reciprocity) plaiting of palm fronds among the mountain Zapotec.

*guarapo.* Pressed sugarcane juice.

*guardamonte.* Armed warden of an hacienda; also a warden who patrols uncultivated community land.

*guardia blanca.* Hired guns of hacendados during the period of agrarian reform after 1917.

*guelaguetza* (Zapotec). Reciprocity in Zapotec Valley culture.

*ixtle* (Nahuatl). Hard fiber made from the processed leaves of maguey.

jacal. A dwelling with a wooden frame and a high, steep roof; its walls and roof are typically constructed of thatched cornstalks, palm fronds, or reeds (*carrizo*).

*jefe de zona*. Head official in district *ejido* bureaucracy.

*jefe político*. Official in charge of a political-administrative district during the Porfiriato.

*jornalero*. A day laborer paid by wage, usually in agriculture. See also *peón*.

*labor*. Small landed estate mostly devoted to agriculture.

*libreta de guelaguetza*. Reciprocity account book.

Licenciado. Typically, a title abbreviated as "Lic." reserved for persons who have completed a higher educational degree program to obtain a *licenciatura*; universally applied to lawyers and regularly applied to predoctoral liberal arts majors, but not to medical doctors, engineers, or architects.

*licenciatura*. Degree awarded for completion of certain undergraduate college programs or law school.

maguey. Agave; the source of *aguamiel* for pulque and mezcal, and hard fiber.

*maíz desgranado*. Shelled corn.

*mandador*. Hacienda foreman.

mano. Stone grinding pin for use with a metate; also a measure, or "handful," of cut palm fronds.

*manojo*. Measure used for cut palm fronds, equivalent to 100 fronds.

*marchante*. A marketplace seller who sells preferably to customers who are regular buyers; commonly used in haggling.

masa. Corn dough, ground on metate from *nixtamal*, for tortillas.

*mayorazgo*. Entailed estate.

*mayordomía*. Saint's cult celebration.

*mayordomo*. Sponsor of a saint's cult celebration; also a foreman.

*mazorca*. Ear of corn with husk.

*mazorca deshojada*. Husked ear of corn.

*medida*. Unit of agricultural land measuring about one-half acre in the Oaxaca Valley; also a gallon jug of mezcal.

*mediero*. Sharecropper.

*merced*. Colonial Spanish royal or viceregal land grant.

*merga*. See *parcela*.

metate. Grindstone.

*metatero*. Maker of grindstones: metates, manos, mortars, and pestles.

*mezcal*. A distilled, highly intoxicating alcoholic beverage made from the maguey plant. The word is of Nahuatl origin, but the beverage is mostly produced and heavily consumed in Oaxaca communities during the annual fiesta cycle.

milpa. Small field planted with corn; also corn plant.

*minifundio*. Small peasant landholding.

*minifundismo*. Condition or system of smallholding peasant agriculture.

*mojonera*. Boundary marker.

*molendera*. Woman who grinds corn on metates to make tortillas for sale (also *tortillera*).

*molino de nixtamal.* Corn-grinding mill mostly producing "dough" (masa) for making tortillas.

*mozo de pie.* Worker assigned to the hacendado for service in the hacienda compound and in the fields.

*municipio.* Municipality, a territorial-administrative unit; also the building where it is housed.

*nixtamal* (Nahuatl). Shelled corn soaked in lime water and then ground for preparation of tortillas.

nopal. Prickly pear cactus.

*nopalera.* Cultivated plot of nopal.

*oficio.* Occupation or trade.

*palenque.* Mezcal distillery.

*palenquero.* Mezcal distiller.

*panela.* Brown sugar cakes (also *piloncillo*)

*par.* Pair of palm strips; measurement for *petate* size.

*paraje.* Named place in a rural landscape.

*parcela* (also *merga*). Parcel or plot of arable land.

*patrón.* Employer; boss.

*pelota mixteca.* Mixtec-style ball game played in a few Oaxaca Valley communities (and elsewhere in southern Mexico) as a team sport resembling netless tennis in which players wear sturdy gloves to strike a small, solid but bouncy rubber ball. It is of pre-Hispanic or early colonial origin.

*penacho.* Feather headdress.

*peón.* Literally one who moves around by foot; general term for a rural day laborer.

*pequeña propiedad.* Small private landed property.

*permuta.* Act of exchanging one thing for another, particularly in legal transactions involving property.

*petate.* Palm mat.

*pistolero.* Political hired gun.

*plaza-mercado.* Marketplace.

*pleito.* Fight, argument, dispute, lawsuit.

Porfiriato. The period from 1876 to 1910 in Mexico when Porfirio Díaz was president.

posada. Inn, usually near a marketplace and with livery services.

*presidente municipal.* Municipal president.

*principal.* Member of indigenous upper class by hereditary succession in preconquest and early colonial period.

*promesa.* Vow to a saint.

*prorrateo.* Act of dividing or distributing proportionately (as of land following a survey).

*pueblo.* A settlement, usually medium or small in size.

*pulseta.* A long steel stone-boring tool with a hammering platform on one end and a cutting point on the other.

*quechquemitl/quechqueme* (Nahuatl). Shoulder cape, shawl, or neckerchief.

*regatón.* Male market trader, intermediary.

*regatona.* Female market trader, intermediary.

*regidor.* Community councilman.

*repartimiento.* Colonial labor draft.

*representante de bienes comunales.* Local official charged with oversight and control of access to communal land or commons.

*restitución.* According to the agrarian reform of 1917, the restitution of lands that were previously possessed by a community and determined by the government to have been illegally appropriated by other individuals or groups.

*riego.* Watering; irrigation.

*síndico.* Elected member of local municipal authority (*ayuntamiento*) with juridical responsibilities.

*sitio de ganado mayor.* Cattle ranch.

*sitio de ganado menor.* Sheep and goat ranch.

*solar.* Residential lot.

*soltero.* Bachelor.

*suarín.* Clairvoyant; diviner.

*sujeto.* Subject community in New Spain.

*suplente.* Substitute for elected or appointed local official.

*surco.* Furrow.

*tablón.* Strip or stretch of arable land.

*talabartero.* Leather crafter.

*tejabana.* House or building with a low-pitched tile roof laid over a tied-reed platform rather than over wooden beams embedded in adobe; the higher back portion of the roof is typically seated on a wall of adobe, whereas the lower front portion is supported by a series of wooden posts or, in some instances, adobe columns.

*tejate.* Beverage made from corn mash and water.

*tejolote.* Stone pestle for use with mortar in grinding chiles and other foodstuffs.

*temporal.* Rainfall-dependent arable land or crop; seasonal (adj.).

*temporada de agua* or *de lluvia.* Rainy season.

*temporada seca.* Dry season.

*tempranero.* A crop, especially corn, planted early in the spring planting season.

*tenate.* Palm basket.

*teniente letrado.* Crown-appointed advisor to a *corregidor-intendente* during the late eighteenth and early nineteenth centuries in provincial New Spain.

*tenocha.* Aztec or Mexica.

*tepache.* Fermented beverage made of water sweetened with brown sugar, pineapple, apples, or other available fruits.

*tequio.* Obligatory communal labor service for male household heads in rural communities.

*terciero.* A tenant cultivator who receives a one-third share of a harvested crop from a landlord.

*terrateniente.* Landlord.

*terrazguero.* Sharecropper or dependent cultivator on an estate paying rent in kind or labor.

*terreno comunal.* Communal land.

*terreno de humedad.* Moist arable land with high water table.

*terreno del santo.* Communal land held in the name of the patron saint of a town.

*tianguis* (Nahuatl). Marketplace or open-air market.

*tierra caliente.* Hot, humid climate zone.

*tierra templada.* Temperate climate zone.

*título.* Title deed to land; often used to refer to the foundational document of a pueblo.

*topil.* Position of errand runner/policeman in local government.

*totomoxtle* (Nahuatl). Corn husks.

*tramo.* Section or stretch of land.

*trapiche.* Sugarcane grinding and processing plant, usually for the purpose of producing *panela*.

*trozo.* Metate-size block of quarry stone.

*usos y costumbres.* Traditional usages and customs.

*vaciar.* To hollow out a solid block of stone (*trozo*) with a *barreta* for the purpose of making a metate.

Vallistocracia. Power elite of the Oaxaca Valley.

*vara.* A length of wood cut for a broomstick; also a Spanish colonial unit of measure equivalent to 33.33 inches (84.66 cm).

*velero.* Candle maker.

*virrey.* Viceroy of New Spain residing in Mexico City.

*vista de ojos.* Colonial land survey and title-granting ceremony.

*yunta.* Ox team.

*yuntero.* Ox team operator (usually its owner).

*zacate.* Forage in the form of stripped, dried leaves of the corn plant.

*zanja.* Irrigation ditch or channel; any long, narrow excavation.

## Preface

1. "Civility" has a dictionary definition that is applicable in general terms to the Oaxaca situation: "Deference or allegiance to the social order befitting a citizen" (*Webster's Third New International Dictionary of the English Language Unabridged.* Springfield, MA: Merriam-Webster, 1993, 413).

2. The nine communities are Magdalena Ocotlán, San Antonio Buenavista, San Juan Teitipac, San Lorenzo Albarradas, San Sebastián Teitipac, Santa Cecilia Jalieza, Santo Domingo Jalieza, Santo Tomás Jalieza, and Xaagá. Most were included in a multicommunity survey project (Proyecto de Estudios Socioeconómicos sobre las Pequeñas Industrias de Oaxaca, or PESPIDEO), conducted in 1978–1981, in which I was the principal investigator. In this book, that project is referenced by the acronym OVSIP (Oaxaca Valley Small Industries Project). OVSIP involved fieldwork and data collection in twenty-three communities in three districts (Centro, Tlacolula, and Ocotlán), and was funded by the National Science Foundation with supplementary funding from the University of Connecticut Research Foundation (Cook and Binford 1990, xiii, 243–249). The choices of research sites were based on data gathered during a comprehensive nine-district survey conducted during the summer of 1977 with funding from the Social Science Research Council, which identified a total of 189 local cottage industries allocated among twenty-four separate branches of production in eighty-seven municipalities (Cook 1978, 292, and Appendix, 319–332).

The two Teitipac communities and San Antonio Buenavista, where I conducted research in the 1960s, were not included in the 1978–1980 OVSIP survey. They were Zapotec-speaking communities according to OVSIP's classification, as were Santa Cecilia Jalieza, Santo Domingo Jalieza, and Magdalena Ocotlán. Xaagá and San Lorenzo Albarradas were classified as "mestizo," and Santo Tomás Jalieza was "transitional" (see Cook and Joo 1995, 38–41).

3. As Sanjek (1991) has shown, "ethnographic present" is not an unambiguous concept. My discussion combines two of Sanjek's definitions (1991, 609): (1) as a mode of presenting ethnography, and (2) as indicative of the ethnographer's presence during fieldwork. John Chance (1996, 403) has reminded us that the effort to sharpen our understanding of the interplay between past and present through questioning, probing, and documenting "requires a balanced approach" free of deterministic bias.

4. Our survey project did not gather information about migration, except for recording absent household members and remittances (Cook and Binford 1990, 40). However, I did address the issue, and reviewed some important studies, in my 2004 book (Cook 2004, 276–291). Of direct interest for the present book are the studies by Cohen (2004), which included San Lorenzo Albarradas as one of twelve communities surveyed, and by Gabbarot and Clarke (2010), which has interesting findings regarding impacts of migration to the United States on the community of

San Juan Teitipac. Symptomatic of the growing interest in Oaxaca migration studies in the 1970s was the fact that three of eight licenciatura theses on social and economic structure by members of the first graduating class of IIS-UABJO (Instituto de Investigaciones Sociológicas-Universidad Autónoma Benito Juárez de Oaxaca) addressed the topic (Benítez Zenteno 1980).

A useful analysis of migration and demographic change in one community, with special relevance for other Tlacolula Valley communities like San Juan Teitipac and San Sebastian Teitipac, is by Eleazar García Ortega (2007) of San Juan Guelavía, his natal community. His analysis is especially important for its focus on relationships between population size and composition, migration, and land use. He found that the Guelavía population tripled from 1930 to 1980, but after 1980 its population began to decline as a result of emigration, going from a peak of 3,645 in 1980 to 2,992 in 2000 (García Ortega 2007, 9–10). Even with the population decline up to 1990, Guelavía was among the municipalities (along with San Juan Teitipac) in the district of Tlacolula with the highest population density (201–250 persons per sq. km), which translated into a high level of minifundismo, a situation worsened by groundwater depletion and low rainfall and resulting in widespread abandonment of agriculture (García Ortega 2007, 13–18) and a corresponding decline in artisanal activity (which in Guelavía means basketry).

Recent evidence suggests a complete inversion of migration patterns in Oaxaca, with migrants avoiding destinations like Mexico City, northern Mexico, and the United States for closer urban and periurban destinations, including, of all places, the pottery village of Santa María Atzompa. By early 2012, this community had experienced a "fast, barbaric and anarchic" demographic explosion from a population of 5,781 in 1990 to more than 27,000 in 2010, due to a flood of new migrants from the hinterland (Cave 2012, A3). This is not a new trend but rather an intensification of a process initiated decades earlier. Indeed, in 1980, I documented how the pieceworking labor force (mileros) of the handmade brick industry in the periurban zone of Santa Lucía del Camino and Santa Cruz Amilpas included a large number of such migrants, known as "avecindados," who were marginalized socially but economically indispensable in those communities (Cook 1984a, 39–45; Hernández-Díaz 2007c).

5. According to Arellanes Meixueiro's guide to AGEPEO (2002), town records for Santa Cecilia Jalieza with six files totaling 655 pages, San Juan Teitipac with five files totaling 160 pages, and San Lorenzo Albarradas with four files totaling 910 pages are most likely to contain documents not included in ASRA files. However, the dates and summaries provided for each AGEPEO file suggest that the main theme or focus corresponds to those covered in the ASRA files, that is, litigation regarding boundary conflicts, land invasions, and destruction of boundary markers from the 1920s into the 1940s. The ASRA files also cover earlier and later periods and contain complete coverage of ejido affairs. It appears that there is a significant correspondence in content between files in AGEPEO and ASRA but that AGEPEO files are more extensive in coverage.

Arellanes Meixueiro's guide (2002) is restricted to coverage of four distinct groupings of documents most frequently consulted by peasant communities: Conflictos por límites, Conflictos por aguas, Conflictos por bosques, and Archivos de pueblos. In short, AGEPEO is an enormous and broad-ranging repository of information on "asuntos agrarios" that was initiated by the Comisión Local Agraria (CLA) in 1916, although "files started being compiled at the end of 1915," and this work was continued by the Comisión Nacional Agraria (CNA), which morphed into the Comisión Agraria Mixta in 1934 until the establishment of the Secretaría de la Reforma Agraria (Arellanes 2002, x–xi) in 1974. Guides to these two collections were also prepared by Manuel Esparza (1991a and 1991b).

6. Inevitably, the neoliberalization of agrarian reform policy and bureaucracy initiated during the presidency of Carlos Salinas de Gortari (1988–1994) transformed the Secretaría de la Reforma Agraria and its documentation and archiving system in Oaxaca and nationally. In 2013, the name of the agency was the Secretaría de Desarrollo Agrario, Territorial y Urbano (SEDATU), and its installations in Oaxaca City have been fragmented and relocated; portions of the archives were moved to Mexico City and other portions moved out of a central location near the Zócalo to Colonia Reforma. Public access to archival materials has been restricted and requires bureaucratic approval. When I and my staff consulted ASRA in 1978–1980, we typically found ourselves in the company of delegations from various pueblos, accompanied by their abogados, seeking official records and conducting business regarding communal and ejido lands. Presumably, that kind of experience is now a thing of the past. On a more positive note, a new computerized system known as the Registro Agrario Nacional (RAN) has been established in Mexico City that offers a comprehensive catalog of agrarian documents for the entire country, listed by state, municipio, locality, and category of documentation (grupo documental).

### Introduction

1. Following Pedro Carrasco (1999, 4), I avoid repetitive use of the popular term "Aztec(s)" and use the more precise term "Tenochca" to refer to the "ethnic group, city, and dynasty that were dominant in the Empire" ruled by the Triple Alliance of Tenochtitlan, Tetzcoco, and Tlacopan.

2. Marcus and Flannery (1996, 12) candidly asserted: "We will never know exactly how many speakers of Zapotec there were when the Spaniards arrived; accurate censuses did not exist." Employing estimates from the Settlement Pattern Project (Kowalewski et al. 1989, 513), they estimate that the entire Central Valleys region and surrounding mountain hinterland may have had a population ranging from 350,000 to 367,000 Zapotec speakers at contact (1996, 13). This is a figure that earlier scholars estimated for the smaller area of the Oaxaca Valley (Taylor 1972, 17). Marcus and Flannery (1996, 27) believe that "the occupants of the Valley of Oaxaca become recognizably 'Zapotec' sometime between 400 BC and AD 100," during the Monte Albán Ia–IIIa periods (Marcus and Flannery 1996, 25).

Carrasco (1999, 305–307) provided a valuable summary of the primary sources regarding the conquest and resettlement of Huaxyacac and located it, together with

Teticpac, on a map of the tributary province of Coyolapan derived from the Codex Mendocino. The Mexica conquest of Huaxyacac occurred during the reign of Moteuczoma Ilhuicamina in retribution for its attack on a group of Mexica royal envoys and merchants.

3. Among the archaeological publications consulted were the following: Paddock 1970; Blanton 1978; Winter 1995; Blanton et al. 1999; Flannery and Marcus 2003; Feinman and Nicholas 2004; Hirth 2009; Joyce 2010. The term "commodity" is not listed in the index of any of these publications. It may be that these archaeologists view the commodity concept as too bound to the culture of Euro-American capitalism to be applicable to the pre-Hispanic economy, but their silence prevents us from knowing the rationale for their avoidance.

Cacao was the most common form of money in the Tenochca economy, but cotton cloaks (*quachtli*) were also commonly used as money (Berdan 2005, 49–50).

4. The geographer Carl Sauer (1969) had a view of change focused on evolutionary transformations and sequences that was eloquently summarized by Rosaldo (1993, 103): "For Sauer, change follows no regular sequence, no lawlike succession, no cultural stages. Changes occur through historical time in a continuous, ongoing fashion, without cessation. Sauer's analysis decenters structures because, with the passage of sufficient time, they either change into other structures or decay and collapse."

I chose the word "civility" as shorthand for compliance with the duties or obligations of community citizenship, which, in Oaxaca's indigenous communities, implies a prevailing regime of usos y costumbres. I am not concerned in this study with the political or electoral implications of civility, which are the central concern of recent discourse about usos and costumbres (see Hernández-Díaz 2007b).

5. My 1978–1980 Oaxaca Valley Small Industries Project (OVSIP) household survey codebook instructed coders to use "1" to code a nuclear family type defined as "husband and wife with their unmarried children"; "2" to code an extended virilocal (extensa virilocal) type defined as "husband and wife with one or more married sons and daughters–in–law. It can include other unmarried children and grandchildren, or father or mother of the head"; and "3" to code an extended uxorilocal type defined as "husband and wife with one or more married daughters- and sons-in-law. It can include other unmarried children and grandchildren, and father or mother of the head's wife." Regarding these two extended-family types, the codebook noted: "Included here are all families with three lineal generations, even though only one of the grandparents is living."

6. House type is also a relevant indicator of household socioeconomic status. In their 1957 study of San Juan Guelavía, Martínez Ríos and Luna Méndez (1960, 224–225) identified three historical house types that corresponded closely to household socioeconomic status from higher to lower: adobe, tejabana, and jacal. Their survey of 80 ejidatario households in 1957 showed that 50 percent of Guelavians lived in jacales, 38.8 percent lived in tejabanas, and 11.2 percent lived in casas de adobe. Household socioeconomic status closely corresponded to house type and construction cost: jacales cost less (323 pesos) and housed the lowest-income fami-

lies; tejabanas cost more (644 pesos) and housed families of intermediate income; casas de adobe cost the most (no figure given) and housed the highest-income families (1960, 265–271).

My 1965 survey of twenty residence lots in San Sebastián with twenty-two households yielded somewhat different percentages: 27 percent of families lived in adobe houses, 13.6 percent lived in tejabanas, 27 percent lived in jacales, and 31.8 percent lived in multiple housing, three each in tejabana + jacal or jacal + jacal, and one in adobe + tejabana. Only one head of household whose principal occupation was metatero lived in an adobe house; the majority of adobe house dwellers listed campesino as their principal occupation, and all of them owned substantial amounts of first-class land.

The 1978–1980 OVSIP household survey employed house type as an analytical tool to address social differentiation. A "house-scale index" was formulated by assigning different numerical values to contrasting house types and taking into account building materials and form of construction (including brick and cement block), flooring, number of rooms, tenure status of residence and lot, and ownership of television set. Assigned values were then summed up to arrive at an overall index value (Cook and Binford 1990, 267n10). This appeared in our book as the "Living Conditions Index" (Cook and Binford 1990, 66–68) and tended to be higher for landed households and households with the most land than for land-poor households with less or no involvement in agriculture. House types were more complex in 1978–1980 than in 1957 and 1965, and are now even more complex with the boom in rural construction and the displacement of the traditional triumvirate of casa de adobe, tejabana, and jacal.

7. By 1957, fifty-nine of one hundred households in Martínez Ríos and Luna Méndez's study included members, mostly children and teenagers, who made baskets. They calculated that over 50 percent of the income of ejido households derived from basketry (1960, 283). In 1979, OVSIP conducted a survey of sixty-nine Oaxaca City craft business proprietors, some of whom specialized in baskets produced through a putting–out system operating in a series of Ocotlán and Tlacolula communities (Cook and Binford 1990, 73–74, 248).

8. Throughout this book, all monetary values will be given in Mexican pesos, sometimes with dollar conversions. Changes in peso-to-dollar exchange rates occurred during the twenty-five years from 1965 to 1990. The peso-to-dollar exchange rate in 1965 was 12.50; in 1977–1980, it varied from 22.74 to 23.26; in December 1985, it was 450.75; and by December 1990, it was 2,941.90. A very useful Internet resource on historical peso-to-dollar exchange rates and annual rates of inflation in Mexico is "Taller de Actualización de la Información Financiera" at http://www.uamcav.uat.edu.mx.

9. Robichaux (2005, 2009) made good use of the essay by Cook and Jong Taick-Joo (1995) as a trampoline for developing and clarifying his own approach to communities he studied in Tlaxcala. He is right to point out that the terms "indigenous" and "mestizo" are not "really accurate ethnic or identity categories but, rather, serve to mask both the Mexican state's language and ethnic policy and specific local his-

tories and identities" and "fail to take into account self-perception of the people studied and their perceptions of the other" (2009, 4). In his opinion, our analysis (Cook and Joo 1995) fallaciously blurred the difference between rural Oaxacans and urban mestizo Oaxacans, creating an illusion of sameness between rural and urban mestizos by failing to recognize "the specificity of social institutions and social relations of towns that historically were *repúblicas de indios*" (Robichaux 2009, 6).

## Chapter One

1. Teitipac (also Teticpac, Teticpaque, and Tetipaque) is the Nahuatl name given in the Codex Mendocino for the Oaxaca Valley community known by the Zapotec as Zeetoba (other sepulchre) or Quehuiquijezaa (palace of stone, of teaching and doctrine; Del Paso y Troncoso 1905, 109; Burgoa 1934, 2:70). The Nahuatl term "Teitipac" is more secular and deviates from Zapotec usage: it means "place situated upon stones" or "stony place" (Peñafiel 1885, 199; Bradomín 1955, 184).

There is some archaeological literature that includes survey and other information on the Teitipac area (see Kowalewski et al. 1989). The only studies I am aware of that include archaeological excavations in San Sebastián Teitipac are by Marcus Winter, Daria Deraga, and Rodolfo Fernández (1975) and Christine McDonnell (2002).

2. The Codex Yanhuitlán contains a picture of a Mixtec carrying a metate on his back supported by a head strap (lam. 12, Museo Nacional, Mexico, 1940). This parallels the practice that prevailed among the valley Zapotec, and suggests that a metate trade may well have existed in the area prior to the introduction of burros and mules in the sixteenth century.

3. According to Olivera and Romero (1973, 239), "The encomenderos formed part of the controlling elite of New Spain and frequently were at the same time high functionaries and wealthy merchants. Only a very few resided on the lands of their encomienda; the majority lived in Spanish cities like Antequera. The relationship with their dependents (sus encomendados) was almost always indirect through their administrators, who worsened the extortion in tribute and services with the collaboration of indigenous authorities. This form of control demanded little change in the forms of local governance and in the culture of dependent indigenous groups." See also Silvio Zavala in Caso et al. 1954, 52.

4. Neither San Juan nor San Sebastián Teitipac was specifically listed in the "Libro de congregaciones" or in accounts of civil congregations undertaken by the Spaniards from 1595 to 1605 (Taylor 1972, 26). Pablo Rojas's foundation story could refer to an earlier period in the sixteenth century when the congregation or reduction of Indians into pueblos was favored by the clergy as the "most appropriate way to Christianize and urbanize or civilize the many Indians that lived unattached or in small groups, very distant and separated from large communities." This policy was applied "without violating the Indians, employing persuasion and not force," as expressed in Real Cédulas of 1538 and 1551 (Zavala 1954, 39; cf. Consejo de Indias 1774, Ley Primera, 198). Indians were, however, reluctant to cooperate with this

policy out of fear of losing their ancestral lands, which, once vacated, ended up being granted to Spanish settlers by mercedaje until that practice was prohibited in 1560 (Consejo de Indias 1774, Ley ix and Ley xiiij, 199).

In referring to the policy during the late years of the sixteenth century, Romero Frizzi (1988, 145) states: "It consisted in bringing together, actually congregating, in a central place the population that inhabited dispersed ranches or small remote hamlets." She then adds: "This was not a new idea by the end of the century; from earlier times the friars and the Crown itself with the intent of facilitating its evangelizing or administrative work had supported it. In Oaxaca some settlements had been congregated earlier. On occasions people were not moved great distances, rather they were taken from their rancherías or estancias to the nearest settlement; still the movement served to destroy 'organización prehispánica.'" This idea of propinquity of original Indian pueblos and congregations is clearly expressed regarding mines (Consejo de Indias 1774, Libro VI, Título III, Ley x, 199). This seems to resonate well with the main points in Pablo Rojas's oral history of the colonial founding of San Sebastián. See also Consejo de Indias 1774, Libro VI, Título III, Ley iii, 198–199; Schmieder 1930, 23; Gay 1950, 1(2):116–128; Zavala 1954, 40–41; Arroyo 1961, 149–152; De la Fuente 1965, 31–32.

5. Jiménez Moreno (1942, 15) sifted through and weighed a lot of the material in the apologetic accounts of the Teitipac rebellion and concluded that "the truth of the matter is that this priest [Grijelmo] had assumed inquisitorial authority and that he had those nine victims burned at the stake."

6. A concise discussion of the role of encomiendas and repartimientos in New Spain is found in Zavala (1954, 52–55). Lesley B. Simpson (1959, 34) defined the encomienda as "a kind of trusteeship, by which a conquistador was given the power to collect tribute from the Indians, while presumably devoting himself to their protection and indoctrination in the Christian religion." See also Gibson 1964, 27; Simpson 1966, 10.

7. Cook and Simpson (1948, 99) calculated that the total Teitipac population in 1565 was 4,318 inhabitants. Cook and Borah (1960, 83), on the other hand, calculated its total population in 1568 as 2,948 inhabitants. They also estimated that the Teitipac population in 1580 was 2,822. Taylor (1972, 233) estimated that Teitipac had between 3,000 and 4,000 tributaries in the pre-1579 period, 581 in 1623, and only 40 in 1670; by 1826, the number of tributaries had risen to 1,325. According to Welte (1973b, 6, 8), in 1580 Teitipac was within the jurisdiction of (suffragan to) Antequera but was absorbed by Chichicapan around 1600 (Welte 1973b, 12). It had a population in 1565–1570 of 2,948 and in 1743–1746 had 872 tributaries.

8. The question of inheritance during the colonial period, and especially the crossover inheritance of cacicazgo lands from patrilines to matrilines, suggests that in precolonial Zapotec society, "descent could be reckoned in both the male and the female lines" (Whitecotton 1977, 154). This, in turn, is supportive of the thesis that Zapotec social organization "corresponded in part to the conical clan" (ibid., 154–157).

9. The term "cacique" is used here to denote a status of respect and power based

on property holdings (land and livestock) and political-economic control in a community or region. Occasionally, I heard this term used by San Sebastianos with reference to Don Matías, but more often he was referred to simply as "patrón" or "rico."

10. Conflicts over land between San Sebastián and Santa Cruz Papalutla are on record at least from 1872, when San Sebastián accused its neighbor of a "despojo de terrenos" (Esparza 1991, 186, citing AGEO file SCP 1872, Leg. 81, exp. 1, 77ff.). It is likely that Matías Marcial was involved in the land conflict between these communities in 1890 (Esparza 1991, 186, citing AGEO Leg. 81, exp. 2, 109ff. with one map). Whitecotton (1977, 223) pointed out that after 1857, the disentailment of communal land "sometimes led to its acquisition by more prosperous local villagers."

11. I made a detailed inventory of Maximiano's landholdings and found that he owned 30 separate parcels of land, 20 of which were classified as first class, mostly de humedad or de riego. He estimated his annual corn harvest as a whopping 150 fanegas, or 30 cartloads. This compared with 43 parcels owned by Wenceslao Gutiérrez Marcial, a grandson of Matías Marcial, 27 of which were first class, either de humedad or de riego, with a total estimated corn harvest of only 18.5 fanegas; Jesús Gutiérrez Marcial, also a grandson of Matías, provided me with his own signed and dated list of his landholdings: 53 parcels, all of which were second- or third-class lands, with a total estimated harvest of about 18 fanegas. Since the two Gutiérrez brothers, direct descendants of Matías Marcial, were certainly among the largest landowners in San Sebastián, it appears that Maximiano, due to his ownership of more acreage of first-class land, which gave him a large corn harvest, was at or near the top of its wealth ladder. According to my informants, he shared this position with a widow, María Díaz, whose data I did not obtain.

12. Martínez Ríos and Luna Méndez (1960), who were unable to find any information regarding land tenure in Guelavía before the second half of the nineteenth century, discussed the rise of Marcial López in San Juan Guelavía and emphasized his role in financing mayordomía sponsorships for household heads who were named but were unable to meet the necessary expenditures. He collected from his debtors by appropriating their land titles (ibid., 216–217). Both Marcial López and Matías Marcial, after dispossessing many of their co-villagers of land through moneylending or extensions of credit for which land was the collateral, were essentially dependent on them to work the land as sharecroppers (medieros) or wage laborers (peones), and generally treated them better (in terms of wages and meals in the case of the peones) than hacienda terrazgueros like those in San Antonio Buenavista. San Sebastianos who worked as peones for Hacienda San Antonio Buenavista, just as Sanjuaneros who worked for the Hacienda de Guadalupe did, had to provide their own food for .50 centavos per day, whereas as wage laborers for López and Marcial they earned less (.31 centavos per day) but were provided with ample and good (suficiente y buena) food (Martínez Ríos and Luna Méndez 1960, 220–221).

There were important differences between the two situations, however. First, Guelavía had very little cultivable communal land (only 6 ha) compared to San Sebastián, and unlike San Sebastián, where the terrenos del santo were affected by the

Disentailment Laws of 1856 (ending up in the hands of Matías Marcial and his heirs until being recuperated in the 1940s), Guelavía's were unaffected. Second, a much larger percentage of households in San Sebastián remained landed during the reign of Matías Marcial compared to Guelavía under López, where most households were either minimally landed sharecroppers or landless peones (Martínez Ríos and Luna Méndez 1960, 217–219). Third, the Lópezes in Guelavía did not operate a "tienda de raya" (ibid., 221), whereas the Marcials in San Sebastián did.

13. See Clarke (2000) for a comprehensive, insightful, and empirically well-documented analysis of change/modernization in Oaxaca's peasantries.

### Chapter Two

1. This remarkable document is entitled "Observaciones y estudios hechos en la práctica del manejo y dirección de los trabajos para la explotación de la Hacienda de San Antonio Buenavista ubicada en el Distrito de Tlacolula, desde el año de 1879." The original, unedited copy is in the Sala Oaxaca of the Fundación Bustamante in Oaxaca City. It consists of twenty-one fojas (sheets of paper) and was handwritten single-spaced by Lic. Carlos Castro Castillo but is undated. The latest dated reference in the text was the "último día del año 1916" (p. 11). All English translations from this document are my own.

In my effort to clarify the twentieth-century ownership of the hacienda, which I knew involved Carlos Castro, Luis Audiffred, and members of the Bustamante family, I corresponded with Manuel Esparza of INAH-Oaxaca regarding his knowledge of the matter, and he referred my query to Contadora Consuelo Bustamante, daughter of Dr. Juan I. Bustamante (former diputado federal and head of Seguro Social), who is head of the Fundación Bustamante. It was Contadora Bustamante who located Carlos Castro's manuscript in her foundation's archives. A scanned copy of same was e-mailed to me by Jorge Hernández of IIS-UABJO. I transcribed the document to a double-spaced Word file. Needless to say, I am grateful to all of the above for their helpful roles in this matter. I have referenced the undated document as (Castro Castillo n.d.) and listed it as such in the bibliography.

2. The peak years of the cochineal trade were 1769–1778 (Hamnett 1971, 30). One of the Magro brothers, Alonso, was a prominent Oaxaca City–based merchant who, as an aviador, invested capital with alcaldes mayores to secure the appointment of his agents as the administrator's lieutenant, especially in the cochineal business in Oaxaca and Veracruz. He was actively engaged in politics and business from the 1770s into the early 1800s, when he held the position of Captain of the Militias of the Costa del Sur and had realistic aspirations of becoming Intendant (Hamnett 1971, 37, 123, 127, 160).

It is not clear from Castro's account (apparently from lack of original documents at his disposal) where the residential/administrative center of Vásquez's San José Guelaviate estate was located with regard to the residential/administrative center of the Magros' mayorazgo that became Hacienda San Antonio Buenavista. Eduardo Mendoza's account, as well as information from local knowledge and physical remains, makes clear that under the ownership of the Castros in the nineteenth century, Rancho Guelaviate was a subordinate but integral unit of the Hacienda San Antonio Buenavista. The latter had its main residential and administrative center 3 kilometers west-northwest of San Juan Teitipac and 2.4 kilometers slightly south-west of San Sebastián Teitipac (see Welte's 1965 map and Welte 1978, 8). I visited the site on only one occasion, and I estimated its location as being about 3 kilome-ters or so south of San Antonio Buenavista, and northwest of Santa Cecilia Jalieza by about an equal distance (see Map 1).

3. I have no proof but suspect that Juan María Acevedo was probably acting on behalf of two masters in this deal: the hacienda and the authorities of his native pueblo of San Sebastián. In any case, it appears that, somehow in the early 1860s, San Sebastián ended up with 200 hectares of land that had belonged to Hacienda San Antonio in 1857. My estimate is based on Castro's estimate of a 2-kilometer change in the boundary.

The financial shenanigans involved in this disentailment process were impres-sive. According to Castro (n.d., 16–17): "Don Manuel Toro obtained the adjudication of the farm for a very low price, only three or four thousand pesos; to facilitate the disentailment, the law provided that the pricing of the farm proceed to auction for a third of its appraised value and, of that third, only one-half was to be paid in cash if the high bidder in the auction (adjudicatorio) had the funds to do so; and if not, 'I owe yous' (pagarés) would be extended through financing controlled by the Jefe de Hacienda who authorized the entire operation; the other half of the settlement value (valor de adjudicación) was paid in public bonds bought at 6 percent of their nominal value."

Castro was referring to the Convent of Santa Catalina de Sena, established in Antequera in 1576, and "especially notable for its aggressive, businesslike approach to land ownership in the seventeenth and eighteenth centuries" (Taylor 1972, 185).

4. In the context of speculating about the process of consolidation of Hacienda San Antonio Buenavista in the period after 1620 and the beginning of the eigh-teenth century, Carlos Castro (n.d., 13) painted an interesting canvas regarding lingering elements of the pre-Hispanic cacicazgo system in that subregion of the Oaxaca Valley: "When the Spaniards took for themselves the land of Mexico by virtue of the conquest, there were some ranches (ranchos) disseminated between pueblos; such well demarcated ranchos and estancias were known as cacicazgos, and were possessed and administered under the direction of the descendants of one or another cacique, who were always respected and sometimes venerated by the in-dígenas of the neighboring pueblos or communes (comunas); and it is not unusual to find titles like some I have seen, from some pueblos established today of lands that belonged to some cacicazgo that they acquired by purchase; or by donation of the cacique, but never by violent occupation. It seems that these cacicazgos were a species of mayorazgos that reigned in accordance with uniform and immemorial custom, by which men and women without distinction inherited property, without being contested or disputed by relatives or strangers. The Spanish crown itself, which found that part of their territory already legally reduced to inherited prop-

erty, did not divest the caciques of their lands; and always recommended to their Virreyes y Audiencias in accordance with the laws of the Indies to respect those properties. In San Juan Teitipac, which appears to be the most ancient pueblo of that region, there existed from time immemorial a cacicazgo, well constituted and operated by hereditary succession before and after the conquest. It embraced a considerable expanse of land and mountains, from the point that is today the boundary between Chichicapan and San Juan to a point that is a boundary with the Hacienda San Antonio, Coyotepec, and San Sebastián Teitipac; within its perimeter was the large Cañada of San Juan, part of the non-mountainous land that it uses together with Santa Cecilia Jalieza, and perhaps including the habitation area of that pueblo, half of which was sold by the last cacica to the owner of San José Guelaviate in order to complete the property of the Hacienda San Antonio."

Gay (1881, 1:153–154), a man of the cloth, had a more militaristic interpretation of the early colonial history of the Teitipac region than Lic. Castro. He alluded to the early historical importance of the corridor between the valley of Tlacolula and Valle Grande (including Chilateca and Ocotlán) in struggles for political control, just as happened in the twentieth-century period of defensas sociales involving caciques like Brito (San Juan Guelavía) and Trápaga (San Juan Chilateca).

5. According to Francie Chassen-López (2004, 182): "There were two types of punishments for laborers: expulsion from the hacienda or, in extreme cases on the Haciendas of San José and Buenavista, the *leva* (consignment to the army)." Eduardo never mentioned the *leva* and denied that worker punishment included being sent into forced labor in places like Valle Nacional.

6. Regarding Carlos Castro, Chassen-López (2004, 460–461) observed: "On July 23, 1902, a second board was elected (the Juárez Association), Guillermo Meixueiro as president. . . . Powerful Porfirian politicians . . . and wealthy entrepreneur (Carlos Castro) joined the middle-class lawyers to honor the memory of Juárez."

7. It is possible that Lic. Jorge Meixueiro, who was instrumental in establishing the ejido in San Juan Guelavía in the 1930s (Martínez Ríos and Luna Méndez 1960, 241), owned considerable land in nearby Santa Cruz Papalutla that was sold to Matías Marcial in 1915, prior to the latter's death. If it was not Jorge, it was surely a close paternal relative who owned land in Papalutla.

8. According to the description of the content of Expediente 264 for San Antonio Buenavista in the Registro Agrario Nacional (RAN) within the document group Dotación de Tierras, definitive possession of San Antonio Buenavista's ejido was granted by a presidential resolution dated June 6, 1929. The petition was initiated by Buenavistans in 1924.

9. It is puzzling that the discussion of San Juan Guelavía's history in the 1920s and 1930s by Martínez Ríos and Luna Méndez made no mention of Juan Brito and the defensas sociales. Their discussion privileged the role of Marcial López and his successors, Wenceslao and Marcelino López, and traced their downfall (1960, 241) but was strangely silent about Brito. López's heirs squandered their inheritance and left Guelavía's peasant population essentially without sources of local employment, but were also opposed to allowing the López landholdings to fall into the hands of

absentee owners. So, in 1936, with the help of Lic. Jorge Meixueiro, at the time a candidate for federal deputy, a petition for a dotación of ejido land was filed with the governor, and a definitive endowment was approved by President Lázaro Cárdenas in 1937 (Martínez Ríos and Luna Méndez 1960, 241–244).

Prior to their discussion of the decline of the López cacicazgo and the establishment of the ejido, Martínez Ríos and Luna Méndez described a situation in which local conflicts were resolved by local authorities (alcalde and síndico) according to norms of common law (normas de derecho consuetudinario) except for extreme matters like homicide that were handled by authorities in Tlacolula. This was the case for "five homicides committed between 1931 [and] 1935" that were "resolved in the Juzgado Mixto de Primera Instancia en Tlacolula," where the perpetrators were sentenced and jailed (ibid., 230). They made no mention in this context of the murder of Juan Brito in his Guelavía store in 1936, much less of his apparent role as the supreme judicial authority of the region during the period of the defensas sociales.

The pre-dotación period in Guelavía was marked by a decline in the age-based ladder system of cargos and a social bifurcation into two groups (ibid., 230). The impulse toward and leadership of the agrarian movement emerged from one of these groups, composed mostly of the landless peons, culminating in the 1936 petition for land redistribution. It is hard to imagine that Juan Brito was disengaged from this process and that his murder in that same year was coincidental. Indeed, his emergence as a regional strongman coincided with the decline of the López family's interests, and in Buenavista and Teitipac, Brito was clearly linked with the agrarian movement.

In short, much remains to be learned about this period in Guelavía's history, which interfaces with the transition from Chicolopismo to Cardenismo in Oaxaca politics—a process in which none other than Lic. Jorge Meixueiro, the son of Guillermo Meixueiro of Villa Alta fame and a virulent opponent of Governor López Cortés, was deeply enmeshed (Smith 2009, 63–134). Benjamin Smith (2009, 237) writes: "Throughout the state, radical leaders . . . were expelled, their places usurped by landowners, caciques, and middle-class bureaucrats such as . . . Jorge Meixueiro, who wanted to harness 'the armed, electoral or organizational power of the campesinos.'" The question is precisely where Juan Brito, Guelavía, and Santa Cruz Papalutla, where Meixueiro himself was a landowner, fit into this scenario.

10. During the agrarian reform process, petitioning communities could either apply for land through "restitución" (restitution) or "dotación" (endowment), both of which involved expropriation of hacienda land. Restitution required more historical documentation, including original titles, whereas dotación could be achieved on the basis of demographic and economic studies supplementing surveys (see Ruiz Cervantes 1988, 385–417, for an analysis of this process in Oaxaca). The 1966 petition was for an "ampliación de ejido" (RAN, Expediente 1856, Ampliación de Ejidos, Legajo 1); apparently a decision was made on the request by December 1967, but it is unclear from the record whether it was approved or denied.

On the effects of ejidatarios on class relations in Tepoztlán, see Lewis 1949.

11. Thanks to the cooperation of a member of the Bustamante family, Consuelo

("Chelo"; personal communication, 2011), the relationships between the Bustamante, the Audiffred, and the Castro Mantecón families have been clarified. "Luis Bustamante León, married to Patricia Cox, had two daughters: Manuela and María Luisa, who married Enrique Audiffred, and from that marriage came Enrique Luis Audiffred Bustamante. But there is a Luis Audiffred who was the older brother of Enrique and six others. The relations of the Castro Mantecón family with the Bustamante Vasconcelos family owe to the fact that a grandmother, Rosa Castro Castillo, was a sister of Lic. Carlos Castro Castillo, who married four times, the last time with a Señorita Mantecón. The Castro Mantecón family had a lot of members, among them: Lic. Ignacio, the dentist Javier, Dr. Armando, and several women."

There is a record of a complaint filed by the residents of San Antonio Buenavista against San Sebastián Teitipac regarding the "cutting of trees" on land of the ejido (Arellanes Meixueiro 2002, 165).

## Chapter Three

1. More precisely, it was the padrino de bautizo, the baptismal godfather of the bride, who had this obligation. Also, the confirmation godfather of the husband was expected to present a second metate to the married couple (see Martínez Ríos and Luna Méndez 1960, 223, re San Juan Guelavía). This explains the two gift metates shown in photo 32 in their book. I have photos showing as many as five metates in the bride and groom's gift array, given by godparents or relatives at their discretion, in accordance with the general custom.

2. Marcus Winter (1995, 20, 23, 24, 89, 93) provided glimpses of the interest metates have for Oaxaca archaeologists. Building on the pioneering work of Hayden and Nelson (1981), Searcy (2011) did an admirable job promoting a new approach in archaeology to metates and manos. He made a plausible explanation for the archaeological record of neglect, and then reported the results of his research in Guatemala, noteworthy for its focus on contemporary patterns of use, discard, and reuse of grindstones as a basis for inferring "archaeological implications" (Searcy 2011, 66–136).

3. Rosendo's inference that stone tools were indicative of pre-Hispanic use is logical but not definitive. One of the most unexpected findings of Hayden's (1987a) pioneering ethnoarchaeological project in Malacatancito in the Guatemala highlands in the 1980s was that metateros there still used chipped-stone tools to manufacture metates and manos (Searcy 2011, 35).

4. The quarry area in Tlacolula, located on the northwestern outskirts of the habitation area since 1930 if not longer, has been plagued by a lack of clarity over boundaries between private and communal lands. The result was a major political and legal struggle in the town between a faction seeking to consolidate and defend communal holdings (los comuneros) and another faction of private property owners (pequeños propietarios) seeking to expand private property interests. The quarrymen were the main comunero constituency, with their interests served by the municipio's representante de bienes comunales (see Cook 1982, 171–172).

5. This pattern still held true in 1980, but by 1990, nearly all of the metate sales in Tlacolula were in the hands of intermediaries and a few producer-sellers from San Juan, with a small representation of San Sebastianos. Even though Inocencio's workshop was out of business by that time, the "style" of metate he developed still dominated the marketplace.

6. I never witnessed a mayordomía sponsorship-naming ceremony in San Juan, but according to Armando, these occurred in the context of a town meeting of all heads of household and involved public input in response to a list of candidates read aloud by village authorities: "They read the list of taxpayers/citizens, and people react by shouting when particular names are read. They hear your name and start shouting '¡Ya va, Ya va!' They really don't know what that person has or doesn't have when they shout '¡Ya va, Ya va!' If one does not accept the sponsorship on the spot, then they start gossiping that 'so-and-so doesn't want to spend his wealth, so it's better for him to leave the town right now.' So, one is really forced to spend." (Dicen, "Pues, ese no quiere gastar, mejor que salga ya." Por fuerza tiene uno que gastar.)

I did witness a town meeting in 1967 held in front of the municipal president's office, presided over by the president accompanied by regidores, where the order of business was, among other things, to name members of committees. It was a raucous affair with periodic shouts from members of the all-male throng of statements like "No estamos en la hacienda, señores" (We're not on the hacienda, gentlemen).

7. Since San Juan had almost twice as many households as San Sebastián according to the 1960 census (2,701 vs. 1,257), San Sebastián had a higher percentage of metateros. By the late 1970s, it appeared that the active metatero population had declined absolutely in both communities, but San Sebastián, with just over forty active metateros, probably had more metateros both absolutely and proportionally than San Juan (Cook 1982, 173n1).

On January 31, 1967, I visited the Frente de Coyote quarry, located on the side of a mountain just above San Antonio Buenavista but within the jurisdiction of San Sebastián west of its habitation area, where the Antonios (Lorenzo, Darío, and Marcelino) worked their quarry. As they worked, Lorenzo (b. 1896) reminisced that his grandfather had told him that the quarry area in San Juan actually belonged to San Sebastián. He said that years ago he had himself been run out of the quarries by the Sanjuaneros. According to him, a fairly recent assassination of a Sanjuanero named Pedro Guerra was a direct consequence of his belief that the San Juan quarry belonged to San Sebastián.

A look at Map 2 shows that in Sector II, between the boundary markers Junto al Bajío and Yevillana, lies Cerrito San Juan, where the quarries are located. Topographically, this is quite close to San Sebastián's habitation area and quite plausibly figured heavily in historic boundary disputes between the two villages. Since San Juan became the center of Spanish power early in the colonial period, and since the Dominican church and monastery was undoubtedly built from stone extracted from this quarry, it is quite feasible that the quarry's "ownership" shifted accordingly—from communal property of San Sebastián, to Dominican property, and then to private property in San Juan.

8. Several references above to wholesale-retail merchants or intermediaries who regularly buy artisan commodities in the plaza-mercado system of the Oaxaca Valley for resale follow a precedent set in 1969, when, in the context of describing the metate market, I referred to them as "itinerant wholesalers-retailers" (257) or "big-lot" buyers (270, 278). I used the same term in subsequent writings (e.g., Cook 1976, 146, 149, 156; and Cook and Binford 1982, 256, 289–290). The term "buyers-up" was also used (Cook and Binford 1990, 195) with regard to the treadle-loom weaving industry in Teotitlán del Valle and Santa Ana del Valle to highlight the role of "weaving intermediaries . . . as much putters-out as . . . buyers-up, since they use their control over the local yarn supply" to stipulate the kind and quality of products they will buy back from the weavers they supply with yarn (ibid., 196). The purpose of these discussions was to highlight the particular way in which merchant enterprises in the Oaxaca Valley intervened in commodity-money circuits (C — M — C, where C = commodity and M = money) in the course of conducting business for a profit.

The term "buyers-up" is free of the implication that merchant transactions involved only big lots. In fact, most such merchants accumulated large commodity inventories by making a series of small purchases, rather than one or a few large purchases, during the course of a typical trading day (día de plaza). In the metate market, for example, large inventories of metates and manos were accumulated through tough bargaining or previously existing credit-debt relationships between merchants and metateros in the Oaxaca City or Ocotlán marketplaces. Inventories were then broken up into small lots for subsequent resale on a retail basis in other marketplaces where the merchants conducted business. This strategy maximized opportunities for assuring high returns on money invested.

9. There was a tragic ending to Ramón Ramírez's career. In the early 1970s, he was invited to a festive celebration in the neighboring ex-hacienda of Santa Rosa Buenavista. The next morning, his lifeless body was found at the bottom of a deep well where, reportedly, he accidentally ended up after imbibing one too many drinks of mezcal.

## Chapter Four

1. In 1966, with a street and block map of San Sebastián showing the name and location of every household residence lot in front of us, I sat down with Luis and Filomeno to compile a comprehensive list of current household heads that were ex-braceros. The list ended up with eighty-one names. This information was confirmed with half of these individuals. See also Cook 1982, 139–154.

2. The distinction made by San Sebastianos between pueblo and campo mirrors official discourse in the state of Oaxaca codified since 1893 (Arellanes Meixueiro 1999, 20).

Map 2 was made from a survey conducted by Cecil R. Welte in January 1967. I arranged the survey with the San Sebastián authorities, who were in need of a new, accurate map of their territorial jurisdiction and boundary markers. Since I was renting space in Welte's Oficina de Estudios de la Humanidad del Valle de Oaxaca in Oaxaca City at the time, and was aware of his cartographic skills, I informed him of San Sebastián's need, and given his curious and generous spirit, he readily agreed to provide his services pro bono to the project. The field survey took one week. I was a member of the survey party, accompanying Welte each day together with several village officials (e.g., the comisariado de bienes comunales, the Comité de Vigilancia) and their assistants. We walked the entire boundary and inspected all of the mojoneras; Welte took transit sightings from the key markers and other prominent triangulation points.

3. The complete list of 144 paraje names is in Cook 1969, 328–331. I employed Spanish phonetics to attempt to spell Zapotec words. The results are less than perfect but better than nothing. It is apparent that several of the Zapotec place-names are Hispanicized (e.g., *skiyn* for "esquina," *zurk* for "surco"). The original discussion of San Sebastián's land types is also in Cook 1969, 77–83.

4. My friend and colleague Martin Diskin, whom I first met in 1965 when he was a predoctoral student working on Ralph Beals's Oaxaca Markets project and conducting dissertation research in Tlacolula de Matamoros, asked me at some point in the early 1970s, when he was a new member of the anthropology faculty at MIT, if I would object to his undertaking a project in San Sebastián Teitipac that would not replicate mine on the metate industry but would focus on agriculture, reciprocity, and the fiesta system, and, further, if I would personally introduce him to the community. I agreed to Diskin's proposal and made contacts for him in San Sebastián. Diskin conducted fieldwork in San Sebastián periodically between September 1974 and July 1976, and to my knowledge the only product of this fieldwork is his 1986 publication.

5. Diskin (1986, 284) counted fourteen "mayordomías del año" compared to my count of eight. Either my count excluded some of the minor saint's days that could be celebrated, or his count included celebrations that my informants considered to be simply gastos rather than mayordomías, since they were not technically saint's day celebrations (e.g., New Year's and Holy Week).

6. I belatedly learned that Saúl Gutiérrez, like his father before him, also served as presidente municipal, from 2002 to 2004. I do not know what other cargos he held after serving as mayordomo of the Virgin of Juquila festival prior to 2002, but my assumption is that he surely served as regidor. Pablo Rojas López, son of the Pablo Rojas who succeeded Saúl's father as presidente municipal in 1966, succeeded Saúl as presidente municipal in 2005.

7. The Virgin of Juquila cult originated in Santa Catarina Juquila and the nearby Chatino community of Amialtepec in the period between 1558 and 1633, but her permanent home in the Juquila church dates from 1719 (www.interfaithmarianpilgrimages.com). Knowledge of that cult in San Sebastián and San Juan, and pilgrimages to Juquila from those communities, came afterward. The cause of the conflict

over the Virgin between San Juan Teitipac and San Sebastián Teitipac may be best understood by its location on contested ground. There was a murder involving a San Sebastiano who claimed that the San Juan quarries located on the south side of the Cerrito had originally belonged to San Sebastián.

Once such a vision occurred, either a shrine might be built on the site for an image of the Virgin or the image would be placed in a niche in a church and become an object of worship. Since San Juan was the head church of the parish that included San Sebastián, and was the permanent place of residence of the parish priest (or priests), the land boundary dispute undoubtedly had repercussions on the role of the church and parish priests in determining the proper location for the saint's image. There was, in fact, conflict between Santa Catarina and Amialtepec, and favoritism by the priests, regarding the original Virgin of Juquila image. The image that ended up in San Sebastián's church was undoubtedly supplied by a friar from San Juan—but was probably originally placed at the site of the vision.

8. For another view of cooperative relationships and community reproduction in a Oaxaca village not far from San Sebastián, but farther along the road to renegotiating "traditional" culture than was San Sebastián in the 1970s, see Jeffrey Cohen's perceptive study of Santa Ana del Valle in the 1990s (1999, 164). Also see Martínez Ríos (1964) now-classic (if tortured) functionalist analysis of "cooperation" and reciprocity in the ejido community San Juan Guelavía.

9. It was quite common for use rights to arable land parcels to be transferred according to an arrangement known as "por empeño," or by pawning; the land so transferred was referred to as "terreno empeñado" or "tierra empeñada." In these cases, the current owner or holder of a parcel received a cash payment from another party who, by virtue of the payment, was understood to have the right to cultivate the parcel and harvest the entire crop from it. It was also understood that the original owner/holder could end the agreement after the harvest by paying back the amount of cash paid for cultivation rights. In many cases, such transactions were never reversed or were reversed several years later, and the land transferred became, de facto if not de jure, property of the payer/lender.

10. The location of the metate sales area had changed by the mid-1960s. From then into the 1970s, metate sellers from San Sebastián lined up their products on the north side of the street directly across from San Juan sellers on the south side. This street, a block or two southeast of the main marketplace, was in an area of permanent shops that sold a variety of utilitarian craft products as well as coffee and chocolate, among other things, and temporary stalls, or puestos, selling the same or other merchandise. See Cook 1982, Chs. 6 and 7, for a comprehensive analysis of metate marketing.

11. See Cook 1969, 195–224, for a detailed analysis of quarry tenure and work organization among the metateros of San Sebastián Teitipac. See also Cook 1982, Ch. 5.

We know from late nineteenth-century archaeologists who explored the ruins of quarries in the Mitla area that quarrying and stonecutting on a monumental scale was accomplished by hand with crude stone hammers and picks aided by wooden levers and wedges. Unassisted by blasting technology, the procedure followed by pre-Hispanic quarrymen/stonecutters is best described as channeling and undercutting of solid masses of bedrock by hand with the above-mentioned tools (research by W. H. Holmes and E. H. Thompson summarized in Chapple and Coon 1942, 164–165).

12. Agustín Hernández, whose father and grandfather were metateros, learned the craft in his father's quarry. In 1966, he was working for a boss in a quarry whose owner was not a metatero. His response to my question about product sharing was: "If the yield is twelve trozos and there are two workers, then six belong to the owner and six to the boss who distributes them among the mozos."

13. A similar threat to suspend quarry activity as a remedy for eliminating conflict among the metateros was voiced by Representante de Bienes Comunales Jesús Gutiérrez Marcial in a second hearing regarding the Mesa Grande dispute (Cook 1982, 225–226). See Cook 1969, 340, for the complete text of an Acta de Conformidad drafted by the síndico to resolve a quarry dispute in San Sebastián.

14. See Cook 1982, 305–314, for a discussion of the metate market cycle.

15. See Cook and Binford 1990, Ch. 2, for a comprehensive and detailed analysis of agriculture and craft production in the Oaxaca Valley. There are various estimates of annual corn-consumption needs for regional peasant-artisan households (with four or five members) that hover around one metric ton or 1,000 kilograms (e.g., Kirkby 1973, 89; Beals 1975, 93; Cook and Binford 1990, 45, 258–259n6). One complicating factor in collecting field data is that the traditional Oaxaca Valley system of measuring crop yields employs measures of volume like almud, fanega, barcina, piscador, carga de burro, and carreta, whereas the official governmental approach relies on the metric system of measures by weight (kilogramos, toneladas). My OVSIP project employed the following approximate sets of equivalencies between these two systems: 1 almud = 4 kg; 1 fanega = 25 almudes = 100 kg; 1/2 carreta = 250 kg; 1 carreta = 5 fanegas = 125 almudes = 500 kg; 1 metric ton = 2 carretas = 10 fanegas = 1,000 kg; 2 barcinas = 1 fanega = 1 carga de burro = 100 kg; 1 piscador = 16 almudes = 64 kg.

16. Regarding the alternation of agricultural work and work in the quarries, Aristeo Gutiérrez in 1990 described the situation for himself and other metateros in the following terms (Cook 1990, Tape 1551): "Planting corn, and going out to the fields with oxen and carts to harvest ears of corn (mazorca); cutting dried cornstalks (zacate); picking up all the harvest and carting it home—agricultural field work is what we do here. When we start the agricultural cycle, we give up the craft for periods of days, weeks, and months while we work in the fields. When that agricultural work is finished, we come back to the quarries and continue working."

## Chapter Five

1. Martínez Gracida (1883) devoted twenty-three pages to Mitla, addressing its pre-Hispanic and early colonial history. On the last page, he wrote: "The sons of this pueblo in 1570 took up arms to contain the eruption of the Mixes that seemed to

threaten death to the Zapotec population, but fortunately they were conquered and all of the Zapotec pueblos were saved. The Spaniards, the Mixtecs of Cuilapan, the Mexicans of Analco, the Zapotecs of the mountains and the Valley, and Oaxaca City all contributed to this defensive effort . . . it is known that the King of Spain conceded many favors to the pueblos that took part in the defense, as well as to individual Spaniards who were rewarded with encomiendas." It is quite conceivable that people of Mixtec, Zapotec, or Nahua ethnicity who were participants in the Mixe War ended up as dependents of the Hacienda Xaagá and were Hispanicized over time in their status as terrazgueros. All quotations from this work are my translation.

2. Taylor (1972) uncovered some relevant information about these two estates, but none about their specific relationships with San Lorenzo Albarradas. The authoritative *Historia de la cuestión agraria mexicana: Estado de Oaxaca*, Vols. 1–2 (Reina 1988b), as well as other specialized histories like Bailón Corres (1999), Arellanes Meixueiro (1999), and Chassen-López (2004), do not include coverage of Hacienda Xaagá. Based on a variety of different sources, Aguilar-Robledo (2009, 40n13) comprehensively reviewed findings regarding the fundo legal in colonial New Spain from 1567 to 1798. Many Oaxaca historians like Taylor (1972, 68) and Berry (1981, 174) follow Mendieta y Núñez's (1966, 59) assertion that "the fundo legal ought to be understood as the minimum and not the maximum extension that a pueblo must have," thereby excluding cultivated lands designated for the subsistence of the inhabitants and those possessed by them prior to being reduced to pueblos.

3. Parsons specifically cited Schmieder (1930, 20) as the source for her attribution of Mixtec origin to the people of Xaagá in this quote. On a visit to the home in San Lorenzo Albarradas of a curandera and loquacious castellana, Catarina Ruiz, Parsons (1936, 376) learned "a lot about that hybrid town, whose people are from the Mixteca, from Santo Tomás and Totolapa, and from Mitla . . . more than we learned the day we spent in San Lorenzo itself, when Catarina was away" (ibid.).

Parsons made several references to residents of San Lorenzo or to particular San Lorenzans as "Castellanos" or "Castilian-speaking" (1936, 30, 76n31, 122–123, 242, 299n21, 376, 568). Her first reference to "Castellanos" in the Zapotec hinterland of Mitla was in a discussion of Mitla traders whom she referred to as "middlemen between Zapotecs, Mixes, and 'Castellanos'" (1936, 14), in which San Lorenzo was mentioned as a place where burro trains from Mitla passed through on their way to Mixe country. The quotation marks Parsons uses for "Castellanos" implied that Mitleños, at the time she was there, considered Lenchanos to have castellano identity. The above "hybrid town" quote suggests that Parsons had not discounted the possibility that San Lorenzo's origins were multiethnic.

4. Martínez Gracida (1883) also said that San Lorenzo Albarradas had a "church of whitewash and stone" (templo de cal y canto) constructed in 1526, a parish house (casa cural) constructed of the same materials in 1623, and a "municipal building of adobe walls and a palm roof" constructed in 1613. He listed a jail built in 1623 of the same materials as the church and rectory, a "cemetery walled with stone and mud" built in 1823, and a "room destined for public instruction, built with adobe walls and a tile roof" in 1872. He provided similar data for all of the Albarradas pueblos,

with dates for founding and titling as follows: Santo Domingo, 1423 and 1517; San Miguel, 1526 and n.d.; Santa Catarina, 1593 and 1614; and Santa María, 1590 and 1701. Unfortunately, his sixteenth-century dating is the least reliable.

5. According to Manuel Esparza (1988, 273), Juárez served as governor for the fifth time from January 2, 1856, to June 30, 1857. This does not include his first period as a member of a governing triumvirate with Luis Fernández del Campo and José Simeón Arteaga from August 11 to September 11, 1846. It does include the period from October 2, 1847, to November 6, 1848, during only a portion of which he was actually Gobernador Constitucional (as of July 6, 1848); the period from December 11, 1848, to January 20, 1849, during which he was back in charge of the government (but not as Gobernador Constitucional); the period from February 1, 1849, to April 1, 1849, as Gobernador Constitucional; and the period from April 24, 1849, to August 12, 1852, also as Gobernador Constitucional. Juárez was Constitutional Governor and Military Commander from June 2, 1856, to June 1857, and was Constitutional Governor from the latter date until October 25, 1857, when according to Martínez Gracida (1884) "he went on leave to go to serve as Ministerio de Gobernación" in Mexico City. Esparza's main source was Martínez Gracida (1884), written when the author was "Oficial Mayor de la Secretaría del Gobierno"; another source was Hernández (1902).

Brian Hamnett (personal communication, January 2012), maintains that Juárez's withdrawals from direct administration during the pre-1857 period were "technical" rather than involving "loss of office and do not denote any instance of instability."

6. It is unclear how San Lorenzo originally acquired the land leased to Guergué, but conceivably it could have derived from a fundo legal defined as "the minimum surface area that a pueblo ought to possess" (Mecinas 1955, 5; Romero Frizzi 1988, 144; cf. Reina 1988, 192–193).

Martínez Gracida (1883) described San Lorenzo as a municipality with an ayuntamiento consisting of a presidente, four regidores, and a síndico procurador, and regarding its territorial limits (3 leguas cuadradas), he wrote: "In the description of the Hacienda de Xaagá it was mentioned that its lands and those of San Lorenzo were in litigation, and for that reason this pueblo finds itself bounded on the North by the Hacienda of San Bartolo, to the South its boundary ends at La Cumbre or el Cerro del Dado where it borders the Hacienda de Xaagá, to the East with San Juan and Santa Ana del Río, and to the West with San Pablo Mitla." It is likely that the litigation referred to involved the "arrendamiento" by Guergué.

7. In San Lorenzo I obtained access to a copy of a uniquely valuable pamphlet written and published in 1955 by Professor Taurino Mecinas, a teacher specializing in adult literacy, entitled *Tierra y libertad: Datos sobre las luchas sostenidas por los agraristas de la población de San Lorenzo Albarradas para recibir las tierras de que hoy disfrutan.* In his foreword, Mecinas explained that to commemorate the nineteenth anniversary of the handing over of lands by ampliación to San Lorenzo, he proposed an activity focused on major events involving San Lorenzo's struggle to obtain land and some of the survivors of that struggle. His proposal was sanctioned and embraced by the local ejido authority (autoridad ejidal). The persons selected to give

testimonials were Crisóstomo Sibaja, Ignacio Olivera, Marcos Olivera, and Ángel Olivera. The first two were the only survivors of the entire struggle and directed the dotación petition process in the period 1916–1923. The other two were involved in soliciting an ampliación of ejidos in the early 1930s.

Mecinas's main informant was Ignacio "Nachito" Olivera, who was president of the Comité Particular Agrario established in 1921. He was born in 1892, was twenty-nine years old in 1921, and sixty-three years old at the time he gave testimony. Olivera's testimony specifically mentioned Joaquín Guergué as the Xaagá hacendado who sold to Iñárritu but did not mention Guergué's son. Mecinas made little use of documentary materials and secondary source materials.

8. The Guardia Rural, popularly known as Los Rurales, was established in 1861 by President Benito Juárez but was more pervasive and notorious after 1877 under Porfirio Díaz. At odds with the record of hostility between the hacienda and the pueblo, in 1909, only one year before the outbreak of the Mexican Revolution, San Lorenzo purchased a parcel of land measuring 751.60 hectares from the Hacienda Xaagá for 400 pesos (Mecinas 1955, 17).

9. The following entry for Luis Iñárritu Flores from the *Diccionario histórico de la revolución en Oaxaca* (Arellanes Meixueiro et al. 2000, n.p.; translation mine) is informative: "Proprietor of the Hacienda Xaagá, one of the most important of the valley of Tlacolula. Member of the Club Reeleccionista de Oaxaca de 1910. Jefe político of Teotitlán in 1914. Diputado suplente in the Twenty-seventh local legislature that functioned from 1913 to 1915 and propietario in the Twenty-seventh Legislatura soberanista in 1915. In this latter year, he codirected the Fuerzas Defensoras del Estado during the sovereignty movement. He obtained the rank of general. During the delahuertista rebellion, he signed, together with Governor Manuel García Vigil, the manifesto to the nation and the revolutionary plan that did not recognize Alvaro Obregón as president."

10. Letter of March 2, 1925, from Saturnino González for the President of the Comité Administrativo Agrario of San Lorenzo to C. Delegado of the CNA-Oaxaca City. A more detailed version appeared in a summary report dated September 6, 1928, entitled "Informe del resultado de la Comisión que se le confirió en el pueblo de San Lorenzo" to Del. CNA-Oax from Zeferino García, mecanógrafo.

11. According to Whetten (1948, 127): "Cárdenas spent a good share of his time travelling among the villagers, frequently by muleback, studying their problems at firsthand and listening to their grievances. On the basis of information thus obtained, he resolved to carry out the Agrarian Reform Laws with utmost dispatch, and he streamlined the governmental machinery for doing so . . . During the Cárdenas regime (1935–40) more land was distributed than in all previous administrations put together." Whetten (1948, 143–151) also outlined contrasting points of view of hacendados and their opponents, and critically analyzed the land redistribution program.

See Smith (2009) for a comprehensive and mixed appraisal of the Cárdenas legacy in Oaxaca; and Ornelas López (1988, 129–130, 187–188) for a more positive appraisal.

12. ASRA: exp. 638, Dec. 18, 1935, Delegación del Depto. Agrario a C. Pres. del Comisariado Ejidal de SLA del ex-distrito de Tlacolula; Dec. 26, 1935, from Ing. Delegado del Depto. Agrario-Oaxaca to C. General González, Jefe de la 28/a Zona Militar with copy to C. Luis Iñárritu Flores.

13. This matches Chassen's generalized description of hacendado-tenant relations on Oaxaca haciendas, including those in the Oaxaca Valley (1986; Chassen-Lopez 2004; cf. Esparza 1988, 323).

**Chapter Six**

1. The household survey in San Lorenzo began on January 30, 1980; the final report was completed on April 14. A total of seventy-five questionnaires were administered from the original randomly selected sample; two additional questionnaires were subsequently administered to palm-product intermediaries (empleadoras), making a total of seventy-seven questionnaires administered and included in preliminary tabulations. Of these seventy-seven questionnaires, there were ten replacement households, but only two of these were refusals. Tape-recorded interviews were conducted with fourteen palm plaiters, four intermediaries, three broom makers, three mezcal distillers (palenqueros), and one hard-fiber worker (ixtlero).

2. The survey in Xaagá was begun on October 3 and completed on October 17, 1980; a total of thirty-eight households were surveyed. A decision was made to expand the survey to include a higher percentage of weavers, so sixteen additional weaver households were surveyed by November 7, bringing the total number of households surveyed to fifty-four. We also tape-recorded thirty-one interviews with weavers (both self-employed and employees), as well as with seamstresses (costureras) and shawl finishers (tejedoras de puntas de rebozo).

3. I am grateful to Loretta O'Connor of Chontal.net and to Danny Zborover of the University of Calgary, Department of Archaeology (personal communication, April 8, 2013), for identifying the settlement referred to by Félix Sibaja as San Pablo Mártir Quiechapa, a Zapotec community immediately to the west of the Chontal highlands. Martínez Gracida (1910) mentioned this community, with the Zapotec etymology of "stone woman," as being one of the most important Zapotec shrines to a local water goddess. It is probable that the community's proximity to the Chontal region meant that historically it had a mixed Zapotec-Chontal population.

4. In discussing the native dress of Zapotec women in Mitla and Tlacolula, Frederick Starr (1900, 47–48) also described the different loom technologies employed by weavers in these two communities: "On gala days or when going to town, the plain cotton enagua is covered by a heavy woolen one a yard or more wide and three yards long, enough to go around the body twice . . . There are two kinds of these enaguas or mantas, one of plain black, the other a crimson red, plain or with black stripes. At Mitla these mantas are woven, under the trees, with the old and simple device so often represented in the ancient Mexican manuscripts. The warp threads are fastened at one end to a tree or post, at the other to the belt of the weaver or to a strap passing behind the body. The weaver may stand or sit while working, but the

threads are held taut by his own weight. A few sticks and loops of string serve to hold the threads apart, to pass the woof threads through the warp, to separate and reverse the sheds, and to beat home the passed woof thread . . . At Mitla this is the prevalent method; at Tlacolula the mantas are made chiefly on old-fashioned Spanish looms. Usually the man who weaves black mantas does not make red ones and vice versa. Prices vary with size: from 6 to 20 pesos. The dyes are home made . . . The mantas are usually woven in rather narrow strips and two are joined side by side, the junction being decoratively stitched with colored wool."

5. The strike that Félix referred to was most likely a fallout of the Movement of January 1947 that involved the formation of the Comité Cívico Oaxaqueño (CCO) and the end of the governorship of Edmundo Sánchez Cano, who appointed Eduardo Vasconcelos as interim governor in January 1947 (Smith 2009, 310–327).

## Chapter Seven

1. The total population numbers from the 1960 and 1970 censuses break down by community as follows: 1970: Santa Cecilia Jalieza—308, Santo Domingo Jalieza—613, Santo Tomás Jalieza—537, and San Pedro Guegorexe—409; and 1960: Santa Cecilia—220, Santo Domingo—644, Santo Tomás—424, and San Pedro—293 (Welte 1973a).

The notion of a Jalieza subregion, including San Pedro Guegorexe, was an ad hoc category generated by our project and is not coterminous with the "Greater Jalieza" concept used by archaeologists. Nevertheless, the terms encompass more or less the same territory.

The Oaxaca Valley population, estimated to be around 160,000 on the eve of the Spanish Conquest, was as low as 40,000–45,000 in the seventeenth century and did not match its historic peak again until the 1940s (Welte 1976, 284). Ironically, the estimate of 160,000 for the Oaxaca Valley at the time of Spanish contact, which is lower than previous estimates of 350,000 (Taylor 1971; 1972, 17; Cook and Diskin 1976b, 13), derives from the same Settlement Pattern Project (Kowalewski et al. 1989) responsible for the Greater Jalieza estimate. Archaeologists have cautioned (Blanton et al. 1999, 71) that regional population estimates based on archaeological surveys cannot be considered completely accurate.

2. One methodological shortcoming of surface survey research in archaeology is that it is apparently incapable of addressing analytically "bulky artifacts" that could not be collected (e.g., manos, metates, and large local chipped-stone cores), especially where they occurred in great numbers (Finsten 1995, 6). Given the importance of these food-processing artifacts in providing insights into critical dimensions of subsistence economics like nutrition and plant collection/cultivation, this incapability does evoke some degree of skepticism about the reliability of the demographic estimates cited above.

3. The OVSIP household surveys in the Jalieza villages were conducted during the fall of 1978 when Alice Littlefield was serving as field director. Participants in the survey, in addition to Littlefield, were Ana Ema Jaillet, Leticia Rivermar, James

Schillinger, Javier Tellez, Rosa María Salgado, Luis García, and Amelia Pacheco. The field report written by Littlefield in January 1979, summarizing the results of the household survey, was consulted in writing sections of this chapter.

4. In the Nahuatl language, an indigenous woman's upper garment is known as a *quechquemitl*. In preconquest times, it was "frequently worn . . . by persons of rank as the sole upper garment or on top of the huipil. Today one or the other is worn, according, not to rank, but to the area in which the person lives" (Cordry and Cordry 1968, 10–11). In Santo Tomás, the garment was called *quechqueme*.

5. Clements (1980, 138–146), without mentioning his name, described in detail Bernardo's dyeing operation (including photos), its trials and tribulations, and noted that he was the second president of the union in about 1970–1973 and 1976–1977. According to her account, which substantially confirms details of my interview, a major impetus for Bernardo's decision to work with colorfast dyes was the visit of two chemists sent to the village by the Ministry of Industry and Commerce to demonstrate the use of such dyes (ibid., 138). Clements (ibid., 140) also reported that Bernardo worked with his teenage son; an older uncle who worked intermittently, probably for a wage; and his wife. She also noted that weavers of Santo Tomás had a tradition of using vegetable and other natural dyestuffs but, for the most part, by the 1970s were using mostly commercially dyed thread.

6. For more detailed accounts of the history and problems of the organization of weavers in Santo Tomás, see Bertocci (1964), Clements (1980), and Aranda Bezaury (1989). For two excellent photos of weavers in Santo Tomás, see Cordry (1968, 138, 240).

### Chapter Eight

1. The document in question was found in Santa Cecilia's municipal agency archive under the care of authorities and the de facto political leader of the community, Marciano García. It was a long document consisting of about fifteen handwritten pages, though several were missing and the rest were in less than ideal shape, and did not include a copy of the 1798 map. The document was read aloud into a tape recorder. A typed transcript was produced from the tape-recorded version at the ovsip office. The typed transcript consists of twenty-five double-spaced pages. The title of the document was "Pleito por tierras entre la estancia de Santa Cecilia Jalieza sujeta a Teozapotlán y el pueblo de Santo Tomás Mecatepeque, 1620–1634." It is held in the Archivo de la Agencia Municipal de Santa Cecilia Jalieza (aamscj). Pagination is from the transcript, not from the original. The July 31, 1923, report submitted by Ing. Sotomayor, "Datos Relativos a la Circular #15" (asra: exp. 7), refers in clause XI to the above document in possession of Santa Cecilia's authorities. This document was also cited in other documents copied by ovsip from Santa Cecilia's files in the Archivo de la Secretaría de la Reforma Agraria in Oaxaca City (asra), identified as Expediente 7, Dotación de Tierras Ejidales, and Expediente 28, Terrenos Comunales. The sixteenth-century reduction of the Santa Cecilia popula-

tion without expropriation of the lands of their original settlement occurred in accordance with the official policy of the colonial administration (Consejo 1774, Libro VI, Título III, Ley ix, 199).

2. Brian Hamnett (personal communication, January 31, 2012) elaborated on the instability in New Spain (and Oaxaca) after 1810 despite the fact that the "three last viceroys were effective and competent." According to him, the "real problem" was that by the "late 1810s and into the early 1820s, the viceregal administration and Royalist military [were] disintegrating, partly under the impact of financial crisis in the metropolis," which put "a terrible strain on New Spain." The viceroyalty, in turn, was "hit by [a] subsistence crisis in 1809–10 and then insurgency and internal war through the 1810s." Inevitably, Oaxaca was "caught up in all this, with a weakened administration (Bishop Bergosa away since November 1812; Intendant Francisco Rendon, on and off, 1816–21, former Intendant of Zacatecas, but now aged)." Nevertheless, in Hamnett's opinion, "It is probably not right to separate creoles and resident Spanish in terms of sentiments and interests in the 1810s and 1820s," and although some Spanish merchants returned to Spain, Oaxaca remained "mainly mercantile-dominated through Independence" (see also Hamnett 1971, 121–155).

3. This type of intimidation of survey parties by mass demonstration was apparently a common tactic employed by Oaxaca Valley Indian communities embroiled in boundary disputes. According to Taylor (1972, 85), "Similar demonstrations took place at San Juan Teitipac in 1692."

4. It should be noted that the 1820 survey party included as a prominent member one of the Magro brothers who was, at the time, hacendado of San Antonio Buenavista, which encompassed Rancho Guelaviate—thus contradicting dates given in the ownership history of the hacienda by Lic. Carlos Castro Castillo related in Chapter 2.

5. The "defensa social," also known as the "defensa rural," apparently was introduced in 1861 by President Benito Juárez, who ordered the creation of four "cuerpos de campesinos rurales bajo la autoridad del Ministro de Gobernación para desempeñar funciones de policía y combatir el bandolerismo" (citation of *Proceso* article, n.d.). Apparently, the institution survived until the Mexican Revolution, when there were twelve such groups located mostly in the central part of the country. On January 1, 1929, under President Emilio Portes Gil, "the regulations for the organization and operation of the defensas rurales was published. It determined that organized agrarianists should form defensas rurales for the purpose of cooperating in the conservation of internal order (con el fin de cooperar a la conservación del orden interno), being constituted on a temporary basis as veterans in the reserves (como el pie veterano de las reservas)." On October 5, 1936, under Lázaro Cárdenas in circular No. 64, the Secretaría de Guerra y Marina stipulated the organization of the personnel of defensa sociales in units denominated reserve battalions or regiments classified as cavalry or infantry and indicated that the personnel constituting defensas sociales as parts of reserve units must be ejidatarios in possession of parcelas and identified with revolutionary principles naming them reservists (www.mexicoarmado.com/leyes).

Frank Tannenbaum mentioned "the Defensa Social" along with the ejido, the school, and the Ligas de Comunidades Agrarias as key institutions of the social movement under Plutarco Elías Calles that boded ill for the "future success of the hacienda as an economic and political system" (1933, 223). Friedrich Katz (1998, 214, 244) defined "defensas sociales" as "local militias" and traced their origin to northern Mexico, particularly the city of Durango, during the revolution as paramilitary units organized by upper-class counterrevolutionaries. He also noted that local participation in defensas was factionalized and led, at least in the case of Namiquipa, to a vengeance killing seventeen years after the fact (1998, 606, 648–649; see also Alonso 1998 and Rocha Islas 1988).

6. Several decades before Malinowski and De la Fuente wrote about the dangers of Cerro Mantecón, José Antonio Gay (1881, 2:372) observed: "The place most frequented by outlaws (malhechores) has always been the summit (cuesta) of Ocotlán, due to the fair (feria) or market (tianguis) that takes place there every Friday, and that is very well attended by the inhabitants of neighboring communities. The thieves hide in brush and thickets, and regularly assault carts due to the slow speed at which they are pulled by oxen that made it impossible for them to flee to safety, and we thus find ourselves forced to lament, due to these attacks, not only the loss of considerable valuables but also wounded and dead." It is noteworthy that Gay connected the delinquency in this notorious corridor to marketing activity in Ocotlán, a connection not made by Malinowski and De la Fuente (Drucker-Brown 1982, 93–94) in their discussion. We may never know the identity of the delinquents; and that may have shifted over time. But my guess is that, at some point, the Guelaviate–San Antonio Buenavista–San Juan Teitipac nexus may have been a source.

## Chapter Nine

1. In a paraje in the northeastern sector of its original fundo legal known as La Peña, there are rock shelters that may well have been early prehistoric sites, but, so far as I know, this has not been confirmed by archaeological investigation. Given the paraje's proximity to San Pedro Mártir, where a large ceremonial mound complex was visible from the Ocotlán–Ejutla highway, it can be inferred that there were pre-Hispanic settlements in the immediate area.

The document cited in Méndez Martínez 1999 is in the Archivo General de la Nación, Tierras collection: Año 1776–1777, vol. 997, exp. 1, fs. 91, Oaxaca Cd.

2. The term "comisariado" is used in rural Oaxaca with reference to either the entire group of local legal and administrative representatives of an ejido, the Comité or Comisión Ejidal, or to the highest ranking official or president of the Comité (who in official parlance may be referred to as "comisario," or commissioner). The comisario has a commission or function to perform in office, hence the term "comisariado," meaning someone "commissioned" to perform his office.

3. A 1776 survey of fundos legales in the Oaxaca Valley was conducted to check for possible encroachments on town sites. Apparently, the 1687 law enlarging the fundo legal to 600 varas (1,650 feet) was still in effect, although several reportedly

exceeded that limit by a substantial amount. Among them was San Pedro Apóstol, which reportedly owned "lands of unknown dimensions extending beyond the 600 varas" (Taylor 1972, 69n). Magdalena was presumably in the same situation, since its fundo legal encompassed 287 hectares. This all remains speculative, however, given the lack of colonial documentation for Magdalena.

4. The same process of congregation and settlement experienced by Ocotlán was probably repeated in the case of Magdalena. According to Gay (1881, 1:380): "The pueblo of Ocotlán that before the conquest was situated on a mountain was brought together around its first temple that was built of thatch in the middle of a valley; but since the site was low and rainfall was heavy in 1556 . . . they moved the site to its present location according to the plan outlined by the Dominicans." Its location near, but not adjacent to, the mines at San José Progreso, raises the possibility that it was established by reduction as stipulated in Law x (Libro VI, Title III of the Laws of the Indies entitled "That close to where there are mines endeavor to found Indian pueblos" (Consejo de Indias 1774, 199). The oral history also coincides with the Laws of Indies stipulations of 1618 "that in each Reduction there be a Church with a door and key" (Consejo de Indias 1774, 198, Libro VI, Título III, Ley iiij) and that pueblos and reductions have "comodidad de aguas, tierras y montes, entradas y salidas, y labranzas, y un exido de una legua de largo, donde los Indios puedan tener sus ganados, sin que se enbuelvan con otros de Españoles" (Consejo de Indias 1774, 199, Libro VI, Título III, Ley viij).

5. The meaning of the term "suarín" (used by Cosme) is unclear. No such word exists in Spanish. Conceivably, it could be a Hispanicized Zapotec term, which, in the context it was used, may refer to a diviner of some sort.

6. In 1967, the largest landowner in Magdalena was reputed to be Luciano Sánchez, who was apparently the only member of the community to be listed on the Padrón Predial, Oficina de Recaudación de Rentas, in Ocotlán as a taypayer on six irregularly shaped parcels in six different parajes (the largest measured 57.50 x 875.90 x 118.40 x 176.16 meters; the most symmetrical parcel measured 96 x 100 x 55.75 x 56.12 meters = 5,488 square meters = .55 hectare). On the ejido rolls in 1964 and 1966, he is listed as planting 6 and 6.5 hectares respectively, with a shelled corn production of 1,000 and 1,025 kilos. On the same rolls there was only one ejidatario who cultivated more land than Luciano, namely, Gonzalo Cosme with 7 hectares, but his harvest were somewhat smaller at 900 and 925 kilos.

7. The ovsip 1979 household survey of ten communities in the district of Ocotlán showed the following mean/median number of hectares for the four case-study communities in this book: Magdalena Ocotlán, 3.22/3.00; Santa Cecilia Jalieza, 2.64/2.62; Santo Domingo Jalieza, 2.05/1.75; Santo Tomás Jalieza, 1.47/0.97.

I conducted fieldwork in Magdalena between July 1967 and July 1968 as Research Associate for the Oaxaca Market Study Project, Ralph L. Beals, Principal Investigator. I first visited the community in 1966 during my doctoral dissertation research project (Cook 1969). Also, my project conducted a household survey of Magdalena in 1979 (Cook and Binford 1990).

**Chapter Ten**

1. The term "jornalero residente" was essentially a form of indentured servitude and, in at least one case on record in Magdalena, that of Atanasio Hernández as a young boy (Cook 1982, 144–147), involved a written "Pagaré" (IOU) agreement between his biological father and his guardian-employer.

2. In a document submitted to the delegado of asuntos agrarios in Oaxaca City by a disgruntled ejidatario from Magdalena dated 9/12/64, also pertaining to the aborted incumbency of Severiano Vásquez as comisariado, he explained that "I am an ejidatario in possession of two small fractions of ejido land, which are not enough to cover the needs of my household, and for that reason I solicited parcels from the comisariado . . . who showed me several vacant parcels, including the parcel abandoned by the ejidatario Abraham Vásquez eight years ago. Being in need, I started clearing and getting the land ready to plant, but it happened that one day when I was with my ox team on the parcel in the paraje known as Río Coyote, ready to start planting, Abraham Vásquez showed up and opposed my planting the parcel, alleging that it belonged to him, and even if he had not cultivated it for eight years, he was up to date in paying his taxes on it. This is why I am writing to you as a Higher Authority to resolve this matter fairly, and suggest the following: If it is not possible for me to retain possession of said parcel, then that my work on it be compensated; it is, after all, a half hectare in size and I did all of the work to clear it and ready it for planting." The next paragraph of this complaint provided the following information for officials to confirm: "The ejidatario A. Vásquez has several fractions of land within the ejido and he has been selling those fractions to other ejidatarios, including Antonio Pérez Aquino, Palemón Vásquez, Domingo Vásquez, and Francisco Colmenares. Regarding this matter, all of those named above, ejidatarios of this community with parcels bordering the one in question, can testify as to its truth."

A later document confirmed the veracity of the above allegations and simply observed that these practices were allowed to occur under the previous comisariado, who was Severiano Vásquez. End of story. The 1966 Padrón de Ejidatarios lists Abraham Vásquez as having a total of 6 hectares of land under cultivation, with total shelled-corn yields of 850 and 875 kilos in 1964 and 1965 respectively, placing him in the top 5 percent in both categories.

Ironically, the disgruntled ejidatario lodging the complaint was none other than the metatero Antonio Rosario who was fated to be expelled from the community in 1969 for allegedly failing to cooperate with tequio obligations. The records do not indicate whether or not he was reimbursed for his parcel-preparation expenditures.

3. Below is a list of the expenditures (lista de egresos) incurred on March 10, 1967, for the celebration of the Mass for the Señor de las Peñas: cura, 123 pesos; músicos, 115 pesos; cantor, 20 pesos; 7 ruedas (fireworks), 35 pesos; 7 cohetones (large rockets), 17.50 pesos; 1/2 gross cohetes (smaller rockets), 15 pesos; 2 libras pólvora (black powder), 5 pesos; flores (flowers), 13 pesos; 22 pliegos esmalte (sheets

of glazed paper) and 2 of crepe (crepe paper), 4.60 pesos; 4 onzas copal (incense), 2 pesos, for a total expenditure of 350.10 pesos.

4. Germán Rosario's *guelaguetza* account book, kept by his wife, distinguished between *guelaguetzas* "secas" and "mojadas." With a *guelaguetza* seca, the recipient asked the donor for tortillas but the recipient-to-be provided the corn. The donor made tortillas and delivered them to the house of the recipient on the assigned day. She was not invited in but was given four tortillas when she handed over her *guelaguetza*. The donor then had the right to a reciprocal provision of tortillas, as well as the ritual obligation of giving four tortillas to the new donor. By contrast, with the *guelaguetza* mojada, the donor provided corn for making tortillas. When the donor arrived with the *guelaguetza* at the recipient's house, she was invited in and given a cup of hot chocolate, two pieces of bread, eight tortillas, and a plate of a special dish made of liver called "higadito."

5. Perhaps it is merely coincidental, but aside from their respective patron saint's mayordomías, Magdalena Ocotlán and San Juan Guelavía share two secondary mayordomías associated with religious societies (also known as cofradías or hermandades), namely, la Virgen del Carmen and el Señor de las Peñas. According to Martínez Ríos and Luna Méndez (1960, 297), these societies and their respective saint's cults were of relatively recent origin, introduced in Guelavía in the 1930s—around the time the ejido was established. This dating is not far off the mark for Magdalena and, consequently, may represent a coordinated initiative by the church to strengthen its influence in two communities heavily influenced by the revolutionary agrarian movement. Edward Wright-Rios refers to these religious societies as "sodalities" and notes (2009, 118): "Individuals in a particular community, often at the urging of the local priest, agreed to form a group dedicated to a particular saint, devotion, or image and to sponsor rituals."

6. The ensuing discussion of the metate market is derived from a comparison of datasets accumulated and analyzed during separate periods of fieldwork, namely, 1966–1968 and 1978–1980. The 1966–1968 and 1978–1980 data were analyzed and discussed in Cook 1982. The 1979–1980 data are analyzed and discussed for the first time in this book, and their discussion involves comparisons with the data presented in Cook 1982.

7. During 1967–1968, I was residing in Magdalena in the old schoolhouse on the south side of the village plaza. Early in the morning on Friday, market day in Ocotlán, as part of my arrangement with the metateros, I would take as many of them to market with their products as could crowd into my VW microbus. I would spend several hours with them there, discreetly photographing and gathering sales data. One spring morning in 1968, we observed an entourage moving toward our section of the marketplace located on the east side of the square under the arches. At first we thought this was just another group of tourists led by tour guides from Oaxaca City, but when we saw a film crew in the midst of the entourage, which had an affluent Southern California look about it, we realized that this was not a routine tourist visit. Attracted by the noise of the metateros who were putting finishing

touches on metates and manos with hand picks, members of the entourage came into the metate sales area to observe the metateros at work. The metateros immediately sensed that they might be rewarded for allowing themselves to be filmed and asked me to negotiate a deal. I avoided that role but inevitably was drawn into a conversation with the celebrity in the entourage, whom I immediately recognized—the radio and television personality (*People Are Funny*) Art Linkletter. He was clearly as curious about my presence and role in the scene as he was about the metateros. He was in Oaxaca on a "working vacation" with his adult son and other family members for the purpose of preparing a documentary episode for a television program. He seemed to have a genuine interest in the metateros and in my presence among them as an anthropologist, and he asked several questions that I answered as best I could. His demeanor indicated discomfort with my emphasis on hard work, low pay, and poverty as constants in the lives of the metateros. Linkletter's last interrogative directed at me is etched in my brain: "But they are happy people, aren't they?" I do not know if any of the scenes filmed ever appeared on TV, but, as I recall, the metateros were unrewarded as photographic subjects of the Hollywood celebrity entourage.

## Conclusion

1. The lack of information about Juan Brito's career in Guelavía in the 1957 study is matched by García Ortega's more recent (2007) *Diagnóstico comunitario*. This silence in key sources is truly strange, considering the fact that Brito is not an unknown figure in Oaxaca's modern political history and, arguably, was the most famous all-time resident of Guelavía.

2. I would not go so far as Rabasa (2011, 1) in characterizing Mesoamerica at Spanish contact as an "elsewhere" populated by beings beyond the Same/Other continuum, but I certainly sympathize with the spirit of his project to attempt to grapple with the possible meanings of images created by Mexican *tlacuiloque* (scribes) under the supervision of Spanish friars in the early postcontact period.

3. According to a 1979 estimate, 10 million peasants in Mexico produced nearly 4 million tons of corn utilized to make tortillas. In that same year, 660 million tortillas were made daily in Mexico—two-thirds of them in automated tortilla factories or tortillerías (Aboites Aguilar 1989, 17–18). So, a process of technological invention and innovation initiated around 1900 and intensified after 1950 regarding tortilla making had become so generalized by 1979 as to support a thesis of "defeminization" of the Mexican workforce involved in tortilla making (ibid., 19). It is clear, however, that in rural Oaxaca, the role of women in preparing and processing corn as *nixtamal* and, ultimately, as ready-to-eat tortillas has not been totally eliminated by the proliferation of molinos de *nixtamal* and automatic tortilla-making machines (máquinas tortilladoras).

4. The changes in the *Constitución Política de los Estados Unidos Mexicanos* referred to by Warman and briefly summarized in this paragraph were in Article 2 and are quite comprehensive, occupying five pages in my copy of the Actualización 2002 (*Constitución Política* 2002, 2–6). Article 2 consists of a preamble, followed by

section A (eight clauses) dealing with guarantees of self-determination and autono-my for indigenous communities; and section B (nine clauses) dealing with guaran-tees of equal opportunity and antidiscrimination policies on behalf of indigenous citizenry (cf. Warman 2003, 289–290). The preamble begins with a declaration, "The Mexican Nation is one (única) and indivisible" (*Constitución Política* 2002, 2), almost as a reassurance that the guarantees of self-determination and autonomy for indigenous communities will not evolve to a possible outcome of separation. This declaration is followed by an attempt to define "pueblos indígenas": "The Nation has a pluricultural composition originally sustained in its indigenous communities, which are those that descend from populations that inhabited the present territory of the country at the time of initial colonization and that conserve their own social, economic, cultural, and political institutions or part of them" (ibid., 2). According to Warman (2003, 278, 288), this definition is applicable to most Mexicans and sim-ply sets the framework for elaborating a "code of laws for indigenous communities with many indefinitions" (un fuero indígena con muchas indefiniciones).

5. Rabasa (2000, 11) discussed the phrase "usos y costumbres" after explaining the contradictory Requerimiento of 1513 but did not specifically cite the New Laws of 1542, which ordered that traditional procedures be used in dealings with Indians rather than "ordinary" Spanish legal proceedings, as the first document in which the phrase was used (see also García Icazbalceta 1866, 2, 212). The concept was introduced to address legal issues in "repúblicas de indios" where Spanish legal norms were inapplicable (wikipedia.org).

In the Oaxaca studies literature, the earliest mention of the concept I have found is in Carriedo (1949, 2: Ch. 12). He employed it originally in an 1843 essay with regard to urban and rural Oaxacans of all social classes, but his most interesting discussion, often patronizing, was reserved for the "communities of Indians . . . where original customs exist" (1949, 2:124–129; see also Clarke 2000, 168–170, Hernández-Díaz 2001, Hernández-Díaz 2007a). According to the 2000 federal census, 418 of 570 municipalities in Oaxaca opted to participate in the electoral system under the "usos y costumbres" rubric. It is noteworthy that just over 52 per-cent of the municipios with 0–20 percent indigenous language speakers took this option, compared to 87 percent of the municipios with 81–100 percent indigenous speakers (Hernández-Díaz 2007b, 46).

I am entirely in agreement with the late Arturo Warman (2003, 11, 38) regarding this new eruption of concern with "la cuestión indígena," the concepts of "indíge-na" and "usos y costumbres," and the collective identity these concepts imprecisely evoke.

# BIBLIOGRAPHY

### Archival Sources

ADAAC. Archivo del Departamento de Asuntos Agrarios y Colonización. Mexico City.

AAMSCJ. Archivo de la Agencia Municipal de Santa Cecilia Jalieza. District of Ocotlán de Morelos, Oaxaca. 1620 land title document.

AGEO. Archivo General del Estado de Oaxaca (also known as the Archivo General del Poder Ejecutivo del Estado de Oaxaca). Oaxaca City.

AGNT. Archivo General de la Nación, Tierras Section. Mexico City.

AMSST. Archivo del Municipio de San Sebastián Teitipac. District of Tlacolula de Matamoros, Oaxaca. Various documents.

ASRA. Archivo de la Secretaría de la Reforma Agraria. Oaxaca City. Magdalena Ocotlán: expedientes 14 and 3325, Dotación de Tierras Ejidales; San Antonio Buenavista, municipio de San Sebastián Teitipac: expediente 264, Dotación de Tierras Ejidales, and expediente 1856, Ampliación de Ejidos; San Lorenzo Albarradas: expedientes 120 and 3334, Dotación de Tierras Ejidales, and expedientes 368 and 638, Ampliación de Ejidos; Santa Cecilia Jalieza, municipio de Santo Tomás Jalieza: expediente 7, Dotación de Tierras Ejidales, and expediente 28, Terrenos Comunales; Xaagá, municipio de San Pablo Villa de Mitla: expediente 955, Dotación de Tierras Ejidales.

FBSO. Fundación Bustamante, Sala Oaxaca. Oaxaca City.

RBC. Ralph L. Beals Collection, National Anthropological Archive, Smithsonian Institution, Washington, DC.

### Published Sources

Aboites Aguilar, Jaime. 1989. *Breve historia de un invento olvidado: Las máquinas tortilladoras en México*. Mexico City: Universidad Autónoma Metropolitana–Unidad Xochimilco.

Aguilar-Robledo, Miguel. 2009. "Contested Terrain: The Rise and Decline of Surveying in New Spain, 1500-1800." *Journal of Latin American Geography* 8 (2): 23–47.

Aguirre Beltrán, Gonzalo. 1970. "Comentario. Indigenismo en México: Confrontación de problemas." *Anuario Indigenista* 30 (December): 280–294.

Alba, Carlos H., and Jesús Cristerna. "Las industrias zapotecas." In Mendieta y Núñez 1949, 493–600.

Alonso, Ana María. 1998. "U.S. Military Intervention, Revolutionary Mobilization, and Popular Ideology in the Chihuahuan Sierra, 1916–1917." In Nugent 1998, 207–238.

Aranda Bezaury, Josefina G. 1989. "Matrimonio, géneros y subordinación de la mujer: El caso de Santo Tomás Jalieza, Oaxaca." Master's thesis in social anthropology, Escuela Nacional de Antropología e Historia, Mexico City.

Arellanes Meixueiro, Anselmo. 1988. "Del Camarazo al Cardenismo (1925–1933)." In Reina 1988b, 2:23–126.

———. 1999. *Oaxaca: Reparto de la tierra, alcances, limitaciones y respuestas*. 2nd ed. Oaxaca City, Mex.: PROOAX/UABJO/Carteles Editores/UNAM.

———. 2002. *Asuntos agrarios del Estado de Oaxaca: Conflictos por límites, bosques y las tierras comunales: Guía*. Oaxaca City, Mex.: SEP-Conacyt/Sibej/ITO.

Arellanes Meixueiro, Anselmo, et al. 2000. *Diccionario histórico de la revolución en Oaxaca*. Mexico City: INEHRM/UABJO.

Arroyo, Esteban. 1958. *Los dominicos: Forjadores de la civilización oajaqueña*. Vol. 1, *Los misioneros*. Oaxaca City, Mex.: N.p.

———. 1961. *Los dominicos: Forjadores de la civilización oajaqueña*. Vol. 2, *Los conventos*. Oaxaca City, Mex.: N.p.

Bailón Corres, Jaime. 1999. *Pueblos indios, élites y territorio: Sistemas de dominio regional en el sur de México: Una historia política de Oaxaca*. Mexico City: El Colegio de México.

Barabas, Alicia, and Miguel A. Bartolomé, eds. 1986. *Etnicidad y pluralismo cultural: La dinámica étnica en Oaxaca*. Mexico City: Instituto Nacional de Antropología e Historia.

Barlow, Robert Hayward. 1949. *The Extent of the Empire of the Culhua Mexica*. Ibero-Americana 28. Berkeley: University of California Press.

Beals, Ralph L. 1975. *The Peasant Marketing System of Oaxaca, Mexico*. Berkeley and Los Angeles: University of California Press.

Belmar, Francisco. 1901. *Breve reseña histórica y geográfica del Estado de Oaxaca*. Oaxaca City, Mex.: Imprenta del Comercio.

Benítez Zenteno, Raúl, ed. 1980. *Sociedad y política en Oaxaca 1980: 15 estudios de caso*. Oaxaca City, Mex.: IIS-UABJO.

Berdan, Frances F. 1989. "Trade and Markets in Precapitalist States." In *Economic Anthropology*, edited by Stuart Plattner, 78–107. Palo Alto, CA: Stanford University Press.

———. 2000. "Principles of Regional and Long-distance Trade in the Aztec Empire. In *The Ancient Civilizations of Mesoamerica*, edited by Michael E. Smith and Marilyn A. Masson, 191–203. Malden, MA: Blackwell Publishers.

———. 2005. *The Aztecs of Central Mexico: An Imperial Society*. 2nd ed. Belmont, CA: Thompson Wadsworth.

Berry, Charles R. 1981. *The Reform in Oaxaca, 1856–76: A Microhistory of the Liberal Revolution*. Lincoln and London: University of Nebraska Press.

Bertocci, Peter J. 1964. "An Artisans' Cooperative: Report on 'Special Problem.'" Tri-Institutional Training Program in Cultural Anthropology. Oaxaca City, Mex. Typescript.

Blanton, Richard E. 1978. *Monte Albán: Settlement Patterns at the Ancient Zapotec Capital*. New York: Academic Press.

Blanton, Richard E., Gary M. Feinman, Stephen A. Kowalewski, and Linda M. Nicholas. 1999. *Ancient Oaxaca*. Cambridge: Cambridge University Press.

Bradomín, José María. 1955. *Toponimia de Oaxaca (Crítica etimológica)*. Mexico City: Impr. "Camarena."

Burgoa, Francisco de. 1934. *Geográfica descripción*. Mexico City: Talleres Gráficos de la Nación.

Carrasco, Pedro. 1951. "Las culturas indígenas de Oaxaca, México." *América Indígena* 11: 99–114.

———. 1999. *The Tenochca Empire of Ancient Mexico: The Triple Alliance of Tenochtitlan, Tetzcoco, and Tlacopan*. Norman: University of Oklahoma Press.

Carriedo, Juan B. 1949. *Estudios históricos y estadísticos del Estado Oaxaqueño*. 2 vols. Mexico City: Imprenta Morales.

Caso, Alfonso, et al. 1954. *Métodos y resultados de la Política indigenista en México*. Memorias del Instituto Nacional Indigenista, Vol. 6. Mexico City: Ediciones del Instituto Nacional Indigenista.

Castro Castillo, Carlos. n.d. "Observaciones y estudios hechos en la práctica del manejo y dirección de los trabajos para la explotación de la Hacienda de San Antonio Buenavista ubicada en el Distrito de Tlacolula, desde el año de 1879." Sala Oaxaca, Fundación Bustamante, Oaxaca City, Oaxaca, Mexico. Unpublished manuscript.

Cave, Damien. 2012. "'Migrants' New Paths Reshaping Latin America." *New York Times*, Friday, January 6, A1 AND A3.

Chance, John K. 1978. *Race and Class in Colonial Oaxaca*. Palo Alto, CA: Stanford University Press.

———. 1990. "Changes in Twentieth-Century Mesoamerican Cargo Systems." In Stephen and Dow 1990, 27–42.

———. 1996. "Mesoamerica's Ethnographic Past." *Ethnohistory* 43 (3): 379–403.

Chance, John K., and William B. Taylor. 1985. "Cofradías and Cargos: An Historical Perspective on the Mesoamerican Civil-Religious Hierarchy." *American Ethnologist* 12 (1): 1–26.

Chapple, Eliot D., and Carleton S. Coon. 1942. *Principles of Anthropology*. New York: Henry Holt.

Chassen, Francie R. 1986. "Oaxaca: Del Porfiriato a la Revolución, 1902–1911." PhD diss., Facultad de Filosofía y Letras, Universidad Nacional Autónoma de México.

Chassen-López, Francie R. 2004. *From Liberal to Revolutionary Oaxaca: The View from the South, Mexico 1867–1911*. University Park: Pennsylvania State University Press.

Chibnik, Michael. 2003. *Crafting Tradition: The Making and Marketing of Oaxaca Wood Carvings*. Austin: University of Texas Press.

Clarke, Colin. 2000. *Class, Ethnicity, and Community in Southern Mexico: Oaxaca's Peasantries*. Oxford: Oxford University Press.

Clements, Helen P. 1980. "'Our Work'; Weaving at Santo Tomas Jalieza, Oaxaca." Unpublished Master's thesis, Anthropology Department, Texas Tech University, Lubbock, Texas.

———. 1987. "Weaving in Two Oaxaca Communities: An Historical Perspective." Paper presented at the 47th Annual Meeting of the Society for Applied Anthropology, Oaxaca City, Mexico, April 8–12.

Cohen, Jeffrey H. 1999. *Cooperation and Community: Economy and Society in Oaxaca*. Austin: University of Texas Press.

———. 2004. *The Culture of Migration in Southern Mexico.* Austin: University of Texas Press.

Consejo de Indias (Spain). 1774. *Recopilación de leyes de los reynos de las Indias.* Vol. 2. Madrid: Antonio Pérez de Soto (3rd ed.). Nabu Public Domain reprint.

*Constitución Política de los Estados Unidos Mexicanos.* 2002. Mexico City: Editores Mexicanos Unidos.

Cook, Scott. 1965. "Toward a Sociolinguistic Analysis of Puerto Rican Clichés." Unpublished paper.

———. 1969. *Teitipac and Its Metateros: An Economic Anthropological Study of Production and Exchange in the Valley of Oaxaca, Mexico.* PhD diss., University of Pittsburgh. Ann Arbor, MI: University Microfilms.

———. 1973. "Stone Tools for Steel-age Mexicans? Aspects of Production in a Zapotec Stoneworking Industry." *American Anthropologist* 75: 1485–1503.

———. 1976. "The 'Market' as Location and Transaction: Dimensions of Marketing in a Zapotec Stoneworking Industry." In Cook and Diskin 1976b, 139–168.

———. 1978. "Petty Commodity Production and Capitalist Development in the 'Central Valleys' Region of Oaxaca, Mexico." *Nova Americana* 1: 285–332.

———. 1982. *Zapotec Stoneworkers: The Dynamics of Rural Simple Commodity Production in Modern Mexican Capitalism.* Lanham, MD: University Press of America.

———. 1983. "Mestizo Palm Weavers among the Zapotecs: A Critical Reexamination of the 'Albarradas Enigma.'" *Notas Mesoamericanas* 9: 39–46.

———. 1984a. *Peasant Capitalist Industry: Piecework and Enterprise in Southern Mexican Brickyards.* Lanham, MD: University Press of America.

———. 1984b. "Peasant Economy, Rural Industry and Capitalist Development in the Oaxaca Valley, Mexico." *The Journal of Peasant Studies* 12 (1): 3–40.

———. 1985. "Craft Businesses, Piece Work, and Value Distribution in the Oaxaca Valley, Mexico." In Plattner 1985, 235–258.

———. 1988. "Inflation and Rural Livelihood in a Mexican Province: An Exploratory Analysis." *Mexican Studies/Estudios Mexicanos* 4 (1): 55–78.

———. 1990. Oaxaca Shoot Audio Transcript (OSAT), handwritten Spanish version. Oaxaca metate footage from "Out of the Past" Project, WQED (Pittsburgh) and Cambridge Documentary Films Production, William T. Sanders, Department of Anthropology, Pennsylvania State University, Project Director.

———. 1993. "Toward a New Paradigm for Anthropology in Mexican Studies." *Mexican Studies/Estudios Mexicanos* 9 (2): 303–336.

———. 2004. *Understanding Commodity Cultures: Explorations in Economic Anthropology with Case Studies from Mexico.* Lanham, MD: Rowman and Littlefield.

———. 2006. "Commodity Cultures, Mesoamerica and Mexico's Changing Indigenous Economy." *Critique of Anthropology* 26 (2): 181–208.

Cook, Scott, and Leigh Binford. 1990. *Obliging Need: Rural Petty Industry in Mexican Capitalism.* Austin: University of Texas Press.

Cook, Scott, and Martin Diskin. 1976a. "A Concluding Critical Look at Issues of Theory and Method in Oaxaca Market Studies." In Cook and Diskin 1976b, 247–280.

————, eds. 1976b. *Markets in Oaxaca*. Austin: University of Texas Press.

————. 1976c. "The Peasant Market Economy of the Valley of Oaxaca in Analysis and History." In Cook and Diskin 1976b, 5–25.

Cook, Scott, and Jong-Taick Joo. 1995. "Ethnicity and Economy in Rural Mexico: A Critique of the Indigenista Approach." *Latin American Research Review* 30 (2): 33–59.

Cook, Sherburne F., and Woodrow Borah. 1960. *The Indian Population of Central Mexico, 1531–1610*. Ibero-Americana 44. Berkeley: University of California Press.

Cook, Sherburne F., and Lesley B. Simpson. 1948. *The Population of Central Mexico in the Sixteenth Century*. Ibero-Americana 31. Berkeley: University of California Press.

Cordry, Donald, and Dorothy Cordry. 1968. *Mexican Indian Costumes*. Austin and London: University of Texas Press.

Dahlgren de Jordán, Barbro. 1963. *La grana cochinilla*. Nueva Biblioteca Mexicana de Obras Históricas, no. 1. Mexico City: N.p.

De la Fuente, Julio. 1965. *Relaciones interétnicas*. Mexico City: Instituto Nacional Indigenista.

Del Paso y Troncoso, Francisco. 1905. *Papeles de Nueva España*. Vol. 4, *Relaciones geográficas de la Diócesis de Oaxaca*. Madrid: Sucs. de Rivadeneyra.

Dennis, Philip A. 1987. *Intervillage Conflict in Oaxaca*. New Brunswick and London: Rutgers University Press.

Diskin, Martin. 1986. "La economía de la comunidad étnica en Oaxaca." In Barabas and Bartolomé 1986, 257–298.

Drucker-Brown, Susan, ed. 1982. *Malinowski in Mexico: The Economics of a Mexican Market System*. Boston: Routledge and Kegan Paul.

Esparza, Manuel. 1988. "Los proyectos de los liberales en Oaxaca (1856–1910)." In Reina 1988b, 1:270–330.

————. 1991a. "Conflictos por límites de tierras, Oaxaca, Siglo XIX." AGEO, Guías y Catálogos #7.

————. 1991b. "Repartos y adjudicaciones, Oaxaca, Siglo XIX." AGEO, Guías y Catálogos #6.

————, ed. 1994. *Relaciones geográficas de Oaxaca, 1777–1778*. Oaxaca City, Mex.: CIESAS and Instituto Oaxaqueño de las Culturas.

Esteva, Cayetano. 1913. *Nociones elementales de geografía histórica del Estado de Oaxaca*. Oaxaca City, Mex.: San Germán Hnos.

Feinman, Gary M. 1986. "The Emergence of Specialized Ceramic Production in Formative Oaxaca." In *Research in Economic Anthropology: Economic Aspects of Prehispanic Highland Mexico*, supplement 2, edited by Barry L. Isaac, 347–373. Greenwich, CT: JAI Press.

Feinman, Gary M., and Linda M. Nicholas. 2004. "Unraveling the Prehispanic Highland Mesoamerican Economy: Production, Exchange, and Consumption in the Classic Period Valley of Oaxaca." In *Archaeological Perspectives on Political Economies*, edited by Gary M. Feinman and Linda M. Nicholas, 167–188. Salt Lake City: University of Utah Press.

Finsten, Laura. 1995. *Jalieza, Oaxaca: Activity Specialization at a Hilltop Center*. Nashville, TN: Vanderbilt University Publications in Anthropology.

Flannery, Kent V. 1968. "Archaeological Systems Theory and Early Mesoamerica." *Anthropological Archaeology of the Americas*, edited by Betty Meggers, 67–87. Washington, DC: The Anthropological Society of Washington.

Flannery, Kent V., Anne V. T. Kirkby, Michael J. Kirkby, and Aubrey Williams, Jr. 1968. "Farming Systems and Political Growth in Ancient Oaxaca." *Science* 158: 445–454.

Flannery, Kent V., and Joyce Marcus, eds. 2003. *The Cloud People: Divergent Evolution of the Zapotec and Mixtec Civilizations*. Clinton Corners, NY: Percheron Press.

Gabbarot, Mariana, and Colin Clarke. 2010. "Social Capital, Migration and Development in the Valles Centrales of Oaxaca, Mexico: Non-Migrants and Communities of Origin Matter." *Bulletin of Latin American Research* 29 (2): 187–207.

García Icazbalceta, Joaquín, ed. 1866. *Colección de documentos para la historia de México*. Mexico City: Antigua Librería, Portal de Agustinos no. 3.

García Ortega, Eleazar. 2007. "Diagnóstico comunitario San Juan Guelavía, Tlacolula, Oaxaca." www.diagnosticocomunitarioguelavia.blogspot.com.

Garriga, Carlos. 1998. "La recusación judicial: Del derecho indiano al derecho mexicano." In *La supervivencia del derecho español en Hispanoamerica durante la época independiente*, 203–239. Mexico City: UNAM (see also www.bibliojuridica.org).

Gay, José Antonio. 1881. *Historia de Oaxaca*. 2 vols. Mexico City: Imprenta del Comercio de Dublan.

———. 1950. *Historia de Oaxaca*. 4 vols. 3rd ed. Mexico City: Talleres V. Venero.

Gerhard, Peter. 1993. *A Guide to the Historical Geography of New Spain*. Rev. ed. Norman and London: University of Oklahoma Press.

Gibson, Charles. 1964. *The Aztecs under Spanish Rule: A History of the Indians of the Valley of Mexico, 1519–1810*. Palo Alto, CA: Stanford University Press.

Hamnett, Brian. 1971. *Politics and Trade in Southern Mexico, 1750–1821*. Cambridge: Cambridge University Press.

———. 1999. *A Concise History of Mexico*. Cambridge: Cambridge University Press.

Hannerz, Ulf. 1992. *Cultural Complexity: Studies in the Social Organization of Meaning*. New York: Columbia University Press.

Hayden, Brian, ed. 1987a. *Lithic Studies among the Contemporary Highland Maya*. Tucson: University of Arizona Press.

Hayden, Brian. 1987b. "Traditional Metate Manufacturing in Guatemala Using Chipped Stone Tools." In Hayden 1987a, 8–119.

Hayden, Brian, and Margaret Nelson. 1981. "The Use of Chipped Lithic Material in the Contemporary Maya Highlands." *American Antiquity* 46 (4): 885–898.

Hernández, Rafael. 1902. *Índice alfabético de la colección de leyes y decretos del Estado de Oaxaca*. Oaxaca City, Mex.: Imprenta del Estado.

Hernández-Díaz, Jorge. 2001. *Reclamos de la identidad: La formación de las organizaciones indígenas en Oaxaca*. Oaxaca City, Mex.: UABJO.

———, ed. 2007a. *Ciudadanías diferenciadas en un estado multicultural: Los usos y costumbres en Oaxaca*. Mexico City: IIS-UABJO-Siglo XXI.

———. 2007b. "Dilemas en la construcción de ciudadanías diferenciadas en un espacio multicultural: El caso de Oaxaca." In Hernández-Díaz 2007a, 35–86.

———. 2007c. "Las elecciones por usos y costumbres en los municipios conurbados de la ciudad de Oaxaca." In Hernández-Díaz 2007a, 328–346.

Hernández-Díaz, Jorge, and Gloria Zafra. 2005. *Artesanas y Artesanos: Creación, innovación y tradición en la producción de artesanías.* Mexico City: Plaza y Valdés.

Hirth, Kenneth G., ed. 2009. *Housework: Craft Production and Domestic Economy in Ancient Mesoamerica.* Archaeological Papers of the American Anthropological Association, Number 19. Washington, DC: American Anthropological Association.

Isaac, Barry L. 1986. "Introduction." In *Economic Aspects of Prehispanic Highland Mexico,* edited by Barry L. Isaac, 1–19. Research in Economic Anthropology, Supplement 2. Greenwich, CT: JAI Press.

Islas Escárcega, Leovigildo. 1961. *Diccionario rural de México.* Mexico City: Editorial Comaval.

Iturribarría, Jorge Fernando. 1955. *Oaxaca en la historia.* Mexico City: Editorial Stylo.

Jiménez Moreno, Wigberto. 1942. "Fray Juan de Córdova y la lengua zapoteca." Introduction to *Vocabulario Castellano-Zapoteco* by Juan de Córdova. Mexico City: Instituto Nacional de Antropología e Historia.

Joyce, Arthur A. 2010. *Mixtecs, Zapotecs, and Chatinos: Ancient Peoples of Southern Mexico.* London: Wiley-Blackwell.

Katz, Friedrich. 1958. "The Evolution of Aztec Society." *Past and Present* 13: 14–25.

———. 1998. *The Life and Times of Pancho Villa.* Palo Alto, CA: Stanford University Press.

Kirchhoff, Paul. 1968. "Mesoamerica: Its Geographic Limits, Ethnic Composition and Cultural Characteristics." In *Heritage of Conquest: The Ethnology of Middle America,* edited by Sol Tax, 17–30. New York: Cooper Square Publishers. (First published by the Macmillan Company, New York, 1952.)

Kirkby, Anne V. T. 1973. *The Use of Land and Water Resources in the Past and Present, Valley of Oaxaca, Mexico.* Ann Arbor: Museum of Anthropology, University of Michigan.

Knight, Alan. 1999. "Political Violence in Post-revolutionary Mexico." In Koonings and Kruijt 1999, 105–122.

Koonings, Kees, and Dirk Kruijt, eds. 1999. *Societies of Fear: The Legacy of Civil War, Violence and Terror in Latin America.* London: Zed Books.

Kowalewski, Stephen A., Gary M. Feinman, Laura Finsten, Richard E. Blanton, and Linda M. Nicholas. 1989. *Monte Albán's Hinterland, Part II: Prehispanic Settlement Patterns in Tlacolula, Etla, and Ocotlán, the Valley of Oaxaca, Mexico.* Memoirs of the Museum of Anthropology, University of Michigan, Number 23. Ann Arbor: Regents of the University of Michigan and the Museum of Anthropology.

Krejci, John. 1976. "Leadership and Change in Two Mexican Villages." *Anthropological Quarterly* 49 (3): 185–196.

Lauria, Anthony. 1964a. "Ethnolinguistic Analysis of Ceremonials of Interpersonal Confrontation in Puerto Rico: Concerning *Cara* and *Vergüenza.*" Paper presented at the 63rd Annual Meeting of the American Anthropological Association, Detroit, Michigan.

———. 1964b. "'Respeto,' 'Relajo' and Inter-personal Relations in Puerto Rico." *Anthropological Quarterly* 37: 53–67.

Lewis, Oscar. 1949. "Aspects of Land Tenure and Economics in a Mexican Village." *Middle American Research Records* 1 (13): 195–209.

———. 1960. *The Children of Sánchez.* New York: Random House.

Limón, José E. 1994. *Dancing with the Devil: Society and Cultural Poetics in Mexican-American South Texas.* Madison: University of Wisconsin Press.

Malinowski, Bronislaw, and Julio De la Fuente. 1957. *La economía de un sistema de mercados en México.* Acta Antropológica Época 2, Vol. 1, No. 2. Mexico City: Escuela Nacional de Antropología e Historia.

Marcus, Joyce, and Kent V. Flannery. 1996. *Zapotec Civilization.* London: Thames and Hudson.

Martínez, Víctor Raúl. 1985. "El régimen de García Vigil." In *La revolución en Oaxaca, 1900–1930,* edited by Víctor Raúl Martínez, 309–373. Oaxaca City, Mex.: IAPO.

Martínez Gracida, Manuel. 1883. *Colección de cuadros sinópticos de los pueblos, haciendas y ranchos, estado libre y soberano de Oaxaca.* Oaxaca City, Mex.: Imprenta del Estado.

———. 1884. *Cuadro cronológico de los gobernantes que ha tenido el Estado de Oaxaca desde la más remota antigüedad hasta el fin del año de 1883.* Oaxaca City, Mex.: Imprenta del Estado.

———. 1910. *Civilización chontal: Historia antigua de la chontalpa oaxaqueña.* Mexico City: Imprenta del Gobierno Federal.

Martínez Ríos, Jorge. 1964. "Análisis funcional de la 'Guelaguetza Agrícola.'" *Revista Mexicana de Sociología* 26 (1): 79–125.

Martínez Ríos, Jorge, and Gustavo M. de Luna Méndez. 1960. "Efectos sociales de la reforma agraria en el ejido de Guelavía." In Mendieta y Núñez 1960, 205–324.

McDonnell, Christine. 2002. "Late I Social Variation: Residential Mobility and Migrant Markets in the Tlacolula Subvalley, Oaxaca, Mexico." PhD diss., Department of Anthropology, University of Connecticut.

Mecinas, Taurino. 1955. *Tierra y libertad: Datos sobre las luchas sostenidas por los agraristas de la población de San Lorenzo Albarradas para recibir las tierras de que hoy disfrutan.* Oaxaca City, Mex.: Privately published.

Méndez Martínez, Enrique. 1983. *Índice de documentos relativos a los pueblos del Estado de Oaxaca: Ramo Tierras del Archivo General de la Nación.* Mexico City: AGN.

———. 1999. *Límites, mapas y títulos primordiales de los pueblos del Estado de Oaxaca: Índice del Ramo de Tierras.* Mexico City: AGN.

Mendieta y Núñez, Lucio, ed. 1949. *Los zapotecos: Monografía histórica, etnográfica y económica.* Mexico City: Imprenta Universitaria.

———, ed. 1960. *Efectos sociales de la reforma agraria en tres comunidades ejidales de la república mexicana.* Mexico City: Imprenta Universitaria.

———, ed. 1966. *El problema agrario de México.* 9th ed. Mexico City: Editorial Porrúa.

Nugent, Daniel, ed. 1998. *Revolt in Mexico: U.S. Intervention and the Domain of Subaltern Rural Politics.* Durham, NC: Duke University Press.

Olivera, Mercedes, and María de los Ángeles Romero. 1973. "La estructura política de Oaxaca en el siglo XVI." *Revista Mexicana de Sociología* 35 (2): 227–287.

Ortega, C. Manuel. 1848. *Carta corográfica del Estado de Oaxaca y de su Obispado.* Mexico City: N.p. Map.

Paddock, John, ed. 1970. *Ancient Oaxaca: Discoveries in Mexican Archaeology and History.* Palo Alto, CA: Stanford University Press.

Palerm, Ángel. 1970. "Respuesta: 'Indigenismo en México: Confrontación de problemas.'" *Anuario Indigenista* 30 (December): 295–306.

Palerm, Ángel, and Eric R. Wolf. 1957. "Ecological Potential and Cultural Development in Mesoamerica." In Palerm and Wolf et al. 1957, 1–38.

Palerm, Ángel, Eric Wolf, et al. 1957. *Studies in Human Ecology.* Social Science Monographs 3, Social Science Section, Department of Cultural Affairs. Washington, DC: Pan American Union.

Parsons, Elsie Clews. 1936. *Mitla, Town of Souls and Other Zapoteco-Speaking Pueblos of Oaxaca, Mexico.* Chicago: University of Chicago Press.

Peñafiel, Antonio. 1885. *Nombres geográficos de México.* Mexico City: Oficina Tipográfica de la Secretaría de Fomento.

Pesman, M. Walter. 1962. *Meet Flora Mexicana.* Globe, AZ: D. S. King.

Plattner, Stuart, ed. 1986. *Markets and Marketing.* Monographs in Economic Anthropology, No. 4. Lanham, MD: University Press of America.

Portillo, Andrés. 1910. *Oaxaca en el centenario de la independencia nacional: Noticias históricas y estadísticas de la ciudad de Oaxaca, y algunas leyendas tradicionales.* Oaxaca City, Mex.: Imprenta del Estado.

Rabasa, José. 2000. *Writing Violence on the Northern Frontier: The Historiography of Sixteenth-Century New Mexico and Florida and the Legacy of Conquest.* Durham, NC: Duke University Press.

———. 2011. *Tell Me the Story of How I Conquered You: Elsewheres and Ethnosuicide in the Colonial Mesoamerican World.* Austin: University of Texas Press.

RAN (Registro Agrario Nacional). Secretaría de Desarrollo Agrario, Territorial y Urbano, Mexico City. intranet.ran.gob.mx/sicoagac.

Reina, Leticia. 1988a. "De las reformas borbónicas a las leyes de reforma." In Reina 1988b, 1:183–268.

———, ed. 1988b. *Historia de la cuestión agraria mexicana: Estado de Oaxaca.* Vol. 1, *Prehispanico–1924,* and Vol. 2, *1925–1986.* Mexico City: Juan Pablos Editores.

Ribeiro, Darcy. 1968. *The Civilizational Process.* Washington, DC: Smithsonian Institution Press.

Robichaux, David. 2005. "Identidades cambiantes: 'Indios' y 'Mestizos' en el Suroeste de Tlaxcala." *Relaciones* 26 (104): 58–104.

———. 2009. "Defining the Indian: State Definitions, Perception of the Other and Community Organization in Southwestern Tlaxcala and Mexico." *Nuevo Mundo Mundos Nuevos.* http://nuevomundo.revues.org/56681.

Rocha Islas, Martha Eva. 1988. *Las defensas sociales en Chihuahua.* Mexico City: INAH.

Rojas González, Francisco. 1949. "Los zapotecos en la época independiente." In Mendieta y Núñez 1949, 159–200.

Romero Frizzi, María de los Ángeles, ed. 1986. *Lecturas históricas del Estado de Oaxaca: Época colonial*. Mexico City: INAH.

———. 1988. "Época colonial (1519–1785)." In Reina 1988b, 1:107–179.

———. 2003a. *Escritura zapoteca: 2,500 años de historia*. Mexico City: CIESAS/Porrúa Grupo Editorial/CONACULTA/INAH.

———. 2003b. "Los zapotecos, la escritura y la historia." In Romero Frizzi 1986, 7–69.

Rosaldo, Renato. 1993. *Culture and Truth: The Remaking of Social Analysis*. Boston: Beacon Press.

Ruiz Cervantes, Francisco José. 1988. "De la bola a los primeros repartos." In Reina 1988b, 1:331–424.

Sanders, William T., and Barbara J. Price. 1968. *Mesoamerica: The Evolution of a Civilization*. New York: Random House.

Sanjek, Roger. 1991. "The Ethnographic Present." *Man*, n.s., 26 (4): 609–628.

Sauer, Carl O. 1969. *Seeds, Spades, Hearths, and Herds: The Domestication of Animals and Foodstuffs*. Cambridge, MA: MIT Press.

Schmieder, Oscar. 1930. *The Settlements of the Tzapotec and Mije Indians: State of Oaxaca, Mexico*. University of California Publications in Geography, Vol. 4. Berkeley: University of California Press.

Schneider, Jane, and Ann Weiner, eds. 1989. *Cloth and Human Experience*. Washington, DC: Smithsonian Institution.

Searcy, Michael T. 2011. *The Life-Giving Stone: Ethnoarchaeology of Maya Metates*. Tucson: University of Arizona Press.

Semo, Enrique. 1973. *Historia del capitalismo en México: Los orígenes, 1521–1763*. Mexico City: Ediciones Era.

Simpson, Lesley Byrd. 1959. *Many Mexicos*. Berkeley and Los Angeles: University of California Press.

———. 1966. *The Encomienda in New Spain*. Berkeley and Los Angeles: University of California Press.

Smith, Benjamin T. 2009. *Pistoleros and Popular Movements: The Politics of State Formation in Postrevolutionary Oaxaca*. Lincoln and London: University of Nebraska Press.

Spielberg, Joseph. 1974. "Humour in Mexican American Palomilla: Some Historical, Social, and Psychological Implications." *Revista Chicano-Riqueña* 2: 41–50.

Spores, Ronald. 1965. "The Zapotec and Mixtec at Spanish Contact." In *Archaeology of Southern Mesoamerica: Part II*, edited by Gordon R. Willey, 962–987. *Handbook of Middle American Indians*, Vol. 3, edited by Robert Wauchope. Austin: University of Texas Press.

Standley, Paul C. 1920. *Trees and Shrubs of Mexico*. Contributions from the United States Herbarium, Vol. 23. Washington, DC: Smithsonian Press.

Starr, Frederick. 1900. *Notes upon the Ethnography of Southern Mexico*. Reprinted from Vol. 8, *Proceedings of Davenport Academy of Natural Sciences*. Davenport, IA: Putnam Memorial Publication Fund.

Stephen, Lynn. 1991. *Zapotec Women.* Austin: University of Texas Press.

Stephen, Lynn, and James Dow, eds. 1990. *Class, Politics, and Popular Religion in Mexico and Central America.* Vol. 10. Society for Latin American Anthropology Publication Series. Washington, DC: American Anthropological Association.

Tannenbaum, Frank. 1933. *Peace by Revolution: Mexico after 1910.* New York and London: Columbia University Press.

Taylor, William B. 1971. "The Colonial Background to Peasant Economy in the Valley of Oaxaca." Paper submitted to the symposium "Market Systems and Economics of the Oaxaca Region" at the joint annual meeting of the Southwestern Anthropological Association and the American Ethnological Society in Tucson, Arizona, April 30. Mimeographed. Personal collection.

———. 1972. *Landlord and Peasant in Colonial Oaxaca.* Palo Alto, CA: Stanford University Press.

———. 1979. *Drinking, Homicide, and Rebellion in Colonial Mexican Villages.* Palo Alto, CA: Stanford University Press.

———. 1986. "Cacicazgos coloniales en el Valle de Oaxaca." In Romero Frizzi 1986, 151–191.

———. 2010. *Shrines and Miraculous Images: Religious Life in Mexico Before the Reforma.* Albuquerque: University of New Mexico Press.

———. 2011. *Marvels and Miracles in Late Colonial Mexico: Three Texts in Context.* Albuquerque: University of New Mexico Press.

Villaseñor y Sánchez, José Antonio de. [1748] 1952. *Teatro Americano: Descripción general de los reynos y provincias de la Nueva España y sus jurisdicciones.* Mexico: Editorial Nacional.

Warman, Arturo. 2003. *Los indios mexicanos en el umbral del milenio.* Mexico City: Fondo de Cultura Económica.

Waterbury, Ronald. 1975. "Non-Revolutionary Peasants: Oaxaca Compared to Morelos in the Mexican Revolution." In *Comparative Studies in Society and History* 17 (4): 410–442.

———. 1989. "Embroidery for Tourists." In Schneider and Weiner 1989, 243–271.

Welte, Cecil R. 1965. *Mapa de las localidades del Valle de Oaxaca (Cuenca Superior del Río Atoyac) según el censo de población de 1960.* Oaxaca City, Mex.: Oficina de Estudios de Humanidad del Valle de Oaxaca.

———. 1966. *Index of Populated Places in the Valley of Oaxaca Listed in the Census of 1960 and Shown on the "Mapa de las Localidades del Valle de Oaxaca".* Oaxaca City, Mex.: Oficina de Estudios de Humanidad del Valle de Oaxaca.

———. 1973a. *Population of Selected Localidades in the Valley of Oaxaca (Censuses of 1960 and 1970).* Oaxaca City, Mex.: Oficina de Estudios de Humanidad del Valle de Oaxaca. Typescript.

———. 1973b. *Welte's Ready Reference Release No. 2.* Oaxaca City, Mex.: Oficina de Estudios de Humanidad del Valle de Oaxaca.

———. 1976. "Maps and Demographic Tables." In Cook and Diskin 1976b, 283–294.

———. 1978. *Welte's Ready Reference Release No. 4.* Oaxaca City, Mex.: Oficina de Estudios de Humanidad del Valle de Oaxaca.

West, Robert C. 1964. "The Natural Regions of Middle America." In *Natural Environment and Early Cultures*, Vol. 1, *Handbook of Middle American Indians*, edited by Robert C. West, 363–383. Austin: University of Texas Press.

Whetten, Nathan L. 1948. *Rural Mexico*. Chicago and London: University of Chicago Press.

Whitecotton, Joseph W. 1977. *The Zapotecs: Princes, Priests and Peasants*. Norman: University of Oklahoma Press.

Winter, Marcus. 1995. *Oaxaca, the Archaeological Record*. 2nd ed. Toluca, Mexico: Editora López Maynez.

Winter, Marcus, Daria Deraga, and Rodolfo Fernández. 1975. *Tumba 74-1 de San Sebastián Teitipac, Tlacolula, Oaxaca*. Oaxaca City, Mex.: INAH.

Wolf, Eric R. 1967. "Levels of Communal Relations." In *Social Anthropology*, Vol. 6, *Handbook of Middle American Indians*, edited by Manning Nash, 299–316. Austin: University of Texas Press.

———. 1969. *Peasant Wars of the Twentieth Century*. New York: Harper and Row.

———. 2001. "The Virgin of Guadalupe: A Mexican National Symbol." In *Pathways of Power: Building an Anthropology of the Modern World*, by Eric Wolf with Sydel Silverman, 139–146. Berkeley: University of California Press.

Wright-Rios, Edward. 2009. *Revolutions in Mexican Catholicism: Reform and Revelation in Oaxaca, 1887–1934*. Durham and London: Duke University Press.

Zavala, Silvio. 1940. *De encomiendas y propiedad territorial en algunas regiones de la América española*. Mexico City: Antigua Librería Robredo de José Porrúa e Hijos.

———. 1954. "Instituciones indígenas en la colonia: 'I. La Población' and 'III. Trabajo.'" In A. Caso et al. 1954, 37–42, 49–58.